SELECTED READINGS ON

The Learning Process

THEODORE L. HARRIS
University of Wisconsin

WILSON E. SCHWAHN

NEW YORK / OXFORD UNIVERSITY PRESS

1961

© 1961 by Oxford University Press, Inc.

Library of Congress Catalogue Card Number: 61–8372

Printed in the United States of America

Preface

The materials in this book have been carefully selected to supplement textbooks in educational psychology by providing ready access to source materials on the central problem of educational psychology—the learning process. These selections on human learning emphasize experimental studies of the learning process in its various forms, the dynamic functions involved in this process, and developmental and evaluational problems related to the study of the learning process. The materials have been chosen for their usefulness in advancing an understanding of how we learn and in illustrating how the learning process may be studied. Each selection is reported in as complete form as possible in order to reflect faithfully the nature, conditions, and methodology as well as the results of the study.

It has been the experience of the authors that the reading of textbook generalizations about the learning process and the highly condensed analyses of associated technical learning problems frequently has little meaning either to beginning or to experienced teachers. Of many possible reasons for such lack of understanding other than the typical generalized text approach, a significant one would appear to be the tendency to treat the general learning process, the different types of learning, the technical problems in learning, and the practical problems of teaching as relatively isolated topics. In such an approach to the study of educational psychology, the student tends to lose sight of learning as process, since the approach is directed toward fragmented aspects of knowledge about learning and teaching rather than toward an understanding of the flow of an on-going process.

v

While meaningful understanding of the learning process may be aided somewhat by classroom illustrations, and by observing and participating in various learning experiences, it would appear that a careful examination of specific studies of behavior changes in learning should materially improve the teacher's understanding of the learning process. Specifically, the study of investigations into how we learn to reason, to create aesthetic products, to develop concepts and generalizations, to acquire skills, to form attitudes, and to work with others in groups, should provide a meaningful basis for understanding the abstraction called "the learning process." Similarly, the study of investigations into the important learning functions of motivation, retention, and transfer, and into the problems of the relationship of development and evaluation to the learning process should help the teacher understand more clearly the significant forces and problems with which he must work. The study of such materials should not only help "bring the text to life" but also should materially assist the student in learning to select desired behavioral changes, and to identify and use instructional approaches appropriate to his desired objectives. Finally, and not least in importance, the study of source materials should contribute to the development of an experimental attitude in the student in his approach to the teaching-learning process. It is in gathering together reasonably complete and detailed studies of human learning which represent a consistent focus upon the learning process, its functions and its problems, that this book of readings should serve a distinctive purpose in the study of educational psychology.

The organization and treatment of the book is such that the chapters may be used in any order desired by the instructor. The correlation chart with textbooks in educational psychology has been prepared for this purpose (see p. 424). The materials in a given chapter may be usefully studied individually or comparatively. As sources, they may be used for examination of the methodology of research in the learning process. Certain selections may also serve as models for replication in the classroom or as a point of departure for further consideration of how learning changes may be studied.

Care has been exercised in the selection of materials to include insofar as possible a range of educational levels—child, adolescent, and adult. The materials have been selected primarily with a view toward their use in courses in educational psychology. However, the nature and scope of the selections are such that they may also prove useful in related aspects of the in-service and graduate education of teachers.

The editors are especially grateful to the authors and publishers whose permission to reprint materials is specifically acknowledged at the beginning of each selection.

T.L.H.
W.E.S.

Madison, Wisconsin
December 1960

Contents

SELECTED READINGS ON THE LEARNING PROCESS

PART : 1

The General Nature of Learning

LEARNING AS PRODUCT, PROCESS, AND FUNCTION

Learning is the heart of the educational process. Educational psychologists seek to develop an understanding of the nature of learning and of those aspects of learning which are of greatest significance for the teacher. While there is considerable unanimity in recognizing that learning is essentially change due to experience, different points of view have arisen regarding those aspects of learning which have the greatest theoretical and practical importance for the teacher and for education. Such differences in point of view have in turn led educational psychologists to prepare materials for use in teacher-education with varying emphases on learning as product, learning as process, and learning as function.

Learning as Product. Materials for teachers which represent a point of view of learning as product emphasize the end-result or outcome of the learning experience. The focus of attention is upon the characteristics of learned behavior. Such aspects of learning as the particular kinds of change, the dimensions of change, and the degree of change in behavior outcomes tend to be described. Similarly, such an emphasis leads to the classification of behavioral change into types, such as learning of skills, concepts or attitudes. A product-oriented description of learning is designed to capture the characteristics of learning as they exist at a certain time or to a certain degree rather than to describe an on-going process.

Learning as Process. A point of view of learning as process emphasizes what happens during the course of a learning experience in attaining a given learning product or outcome. The sequence and pattern of change in behavior now become the focus of attention. Emphasis is placed upon

1

the dynamics of the learning situation for the individual or group. A process-oriented description of learning attempts to show to what aspects of the learning situation the learner is reacting, how the learner organizes and focuses his behavior in a learning situation, and how such activity leads to change in behavior.

Learning as Function. A point of view which describes learning as function emphasizes certain critical aspects of learning which presumably make behavioral change in human learning possible. Motivation is a functional concept which is useful in describing certain preparatory, dynamic and directive characteristics of learning. Similarly, such concepts as transfer, retention, and meaningful interpretation and organization by the learner are concepts of great utility in describing other on-going functions involved in the learning process. A description of learning as function tends to emphasize certain important features or highlights of learning, several of which may occur concurrently, but none of which describes fully or completely the total pattern and sequence of change in the learning process.

A Point of View. Each of the foregoing ways of viewing learning— as product, as process, and as function—possesses certain values which are recognized in this selection of readings. The emphasis, however, is placed on processive and functional aspects of learning, for these are the aspects of learning which the teacher must understand and work with to promote effective learning. Classification by products or types of learning is used merely as a means of grouping studies in which differences in specific learning processes and outcomes are useful for understanding the nature of behavioral change in learning.

The Role of the Teacher. The teacher is responsible for the management and direction of learning in a way that brings about certain desired results or outcomes. An understanding of learning focused primarily upon the nature of the end-result or product contributes little to the effective functioning of the teaching-learning process, a point repeatedly emphasized by Dewey and his interpreters.[1] It is apparent that the teacher also basically needs to know how and why changes in behavior occur to determine what can be done to bring about desired changes. Thus, an understanding of what happens during the course of a learning experience—the pattern and sequence of change in behavior and the functional concepts and problems which illuminate key aspects of behavioral change —is essential to the professional preparation and work of the teacher who

---

[1] See, for example, the manifesto "John Dewey and Creative Education" in the *Saturday Review,* November 21, 1959, pp. 19 ff.

is more than a mere technician. Such a teacher needs to understand the general nature of the learning process itself, to note its outstanding features or characteristics, to study variations in the learning process as well as its common elements, and to consider the implications of the learning process for the management and measurement of the learning experience.

CHAPTER : 1

The Learning Process

1. A Description of the Learning Process*

> This description of the learning process is taken from a study by a national committee of the relationship between learning and instructional processes. After suggesting a definition of learning, the authors outline the structure of the learning process in a simplified schematic diagram, discuss its interpretation, and indicate the key processive concepts which they believe to be useful in understanding the characteristics of change in learning.

Learning may be considered in its broadest sense as a process of adaptation. Through the process of learning, men acquire new ways of behaving or performing in order that they can make better adjustment to the demands of life. But we need to know what happens during the process of learning. How do responses change? How is behavior modified?

The essential elements in a learning situation are shown in Figure 1. They are: environmental stimulation of a living, motivated organism; incentives which when attained will lead to satisfaction of the motives; and at least a temporary blocking or inability of the learner to respond in ways that will enable him to gain the incentive. Motivation is assumed to be an inner state of need and is a necessary condition if the learner is to engage in learning activity. Needs, wants, interests, and sets are terms

---

* G. LESTER ANDERSON and ARTHUR I. GATES. Reprinted with permission of the authors and publisher from The general nature of learning, pp. 16-21. N. B. Henry (Ed.), *Learning and Instruction.* Forty-ninth Yearbook, Part I, National Society for the Study of Education. Chicago, Ill.: University of Chicago Press, 1950.

which are used to refer to motivating conditions. Satisfaction of a motive
may be blocked by the learner's inability to attain the incentives which
could satisfy the need.

When satisfaction of a motive is blocked, the learner, under appropriate
stimulation, makes a series of responses. These responses may or may not
be approximations of successful goal behavior. They are "provisional
trys." In Figure 1 the responses are labeled R_1, R_2, R_3, and R_n. At first,

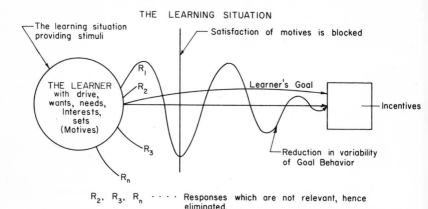

THE LEARNING SITUATION

R_2, R_3, R_n · · · · Responses which are not relevant, hence
                    eliminated.

FIG. 1. ESSENTIAL ELEMENTS IN A LEARNING SITUATION.

this behavior is variable; the responses may be extraneous or irrelevant,
confused or inefficient. As learning proceeds, some responses are eliminated, and appropriate responses are selected. These successful responses
are ultimately stabilized as variability is reduced. This reduction in variability is characterized by the processes of differentiation, integration, and
generalization. The attainment of the incentive, which frequently involves seeing the relation between means and end, with the consequent
satisfaction of the motive is the condition that determines which responses
will be retained (learned) and which will be eliminated.

The circumstances under which learning, as we have briefly outlined
it, takes place in its least cluttered although often more complex forms
are most readily observed in nonlaboratory, or even nonschool, situations.
As a child learns to ride a bicycle, to put a jig-saw puzzle together, to
count and otherwise quantify his environment, to spend his money wisely,
to tell time, to respect the property of others, to feed and dress himself,
or to secure status in a group of his peers, the process operates as we have
outlined it. Involved in the learning experience are: motives which are

temporarily blocked; the incentive or incentives, the attainment of which will ultimately lead to satisfaction of the motive; variable, often irrelevant behavior; and, finally, better organized and smoother behavior appropriate to the goal. All this is called the process of learning[1] . . .

REFERENCES

1. GATES, A. I., JERSILD, A. T., McCONNELL, T. R., CHALLMAN, R. *Educational Psychology*. New York: Macmillan, 1948 (revised).
2. HILGARD, E. R. *Theories of Learning*. New York: D. Appleton-Century-Crofts, 1948.
3. KINGSLEY, H. L. *The Nature and Conditions of Learning*. New York: Prentice-Hall, 1946.
4. *The Psychology of Learning*. Forty-first Yearbook of the National Society for the Study of Education, Part II. Chicago: University of Chicago Press, 1942.

2. A Description of Active Learning*

In this description of the learning process, Cronbach uses seven key concepts derived from an analysis of behavior to describe the sequence of change occurring in learning. The nature of these concepts is worthy of note in terms of their potential meaningfulness and usefulness to the teacher. Similarly, his discussion of what is meant by learning as a change in behavior is clear and readable.

WHAT WE MEAN BY LEARNING

. . . Behavior involves a response to a situation. If the person makes a different response this month than he made a month ago, we say that he has learned something. Or, more precisely, *learning is shown by a change in behavior as a result of experience.*

The sound of an ice cream wagon coming down the street is to the child a signal. He can make a tremendous number of possible responses. Different children may be observed to call to the man to stop, or to run

---

[1] Many experimental studies, especially those done under laboratory conditions, often fail to show a learning process that seems to fit our scheme. However, studies of children's learning in the school and studies of social learning often reveal a form which fits the pattern we have outlined.

* LEE J. CRONBACH. Reprinted and adapted with permission of the author and publisher from *Educational Psychology*, pp. 46-51. New York: Harcourt, Brace and Co., Inc., copyright, 1954.

into the house for a dime, or to scamper along beside the wagon, or to go on with whatever game they are playing. If we observe a single child on dozens of days, we find that his responses are not always the same. He makes one response 50 per cent of the time, a second response on 30 per cent of the occasions, a third response 10 per cent of the time, and other responses very rarely. The differences from day to day probably reflect small differences in the situation or in his desires (he isn't hungry, or is especially hot, or knows that his mother is in a bad mood and he'd better not ask for money).

Learning is shown when some responses occur with increased frequency in a repeated situation. A child moving into the neighborhood, who has not previously seen this kind of wagon, may during his first week consistently glance at the wagon and go back to his game. Then, from the other children, he finds out that the wagon is a source of ice cream and that their mothers sometimes give them money. So his interpretation changes, and during the next week we find him streaking for home to request a dime whenever the wagon is heard. If his mother refuses the money, this trial response may be dropped, but he probably will not go back to his original indifference. Instead, we may find him stopping his play and watching the others envyingly, or we notice that when the wagon comes in sight he bites his nails or becomes irritable for a spell. Some responses have become more probable, and others have become less probable. Learning has taken place.

Many different changes take place when we learn. We may acquire new goals or ideals which make a response more attractive than it used to be. (The classic example is the boy making a detour to pass the house of a girl to whom he paid no attention a month ago.) We may become sensitive to new signs or discover a new interpretation. We may acquire helpful or harmful emotional reactions, and these help to determine our response. Confidence, fear of looking foolish, sensitivity to small discomforts, or an enthusiastic outlook are all learned. All these types of learning are recognized by the change in response that results.

It is somewhat unusual to say that a person learns the *mis*interpretation that causes him to make a wrong response, but this is also learning and it can be explained by the same laws. If a pupil consistently says that the capital of Kentucky is Lexington, he obviously has learned this response, even though his teacher wishes he had learned to respond "Frankfort."

The probability of giving a particular response can increase or decrease. There are occasions when the hardest job of the teacher is to break up a response pattern which is already fixed, reducing its probability of occurrence. When Johnny learns *not* to hit another child who annoys him, the way is paved for teaching him more intelligent ways of handling conflicts. He has learned something when he abandons the old response, even though he has not yet learned what he should do.

One learns through encountering situations, trying responses, and discovering what consequences each response leads to. We shall use seven concepts to describe the process of learning, and to do so we need to define the terms and indicate the part each one plays in learning.

a. *Goal. The goal of the learner is some consequence which he wishes to attain.* This target may be defined in terms of some object to be obtained, some response desired from another person, or some internal feeling such as the enjoyment of an entertaining show. The person has many goals at the same time, and usually thinks of some immediate goal (such as completing an assigned task) as related to a whole series of future goals (such as earning a respectable grade in the course, finishing school, and succeeding in a career). Goals direct the effort of the learner.

b. *Readiness. A person's readiness consists of the sum-total of response patterns and abilities he possesses at any time.* Readiness depends upon physical and mental maturity, and upon the responses the person has already learned. The person's readiness determines what responses he has at his disposal in any new situation. Therefore, his readiness limits what he can do. Readiness determines the choice of goals; a more mature person has different wants and is more likely to direct his efforts toward distant goals.

c. *Situation. The situation consists of all the objects, persons, and symbols in the learner's environment.* Experience in one situation prepares a person to respond to similar situations in the future.

d. *Interpretation. Interpretation is a process of directing attention to parts of the situation, relating them to past experiences, and predicting what can be expected to happen if various responses are made.* Interpretation may be conscious and deliberate. But the person also makes many interpretations without putting them into words or giving them his full attention. The interpretation suggests what response to try.

e. *Response. A response is an action or some internal change that prepares the person for action.* By this definition, a response might be an observable movement, a spoken remark, or an increase in tension that is concealed from the observer. The response chosen is that which the learner thinks will most nearly satisfy his wants. If the learner is in doubt about his interpretation, as he often is in a strange situation, he makes his response tentatively and we speak of it as a provisional try.

f. *Consequence: confirmation or contradiction. Some events that follow the response are regarded by the learner as the consequences of the response.* If these are the consequences he predicted, the learner's interpretation is confirmed. If the consequences are not what he expected, his interpretation is contradicted and he usually is dissatisfied. If an interpretation is confirmed, the person will make a similar interpretation on another occasion of this type. Consequences include the direct effect of the response, such as getting the basketball through the hoop, and some less direct accompaniments, such as the popularity attained by a good player.

g. *Reaction to thwarting. Thwarting occurs when the person fails to attain his goals.* If his first try is not confirmed, he may make a new interpretation and adapt his response. If he cannot deal with the situation in a way which attains his goals, he is likely to become disturbed. He may give up, or act erratically. This disturbance can eventually result in misconduct, loss of interest, or inferiority feelings. Any such reaction which does not help him satisfy his need is called *nonadaptive*.

Reaction to thwarting is not really the end of the chain, although we have had to place it there. Always, the thwarting is followed by other behavior. The person makes new interpretations and finds some new way to satisfy his wants. Or, if he cannot, he abandons that goal and tests some other expectation. Sooner or later he does find an interpretation that is confirmed. When he is acting in harmony with reality and with his own ability, confirmation is the final step in the chain of behavior.

REFERENCES

1. MILLER, N. E., DOLLARD, J. *Social Learning and Imitation.* New Haven: Yale University Press, 1941. Chapter II.

3. The Learning Process*

Woodruff presents a highly detailed description of a series of steps or phases in learning presumed to be common to all types of learning. He also advances the idea that emphasis upon certain of these phases

* ASAHEL D. WOODRUFF. Reprinted and abridged with permission of the author and publisher from *The Psychology of Teaching*, pp. 59-75. Second edition. New York: Longmans, Green and Co., 1948. (Please note that the copyright date of the Third Edition is 1951.)

varies with the type of learning. An elaboration of this concept of variation within the learning process as a function of the type or end-product of learning is found in the text from which this selection is taken.

LEARNING

The process of learning is the vehicle by which the individual is changed from a bundle of potentialities to an acting organism with ideas, habits, skills, preferences, and other distinguishing personality characteristics. The various factors in learning wield influences which have much to do with the *direction* in which the learning process moves. Some of them have much influence, some little, but they only modify the learning process; they do not take its place. Figure 1 illustrates one way of visualizing this idea. The first step in becoming an effective teacher, then, is the development of thorough understanding of the learning process.

No one lives or learns in a vacuum. Therefore learning never takes place apart from the many modifying factors which determine its direction. As a means of becoming familiar with any phenomenon, however,

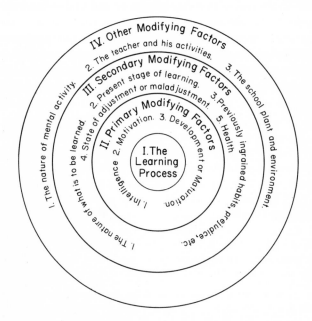

FIG. 1. FACTORS WHICH INFLUENCE THE LEARNING PROCESS.

it is helpful to lift it out of its natural setting and examine it as if it were in a vacuum. When this is done, there is always the obligation of putting it back into its natural setting after such familiarity is developed, and there continuing the examination until it is possible under natural conditions to recognize the phenomenon itself, as well as the ways in which it is changed or modified by each of its important modifying factors . . .

The steps in learning. When all theories and schools of thought are peeled aside, and the bare facts about learning are exposed, it becomes clear that regardless of theoretical points of view, the learning process contains certain common sequential steps. These steps seem invariably to be present when learning occurs. One version of the steps is presented in Table 1. Each step will be discussed separately, although it must be remembered that any attempt to separate them into discrete parts of the learning process is wholly artificial and academic, and is to be justified only in terms of its ability to help the student become familiar with the process in its entirety. At times the learner seems to rush through the steps in a manner which suggests they are all parts of one movement or that some of them are missing. At other times learning seems to bog down on one step or another for varying lengths of time and for various reasons. In still other cases it seems as if the learner shifts back and forth over a few of the steps until some condition is satisfied before the process moves on to completion. In other words, there is no apparent uniformity of movement from one step to another during learning, and yet in spite of the many different ways in which a learner may run through these steps, there is uniformity in the fact that the steps are always there and can be identified by a trained observer.

Step 1. Motivation within the learner makes him receptive to stimulation. There are four facts about motivation which are of importance here: (1) A motive is any condition within the learner which arouses and sustains activity. (2) It is always within the learner and never exists apart from his own mental processes. (3) It is not put there by the teacher, but grows within the person as a direct result of his experiences throughout life. (4) All purposive behavior (goal-seeking activity) begins with a motive; there is no such behavior without motivation . . .

Step 2. A goal becomes related to the motivation. Often the urge to act is something as indefinable as a general physiological restlessness. At such times the individual seems to be actively seeking some kind of a goal which will satisfy his restlessness. When a goal is selected, such as a beefsteak or a glass of water, action toward that goal can begin. Motives of

TABLE I

Sequential Steps in Learning

1	2	3	4	5	6
Motivation within the learner makes him receptive to stimulation.	A goal becomes related to the motivation. A. The goal is not at once attainable. B. A barrier exists.	Tension arises. A. Energy is released within the learner; he is ready to act. B. The barrier prevents an appropriate discharge of the energy and creates tension.	Learner seeks an appropriate line of action to reach goal. A. In every situation there are a number of possible ways of acting. B. The selection of one of those ways of acting will involve elements of chance and/or analysis. C. When the selection is made action toward the goal is attempted. D. If the selected line of action is inappropriate, steps A, B, and C will be repeated until an appropriate action occurs. E. When an appropriate action occurs it will involve: 1. Some degree of success in terms of the goal. 2. A sense of satisfaction and a reduction of tension to the extent that the motive is satisfied.	Learner fixes the appropriate line of action. A. Skills are acquired by drill or practice. B. Concepts are developed by becoming familiar with the referent. C. Memorization is accomplished through meaningful repetition. D. Tastes and preferences are established by the satisfyingness or annoyingness of the experience. E. Ability to think is a product of A and B above.	Inappropriate behaviors are dropped. A. Yielding no satisfaction they lose attractiveness.

Speed of Learning Varies
A. May be relatively sudden.
B. May be very slow.
C. Depends on:
  1. Nature of the problem.
  2. Degree of motivation.
  3. Capacity of the learner.

value in school work are more often in the social and personal realms. Examples are the desire to be a success in life or in some particular area, the desire to be recognized or approved, the urge to make some change in one's knowledge or skills to meet a particular need, or the desire to pursue some special interest which has developed over a period of time. When the learner is led to see and desire to reach an attainable goal which is obviously contributory to his strong motives, the second condition or step in learning has been satisfied, and action can then proceed toward the goal . . .

(a) The goal is not at once attainable. (b) A barrier exists . . . There are many kinds of barriers which interfere with the immediate mastery of a goal, and they may be usefully divided into educational barriers and psychological barriers. Educational barriers consist almost solely of the absence in whole or in part of the particular knowledge or skill involved in the learning situation. Such barriers may be overcome by the usual educative procedures such as reading, drill, and practice. Psychological barriers are always potentially dangerous to good adjustment. There are several kinds. (1) Some of them consist of an inadequacy on the part of the learner, such as low intelligence, lack of fine neuromuscular coordination, specific inaptitude, prejudice, or faulty concepts. These barriers may not always be fully overcome and may succeed in permanently thwarting one's mastery of a given goal to some extent. (2) Other barriers grow out of a disturbed condition of the learner, such as emotional blocking, fears, or other conditions of maladjustment. (3) The teacher's personality may be a barrier for some students. (4) Poor teaching techniques constitute barriers to learning. They may be due to ignorance of the effective motives of pupils, disregard of a student's level of attainment in a subject, or lack of effective ways of organizing and presenting the materials of learning, including the use of poor textual materials.

When the barrier consists only of a lack of the particular knowledge or skill involved, learning usually proceeds normally to the point where the goal is attained and the motivation satisfied. When the barrier is of the other kinds described here, unpleasant tension usually arises and something other than the usual techniques of study is required before a wholesome adjustment can be achieved . . .

Step 3. Tension arises. (a) Energy is released within the learner; he is ready to act . . . There is considerable evidence for the statement that it is satisfying to act when one is ready to act, and annoying to be prevented from acting.

(b) The barrier prevents an appropriate discharge of the energy and creates tension. Regardless of its nature, a barrier which prevents the student from moving toward his goal operates as a dam behind which the energy which would normally be used in making an adjustment is allowed to build up under pressure. It must be remembered that a true motive is a condition which will not stop agitating until it is satisfied or otherwise removed . . .

Mild tension may be an aid in learning. It tends to organize one's energies and facilities into an efficient and vigorous attack on the problem. [On the other hand] strong tension is often disruptive in its influence on the learner.

Step 4. The learner seeks an appropriate line of action to reach his goal. (a) In every situation there are a number of possible ways of acting. For example, if one has to find the meaning of a new word he can use the dictionary, ask someone, see how the word is used in a sentence, guess at its meaning, or try something else . . . It is theoretically possible for the individual to try any one or more of the possible courses of action in any given situation.

(b) The selection of one of those ways of acting will involve elements of chance or analysis or both. Chance implies random selection without the aid of logical indicators of what it may be appropriate to do. It may show up in behavior in two ways. (1) Mental exploration is often the random sampling of various lines of action . . . (2) Random physical activity often involves many kinds of movement which may have little or no real relationship to the problem . . .

Analysis implies a more or less organized examination of the known parts of a problem to see what they have to offer as leads toward the solution . . . The amount of random activity of the purely chance variety will probably diminish as the learner's familiarity with his problem increases. Conversely, logical analysis will probably tend to become an increasingly prominent part of the learning process as familiarity increases.

(c) When the selection is made action toward the goal is attempted. The fact that the student has decided on a line of action does not necessarily mean he has selected the appropriate or best action. Nevertheless having decided to try a certain approach, he will begin what he thinks to be a movement toward his goal. If he has selected a sound approach, he will probably get through to his goal in time, but if he has selected an unsound approach, he will find himself blocked by some barrier.

(d) If the selected line of action is inappropriate, steps 4a, 4b, and 4c will be repeated until an appropriate action occurs. These steps are often called the trial-and-error process because so often the learner decides to try something only to discover he has tried the wrong thing and must try something else. Trial-error-trial-error-trial-success would be a more accurate and enlightening term . . .

Regardless of how this process is designated, then, any line of action which does not offer satisfaction to the motive or any useful solution to the problem or lead to the goal is discarded and another line of action is sought in the same general manner as that used to find the first one. This will ordinarily continue until a useful line of activity is found. In cases where the barrier is too great, learning may break down or move in an unexpected direction at this point . . .

(e) When an appropriate action occurs, it will involve some degree of success in terms of the goal, and a sense of satisfaction with reduction of tension to the extent the motive is satisfied.

(1) Any act which moves the learner toward his goal may be regarded as successful to some degree. That is, it brings about a condition which is satisfying to the organism because it tends to fill the need which is motivating the behavior. It is the nature of most goals in the learning process that they do not recur once they have been achieved, dismissing for the present the tendency to forget. For example, one may learn to read the daily newspaper. This learning need not be repeated. When once fully achieved such a goal (*ability* to read) ceases to be a motivating force in behavior and may become a tool for the achievement of another goal. On the other hand, it is the nature of many goals set up in an effort to maintain a state of equilibrium in life that they recur with varying degrees of regularity and frequency and need new satisfaction each time they recur. For example, one needs to eat each time hunger recurs. The fundamental difference between these two types of goals is that one requires the mastery of a new *way* of doing something, while the other merely requires the repeated use of some process already learned. The first is a goal in the learning process. The second is a goal in the continuous process of maintaining a state of adjustment . . . Any motivating drive is ended when the sought-for condition is fully or adequately produced.

(2) Tension is relieved in proportion to the satisfaction of the motive. Most goals in learning are won by degrees rather than all at once. Each degree of success seems to have the power to bring some degree of satisfaction to the learner and therefore to temper the agitation produced by the motive. Since tension is directly related to inability to satisfy a motive, release of tension is directly related to satisfaction of a motive. When a motive is fully satisfied, the tension related to it is fully released, and the effort to learn stops. If the motive is *not fully* satisfied the student will continue his efforts to master the problem, but only up to the point where

is motivating need is satisfied, regardless of whether that point is short of or beyond the goal set by the teacher. This is not to say that any other tensions due to still unsatisfied motives will disappear . . .

Step 5. The learner fixes the appropriate line of action. The processes by which students fix learning vary with the type of goal sought . . . Five common types of goals are motor skills, concepts, memory, tastes and preferences, and ability to think critically.

(a) Skills are acquired by drill or practice. Fingers learn to coordinate in the act of writing through actually performing the act over and over until it becomes established in a certain pattern. Most skills require some degree of neuromuscular coordination, which means that the various separate muscles involved in a given act have to be brought into unified action. One muscle must contract while another relaxes in order to get a certain movement. Each muscle is capable of acting alone without practice, but when cooperation is required there must be rehearsal. The higher the skill sought, the more drill or practice is required, because higher skill usually means that a more complex or exacting type of muscular cooperation is required.

(b) Concepts are developed by becoming familiar with the referent. This puts a premium on personal experience with the thing to be known. A student handling a book is having a personal experience with that book. From the acts of opening it, turning pages, feeling it, smelling it, hefting it, examining the printing in it, and so on, he will develop an understanding of what a book is. This understanding is a concept. The real book is the referent. The word "book" is the symbol by which the concept is known.

(c) Memorization is accomplished through meaningful repetition. Memory is the product of associational learning. That means that two or more things have been associated together in the experience of the learner until he always thinks of those things as belonging together. A word is associated with an object, and becomes known as the name of the object. The words of a poem become associated together and the poem becomes memorized. A list of ingredients become associated together and a recipe learned. The presence of meaning and belongingness aids this process greatly, but repeated experience with the associated items is necessary in most cases before memory is established.

(d) Tastes and preferences are established by the satisfyingness or annoyingness of the experience. Most tastes and preferences are by-products of an experience which had as its goal another end product such as knowledge or skill. If the search for the end product was satisfying, the learner is apt to come to like the circumstances under which that search was carried on. Thus students develop likes and dislikes for various subject and other things.

(e) Critical thinking is a mental skill which involves manipulating ideas in the mind and arriving at sound conclusions. It involves also number of specific techniques, such as the evaluation of evidence and the weighing of values. Since it is primarily a technique for use in making decisions and drawing conclusions, it involves both a direct and an indirect approach. The concepts involved in critical thinking must be developed as any other concept is acquired, by becoming familiar with the referent. Those concepts include evidence, propaganda, induction, hypothesis, and others, and they are direct goals which require special attention in the usual manner for conceptual problems. The development of facility in the use of those concepts depends on practice, and is therefore best thought of as a by-product of the carrying out of any other purposive work, providing that work is so arranged that it allows for or requires the use of critical thinking by the participants.

Step 6. Inappropriate behaviors are dropped. Yielding no satisfaction they lose attractiveness. This is in a sense a form of forgetting but it differs from the usual problem in that the items which are forgotten were not learned to any significant degree. Even granting the hypothesis that everything one does leaves some trace in his biological make-up, the trace left by a trial-and-error exploration into an unsuccessful line of action is very slight indeed. It requires no measurable amount of forgetting to render it unlikely to produce such behavior again. Therefore, the fact of interest here is that behaviors which yield no progress and no satisfaction to the motive seem to be dropped almost as if they had never been tried. Whether the learner avoids them in the future because he knows they won't work or because he becomes unaware of them after he finds a successful line of action is not clear . . .

The speed of learning varies. . . . The speed of learning depends on several factors: (1) Learning proceeds more rapidly when the learner's intelligence is high than when it is low. (2) Learning proceeds more rapidly when motivation is intense than when it is mild or weak. (3) The speed of learning is related to the nature of the problem and the material being learned. For example, most motor skills require some drill scattered over a period of time whereas many simple associational or conceptual learnings are complete with one brief experience. A finger applied to a hot stove tells its owner all at once and in a very final manner that stoves are hot . . .

Common points in learning and adjusting. At this point it will be profitable to emphasize the similarity between ordinary on-going behavior, and behavior involved in learning something new. They share in common these sequential steps: (1) motivation, (2) the setting-up of a goal toward which action is directed, (3) the development of tension and readiness to act, (4) discovering a way of acting which brings progress, and (6) throwing aside or ignoring other ways which seem less promising. Whether the fifth sequential step (fixing the successful act) is present in behavior depends on whether one is trying to learn a line of behavior or is just trying to use one at the moment. No doubt everything the individual does leaves some sort of residue akin to learning, but a good deal of it is so casual and so insignificant when compared to one's total experience, that the residual effect is slight. Nevertheless, it is true that for both deliberate learning, and daily living and adjusting, the sequential steps are a sound basic formulation . . .

REFERENCES

1. DASHIELL, J. F. 1935. A survey and synthesis of learning theories. *Psychol. Bull.* 32:261-75.

4. The Biological Basis of Learning*

The basis of learning is biological in nature. Thus, a description of certain of the anatomical and physiological characteristics that make a high order of learning possible in humans is important and useful. Gerard, a noted physiologist, writes in a lucid fashion about a very complex and difficult subject. He also offers a number of shrewd estimates about the nature and direction of further research into the neural mechanisms of learning. (Another portion of this essay, on the nature and psychology of imagination, is included in the chapter on Aesthetic Creativity.)

ANATOMY

The introspective psychologists have distinguished between crude sensation, organized perception, and full-formed imagery on the sensory side; reason, will, and action on the motor side. The boundaries are not sharp,

---

* RALPH W. GERARD. Adapted and abridged with permission of the author and publisher from The biological basis of imagination. *Scientific Monthly,* 1946, 62:489-98.

to be sure, yet one can almost follow the one into the other one moving with nerve messages along the nervous system. From the single receptor, or sense organ—tactile corpuscle of the skin, eye, ear, etc.—comes but one modality of sensation—touch, light, sound. This has the attribute of intensity, given by the frequency or closeness with which impulses follow each other in each nerve fiber and, less, by the number of fibers activated. When the message reaches appropriate regions of the nervous system, the sensation also has its particular quality of touch or pitch, and this much of pattern that a "local sign" is attached, so that the region of the body (touch) or receptor (eye) from which the messages come remains identifiable. As nerve fibers from receptors gather into nerve bundles (along with motor fibers for much of the way, but separating at the ends, especially where they join the central nervous system), sensory messages are grouped together either by modality, in special cases like those of seeing in the optic nerve and those of hearing in the auditory nerve, or more generally by region, as all the skin and other sensations from one finger in a particular nerve or nerve branch.

Yet as soon as these latter nerves enter the nervous system, mainly along the spinal cord, the relay fibers are shuffled about so that they also become grouped by modality. Thus, if a nerve to the leg is cut, some portion of the leg skin (and muscle) will have lost all sensation of touch, pressure, temperature, pain, position, vibration, etc. But if one of the relay bundles in the spinal cord is damaged, the entire limb will lose only the sense of touch or of pain or of position, as examples, depending on which part of the cross section of the cord is injured, while retaining the other senses unimpaired. When these second relay fibers pass on their messages to the third member of the team, in the thalamus at the base of the great cerebral hemispheres, there is another reshuffling so that region again enters strongly into the arrangement. And from here the nerve wires fan out to reach the cerebral cortex, each to its own particular spot . . .

These cortical areas to which sensory nerve messages are projected from the thalamus, or from which motor messages project through the thalamus, are called the projection areas. They occupy but a small portion of the cerebral cortex, being surrounded by various association areas; and indeed both the microscopic characteristics and arrangements of the nerve cells and the functional influences that have been traced between them show that some half a hundred individual and distinctive areas are present in the cortex of man. Some of the association areas, in close relation to projection areas, are primary and concerned directly with an elaboration of the particular projected messages. More of them, the secondary association areas, are concerned with the most general inter-relation and reworking of the elaborated sensory clues, present and past . . .

Now what of sensation, perception, and the like, and especially imagination, in relation to this sketched-in organization of the nervous system? Clearly, a knowledge of structure and localization of function is not enough; for a single nerve impulse running in a single nerve fiber in one or another part of the brain is much the same thing, and a billion of them simply added together are only a billion of the same things. But nerve impulses are not simply added. Messages set up from a single hair on a cat's paw—by touching it with a hair on the observer's hand so lightly that the observer feels nothing—run up a sensory nerve fiber to the spinal cord and there "explode" into many impulses running up to the brain in many fibers, which further interact along the way. A person listening to a watch tick hears it as louder while a light is being looked at; and experiments on cats show a similar enhancement of messages in the auditory sensory paths when the nearby optic paths are simultaneously active. The point is that as sensory messages ascend toward and into the cerebrum they are not merely relayed and regrouped, they are also reorganized and reworked; in fact, we shall see they even reverberate . . .

Between perception and imagery on the one hand and volition on the other lie the great mental territories of imagination and reason. It might be useful to consider imagination as the culmination of sensory events, reason as the origin of the motor ones. Or perhaps reason, with its attendant logic, verbalization, decision, and willing, is more properly the start of motor events, and imagination is the more pervasive and encompassing mind work which is the keystone of the sensory-motor arch. Men with moderately severe brain injuries may perform well on the usual intelligence tests, while falling down on those which sample imagination. Indeed, imagination may include a "power" factor of intelligence underlying the others, as Spearman believed, and depending on the mass functioning of the whole brain, as Lashley's work on animals suggests.

Certainly, as earlier outlined, imagination depends on sensory information. Man cannot use the world other than as it unfolds itself within the sensory projection areas of his brain. These determine his basic orientation to externality. In the very spatial arrangement of the areas of vision, skin, and muscle sense is embedded an unformulated geometry. The basic units of physical science are distilled from these areas: space (centimeters) from vision, touch, muscle sense, and vestibular system (the balance organs located within the ear); substance (mass, grams) from smell, taste, touch, muscle sense, and, secondarily, vision—a congenitally blind person, on achieving vision, feels objects "hitting" his eyes until he learns to project his experience into the third dimension, as we all project the sense of touch to the end of a stick with which we explore the bottom of a pond—and perhaps, even the notion of force comes from touch and muscle sense, of matter more from taste and smell; and time (seconds) most directly from hearing. At least, as evidence for this last, is the powerful reaction to heard rhythm, tapping to a tune, and the fact that a sound track of words or music run backwards is completely meaningless, whereas a reversed light track, though often ludicrous or impossible, is perfectly meaningful. Moreover, one's subjective judgment of time certainly depends on a brain clock, which runs fast in fever according to a precise mathematical function of the brain temperature (Hoagland) . . .

Physiology

What, then, of the mechanisms of brain functioning, of the generation of thought? Granting, again, that the exact relation between neural processes and conscious events remains unknown, it is still possible to recognize some striking parallels. Are closure and patterning basic to imagination? They are simply shot through the entire felt-work of the nervous system! Not only in the large-scale organization we have already noted but in the small-scale one no less. True, particular nerve fiber bundles connect each of the separate areas of the cortex with all; many directly, the others by relays. True, some of the bundles carry messages which excite the nerve cells they reach, so that when cells in area X fire messages to area Y the cells in Y become active. But it is also true that comparable nerve bundles connect cortical areas with thalamus, with spinal cord, with all parts of the nervous system; so that a nerve impulse entering the central mass along any fiber path could, in principle, find its way by one route or another to every part of the nervous system. (And in fact, too, under some conditions; as when strychnine has rendered the whole neural apparatus more sensitive, and a slight irritation anywhere can set off a general convulsive reflex contraction of all the muscles of the body.) And it is further true that the nerve impulses running from area X may not excite but inhibit or suppress the cells in area Y so that these stop their current action and cannot be re-excited for a time . . .

Each nerve cell is so richly supplied by nerve fibers reaching it from all sorts of local and distant neural regions, reaching it and making functional connection (synapse) with it, that it is rather like an egg packed in sticky excelsior. Messages bombard it along these many paths, some pushing it to action and some to quietude, some perhaps powerful enough to tip and balance individually but most surely requiring the help of their like fellows. Further, the nerve cell is being influenced by the blood passing it, by the oxygen and sugar it receives, the salts that bathe it, the electric currents from its neighbors, the temperature at which it finds itself, by drugs which reach it. And from this welter of influences—its state of health, the condition of the environment in which it is living, and particularly, the clamor of allied and opposed messages reaching it—from all this comes a single result: the cell fires messages along its own fiber to still other cells, or it does not fire. There is, to be sure, some gradation in number and frequency of impulses sent or in duration of inactivity and depth of inactivability, but essentially the balance is between action or no action. Just so the judge, depending on the state of his stomach, or the temperature of the courtroom, or the bombardment of arguments on each side of the case, renders a single decision for or against. (Freedom of the individual to make the decision is equally easy or hard to discover in the nerve cell and in the judge.) It is the collective and patterned actions of the several billion nerve cells of our brains that determine our behavior and accompany our thoughts. We must explore further this neural patterning.

A few years back, the only well-recognized pattern was the reflex arc. A message entered along a sensory nerve, continued through the nervous system along direct or relayed connections, and finally emerged in a motor nerve. Except as messages were in transit, the nervous system was presumably quiet. Today we know, largely from the electrical pulses of the "brain waves," that nerve cells are continuously active in wake or sleep, and many beat on like the heart. In part, this beat depends on the chemical and physical state of the cell and its surrounding fluid; in part, on the nerve messages playing on it. Suppose cell A sends its fiber to connect, among others, with cell B, B with C, C with D, and D with A. If A were once activated by a message from X it would excite B, and so through C and D be re-excited itself. Another branch from D might excite Y. Then, once started, such a circuit might continue active, with excitation going round and round like a pin wheel and throwing off regular sparks of activity on each cycle. Of course this picture is too simple—the circuit would not be set off so singly, it would vary in its path and speed of spinning, it would have to stop by cell fatigue or other impulse interference, it would involve many more cells and connections, were it to accord with the actual behavior of the brain. But what is important is that just such circuit patterns, with all the needed complexities, have been shown to exist and function in this manner (Lorente de No). Closure in mental processes, did we say? Here is closure woven into the very fabric of the nervous system!

These closed circuits are mostly over minute distances, in single centers of the nervous system, but comparable ones exist on a gross scale. In many cases, also, a nerve cell cannot be made to fire by impulses reaching it along a single fiber but requires a nudge from two or several arriving at the same time (the main effect of a single impulse is expended in a few ten-thousandths of a second) and even from different regions. Again, what a beautiful basis for making new gestalts or recombinations of sensory material! As one example, recall that light can make sounds seem louder; as another, how association areas rework and embroider the activity of projection areas. A further instance shows that messages from the frontal lobe of the brain, as well as from the optic nerve and thalamus, must reach the visual centers for them to become fully active; for after injury to the front of the cerebrum the field of vision is narrowed, even though the retina and its immediate brain connections to the optic brain areas remain intact (Halsted).

Several important interactions occur between the cerebrum and thalamus, besides those already mentioned. Through the latter pass all sensory messages on their way to the projection areas and to full consciousness; and in another part of the thalamus are coordinated the bodily responses and perhaps the subjective aspects of emotion and other primitive feeling. When the cerebrum of an animal is removed, affective behavior is grotesquely exaggerated; so nerve paths from the cerebrum hold the thalamus in check. Other fibers from the cortex can activate the thalamus, and, indeed, even as sensory messages relay up through this part of the brain, other messages coming down to it from the cortex can block or enhance their passage (Dusser de Barenne). Perhaps what we call attention is in action through these paths which functionally open or close the gates of the thalamus and allow now one, now another, group of sensory messages access to the cortex and full consciousness while relegating the others to the fringe of awareness or even to the unconscious. (This is not to say that all cortical activity is conscious or self-conscious, for such is not the case. James's figure of consciousness, as a single lighted candle carried from place to place in the cavernous darkness of a great building, is still a good one.) And, a final example, certain paths from the thalamus radiate out to much of the cerebral cortex and, when stimulated, set the whole cortical sheet into vigorous electrical beating (Morison and Dempsey).

Perhaps this mechanism is responsible for the overactive mind work that follows an emotional shock. Perhaps just this occurred in Goethe's brain when news of his friend's suicide "crystallized" the plan of "Werther" as, "the whole shot together from all directions and became a solid mass." And surely here again is a neural basis for closure.

Besides such provocative nerve messages, able to influence the action of millions of nerve cells, other integrating mechanisms exist in the brain. Waves of action can be made to travel slowly over the cerebrum, for example, even when all anatomical connecting paths have been severed. Electric currents are probably involved here, and, indeed, these are a major factor in that environment which influences the discharge of the single nerve cell and the coordination of the many. Electrical fields have been richly demonstrated in brains; have been shown to vary their pattern with state of activity, chemical environment, drug action, and the like (Gerard); and have even been successfully invoked to explain in detail a variety of optical illusions in man (Köhler). By such various mechanisms, then, great masses of nerve cells—the brain as a great unity —act together; and not merely do two or a billion units sum their separate contributions, but each is part of a dynamic fluctuating activity pattern of the whole. This is the orchestra which plays thoughts of truth and beauty, which creates creative imagination.

Plenty of problems remain; some demand attention. Most urgent to our present theme is how novel neural patterns originate, since they must accompany novel thoughts or learning in general. Much attention has been given to the phenomena of learning: by "at sight," the slow cumulation of a new "correct" response in the course of conditioning experience, the conditioned reflex, and by insight, the sudden grasp of a solution and abrupt performance of the correct response, the gestalt or closure or imaginative act. They seem very different, and, as Terman put it, conditioning serves admirably to explain stupid behavior; gestalts, intelligent behavior. The mechanisms may indeed be quite different, but it is possible, perhaps probable, that they are basically quite similar. In both cases, new functional connections must be established in the brain; and this process may be more gradual and cumulative in the case of insights than appears. For here, also, much brain work precedes the imaginative flash —the theory of gravitation may result only when the metaphorical apple falls on the prepared mind—and only when the process has progressed to some threshold level does it overflow into a conscious (self-conscious) insight.

So long as our picture of the nervous system was that of the telephone exchange, with reflex plugs all set and each sense organ subscriber connected with, and able to call to action, its allotted muscles, the appearance of new responses seemed to demand the presence in the brain of rather mysterious telephone operators to shift the plugs. Now, with our discovery of a far more fluid nervous system, one unceasingly active and with neural and electrical messages rippling the whole into dynamic patterns, which flow from one contour to another as present influences play upon the condition left by past ones—with such a picture the arrival of new neural relationships is no great problem. Schemata have been offered—in terms of nerve impulse balance, electrical fields, fiber growth—which at least indicate reasonable avenues for further exploration . . .

Perhaps learning is initially a function of the whole brain and as ephemeral as a pattern of activity. But even activity leaves some more permanent change in the active part . . . and brain regions which are most active in particular patterns . . . might well acquire, with repetition of these patterns, alterations which are both more local and more enduring than the initiating disturbance. With such regions located it will become practicable to look for the kind of change which endures; change in chemical composition or metabolism, electrical potential or resistance, cell structure or connection, or whatever it turns out to be when found . . .

A final problem: . . . What is the neural basis for the striking quantitative differences between man and man in intelligence or in the several abilities which constitute intelligence or its component, imagination? Surely brain size as such is not the answer, as many studies have demonstrated. Perhaps absolute or relative size of the association areas would show better correlation with intelligence; or perhaps the richness of fiber connections and the architectural intricacy—as the more elaborate circuits make the better radios, large or small. And the factor of activity level is almost surely involved; not only the size and number of nerve cells but their rates of beat, maintained potentials, irritabilities; their functional vigor. This, in turn, depends on their composition (make what you will of the fact that the brains of women contain a higher percentage of lipins—fats—than those of men) and on their metabolism; and this, on the blood supply and the amount of oxygen and sugar it brings on the salt and acid and other components of the tissue fluids, on particular stimulants or depressants, as the thyroid hormone or anesthetic drugs, and the like. The influence of caffeine, alcohol, strychnine, cocaine, morphine, hashish, absinthe, and mescaline on brain metabolism and activity are being steadily worked out; their dramatic effects on the mind, especially on hallucinations and imaginings, are commonly enough known and are also being further studied (Kleuver). As the sets of facts are brought together new understanding will arise. Possibly from this direction we shall get a clue as to the finer differential between brains: what gives one man a vivid imagination but a poor memory, another an encyclopedic memory but dull imagination. And when that answer is at hand science will indeed have established the biological basis of imagination.

Processes of Behavioral Change

VARIABLE PROCESSES IN LEARNING

Important modifications of the generalized learning process described in Part 1 occur in the act of acquiring various learning outcomes. Indeed, it is perhaps more accurate to think of the learning process as a complex set of variable processes of behavioral change, some occurring sequentially and others concurrently. In Part 2, emphasis is placed upon selections which illustrate differential aspects of sequential change in learning of various types. To study the distinguishing features of different learning outcomes and the variable processes involved in attaining them, it is convenient to classify the more educationally significant of these into corresponding types of learning.

Five types of learning have been selected for emphasis in Part 2, plus a sixth category having to do with group learning processes. One type of learning is reasoning, a form of learning in which a rational approach to the solution of problem situations is sought. A closely related type of learning is aesthetic creativity, or the application of creative or original thought in aesthetic production. A third type is conceptual learning, the interpretation of situations, signs and symbols; and the representation of their meaning in terms of definitions, generalizations and qualities. A fourth type, skill learning, involves the coordination of appropriate sensory and perceptual functions in motor performance. A fifth type of learning, attitudinal learning, has to do with changes which involve a person's values. The sixth category indicated—group learning processes—refers to learning in situations, often problem-oriented, in which interpersonal or social interaction plays a prominent role in the course of learning. A separate chapter is devoted to each of these forms of learning.

29

CHAPTER : 2

Reasoning

5. Reasoning in Humans *

> Maier's research into the human reasoning process led him to conclude
> that the way in which a problem is attacked depends upon the way
> in which it is seen. Even when the necessary experience was provided,
> obvious solutions were often missed because the problem was inter-
> preted and attacked in an habitual way. Maier stresses the importance
> of "direction" in problem solution and shows that successful reasoning
> requires that a new "direction" be found when necessary.

PROBLEM

. . . The part experience plays in reasoning is not agreed upon. Either
specific experiences must be recalled or a general background of experience is taken for granted. Whether or not experience is conditioned, and
if so, under what conditions it plays its part in the reasoning process,
seems to have been neglected. The problem in this study is to find
whether or not experience, if recalled, is the sufficient fundamental factor
in problem solving, and if not, to discover, if possible, what the conditions are under which experience can best function.

PROCEDURE

If the experience as a whole is previously given to the reasoner then,
naturally, reasoning is not necessary. The application of an old experi-

---

* NORMAN R. F. MAIER. Reprinted and abridged with permission of the author and
publisher from Reasoning in humans. I. On direction. *Journal of Comparative Psychology*,
1930, 10:115-43.

ence must be new for the individual. If this were not the case, then learning and habitual responses would be no different from reasoning. (In fact, most of our so-called reasoning problems are nothing more than the selection of one out of several memories.) To test the influence of experience in the solution of a new problem, without unnecessarily hiding it in complex patterns, the solution of a [construction] problem was presented to the subjects in three separate parts. All the subject had to do, in order to solve the problem, was to recombine the parts in the right manner and thus obtain a unity which was the solution. Thus if the solution of the problem was ABC, the experience given was A, B, and C. In this manner all the experience necessary for the solution was given to the subject and did not have to be recalled by him . . .

The room in which the construction was to take place was 6.5 m. by 5.6 m. and was 2 meters high. It contained a large table which was not to be moved by the subject, 2 poles 1.9 meters long and 2 cm. square in cross-section, 2 other poles each about 1 meter long, 1 table clamp, 2 burette clamps, 2 pieces of electric bell wire about 2.3 meters long, 8 pieces of lead tubing 1 cm. in diameter and from 5 to 15 cm. long, and several pieces of chalk. The material was scattered about the table. There was a chair for the subject. The experimenter sat at a table in the far corner of the room . . .

The subject when taken into the room was informed that he or she would be asked to do some building, that there were several ways of making the construction, but that we were interested in how different people went about it. There would be the difficulty of not always having all the material that might be desired, but that made it all the more interesting. A good, firm construction would, of course, be the best. This was not a "catch" problem, there was to be no time limit. We were only interested in the qualitative side.

The problem was then stated (and elaborated so far as was necessary, until it was perfectly clear to the subject), as follows: "Your problem is to construct two pendulums, one of which will swing over this point (cross indicated on the floor, see Figure 1) and one which will swing over this other point (other cross indicated). These pendulums should be so constructed that they will have a piece of chalk fastened to them which will make a mark (which can be seen) on the points on the floor just indicated. Naturally you must have something to hang the pendulums to. That is for you to worry about. Don't try to move the table about. Otherwise do anything you want to. This material is at your disposal. That chair, however, is not to be part of your construction; you may use it for a workbench or a place for meditation, or anything you wish so long as it is free when you are through. Ask any questions you wish. I'll be glad to assist you in building, only you must tell me what to do." These specifications were repeated and explained until everything was perfectly clear to the subject.

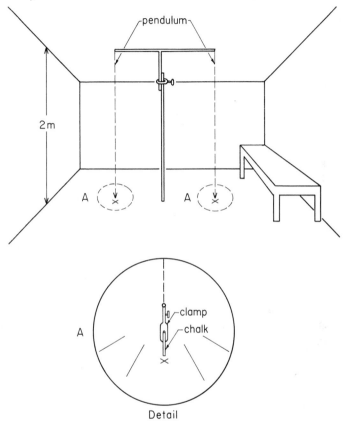

Fɪɢ. 1.

The three parts which were given as separate experiences were given under different conditions for the different groups used. These conditions will be described later. The separate parts may be called A, B, and C.

Part A. "In making a plumb line (a plumb line was explained if unfamiliar to the subject) one can, if he has not the desired material, combine this clamp (demonstrated with a burette clamp) with a pointed object such as a pencil and so have something which is both heavy and pointed at the same time and so will have the qualities of a plumb bob. Then we can fasten a cord or this wire to the thing and have a plumb line. This is to show you how it is possible to combine certain objects and so get the qualities we desire."

Part B. "If you were confined in a cage and wanted to reach a banana which was farther away than the longest of these poles what would you do? Most likely you would do what Koehler's apes did, combine two poles and make a longer one. This you can do very easily with the use of this table clamp. (This was demonstrated.) Thus you see how nicely we can make one long pole out of two short ones."

Part C. "Now I will show you a way to do without hammer and nails. If, for instance, you wanted to make a lantern screen, you naturally would like to have nails with which to fasten the screen to the wall. If there are none to be had you could take these two poles, place one flat against the wall of the doorway, like this, and so keep your white cloth taut up and down, then place this stick at right angles to it and wedge it in the doorway. (This was demonstrated by placing one of the sticks against the side of the doorway and wedging the other against the center of the first and opposite wall of the doorway. Thus a "T" in a horizontal position was formed.) In the same way you could fasten the other side of the screen and so keep the cloth taut sideways. Thus we could do it without hammer and nails, do you see?"

In some cases the subject was also given the following experience which will be called "direction."

Direction: "I should like to have you appreciate how simple this problem would be if we could just hang the pendulums from a nail in the ceiling. Of course, that is not a possible solution but I just want you to appreciate how simple the problem would be if that were possible. Now that it is not possible the problem is, as you may find, really quite difficult." This was demonstrated by holding one of the wires against the ceiling . . .

The subjects used were advanced students at the University of Berlin, most of them working for a doctorate in Psychology, Physics, or Chemistry (several already had their degree) and students in an advanced course in experimental psychology at the University of Michigan. The subjects were made to feel at ease and most of them enjoyed the problem. The German students were all volunteers . . .

The subjects were divided into the following five groups, each group being given the problem, the solution of which was ABC:

Group 1. The problem only was given. (Control group.)

Group 2. Parts A, B, and C were given, but the subject was told that these preliminary problems were given in order to get him acquainted with the situation and the material. They were given as separate experiences and he was asked to judge whether or not he found them clever or neat ways of doing things. He was also told that he would be given a problem to solve and when he had finished would be asked to judge his own solution in the same manner. (After A, B, and C had been demonstrated the problem was given.)

Group 3. Each member of this group was told, "I'm going to give you a problem to solve. You will have to construct something. (Problem was then given.) Before you start on the solution I should like to show you three separate things, each of which will involve a principle. If you combine the ideas, which I thus give you, in the right manner, you will have the best solution to the problem. Try to use them; they are the solution in three separate parts. You do not have to use them, but only by using them will you get the most satisfactory solution. So try to use them."

Group 4. Following a statement of the problem the "direction" (described above) was given.

Group 5. Same as Group 3 except that the "direction" was also included.

In every case the subject was given to understand that the problem or any of the instructions would be repeated if he was in doubt or had forgotten something . . .

Into which group a subject was to be placed was determined before the subject made his or her appearance. In case the subject was known and was considered intelligent he or she was not placed in Group 5. Group 5 was, therefore, not a group superior in intelligence.

Each experiment was individual. Some subjects worked as long as three hours; those who got the solution worked five or ten minutes. If the subjects did not solve the problem after one and a half hours or if completely out of ideas before then, other variations were introduced and new suggestions given. This will be indicated if such results are discussed.

RESULTS

. . . The attempts at solutions were of the following types:

1. An attempt was made to use the ceiling in the solution. Two pieces of wood would be clamped together and wedged between the floor and

ceiling. This required two pairs of sticks in order to have the two pendulums in their proper positions. For this there was a shortage of material.

2. Poles would be clamped or tied together with one of the pieces of wire, and thus wedged between the walls of the room. In the Berlin laboratory the room was wide and required three poles. This combination could be made to pass over the two points indicated for the pendulums, but would never stay in place. At the University of Michigan laboratory the poles could only be clamped across the hallway and therefore two separate pairs of poles were necessary. Only one pair would, however, reach across the hall.

3. The table was often used as part of the structure. One of the poles was just long enough to span the distance between the points over which the pendulums were to hang. If this pole was clamped to the table it was not long enough to reach, because the table could not be moved. This necessitated clamping a piece to the longer pole, a procedure which made the poles too heavy to be firm, as well as used up an extra clamp.

4. The German subjects also attempted to wedge poles between the table and the opposite wall. The poles would never stay in place.

5. Building up from the floor was also a common attempt at the solution. A leg, tripod, or sticks crossed to form an "X" were used to support the longer pole, in a horizontal position, from which pole the pendulums were expected to be hung. These attempts were unsuccessful because they either necessitated more material than was available or else they were so poorly constructed as to fall over. Making them just balance was often attempted, but such a structure would not support pendulums.

6. The solution consisted in placing the longer pole (which spanned the distance between the two points) flat against the ceiling and then holding it in place by clamping two of the other poles together in such a manner that they were just long enough to reach the floor when one end was placed against the middle of the pole which was flat against the ceiling. Thus the pole was wedged against the ceiling and the poles formed a large "T." The pendulums could then be hung from either end of the pole placed against the ceiling. A piece of chalk was then fastened in each burette clamp which formed the pendulum weight. The pendulum was made just long enough to allow the chalk to touch the floor. The structure was very simple and stable and required even one pole less than was given. All the subjects were surprised and pleased with the solution, whether it was shown to them or whether they found it themselves. Many were astounded at their "dumbness," and said they could not ex-

plain why they hadn't done it themselves. (See Figure 1 for diagram of solution.)

These types of solutions are indicated in Table 1. Often many different things were tried out that obviously would not work, but finally one variation of the above solutions would dominate the attention and would be rebuilt and revised for hours. The subject was always permitted to try until apparently altogether out of ideas or ready to give up.

TABLE 1

	Number of Subjects	Number Using Solution					
		1	2	3	4	5	Correct
University of Berlin:							
Group 1 (no parts)	15	1	0	8	3	3	0
Group 2 (parts A, B, C)	9	0	0	6	0	3	0
Group 3 (use A, B, C)	18	0	3	3	6	5	1
Group 5 (A, B, C and direction)	10	3	0	0	0	3	4
University of Michigan:							
Group 3	10	1	4	3	0	2	0
Group 4 (direction only)	10	0	1	7	0	2	0
Group 5	12	1	4	2	0	1	4

No difference between men and women as to resourcefulness was found. Many of the cleverest solutions came from women and many men were as unhandy as it was possible to be. The types of excuses, however, differed. The men said that they could do it if they had the proper material, the women said that they were inexperienced with carpenter work . . .

Thus it is clear that only when parts and "direction" are given is the solution at all likely to appear. Only one out of 62 subjects in the first four groups found the solution, but 8 of the 22 subjects in Group 5 were successful. It should also be noted that 4 of the 14 remaining subjects in Group 5 tried to use the ceiling and so were near the solution, and that only 2 of the 61 remaining subjects in the other four groups tried to do this . . .

In order that the reader may better understand the way in which the subjects attempted to solve the problem, and how, in the case of failure, suggestions were continually given until the solution was obtained, the proceedings in two typical cases are given in detail.

Subject 14 in Group 3

Begins to work after having been given A, B, and C.

Measures across room.

Measures from table to chalk marks on floor. Says, "I don't see where what you did in the doorway comes in" (referring to part B). Clamps the longest and shortest poles together and wedges them between the walls. Tries to figure out how the same can be done at a different point, but everything tried needs more wood than is to be had. Takes poles apart again.

Tries to use the table; rests one end of long pole on edge of table and holds other end. Stands thus and thinks. Makes feeble attempt at using walls again. Says she can't see how it can be done with what she has. (She is told that it can be done.)

Tries to find some way of using hall door (which is about halfway between the chalk marks). Measures between walls again, trying to find a narrower place or some projection from the walls.

Measured distance to ceiling and suggested clamping two poles together and wedging them between floor and ceiling. "If this could be done in two pieces a wire could be stretched across the two and the pendulums hung from it." Sees that she has not material for this. Tries walls and table again. Loses interest.

At the end of one hour direction was given.

This made no difference in her procedure. She listened and admitted that she appreciated how simple that would make the problem.

She was then told that she already had done two things, which if put together, would lead to the solution. She wondered which things were referred to and asked if this or that was correct.

She was then told to use part C, that a pole must rest against the ceiling, that her idea of wedging poles between floor and ceiling was correct, and that it was necessary to know how to hold a stick in place without nails.

This gave her no idea. After awhile she tried to hold a pole to the ceiling by running braces from the wall which, of course, would not stay in place any more than the pole at the ceiling.

She was then asked to recall how we got along without nails before. This only confused her (apparently).

The pole was then held to the ceiling by the operator who held it with his finger against the center of the pole.

She showed no signs of having thought of the solution.

The operator then said, "See, it stays there now."

She stood looking an instant, then quickly placed a pole so as to take the place of the operator's finger. She then lengthened the pole so as to reach the floor.

Correct solution.

Subject 26 in Group 4

He begins measuring across walls trying different combinations of poles.

Sets tripod, made from poles, in middle of floor and holds them.

Tries walls again. Clamps two shorter pieces together and tries to fill in the few inches, they are too short, by wedging in a short bolt. This is soon given up. The combined poles are turned about end for end. He has to avoid hitting the ceiling because this same combination of poles more than reaches between the ceiling and the floor. This, however, gives him no idea. Tries using bolt with poles between walls again and after some time gets the poles to just stay in place.

He then said that he ought to have a clamp so that he could do the same over the other chalk mark. When asked about the burette clamps, he said that he was saving them for the pendulum.

Tries to figure out how to tie the poles together and still have wire for the pendulum. Tries different schemes. Finally says he doesn't believe he can do it.

After awhile he sets all poles side by side, on the floor, in order to compare their different lengths. Then different combinations across the room are again tried out.

Next he tries making a pair of poles stand in the middle of the floor by leaning them against each other. He then varies this by supporting their bases against the walls.

After this possibility was exhausted direction was given.

He returned to what he had done just before, but instead of leaning two poles against each other, with their bases against the walls, he places an extra one at one end.

After a little while he again tried clamping between walls as in the beginning.

He was then told, "You'd like to drive a nail in the ceiling, well, you've been shown how it is possible to get on without nails."

Then he thinks awhile and tries to see how this can be applied to walls.

He was then told, "You've had the wrong idea so far, get rid of that one idea and its variations; it will not give a satisfactory solution."

Then he set a short pole on the floor and placed the long pole horizontally over the top. Next he tried placing the same long pole on a tripod, which he held together, in the center.

The operator then told him that his idea of using the walls would have been a good one if the ceiling and the floor had been the walls. Also that the three parts given in the beginning would have to be used more exactly.

He then tried placing a short piece cornerwise against the wall and ceiling and then placing a long pole under this cross piece to hold it in place. He tried many variations of this.

Then he tried to make the long pole stand by placing a bolt on one end to make it reach the ceiling, but the two together were too short. He returned to trying the cross piece again.

He was then told to get along without using the walls.

Clamps long and short pole together and wedges between floor and ceiling. Can't figure out how he can have a support for second pendulum.

Told to use the three parts more exactly.

Leans long pole against wall, holds onto it and thinks.

Told that the long pole must be horizontal and the pendulums hung from it.

No response, stands and thinks.

Operator asks for a description of part C. Subject describes and operator asks subject to use it. Subject says he needs walls. Operator says that he told him to use floor and ceiling for walls. Subject says, "That gives me an idea." Then he proceeds with the solution . . .

Discussion of Results

From the results it is obvious that the mere conscious presence of the necessary experiences or data is not sufficient to solve certain problems. Some other factor is necessary before the elements can be integrated into a unified whole, the solution of the problem. This factor we have called "direction." "Direction" is the way the problem is attacked and depends on the way the problem is seen or what the difficulty of the problem is seen to be. Experiences are only useful if they aid in overcoming the difficulty. By giving "direction" it was intended that the subject should see the problem in a certain way . . .

Only when experience fits the "direction" or the way the person has attacked the problem will it aid in the solution of the problem. Otherwise experiences given or called up by association have nothing to do with the problem and at best can only be made over so as to fit the "direction" which has been taken . . .

6. An Experimental Study of Problem Solving *

The conception of Durkin's experimental study of problem-solving processes was broad enough to allow her to distinguish three "forms" or characteristics of thinking. Using a series of puzzle construction tasks, she identifies the processes involved in problem solution as "trial and error," "sudden reorganization," and "gradual analysis." This study is useful in examining such questions as the effect of the nature of the problem upon problem-solving processes, and the appropriateness of the concepts used to describe the behavior involved.

Technique

. . . A glance at the experimental literature indicated that it would, for my purposes, be best to begin with a very simple level of thinking, for even then it is complex, rapid and not, at each point, clear to the subject. Anything on a more complex level, as verbal, numerical, or even three-dimensional construction puzzles, would be extremely difficult to follow through minutely in the attempt to reduce thinking to its lowest terms.

I chose, accordingly, a rather simply organized series of two-dimensional construction puzzles, which seem at first glance to offer a problem only in perception, but whose patterns and form of disarrangement are conceived to necessitate a roundabout process for solution. The subject's problem was to find the roundabout path; mine, the means by which he reached it. This set-up had the further advantages that no factor of skill could cut across the results; that verbal description could be comparatively accurate and easy to follow; and that the situation confronting observer at any stage of the solving would be visible and could be photographed.

* HELEN E. DURKIN. Reprinted and abridged with permission of the author and publisher from Trial-and-error, gradual analysis, and sudden reorganization; an experimental study of problem solving, pp. 10-84. *Archives of Psychology,* Vol. 30, No. 210, 1937.

There were six puzzles in all. Each of five consisted of several (4 or 5) pieces so cut that they could be made into squares (4″ by 4″) or into Maltese crosses. The sixth puzzle consisted of all these pieces to be made into one large Maltese cross. Of the first five puzzles, A, B, C, D and E respectively (see the diagrams), all but B were based at least partly on the diagonal principle, i.e., the apparently straight edges were to be used

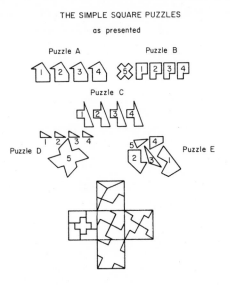

THE SIMPLE SQUARE PUZZLES

as presented

Puzzle A   Puzzle B

Puzzle C

Puzzle D   Puzzle E

The Completed Total Cross Puzzle

THE SIMPLE SQUARE PUZZLES AS PRESENTED AND THE TOTAL CROSS PUZZLE.

on the diagonal, and vice versa. All except E were based also on the circular principle, that is, the pieces were to be used pin-wheel fashion. Since they were so presented as to avoid suggesting these principles of construction, and in the case of the diagonal principle to suggest the opposite, these factors contributed to the necessity for finding a roundabout path to solution. The pieces were cut to specification out of bristol board and lacquered black on both sides.

. . . Observer worked at one end of a long wooden table; experimenter at the other. Separating them, about midway, was a one-way screen made of rayon. From this screen to the observer, attached to either side of the table, and held in a wooden frame, were two large black lacquered sheets of cardboard. They reached about as high as observer's head and were meant to isolate observer for the purpose of concentration, while the one-way screen served to minimize his consciousness of being observed. A noisy electric fan sounding continuously, masked intercurrent sounds which might be distracting.

After experimenter had arranged the pieces of puzzle A in prescribed order (see the diagram) on a large sheet of white cardboard, and covered them with a similar piece, observer was asked to come in. Experimenter put him as much at ease as possible and then asked him to sit down to the work, told him it was a study of problem solving, and read the following instructions:

This is not in any sense a mental test. I am not interested in how well any individual does, but in the general methods used in solving. Your results will not be evaluated, nor your ability compared to anyone else's. As you solve, please think aloud. Express every idea that comes to you as you work even if it seems irrelevant. Try to tell me also how you feel about it as you go along. My chief interest is to find out as fully as possible just what goes on in your mind as you work. Now, when I say ready, please remove the cover, look at the pieces of the puzzle you will see before you, and try to make a square with them. Before you move any piece, make a plan of what you are going to do. When you have a plan, let me know. Later you will have a chance to work it out. Do you understand, or would you like me to explain any point?

(Experimenter then repeated chief ideas, and answered any question.)

As soon as one puzzle was finished, observer, with the pieces as originally presented before him, was asked to *retrace* his solution, and any point of interest was discussed.

Observer was now asked to step outside until experimenter prepared the next puzzle. The same instructions were given for Puzzles B, C, D, and E in turn. After Puzzle E, observer was allowed to walk down the hall to relax, while experimenter arranged the entire assortment of pieces either as small crosses or in mixed order . . . Upon his return, experimenter said:

Now, I've given you quite a different puzzle. (This was an attempt to cancel the square-making set.) Put all the pieces together to form a large Maltese cross. Please express verbally every idea that comes to you, in order to help me see just what is going on in your mind as you work. As before, make a plan, before you move the pieces.

This last requirement was not, however, insisted on rigidly. When observer did reach a plan, or when he was finished, if he did not formulate a plan, he was asked to retrace . . .

The moves made in solving supplied a natural and explicit record of the progress of the solution, and were noted as to number and kind. Snapshots were taken at crucial stages. To find out as completely as possible the "how he did it," experimenter asked observer to think aloud, and took a full record of his verbal report. The retrace added much valuable material, unreported during the solution, and I strongly recommend it as an integral part of any talking-out method. The experimenter must, of course, remain constantly alert to the possibilities of inaccurate report, but with experienced and cooperative subjects who know there is nothing to be gained by appearing smarter than they are, one should be able to gain a fair understanding of what has gone on. Experimenter must always interpret the verbal record strictly in light of what observer did with the pieces . . .

TRIAL-AND-ERROR AS A METHOD OF APPROACH

. . . What is the experimental evidence about trial-and-error as a method of solving? It is rarely used throughout a whole puzzle, but when it is, it is slow and inefficient. However, in spite of the method, the problem is eventually solved, but not till the basic relationship of the puzzle is recognized. Thus we bring into high relief the difference between mere manipulation of the material and manipulation guided by observer's idea of the goal, which we have called trial-and-error. Manipulation is merely the most obvious of observer's responses in a trial-and-error solution.

Let us examine in detail such a solution by trial-and-error.

Protocol 1—E.V.O. on Puzzle A

Plan: 2 minutes

> 1. Oh, my word (laughs in an embarrassed way).
> 2. – – – – I don't see anything – – –.
> 3. – – – – can make no plan till I touch them – –.
> 4. – – I'll have to move them.

Solution: 8 minutes

26 moves

Remarks 1–4 are accompanied by manipulation during the long pauses.

At 5 lifts one up into the air and examines it (manipulation).

Another series of rapid moves (1 correct unrecog.) (Manipulation)

Puts 2 together wrong but adds third correctly, recognizes it, and very slowly; the last 2 moves are correct (foresight).

Remarks

1. – – – – Experimenter prompts – – "I can't talk – – –.
2. – – – don't see how – – – –.
3. – – feel warm – – – laughs – –.
4. – – – have no idea – –.
5. – – must stop and try to think.
6. – – – don't think I can do it.
7. – – – – feel ashamed – – –.
8. – – Experimenter: "You had it once." Observer: "Yes, there were 2 that went together perfectly – – but can't repeat it."
9. – – – – Experimenter prompts – – "Just sitting here stupidly just moving pieces – – a vain attempt to do it without thinking – – –."
10. – – – thinking mostly that I'm stupid.
11. – – – Oh, I see it now" (recognition) (after the correct move occurs for the 3rd time.)

Retrace:

I didn't think—just luck—found two edges of the same length on a slant. Now I can see that if you stopped for a plan, you could see that they were cut the same way; if you arranged the straight edges, the points would fit together inside. Did last slowly because thought it didn't fit accurately enough . . .

ANALYSIS AS A METHOD OF SOLVING

M.M.E.'s work on Puzzle A is a typical example of solving by analysis and yields a suitable case for minute study of the method. It contrasts vividly with Protocol 1.

Protocol 2—M.M.E. on Puzzle A

Plan: 1 minute

1. Well, all same—pause—yes, all same.
2. Doesn't look bad—smiles.

3. Just seeing which is the probable corner (A implied).
4. Obviously longer corners (A implied).
5. Yes, I'll take a crack.

Solution: 13 seconds

5 moves	*Remarks*
Immediately put 2 together correctly, then 2 more, which he turned upside down and fitted in. No errors.	"I licked that by inspection."

Retrace:

Since a square was called for, a certain edge must be a corner. Saw by inspection that if I used the short side as corner the longer would not fit in with the rest of the pattern. Also could see that the 2 short sides would fit together. Can do same for other 2 and turn upside down. No feeling, because too simple. Absolutely certain before moving a piece. The moving of the pieces was entirely unnecessary to the solution. Did it by inspection . . .

COMPARISON OF TRIAL-AND-ERROR AND ANALYSIS AS FORMS OF "THINKING"

The most easily recognized distinction between this "analytic" form of thinking and the trial-and-error variety is that in analysis, observer sees the reason for his moves before he makes them, instead of making them to see what will result. He makes enough observations and inferences about his goal to know what is needed to reach it, and about his material to meet those requirements. Consequently he comes to see the basic puzzle relationship (rightly or wrongly) before he moves the pieces instead of after he does so. Seeing the relationship is the crucial factor in both, but in analysis it is seen before manipulation, in trial-and-error, after.

A second quite obvious difference is that in analysis observations and inferences play the role of means to the desired end, while in trial-and-error, manipulation plays that role.

Probing deeper, we find at the root of these differences the fact that in analysis, observer centers his attention on the goal, becoming aware of its specific requirements and looking at the material only in light of this knowledge, while in trial-and-error he centers his attention on the material and keeps the goal at the "rim" of attention—to use Titchener's phraseology. As a result, he is more fully conscious in analysis of the steps that bring about the solution; his search is more highly selective, and he is apt to speak of this method as "figuring it out" as compared to what he calls "just playing around" in trial-and-error.

It seems to me that such differences as these justify and even demand a separate term for the method, and that, if we call the method in Protocol 1 trial-and-error, because it depends chiefly on trial moves, the term analysis is appropriate here because the solution is based chiefly on logical reasons and only secondarily on trial moves whether imaginal or actual. Whether the logic was correct or not does not affect the question of whether it was used. If the logic was correct, there was a minimum number of moves while, if it were not, the moves were wrong and observer had to begin again, either returning to "the figuring it out" procedure or changing to moving the pieces more at random (trial-and-error). "Figuring it out" can, of course, in a general sense be called exploratory, but that designation hits only the external of observer's work, not the specific processes which are responsible for this final solution.

Analysis and trial-and-error have several processes in common—attention to the goal, observation of the material, recall, if the problem calls for it, manipulation, and seeing the crucial puzzle relationship. But in trial-and-error, observer's attention to the idea of the goal is rather remote and diffuse; in analysis it is specific and concentrated; in trial-and-error seeing the relationship is merely a matter of recognition; in analysis, by means of inferences. In trial-and-error the moves are made before the resultant relation to the goal is clear; in analysis, after. Since most of these differences seem to be a function of attention, which is capable of variations as to direction and intensity, there is no claim made for mutual exclusiveness of these methods. The indications are, rather, for a continuum . . .

SUDDEN REORGANIZATION

Among the observers who had experience with the squares first, most solved by sudden reorganization. It is to those cases that I would like to give special attention in the following section, for it is there that the phenomenon of "foreshadowing" occurs. Later, these sudden reorganization solutions will be compared to those by gradual analysis.

To make quite clear just what I mean by sudden reorganization, to show its unique nature and to study its developmental course, I shall quote and examine minutely the following example:

Protocol 10—B.C.* on "Total Cross" Puzzle

Moves	*Remarks*
1. Looks over whole board. Eyes move rapidly. Fingers many pieces, particularly D (observation).	1. Seems to be all the pieces I've used before – – – – I wonder if all really here. (Recall, not in relation to present goal.)
2. Picks up D.	2. Logical to start with big cross (D) (implied analysis).
3. Fingers B.	3. Maybe the little cross will complicate the thing. (Analysis)
4. Places D at bottom center so it looks like a cross and would not make a square.	4. No ready solution but will start with this (D).
5. Piles them up in assorted order.	5. Get all similar pieces together so if one works all will.
6. Looks around at all pieces and fingers the little cross.	6. Maybe with little cross as center – –. This has to be much broader than these arms at center. (Analysis)
7. Fingers B.	7. Maybe this little cross ought to be started out as a square, because so many pieces need a big center. (Analysis)
8. Picks up B – – stops, hesitates, and is very quiet a moment – – –.	8. (Raised his voice and said excitedly) This is a good one, the real solution finally hits me. Make five squares and this can be the center.
9. Makes the five squares with only one error and puts them together to form the Greek cross.	

Retrace:

I was thrilled when it finally dawned on me, but should have thought of that first because I had been making squares. While working I had noticed there were 5 squares but didn't tie it up to the present problem. I recognized parts to go with the various squares. The clue came from the square to be used in center—because to use up all the pieces would have to get a large center. At that the idea came to me that I had the material for the square and the fact previously noted that with the little cross I had thought of using in the center none would fit in except the 4 used before as a square. Then it suddenly

---

* Observer does not stop to make a plan. Experimenter did not interfere when this happened on the final "total cross" puzzle.

dawned on me that it would be one arm and I had the material for other arms. I remembered pieces very well to sort them. I had already sorted them at the beginning though with different plan in mind—merely that if one could be used probably the others of its kind could . . .

What we have, then, is a distinctive pattern of problem solving descriptively designated as sudden reorganization . . . involving a dynamic readjustment of the field which seems sudden because the reactions that led up to it are concealed. Either they are not, when they occur, clear in relation to the goal or they occur too swiftly and fleetingly to be verbalized. At a certain point the errors drop out and the solution has virtually been reached. The essential pattern is stable but its form varies considerably . . .

GRADUAL ANALYSIS

In our attempt to classify gradual analysis solutions by separating them from sudden reorganization, we find many cases falling between the two groups. In some gradual analysis the subject's retrospective report indicated a very gradual development, though his remarks and behavior during the process seemed to show one or more sudden turning points. In others, observer did not, at the turning point, see his way clear to the solution. He may have reached the turning point by a series of inferences, well aware all along that he was making progress, and therefore with no sense of sudden discovery at the turning point. Still others experienced no particular turning point at all. We may therefore postulate a continuous series running from sudden reorganization to gradual analysis. The difference between the end cases in this series is that the steps leading up to the sudden reorganization are hidden, whereas those leading through gradual analysis are clearly revealed.

The most obvious characteristic of gradual analysis is a zigzag quality (described by Claparède) with so many trial moves as to suggest the term trial-and-error. But this appearance is superficial; the trial moves are auxiliary rather than primary and serve mainly to discard hypotheses, rather than to form them; they do not carry the real progress of the solution.

What does then? The implications of the goal and of the material are seen in relation to each other. The essential process is seeing relations, making inferences based on observation and recall, all within the framework of the problem. We might speak of "inferential behavior." The zigzag procedure, carefully examined, reveals a series of steps, spiral perhaps, but leading nearer and nearer to the solution. Each step is a clear advance toward the goal. Confusion gives way to clear vision gradually rather than at any single point . . .

Our next step must be to compare in detail some of the actual solutions by gradual analysis to the sudden reorganizations we have been examining. Protocol 20 provides a satisfactory example.

Protocol 20—C.D. on the "Total Cross" Puzzle

Moves*	Remarks
1. *Observer didn't stop to plan.	1. I notice 2 (C 1, 2) alike and 4A also (observer). So while this may be large, there is some similarity in the way it is made (analysis).
2. Piles the similar ones together.	2. Proceeding on theory that each side is like the other, all equals, and sees what's left—try to make a center out of that (analysis).
3. Looks at 4 piles.	3. That's an extra reproduction. It's composed of 5 squares (analysis).
4. Looks at left-overs, then at sample.	4. I'm debating 2 theories—that of 5 squares, and 4, with miscellaneous inside.
5. Fits them in (manipulation).	5. Obvious the little triangles fill out the D 5.
6. Moves E 1, 2, 4, 3 in various positions (manipulation).	6. Trying to make a square of the remains which doesn't seem successful.
7. Adds triangle.	7. Oh. (merely because last piece fits).
8. Puts 2 pieces in various positions.	8. Goes to C and measures sides to see which side is the right length.
9. Adds long side to side of made square, then adds the 2nd correctly and finishes it.	9. Getting into all sorts of difficulties—can't get beyond 2 sq. Too lazy to figure out size of the whole.
10. Observer goes on with too little verbalization to give clear idea of his processes. He seems to continue to fall back on trial-and-error for making the specific square.	10. I was working to make square of same size when 2nd piece fit knew the same sequence would work. How 2nd fit in is more than I can tell. It was the acute angle making a right angle.

Retrace:

Not sure if center would be regular, therefore sorted out regular ones and tried that. When they fitted – – – (probably meant irregular ones) E 4, 5, fooled me. The main thing is not to let them throw you. Got to start on system based on preliminary surveys as to what the problem consists of. Got the idea of 5 squares from the sample and proceeded fairly clearly from this and the fact that there were similar pieces. Assumed there must be some relation between them . . .

GENERAL CONCLUSIONS

These results lead inevitably to the conclusions that:

1. Problem solving in human adults is never completely blind or random, although observer may proceed to his goal by manipulating the material without seeing ahead the relation of his moves to the goal. At the worst he *recognizes* it by hindsight.

2. On the other hand, it is, except in the simplest case, to some degree exploratory, and always requires some manipulation, if only for verifying a correct hypothesis.

3. It is not that a new kind of process, that of seeing the relationship of the material to the goal, enters in at the level of so-called "insightful" thinking, but that that process was there in nucleus, though but vaguely, from the beginning, in the "blindest" variety of trial-and-error. Whether this is an independent process or is based genetically on trial-and-error or conditioned response, is not established.

4. One can distinguish three main types of solution, which can be considered as three "forms" of thinking, whose characteristics are sufficiently different to warrant the application of three separable names. I suggest: Trial-and-Error, Sudden Reorganization, and Gradual Analysis. The differences are listed in the chart [below].

5. Each sudden reorganization is preceded by a short intent pause during which observer seems to try to grasp a series of rapid, fleeting inferences and recalls which bring the sudden reorganization to focus.

6. Sudden reorganization, which parallels closely the usual descriptions of sudden insight, can, whenever the problem situation is beyond observer's "apprehension span," be found to be related to certain previous responses to the material. These responses are in the form of observations, recalls, and inferences and may have occurred earlier during the solution or in previous experience.

Trial-and-Error	Sudden Reorganization	Gradual Analysis
1. "Blind" groping.	Groping suddenly stopped.	No groping but a gradually developing understanding.
2. Hindsight.	Sudden foresight.	Foresight.
3. Confusion till the last moment.	Confusion suddenly cleared.	Cleared step by step.
4. Hopeless feeling.	Excitement, elation, sometimes relief.	Satisfaction.
5. Aim—to match pieces.	To look for wholes or interrelations.	To satisfy goal needs.
6. Attention to goal distant, diffuse.	Attention not centered on goal.	Attention concentrated on specific goal needs.
7. Attitude not definite, but wandering, haphazard.	Passive, receptive.	Active, directed search.
8. Error curve irregular, may not drop out after solution; transfer poor.	Curve irregular, then sudden drop; transfer good.	Error curve step-like; transfer good.
9. Manner baffled.	Baffled, then suddenly well organized, efficient.	Calm, well-organized.

7. Underlying these, however, we find the same processes throughout. These are, observation, recall, seeing relations, and attention to the goal. To this manipulation can be added, and inferences can be considered as a higher level of seeing relations. Furthermore, we find sufficient transitional cases so that we have here a basis for considering our three "forms" of thought as points on one continuum, rather than mutually exclusive kinds of thinking.

REFERENCES

1. BULBROOK, M. E. 1932. An experimental inquiry into the existence and nature of insight. *Amer. J. Psychol.* 44:409–53.
2. HEIDBREDER, E. 1924. An experimental study of thinking. *Arch. Psychol.* No. 73.
3. HENRY, L. K. 1934. The role of insight in the analytic thinking of adolescents. *U. Iowa St., Educ. Psychol.* Ser. 2:65–102.
4. MAIER, N. R. F. 1931. Reasoning and learning. *Psychol. Rev.* 38:332–46.
5. MATHESON, E. 1931. A study of problem solving behavior in pre-school children. *Child Devel.* 2:243–62.
6. MORGAN, C. L. 1934. Characteristics of problem solving behavior of adults. *U. Iowa St., Educ. Psychol.* Ser. 2:105–43.

. The Solution of Practical Problems*

The concept of "productive thinking" is usually associated with Duncker's studies on how people go about the solution of practical problems. He suggests that such thinking requires an active process of formulation and reformulation of the problem, certain solutions having greater functional value than others and hence being more "productive." Duncker's discussion of how the functional value of a solution is related to understanding, and why learning from errors has great utility in the solution process is stimulating and thought-provoking.

Introduction and Formulation of the Problem

A problem arises when a living creature has a goal but does not know how this goal is to be reached. Whenever one cannot go from the given situation to the desired situation simply by action, then there has to be recourse to thinking. (By action we here understand the performance of obvious operations.) Such thinking has the task of devising some action which may mediate between the existing and the desired situations. Thus the "solution" of a practical problem must fulfill two demands: in the first place, its realization must bring about the goal situation, and in the second place one must be able to arrive at it from the given situation simply through action.

The practical problem whose solution was experimentally studied in greatest detail runs as follows: Given a human being with an inoperable stomach tumor, and rays which destroy organic tissue at sufficient intensity, by what procedure can one free him of the tumor by these rays and at the same time avoid destroying the healthy tissue which surrounds it? . . .

In the present investigation the question is: *How does the solution arise from the problem situation? In what ways is the solution of a problem attained?*

Experimental Procedure

The experiments proceeded as follows: The subjects, who were mostly students of universities or of colleges, were given various thinking prob-

* KARL DUNCKER. Reprinted and abridged with permission of the publisher from On problem solving, pp. 1-14. *Psychological Monographs,* Vol. 58, No. 5, Whole No. 270, 1945.

lems, with the request that they think aloud. This instruction, *"Thin. aloud,"* is not identical with the instruction to introspect which has been common in experiments on thought-processes. While the introspected makes himself as thinking the object of his attention, the subject who is thinking aloud remains immediately directed to the problem, so to speak allowing his activity to become verbal. When someone, while thinking says to himself, "One ought to see if this isn't . . . ," or, "It would be nice if one could show that . . . ," one would hardly call this introspec tion; yet in such remarks something is revealed which we shall later deal with under the name of 'development of the problem.' The subject was emphatically warned not to leave unspoken even the most fleeting or foolish idea. He was told that where he did not feel completely informed he might freely question the experimenter, but that no previous specialized knowledge was necessary to solve the problems.

A Protocol of the Radiation Problem

Let us begin with the radiation problem . . . Usually the schematic sketch shown in Fig. 1 was given with the problem.

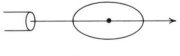

Fig. 1.

Thus, it was added, somebody had visualized the situation to begin with (cross-section through the body with the tumor in the middle and the radiation apparatus on the left); but obviously this would not do.

From my records I chose that of a solution-process which was par ticularly rich in typical hunches and therefore also especially long and involved. The average process vacillated less and could be left to run its own course with considerably less guidance.

Protocol

1. Send rays through the esophagus.
2. Desensitize the healthy tissues by means of a chemical injection.
3. Expose the tumor by operating.
4. One ought to decrease the intensity of the rays on their way; for example —would this work?—turn the rays on at full strength only after the tumor has been reached. (Experimenter: False analogy; no injection is in question.

5. One should swallow something inorganic (which would not allow passage of the rays) to protect the healthy stomach-walls. (Experimenter: It is not merely the stomach-walls which are to be protected.)

6. Either the rays must enter the body or the tumor must come out. Perhaps one could alter the location of the tumor—but how? Through pressure? No.

7. Introduce a cannula.—(Experimenter: What, in general, does one do when, with any agent, one wishes to produce in a specific place an effect which he wishes to avoid on the way to that place?)

8. (Reply:) One neutralizes the effect on the way. But that is what I have been attempting all the time.

9. Move the tumor toward the exterior. (Compare 6.) (The experimenter repeats the problem and emphasizes, ". . . which destroy *at sufficient intensity.*")

10. The intensity ought to be variable. (Compare 4.)

11. Adaption of the healthy tissues by previous weak application of the rays. (Experimenter: How can it be brought about that the rays destroy only the region of the tumor?)

12. (Reply:) I see no more than two possibilities: either to protect the body or to make the rays harmless. (Experimenter: How could one decrease the intensity of the rays en route?) (Compare 4.)

13. (Reply:) Somehow divert . . . diffuse rays . . . disperse . . . stop! Send a broad and weak bundle of rays through a lens in such a way that the tumor lies at the focal point and thus receives intensive radiation. (Total duration about half an hour.)

Impracticable "Solutions"

In the protocol given above, we can discern immediately that the whole process, from the original setting of the problem to the final solution, appears as a series of more or less concrete proposals. Of course, only the last one, or at least its principle, is practicable. All those preceding are in some respect inadequate to the problem, and therefore the process of solution cannot stop there. But however primitive they may be, this one thing is certain, that they cannot be discussed in terms of meaningless, blind, trial-and-error reactions. Let us take for an example the first proposal: "Send rays through the esophagus." Its clear meaning is that the rays should be guided into the stomach by some passage free from tissue. The basis of this proposal is, however, obviously an incorrect representation of the situation inasmuch as the rays are regarded as a sort of fluid, or the esophagus as offering a perfectly straight approach to the stomach, etc. Nevertheless, within the limits of this simplified concept of the situation, the proposal would actually fulfill the demands of the problem. It is therefore genuinely the solution of a problem, although not of the one which was actually presented . . .

CLASSIFICATION OF PROPOSALS

If one compares the various tentative solutions in the protocol with one another, they fall naturally into certain groups. Proposals 1, 3, 5, 6, 7 and 9 have clearly in common the attempt to *avoid contact between the rays and the healthy tissue*. This goal is attained in quite different ways: in 1 by re-directing the rays over a path naturally free from tissue; in 3 by the removal of the healthy tissue from the original path of the rays by operation; in 5 by interposing a protective wall (which may already have been tacitly implied in 1 and 3); in 6 by translocating the tumor towards the exterior; and in 7, finally, by a combination of 3 and 5. In proposals 2 and 11, the problem is quite differently attacked: the accompanying destruction of healthy tissue is here to be avoided by the *desensitizing or immunizing of this tissue*. A third method is used in 4, perhaps in 8, in 10 and 13: *the reduction of radiation intensity on the way*. As one can see, the process of solution shifts noticeably back and forth between these three methods of approach . . .

FUNCTIONAL VALUE AND UNDERSTANDING

. . . The functional value of a solution is indispensable for the understanding of its being a solution. It is exactly what is called the sense, the principle or the point of the solution. The subordinated, more specialized characteristics and properties of a solution embody this principle, apply it to the particular circumstances of the situation. For example, the esophagus is in this way an application of the principle: "free passage to the stomach," to the particular circumstances of the human body. To understand the solution as a solution is just the same as to comprehend the solution as embodying its functional value. When someone is asked, "Why is such-and-such a solution?" he necessarily has recourse to the functional value. In all my experiments, aside from two or three unmistakable exceptions, when the experimenter asked about a proposal: "In what way is this a solution of the problem?" the subject responded promptly with a statement of its functional value . . .

. . . To the same degree to which a solution is understood, it can be transposed, which means that under altered conditions it may be changed correspondingly in such a way as to preserve its functional value. For, one can transpose a solution only when one has grasped its functional value, its general principle . . .

THE PROCESS OF SOLUTION AS DEVELOPMENT OF THE PROBLEM

It may already have become clear that the relationship between super-ordinate and subordinate properties of a solution has *genetic* significance. *The final form of an individual solution is, in general, not reached by a single step from the original setting of the problem; on the contrary, the principle, the functional value of the solution typically arises first, and the final form of the solution in question develops only as this principle becomes successively more and more concrete. In other words, the general or "essential" properties of a solution genetically precede the specific properties; the latter are developed out of the former . . .*

The finding of a general property of a solution means each time a *reformulation of the original problem.* Consider, for example, the fourth proposal in the protocol above. Here it is clearly evident that at first there exists only the very general functional value of the solution: "one must decrease the intensity of the radiation on the way." But the decisive re-formulation of the original problem is thereby accomplished. No longer, as at the beginning, does the subject seek simply a "means to apply rays to the tumor without also destroying healthy tissue," but already—over and above this—a means to decrease the intensity of the radiation on the way. The formulation of the problem has thus been made sharper, more specific—and the proposal not to turn the rays on at full strength until the tumor has been reached, although certainly wrong, arises only as a solution of this new, re-formulated problem. From this same reformulation of the problem there arises, at the end of the whole process, the practi-cable solution, "concentration of diffuse rays in the tumor." With the other proposals in the protocol, the case is similar: the solution-properties found at first, the functional values, *always serve as productive reformulations of the original problem.*

We can accordingly describe a process of solution either as development of the solution or as development of the problem. Every solution-principle found in the process, which is itself not yet ripe for concrete realization, and which therefore fulfills only the first of the two demands given [earlier], functions from then on as reformulation, as sharpening of the original setting of the problem. *It is therefore meaningful to say that what is really done in any solution of problems consists in formulating the problem more productively.*

To sum up: *The final form of a solution is typically attained by way of mediating phases of the process, of which each one, in retrospect, possesses the character of a solution and, in prospect, that of a problem . . .*

LEARNING FROM MISTAKES (CORRECTIVE PHASES)

As yet we have dealt only with progress . . . along a given geneological line. That this is not the only kind of phase succession is . . . sufficiently indicated by the protocol given above. Here the line itself is continually changed, and one way of approach gives way to another. Such a *transition to phases in another line* takes place typically when some tentative solution does not satisfy, or when one makes no further progress in a given direction. *Another* solution, more or less clearly defined, is then looked for. For instance, the first proposal (esophagus) having been recognized as unsatisfactory, quite a radical change in direction takes place. The attempt to avoid contact is completely given up and a means to desensitize tissues is sought in its place. In the third proposal, however, the subject has already returned to old tactics, although with a new variation. And such shifting back and forth occurs frequently.

It will be realized that, in the transition to phases in another line, the thought-process may range more or less widely. Every such transition involves a return to an earlier phase of the problem; an earlier task is set anew; a new branching off from an old point in the family tree occurs. Sometimes a subject returns to the original setting of the problem, sometimes just to the immediately preceding phase. An example for the latter case: From the ingenious proposal, to apply the rays in adequate amounts by rotation of the body around the tumor as a center, a subject made a prompt transition to the neighboring proposal: "One could also have the radiation apparatus rotate around the body." Another example: The subject who has just realized that the proposal of the esophagus is unsatisfactory may look for another natural approach to the stomach. This would be the most "direct" transition, that is, the transition which retrogresses least. Or, renouncing the natural approach to the stomach, he looks for another method of avoiding contact. Or, again, he looks for an altogether different way to avoid the destruction of healthy tissue. Therewith, everything which can be given up at all would have been given up; a "completely different" solution would have to be sought.

In such retrogression, thinking would naturally not be taken back to precisely the point where it had been before. For the failure of a certain solution has at least the result that now one tries *"in another way."* While remaining in the framework of the old [problem situation], one looks for another starting point. Or again, the original setting may itself be altered *in a definite direction,* because there is the newly added demand: From now on, that property of the unsatisfactory solution must be avoided which makes it incompatible with the given conditions . . .

Such learning from errors plays as great a role in the solution-process as in everyday life. While the simple realization, *that* something does not work, can lead only to some variation of the old method, the realization of *why* it does not work, the recognition of the *ground of the conflict,* results in a correspondingly definite *variation which corrects* the recognized defect.

REFERENCES

1. DUNCKER, K. 1926. A study of productive thinking. *Ped. Sem.* 33:642–708.
2. MAIER, N. R. F. 1931. Reasoning in humans. II. The solution of a problem and its appearance in consciousness. *J. Comp. Psychol.* 12:181–94.
3. MAIER, N. R. F. 1933. An aspect of human reasoning. *Brit. J. Psychol.* 24:144–55.

8. Problem-Solving Processes of College Students*

In this investigation, the authors identify certain differences in the problem-solving processes of college students who were successful or unsuccessful in solving problems faced in academic examinations. Bloom and Broder discuss the need for greater understanding of such processes and stress the importance of the proper selection of types of problems, of methods of gathering the data, and of analysis of results in order to gain insight into the factors affecting success or failure in problem solving. An analysis of the differences in methods of problem solving enables the authors to identify four critical aspects of the problem-solving process.

INTRODUCTION

Mental processes represent a very difficult and complex subject for study. To a large extent, we have been limited in this study by the widespread emphasis on overt behavior as the major acceptable type of evidence on the workings of the mind. Much of psychological research attempts to infer

* BENJAMIN S. BLOOM AND LOIS J. BRODER. Reprinted and abridged with permission of the authors and publisher from *Supplementary Educational Monographs,* No. 73, pp. 1-31. Chicago: University of Chicago Press, 1950.

from the observed behavior of the individual what the mental processes must have been. This attempt to make an objective science of psychology not only limits the kinds of data acceptable to the psychologist but must necessarily make for many inaccuracies in his inferences about the nature of the mental processes . . .

The educator and the psychologist are faced with three alternatives:

1. They can, as they are now doing, give their primary attention to the products of thought and almost completely ignore the processes of thought. This, in the writers' opinion, must inevitably mean educational procedures and psychological research which are inappropriate, superficial, and, in all likelihood, incorrect.

2. They can perform experiments which may enable them to establish a high relationship between the products and the processes of thought. If such a relationship can be established, they will need to be concerned only with the more readily observed products and can infer the processes from these observations. Such a relationship is, in the writers' opinion, not likely to be established. However, it should be possible to set up methods of observing the products of thought which will enable the educator and the psychologist to make somewhat more accurate inferences about the processes of thought.

3. They can develop techniques which will make possible the securing of evidence on both the processes and the products of thought. Much difficulty can be anticipated in securing evidence about the processes, and perhaps the nature of the human organism is such as to prevent the securing of any clear-cut and objective evidence on these processes. In any case, attention on the processes of thought must mean the development of new techniques for psychological research. It may also require a change from large-scale testing and mass studies to those which involve small numbers of subjects studied by rather intensive techniques . . .

A possible point of departure in analyzing the nature of mental processes in relation to the products of thought is through investigations of problem solving. Problems can be selected for which only a limited number of solutions are appropriate, although the methods by which the solutions are reached cannot be so easily limited. It is possible to select problems such that some can be solved quickly and simply by the subject, while others tax the subject's mental resources to the utmost. It would also seem possible to find problems which require the subject to make use of relatively clear and easily reported mental processes.

For this type of investigation, problem solving may be regarded as the process by which the subject goes from the problem or task as he sees it to the solution which he regards as meeting the demands of the problem. A problem may be regarded as a task which the subject is able to understand but for which he does not have an immediate solution. It is expected that, although the subject will be somewhat perplexed, he will not be utterly confused.

In an effort to understand more about the nature of problems and the processes of thinking involved in problem solving, an investigation was started at the University of Chicago in the spring of 1945. Since we were primarily interested in the problems that students must solve in an academic environment, the problems were selected from the various tests and examinations which are given to students in the College of the University of Chicago.

For the purposes of this investigation, we rejected examination questions in which memory for specific information appeared to be the sole factor in securing a solution. We were not interested in studying the ways in which an individual recalls specific information, nor did we believe such questions would reveal much about the nature of the mental processes . . .

We also rejected, for purposes of this study, problems which appeared to be merely puzzles and which required little more than the proper manual or mental manipulations. By puzzles we are referring to problems which can be solved only through trial and error because it is impossible to see in advance the consequences of particular actions and manipulations.

We attempted to select problems for which the subject would have clear-cut, although perhaps quite complex, goals to achieve and for which he could make a conscious plan of attack . . . We limited the problems to questions and test situations taken from various academic tests and examinations. This was done because students in school are expected to solve such problems, and most of the students accept them as problems to be solved. Although it is expected that problem solving is just as real and far more earnest when the student encounters "real-life" problems, the very nature of these problems makes it difficult to analyze them. In "real-life" problems, the values and goals of individuals play a large part in the attack and many solutions are equally appropriate and correct, depending upon the point of view from which the individual has started. The examination problems, on the other hand, involve rather clear-cut solutions, and to a large extent, are so oriented as to divorce values from the problem-solving situation. The examination problems are very clearly structured, and competent individuals in a subject field can agree on the solution regarded as most correct or adequate . . .

In order to secure data on the thoughts, feelings, and methods used by students when attacking this group of problems, an attempt was made to get each student to "think aloud" as he worked the problems. The students were given a brief training period on the technique of thinking aloud as they attacked simple arithmetical problems. When the student was asked to multiply 5 × 6, he gave the answer at once and was unable to report the steps by which he solved the problem. However, when presented with a more complex problem, 34 × 89, the student was able to tell what he was doing as he multiplied the numbers and added the products of 4 × 89 and 30 × 89. After a series of problems like this, the student was given several simple verbal problems. When the interviewer judged that the student was giving a relatively adequate picture of his mental processes as he attacked each problem, the student was given the selected problems for which data were to be secured.

As the student thought aloud on each of the problems, the interviewer took as complete notes as possible on everything the student said and did. From time to time, it was found necessary to supplement these notes by asking the student to recall what he had done after he had completed a problem. This was necessary when the student spoke too rapidly for the interviewer to take notes and when the student's report on his thoughts did not yield a complete picture of the problem-solving process. Best results were obtained when the student reported his thoughts by mumbling. If he spoke loudly and clearly, it was noticed that he seemed to be doing many of the operations twice—once for himself and once for the interviewer.

A few of the problems included in this study are presented below. These problems are accompanied by the solutions and the reports on the methods by which they were attacked. The reports were almost verbatim recordings and, in many cases, appear to be rambling and confused. In many cases, the reports are incomplete and do not reveal all the considerations the subject must have had in mind in order to reach his solution. Frequently the subject expresses his thinking in incomplete sentences, and occasionally the grammatical form is quite incorrect . . .

The three problems to be presented were selected because they illustrate some of the characteristics revealed by the techniques of problem-solving analysis discussed in this monograph . . .

In most cases, the reports or protocols are arranged in order of scores on the problem as well as in order of clarity and effectiveness of problem solving. Thus, some of the first protocols are vague, wandering and, to a large extent, not productive of correct solutions. These first reports also reveal little about the process of problem solving. The later reports in a series are usually more clear, direct, and productive . . .

Responses on Problem 1. The responses of certain students to the first problem are presented below.

Problem 1

Rank the following life forms in the order of their appearance in the geologic record. *Blacken* the answer space *A* for the one that appeared first, etc.

81. Mammals
82. Sponges
83. Amphibians
84. Fishes
85. Flowering plants

Pauline M. (Score 0):

(Read the directions—laughed.) "Something I don't know anything about —guess on all problems—seems plants would be first—don't know what the sponges are since I don't know sponges—would probably get them all mixed up—might say sponges second, only guessing—say amphibians—last, I believe, mammals and fishes—all guesswork, though."

This student looked at the problem and apparently decided that this was a totally unfamiliar field and that her plan of attack would be one of guessing. Her placement of the plants first would seem to indicate some basis other than guesswork for the ranking, although she was apparently unaware or unable to report it. It is probable that she divided life forms into plants and animals and regarded plants as coming first. Her claim of lack of knowledge about sponges may have represented a defense in case the solution was incorrect. She ranked the remaining items in some order without revealing a basis for the order, although she again repeated that it was all guesswork. Throughout the attack there was evidence of very little confidence in her ability to get the correct answers and little evidence of an attempt to reason through to a solution . . .

David F. (Score 1):

"Rank—(Read the directions.) Does that mean phylogenetic tree—I know the phylogenetic tree better than the geologic record—mammals late in the animal kingdom—flowering plants late in the plant kingdom—sponges is the answer—check—mammals after sponges, sponges before amphibians, amphibians before fishes, fishes before flowering plants, sponges before all of them, so sponges first."

In spite of his emphasis on the word "rank," it is not clear whether David ever clearly understood the nature of the problem or whether he forgot what he was to do. This student translated the problem from one of ranking the items in order of appearance in the geologic record to one of ranking them in order of their position on the phylogenetic tree. This equating of the phylogenetic tree and the geologic record appears to be a legitimate method and is apparently an effective method of changing a problem into a more workable form. It is not clear whether the student remembered the positions of the various life forms on the phylogenetic tree or whether he was considering the characteristics of each as the method of placing it on the tree. The distinction between animal and plant kingdom and position within each kingdom appeared to be a helpful organization and guide to further thinking about the problem. After considering three of the five life forms, the student selected an answer and then went through a fairly elaborate checking process in which he compared pairs of items.

Ned M. (Score 2):

(Read the statement. Read the alternatives, mispronouncing "amphibians.") "Mammals last and fishes next—no, mammals last—no, my biology course in the ninth grade—mammals, no flowering plants last because had cavemen and animals when only had ferns—third, phyla, and flowering plants in the fourth—then mammals, fishes, going backwards—flowering plants, mammals, fishes, don't know what amphibians are, but sponges are third from the bottom of lowest animal life, so amphibians last along with amoeba—amphi, amphia, can't remember."

This student was apparently unfamiliar with the term "amphibian," and it became a source of difficulty. It is interesting to observe that he started from the most recent and attempted to work back, which is the reverse of the method by which the answers are to be recorded. The system of placing flowering plants last appeared to involve a kind of proof based on his evidence that mammals existed when primitive forms of plants also existed. This student seemed to have a mental picture of phyla, since he talked about third and fourth phyla and also spoke of lowest animal life in terms of "bottom." He seems to have attempted to place the one unknown item (amphibian) by establishing a relationship with a known form which sounds similar (the amoeba). In general, then, this student seemed to have a mental picture of phyla in mind, and his task was that of relating the specific forms given to their possible position in the order of phyla. (After the problem had been completed, the student was asked whether he knew what an amphibious tank was. He replied immediately and quickly grasped the correct order of the amphibians in this problem.)

Bernice Y. (Score 3):

> (Read the directions. Read the alternatives.) "Fish before the land animals, therefore fishes first—no, sponges first, sponges on the cellular level of development—well, minimum of differentiation—then fishes, differentiated structures, gill—amphibians, the bridge—life from water to earth—flowering plants next, no, flowering plants are plants, rest are animals—either flowering plants late on the evolutionary scale—flowering plants 4, and mammals 5; very latest, highest degree of development."

Here the subject appeared to be using two bases for decisions and using them interchangeably. One was that water life forms preceded land life forms while another basis was that life forms should be in the order of level of development. She began with the distinction between water and land forms but, as this basis proved inadequate, she made use of the level of development and differentiation. In each case, she had a principle in mind, as well as the characteristics of each of the life forms which enabled her to make use of the principle. Her method of resolving the position of mammals and flowering plants was not clearly indicated. In general, however, this represents a fairly complete picture of her method of attack on the problem. It reveals an attack of a very high order; the student had a systematic method which she was able to keep in mind throughout the problem-solving process.

Comments on Problem 1 and the reports. In solving this problem, the student must first realize that it is one in which he is to rank items in a particular order. The fact that the directions are somewhat abbreviated may have proved a stumbling block for some of the students. However, a careful student should have little difficulty in understanding the problem from the directions given here. After the student has the problem in mind, he may use different bases for his ranking. Thus, he may place them in order on the basis of memory of the geologic record or the evolutionary tree. He may also make use of such bases as differentiation between water and land forms, between plant and animal kingdom, and between more complex and less complex life forms. In addition to having a particular principle or basis for ranking, the student must know a sufficient amount about each of the life forms to select the characteristics which enable him to apply the principle in each case. This involves the isolation of the particular characteristics of the life form which are most relevant to the principles he is using . . .

Responses on Problem 2. The problem-solving techniques employed by certain students in another problem are analyzed below.

Problem 2

DIRECTIONS: In each of the following items you are given *statements* and *four conclusions. Assume that the statements are true.* You are to judge which of the conclusions then logically follows, i.e., must be true if the statements are true. *Blacken* the answer space corresponding to the one conclusion which logically follows. If none of the conclusions logically follows, blacken answer space *E.*

STATEMENTS:

Any action that impedes the war effort of the United States should be made illegal.

All strikes impede the war effort of the United States.

CONCLUSIONS:

A—All strikes should be made illegal.
B—Some restrictions should be placed on the right to strike, but it would be unwise to make them all illegal.
C—Some strikes should be made illegal.
D—Unjustifiable strikes should be made illegal.
E—None of the foregoing conclusions follows.

Roy C. (Score 0):

(Read the directions.) "Don't do that (blacken answer space). (Read the statements. Read the alternatives.) Say D—Usually when men strike they have a reason for it—if they don't, then their jobs are at stake."

Although this is not a very complete report on the student's problem solving, it is clear that he lost sight of the true nature of the problem and selected a conclusion for reasons other than those of logical relation to the original statements. The conclusion he selected apparently involved a personal judgment about the desirability of strikes. This lack of objectivity when faced with a problem set in a context involving value considerations is a frequent source of error for many students . . .

John D. (*Score 1*):

(Read the directions and the statements. Read the list of conclusions.) "According to these statements, say A because strikes impede the war effort, so should be illegal—not my comment, but according to what the statements say."

This student recognized his own attitude on the subject, but he was fully aware of the basis on which he was to select a conclusion to satisfy the requirements of the problem. He appears to have substituted the word "strike" from the minor premise for the phrase "any action" in the major premise—probably as a test of the correctness of the conclusion. Although he gave some consideration to the other conclusions, this record does not reveal the nature of his thinking about them . . .

Allen G. (*Score 1*):

(Read the directions and the statements.) "Then say, if a strike impedes the war effort of the U.S., then strike should be made illegal because it is an action—studying now in mathematics—knew the answer before looking."

This student recognized the relationship between "strike" and "action." He, unlike the previous students, managed to determine the correct conclusion before even examining the alternatives given. This would indicate a relatively high degree of confidence in his ability to solve the problem.

Comments on Problem 2 and the reports. This problem is relatively simple and does not yield much information about the students' mental processes. We have found that, whenever a problem involves only a straightforward and mechanical manipulation of symbols, the student is unable to report much about this thinking . . .

This problem requires the student to work with the terms of a fairly simple syllogism. Some complexity is added to the problem by its emotional or value context. The problem and the methods of solution here reported are of value in revealing:

1. The extent to which the individual has difficulty in keeping the requirements of a problem in mind when they are in conflict with his attitudes or values.

2. Some of the techniques by which students manipulate the terms in a simple syllogism. In this problem some students used a method of substituting one term for another; others used a method of equating certain of the terms and propositions; and another student either attempted to remember a similar syllogistic form or substituted letters for the terms in the syllogism.

3. The extent to which students differ in confidence about their problem solving. Some students apparently find it unnecessary to read the alternatives offered and are able to determine a correct answer before referring to the alternatives. This appears to be a very different type of problem solving than one where the student examines each of the alternative answers and then makes a choice.

Responses on Problem 3. The thought processes of [certain] students solving Problem 3 are analyzed below.

Problem 3

Some economists feel that there is danger of an extreme inflationary boom after the war. It is the opinion of such economists that the government should control the boom in order to prevent a depression such as the one following the stockmarket crash of 1929.

Below are a number of specific suggestions. For each of the following items, *blacken*

answer space 1—if it would be *consistent* with the policy of controlling the boom;
answer space 2—if it is directly *inconsistent* with the policy.

26. Lower the reserve that banks are required to hold against deposits

27. Reduce taxes considerably

28. Encourage the federal reserve banks to buy securities in the open market

John N. (Score 0):

(Read the introductory statements and read the directions incompletely.)

(Read item 26.) "No.

(Read item 27.) "Think about that.

(Read item 28.) "No—must be number 27, by the process of elimination."

This student, who evidently did not understand the nature of the problem, made it one of selecting the best of three statements rather than one of judging the relation of each statement to the policy of controlling the boom. In this report there is practically no evidence on the process of problem solving. It is of little value in determining why the student misunderstood the problem or on what basis he made his decision about item 27.

Stephen N. (Score 1):

(Read the statement and directions.)

(Read item 26.) "Forget that reserve ratio—if you lower the reserve ratio would tend to control inflation—consistent, I think—would let less deposits out of the bank.

(Read item 27.) "Inconsistent—people would have more money for other things—would be runaway inflation.

(Read item 28.) "Forgot open market—if you buy in the open market—know three ways for banks to have more reserve on hand—reserve ratio, something else, and open market—would be consistent, I think—can't remember how it operates—have to study economics some more."

This student attempted to remember relevant material he had studied at one time and made little effort to solve the problem on the basis of the given material. It is interesting to note that he translated the reserve into a reserve ratio. He did not, however, grasp the correct relation between changes in reserves and release of deposits from the bank. In item 28 the student correctly related reduction in taxes to amount of money available and to inflation. In item 28 the student attempted to remember particular subject matter rather than think through the consequences of the item. He had great difficulty in solving other problems presented to him; to a large extent, this difficulty can be accounted for by his lack of independent thinking. In attempting to solve most problems, he tried to remember specific answers from textbooks, lectures, and discussions rather than make an effort to think through each problem on the basis of the given material. This student was not at all confident about his problem solving and apparently found it necessary to make several excuses about his lack of memory for certain specifics . . .

Dora Z. (Score 2):

(Read the statement and the directions—emphasizing the key words.)

(Read item 26.) "Lower the reserve, raise the amount of money in circulation—if you raise the money in circulation—inconsistent. By raising the money in circulation you don't control a boom.

(Read item 27.) "Also inconsistent for the same reason.

(Read item 28.) "Open market—think what the open market is. Think would take money out of circulation, therefore would be consistent."

In her reading of the statements and the directions, this student very quickly focused attention on what she considered to be the key words or ideas. She managed to reduce the three items to a single problem by relating the amount of money in circulation to the control of the inflationary boom. In each case she attempted to determine how the amount of money in circulation would be affected by each of the items. Although the report is not complete and it is not clear how item 27 was answered or what she thought the open market is, a rather high order of problem solving is evident. The ability to reduce three items to a single problem and attack it on the basis of a single rule or principle would appear to be evidence of a very efficient method of dealing with the material. This would seem to be a good method for getting to the heart of a problem and is likely (if the correct elements are selected) to produce correct solutions. In the present instance, however, the student was unable to see the relationship between the purchase of securities on the open market by the federal reserve banks and the amount of money in circulation.

David F. (Score 3):

"Will read the statement. (Read the statement and the directions.) Statement of possible policy. See if the suggestions are consistent or inconsistent with the policy.

(Read item 26.) "If they did that, what happens?—Possibility that the banks would crash, so it's inconsistent.

(Read item 27.) "People would have more money to spend, prices would go up, so inconsistent.

(Read item 28.) "Intuitively, I feel that 28 is also inconsistent—can I find a reason—if they do—stocks will go and federal reserve banks, no, inconsistent. Lot of hazy ideas—don't know enough about federal reserve banks or securities in the open market to definitely say inconsistent."

David was a student who stuttered a great deal. This stuttering appeared to get worse when he attempted to *describe* his problem solving to the interviewer, but when he was "thinking aloud" as he worked through the problem, there was no sign of speech difficulty. In this example, he restated the directions in such a way as to clarify for himself what the problem involved. He apparently did a great deal of his thinking by asking and answering his own questions. He answered all three items correctly but approached them as involving three independent questions. Thus, in item 26 he related the reduction of reserves to the possibility of bank crashes. This enabled him to answer the item correctly but did not bring into focus the effect of less extreme reductions in the reserve. In item 27 he related reduction in taxes to increases in money available for spending and the consequent rise in prices. Here, without stating it, the student implied that rise in prices is related to an inflationary boom. The student "intuitively" determined that item 28 is inconsistent and then searched for a reason. (This was a characteristic method for many of the students.) He explored one possible consequence of the buying of securities by the federal reserve bank and then rejected it. Although this report of process of problem solving is somewhat incomplete, it gives a fair idea of how the student attacked the particular problem.

Comments on Problem 3 and the reports. In this problem the student is called upon to know the meaning of certain key terms such as "inflationary boom," "reserves," "open market." In addition, he must recognize that the problem is not one of deciding whether or not the boom should be controlled but one of determining what is or is not consistent with the policy of controlling a boom. The problem may be attacked by an attempt to remember the exact way in which each of the terms might have been discussed in a class or a textbook or by an attempt to work out some general ideas of how an inflationary boom operates and the relation of these ideas to each of the items. Thus, it is possible to relate the inflationary boom to the amount of money in circulation and then to determine the consequences of each of the items in terms of amount of money in circulation. A number of the students had this principle in mind, but only one seemed to be able to follow through on it consistently.

This problem and the reports on the problem solving are of value in revealing a number of things:

1. The extent to which the same directions may be misleading to some students while completely clear to others . . .

2. Some students find it necessary to modify the problem or to delimit it before proceeding to a solution . . .

3. Some students have difficulty in organizing their thought in any systematic way . . .

4. Although it is not frequently apparent from the reports, some students appear to proceed in their problem solving by asking and answering specific questions . . .

5. When given a number of questions on the same topic, students have difficulty in detecting a single idea which runs through all the items. They proceed to attack each question or item separately and independently rather than to attack all as a group. Only one of the students appeared able to attack the questions here on the basis of a central idea . . .

VARIATIONS IN THE PROBLEM-SOLVING CHARACTERISTICS OF STUDENTS

. . . A major task in this study was the simplification, classification, and analysis of results. Verbatim reports were made as the student attacked each problem. These reports were extremely lengthy and specific and were of value primarily as raw data.

The attempts at analysis of the protocols were aided by the first study in this investigation, in which the participating students came from two sharply defined academic-achievement groups. These included six academically successful students with high scores on aptitude tests and grades of A and B on the achievement examinations. At the other extreme were six academically nonsuccessful students with low aptitude scores and grades of D and F on the comprehensive achievement examinations. Each protocol was examined carefully, and an effort was made to list specific characteristics which tentatively seemed of importance in describing the attack, in explaining failure on the problem, or in appraising the quality of the mental processes involved. The characteristics of the extreme groups were then studied to determine the consistency within each group as well as differences between the groups . . . In discussing differences between the two groups, we have frequently referred to them as successful and unsuccessful problem-solvers. It was our judgment that the differences in their success in problem solving were as marked as the differences in their academic achievement.

Analyses of the differences in methods of problem solving were made in various ways, including attempts to fit the data into previously defined classifications . . . However, none of these classifications seemed to summarize adequately the specific data obtained in this study. After several attempts at classification of the data, four major headings were selected:

1. Understanding of the nature of the problem
2. Understanding the ideas contained in the problem
3. General approach to the solution of problems
4. Attitude toward the solution of problems

Each of these categories is discussed in some detail in the following sections.

1. *Understanding of the nature of the problem.* By "understanding of the nature of the problem" is meant understanding the kind of problem to be attacked—more or less a clarification of what is involved or required in the problem. In this general area the successful problem-solvers usually differed from the nonsuccessful problem-solvers in two ways: in their ability to start attack on a problem and in their ability to solve the problem in its own terms.

A major difference between the two groups was found in *their ability to start the attack on a problem.* The successful problem-solvers seemed able to read the directions and the statement of a problem and almost immediately to choose some point at which to begin their attack—some word or phrase on which to begin their process of reasoning . . . The nonsuccessful problem-solvers, on the other hand, would read the same statement of the problem and then begin to flounder. They might read and re-read the statement and complain, "I don't understand what it means," or "This doesn't make sense." In general, the nonsuccessful students seem to have established no effective technique for starting the solution. Rarely did they pull out some key word or break the statement into lesser parts which they might find easier to understand . . .

In many cases the inability of the nonsuccessful problem-solver to begin the solution of the problem resulted from lack of comprehension of the directions. In some cases this lack of comprehension was evidently due to failure to read the directions or to a misunderstanding of terms or phrases in the directions. It was noted that many of the nonsuccessful problem-solvers "skipped" the directions in whole or in part. Frequently, failure to read the directions seemed to be part of an effort to hasten the problem solving and to save time. The successful problem-solvers did a certain amount of shortening of the directions, but it was done in a different manner. Thus, they would omit repeated phrases or scan the directions in such a way as to select ideas. In their shortening of directions, they lost none of the essence, while the nonsuccessful problem-solvers seemed to skip indiscriminately. For the successful students, this condensing or shortening seemed to bring the major elements into focus . . .

The two groups differed considerably in *their ability to solve the problem as presented*. The nonsuccessful student would frequently present an acceptable or correct solution to the problem he had attacked, but this problem was not the one he had been asked to solve. Failure to attack the problem as posed was due, in some instances, to a neglected or misinterpreted term in the directions. In other instances it resulted from a failure to keep the directions in mind as the problem was being solved. Thus, in one problem which was presented, a statement and three comments on the statement, the student was directed to choose the one comment which showed best understanding of the subject discussed in the statement. Many of the nonsuccessful students lost sight of these directions as they proceeded with the solution of the problem and chose the comment which most nearly expressed the same ideas as the statement. For the problem they were solving, they had achieved a good solution, but for the problem originally posed, they had achieved a poor solution. When their attention was called to the directions for the problem, these students were usually able to determine the correct solution . . .

2. *Understanding of the ideas contained in the problem.* By this we mean possession of the basic information necessary for the solution to a problem as well as the ability to bring this knowledge to bear in attacking the problem.

In this general area the outstanding difference between the successful and the nonsuccessful problem-solvers was not, as might have been expected, a difference in the amount of relevant knowledge possessed by the two groups. The major difference was in *the extent to which the two groups could bring the relevant knowledge they possessed to bear on the problem.* Often the nonsuccessful students had within their grasp all the background and technical information necessary for the solution of a problem but were unable to apply the knowledge to the problem. One student, for instance, was given a complex problem involving a set of observations and requiring judgment about a list of possible conclusions to be drawn from the observations. After reading the problem, the student felt that she "just didn't have enough information to solve it." When the experimenter prodded, encouraged, and questioned her further, the student discovered that she did possess the necessary information. She finally solved the problem correctly, much to her surprise.

The nonsuccessful students seemed unable *to realize fully the implica-*

tions of the ideas of the problem. For example, when these students were asked a question concerning "corporate enterprise in America," they were confused and seemed unable to answer the question. If, however, as a result of a series of questions by the experimenter, they came to realize that the Ford Motor Company or some other specific corporation could be considered an example of "corporate enterprise," they were able to deal adequately with the question posed. On a problem dealing with methods for the control of inflation, they would say, "We haven't studied that yet," or "I don't know about that." When, however, they were questioned about specific wartime controls, they seemed fully aware of the purpose of those restrictions. After these specific questions they appeared to have little difficulty in putting the various pieces of information together and correctly solved the problem. They had gained no information but had acquired a new orientation to the problem. Apparently, they were unable to deal with or to comprehend ideas in the form present in the problem.

The unsuccessful problem-solvers had difficulty in *relating their readings and lecture notes to the problem* if the problem material was presented in a form different from the form they had encountered in their studying. For instance, one student had great difficulty with a genetics problem because of changes in the symbols used. In the problems she had worked at home, the recessive individuals were represented by black symbols and the dominant by white, whereas in the examination this symbolism was reversed. In a problem dealing with state rights, the nonsuccessful students were reluctant to attack the problem, saying they didn't know what state rights were. But, if asked to tell some of the rights of states or if asked to contrast state rights with the rights of the federal government, they could proceed with the solution to the problem. This ability to put relevant knowledge to use is apparently related to the individual's self-confidence.

It seemed, then, that the ideas which the nonsuccessful problem-solvers possessed were huge, unwieldy things, figuratively capable of fitting into only one particular space—that in which they had originally been framed. The ideas of the successful problem-solvers, in contrast, were many-faceted things which could be turned this way and that, expanded or contracted, and made to fit the space in which they were needed.

In some few instances, the students had difficulty *using the relevant knowledge at their command,* due to the presence of totally unfamiliar or highly abstract terms or ideas. Under such circumstances, the successful problem-solvers attempted to translate the difficult and abstract terms of the problem into simpler, more concrete, or more familiar terms.

Frequently they made tentative assumptions about the meaning of un-familiar terms, even though they recognized that some of these assumptions were probably not entirely correct. In contrast, the nonsuccessful problem-solvers quickly gave up and prepared to "go on to the next problem." Frequently the successful problem-solvers would substitute an illustration or example for a difficult or vague concept and then think in terms of these illustrations and examples. This kind of thinking appeared to help them solve the problem. In contrast, the nonsuccessful problem-solvers treated vague or unfamiliar concepts as given and appeared unable to do anything further with them.

3. *General approach to the solution of problems.* By this we mean the procedure of the student during his attack on a problem. The analysis of the protocols indicates that the successful and the nonsuccessful problem-solvers differ in three general respects in their approach to the solution of problems. These are: extent of thought about the problem, care and system in thinking about the problem, and ability to follow through on a process of reasoning . . .

The major difference between the successful and the nonsuccessful problem-solvers in their *extent of thought about the problem* was in the degree to which their approach to the problem might be characterized as active or passive . . .

The successful problem-solvers would read the statement of the problem and then set up their own hypothesis as to the correct solution, or, where the nature of the problem made this an impossibility, they would set up the criteria which the correct answer must fulfill. Where the problem contained unfamiliar terms, the successful problem-solvers would make an assumption with regard to their meaning and proceed with a solution based on these assumptions.

In contrast, the nonsuccessful problem-solvers were almost completely passive in their thinking about the problem. They gave little time to a consideration of the problem, selecting an answer on the basis of very few clues or on superficial considerations. There was a definite tendency on the part of these students to select an answer on the basis of "impression" or "feelings" about which choice might be correct. They attempted to remember the solution to a similar problem rather than solving each new problem independently. They used a negative approach—that of selecting one answer because none of the others appeared attractive. The nonsuccessful problem-solvers might look at the choice of answers and select one purely on a guesswork basis . . .

There was a noticeable difference between the successful and the non-successful problem-solvers in their *care and system in thinking about the problem*. As might be expected, the successful problem-solvers were careful and systematic in their method of attack on the problem. They seemed to take the problem as given and reorganize it to simplify it, pulling out the key terms or ideas, or breaking the problem into simpler and sub-problems, in order to gain an understanding of the material. They attempted to eliminate some of the given answers as clearly incorrect. They then attempted to determine which of the remaining answers was correct, apparently finding it more efficient to decide between one of two or three choices, than one of five. Further, they attempted to deal with each part of the problem separately, if the whole were too complex for easy manipulation.

The nonsuccessful problem-solvers, on the other hand, started the problem with no apparent plan for solution, more or less plunging in, not knowing what was to come next. They jumped from one part of the problem to another, giving insufficient consideration to any one part to enable them to find a beginning point of attack. They would attack the problem as a whole, reading the directions, the statement of the problem, and the alternatives again and again, searching for some clue to the solution. The nonsuccessful problem-solvers neglected to consider important details in the solution or were extremely careless in considering these details. They were easily sidetracked by external consideration—some word might suggest a book they had read or an interesting incident, and their thoughts would go off on this tangent, coming back to the problem at hand only with considerable difficulty . . .

A further point of difference between the successful and the nonsuccessful problem-solvers was evident in their *ability to follow through on a process of reasoning*. The nonsuccessful problem-solvers might begin their attack on a problem in much the same way as the successful problem-solvers, carry their reasoning part way through to completion, and then give up. They would start to solve the problem with a definite plan for the solution in mind, but would then lose sight of the original plan as difficulties were encountered and never return to it. If they had carried it through, the plan probably would have led to a successful solution. The nonsuccessful problem-solvers occasionally elaborated a hypothesis as to the correct solution or set up criteria that the correct solution must fulfill, just as the successful problem-solvers did, but they neglected to apply this reasoning to the selection of a final answer.

4. *Attitude toward the solution of problems.* By "attitude" the writers mean the emotions, values, and prejudices of the student as they are involved in the attack on problems. These attitudinal characteristics are observable in the student's reactions to the form and content of the problem. The attitude of the student toward the solution of problems and the nature of the problem material was found to be another point of differentiation between the successful and the nonsuccessful students. In many instances, it was an important factor in determining the success of the problem solving. It was possible to identify at least three distinct kinds of attitudes: attitude toward reasoning, confidence in ability to solve problems, and introduction of personal considerations into the solution of problems.

The writers found that many of the nonsuccessful problem-solvers had difficulty because of their *attitude toward reasoning*. These students were inclined to take the view that, in solving problems, reasoning is of little value and that either one knows the answer to a problem at once or one does not. These students would look at a problem and quickly decide that they could or could not solve it. They appeared to make such judgments largely on the basis of whether or not they thought they possessed all the necessary information. Unlike the successful students, they could see no way of manipulating the parts of the problem if they were not certain of their knowledge of the subject. They could not see problems as things to be broken down into subproblems, nor were they willing to make assumptions to fill gaps in their information. Many of the students who refused to attempt problems because they *felt* they did not know the answer did, in reality, have sufficient information. One student in particular, after refusing to attempt a problem in reasoning which she felt was beyond her, was persuaded to attack it piece by piece, just to see how far she could get. She found that, following this piecemeal approach, she was quite capable of solving the problem.

The nonsuccessful students had little *confidence in their ability to solve the problems*. They were easily discouraged and made little or no attempt to attack problems which appeared complex or abstract. The format of the problem was sufficient to discourage them from attempting any attack. Thus, many of them would look at a complex graph or table of figures in the problem and quit at once. Sometimes they would make a superficial attempt to reason through a problem and then would just give up and guess, for no apparent reason. Lack of confidence in their ability to solve problems extended to lack of confidence in the correctness of the solution they had obtained. They went back to the problem and changed their answer over and over again. Sometimes they were unable to come to a definite conclusion or to decide between one or two alternatives. These students indicated that in a test they would put down an answer just on the chance it would earn an extra point but that, in the interview situation, this was not necessary, and they were willing to leave the decision unmade.

Again, there was a difference between the successful and the non-successful problem-solvers in the frequency with which they *introduced personal considerations into their problem solving*. The nonsuccessful problem-solvers had difficulty in maintaining an objective attitude in certain problems because their personal opinions played such an important role. Thus, although the directions to the problem might clearly state, "Assume the statements are true," the student was unable to sufficiently divorce his personal convictions from the problem to enable him to solve it objectively. Some of the students also had difficulty in differentiating between correct answers and answers that seemed desirable on the basis of their personal value patterns. For example, in a syllogistic problem where the two premises are given and the student is to choose the logical conclusion, one student reported, "Answer A is the one that logically follows, but C is the one I believe, so I take C."

REFERENCES

1. BILLINGS, M. L. 1934. Problem solving in different fields of behavior. *Amer. J. Psychol.* 46:259–72.
2. BUSWELL, G. T., JOHN, L. *Diagnostic Studies in Arithmetic.* Supplementary Educational Monographs, No. 30, Chicago: University of Chicago Press, 1926.
3. HEIDBREDER, E. F. 1928. Problem-solving in children and adults. *J. Genet. Psychol.* 35:522–45.

CHAPTER : 3

Aesthetic Creativity

9. What Is Imagination?*

A distinguished physiologist here considers the nature of imagination in a brilliant synthesis of ideas from several fields of knowledge. Gerard discusses some aspects of the psychology of imagination, and what has been learned from brain pathology about disturbances in the functioning of imagination. He concludes his discussion by suggesting certain implications for education. (Another portion of this essay, on the anatomy and physiology of the brain, is included in Chapter 1 on The Learning Process.)

Imagination is more than bringing images into consciousness; that is imagery or at most hallucination. Imagination, creative imagination, is an action of the mind that produces a new idea or insight. "Out of chaos the imagination frames a thing of beauty" (Lowes' *The Road to Xanadu*) or of truth. The thing comes unheralded, as a flash, full-formed. We have all had this experience, and famous or important cases abound . . .

Imagination, not reason, creates the novel. It is to social inheritance what mutation is to biological inheritance; it accounts for the arrival of the fittest. Reason or logic, applied when judgment indicates that the new is promising, acts like natural selection to pan the gold grains from the sand and insure the survival of the fittest. Imagination supplies the premises and asks the questions from which reason grinds out the con-

* RALPH W. GERARD. Adapted and abridged with permission of the author and publisher from The biological basis of imagination. *Scientific Monthly,* 1946, 62:477–99.

clusions as a calculating machine supplies answers. Wood's story of how a plausible answer to a perplexing problem came to him while dozing, only to be later exploded by his experiments, is illustrative. Dryden, presenting *The Rival Ladies,* to the Earl of Orrery, said:

"This worthless Present was design'd you, long before it was a Play; when it was only a confus'd Mass of Thoughts, tumbling over one another in the Dark: When the Fancy was yet in its first Work, moving the Sleeping Images of things towards the Light, there to be distinguish'd, and then either chosen or rejected by the Judgment." And Coleridge's artistry has compacted the matter into the phrase, "The streamy nature of association, which thinking curbs and rudders." . . .

Simple imagination is observable in a pure and untrammeled state in dreams, in the hallucinations of drugs and other agents, in those hypnagogic states which interpose between wake and sleep or in the slightly-fettered day-dreaming while awake, in the free fancies of the child and the less free fancies of the amateur. For ideas, like mutations, are mostly bad by the criteria of judgment, and experience or expertness suppresses them—unless imaginings get out of hand and displace reality, as in the insanities. But the imaginative hopper is fed from and feeds back to the conscious and critical level. There the heat of mental work transforms the soft ingots of fancy into the hard steel of finished creations. Baudelaire refers to "the labor by which a revery becomes a work of art," and Mary Boole has likened the alternate conscious and unconscious digestion of a problem to the rumination of a cow—as indeed our language does in using "rumination" for a loose form of mental activity . . .

Clearly, then, pursuit of imagination leads us into the unconscious and its mechanisms. Nor is this any longer a completely uncharted wilderness, for psychoanalysis especially has even now developed a usable body of knowledge to guide the explorer. It has recognized and isolated such unconscious mechanisms as condensation, displacement, projection, and identification—as well as repression, sublimation, substitution, rejection, denial, introjection, suppression, and conversion, to extend the list—which often enable the student not only to see further into the how of imagining but even to account for what is imagined. This is true for the normal and perhaps more strikingly for the disturbed; the previously meaningless chatter of the schizophrenic patient, for example, is quite intelligible in terms of known dynamics. Condensation and identification, respectively, are clearly revealed in the following statements by Coleridge concerning himself: "Ideas and images exist in the twilight realms of consciousness, that shadowy half-being, that state of nascent existence in the twilight of imagination and just on the vestibule of consciousness, a confluence of our recollections, through which we establish a centre, as it were a sort of nucleus in (this) reservoir of the soul." And: "From my very childhood, I have been accustomed to abstract, and as it were, unrealize whatever of more than common interest my eyes dwelt on, and then by a sort of transfusion and transmission of my consciousness to identify myself with the object." And Lowes, in a painstaking study of the materials Coleridge had immersed himself in during the years prior to his writing "The Ancient Mariner," was able to trace to these sources every word and phrase of the poem's most vivid stanzas. As Lowes says:

"Facts which sank at intervals out of conscious recollection drew together beneath the surface through almost chemical affinities of common elements . . . And there in Coleridge's unconscious mind, while his consciousness was busy with the toothache, or Hartley's infant ills, or pleasant strollings with the Wordsworths between Nether Stowey and Alfoxden, or what is dreamt in this or that philosophy—there in the dark moved the phantasms of the fishes and animalcules and serpentine forms of his vicarious voyagings, thrusting out tentacles of association, and interweaving beyond disengagement." This is not, of course, to detract a grain from Coleridge's achievement; it is only a recognition and demonstration of the sensory components on which imagination operates. For the components had to be integrated, the poem given form. Again to quote Lowes:

"Behind 'The Rime of the Ancient Mariner' lie crowding masses of impressions, incredible in their richness and variety. But the poem is not the sum of the impressions, as a heap of diamond dust is the sum of its shining particles; nor is the poet merely a sensitized medium for their reception and transmission. Beneath the poem lie also innumerable blendings and fusings of impressions, brought about below the level of conscious mental processes. But the poem is not the confluence of unconsciously merging images, as a pool of water forms from the coalescence of scattered drops; nor is the poet a somnambulist in a subliminal world. Neither the conscious impressions nor their unconscious interpenetrations constitute the poem. They are inseparable from it, but it is an entity which they do not create. On the contrary, every impression, every new creature rising from the potent waters of the (unconscious) Well, is what it now is through its participation in a *whole,* foreseen as a whole in each integral part—a whole which is the working out of a controlling imaginative design. The incommunicable, unique essence of the poem is its *form."* . . .

Form, structure, relationship, organism, part-whole systems, gestalt, or closure is basic for the product of imagination and for its process. To see star groups, constellations, instead of unrelated stars—the literal meaning of "consider"—is the gist of closure, of a confluence of elements. Since imagination only regroups sensory material, there is truly nothing new under the sun. Perception is really a harder problem, for red rays and green rays, even falling on separate eyes, do give the "new" sensation of yellow; but imagination cannot conjure a hue for ultraviolet. A mermaid, griffin, or centaur, as Lucretius recognized, are only recombinations of familiar elements. Yet when we recall that a single inning of a chess game may offer some four hundred choices, that all literature is built from the same words and these of the same letters, as all material is of the same elements and their handful of subatomic particles, novelty in combination does not seem too barren. A new and fertile pattern of thought may come from a conceptual reslicing of the universe into fresh classes and the making of new combinations of them . . .

THE PSYCHOLOGY OF IMAGINATION

The gestalt school of psychologists, especially, has emphasized the importance of closure or structuring—of "considering"—in insight. Insight is an imaginative way of learning or problem solving, in contrast to the blind and buffeted way of trial and error, often called "at-sight" for contrast. (A neurotic behavior development, inappropriate to the actual situation and, in a sense, no longer goal-directed, might similarly be called "out-sight.") Beyond sensation and even simple perception, involving the correlation of current sense data and of past experience, closure is a basic property of mind. It is, in Goldstein's formulation, the ability to separate a figure from its ground, to formulate a gestalt, or form, to identify an entity. (It operates in seeing three separated dots as the corners of a triangle.) From this flows the setting up of classes and the recognition of spatial—or temporal—relations. Thus Conrad notes the ability to combine parts or elements into a whole, to integrate systems; and also the converse ability to identify parts or elements in the whole, to fragment or differentiate systems. And Wertheimer further recognizes the ability to shift from one whole to another one, to restructure a system . . .

Some examples of imagination at the comfortable and familiar level of parlor problems will serve best, perhaps, to illustrate the points made above.

The victim is asked to draw four straight lines which shall pass through all nine dots arranged in a square of three rows of three dots. The presentation sets the gestalt of the square, but within that pattern a solution is impossible. When the imagination overcomes this restriction, however, and extends lines beyond the self-imposed margin of the figure, the answer is given almost by inspection. Entirely comparable is the problem of constructing from six matches tossed on a table four equilateral triangles, each having its sides the length of a match. So long as the solver limits himself to the suggested plane of the table he struggles in vain; as soon as he adds a third dimension in his consideration the tetrahedron almost leaps at him . . .

If imagination is a definable property of the mind it should also be measurable; and as the definition progresses from the vague impressions of ordinary human dealings to that offered by standardized situations, so the measure moves from the subjective judgment of a person, as having a good or poor imagination, to a fairly quantitative statement about performance. Thurstone, especially, has pressed forward the analysis of mental abilities. By extensive testing with a rich variety of problems he has shown at least seven such abilities which are independent of each other. Thus, individual A may outperform individual B by ten- or a hundredfold on tests which utilize ability 1, while B may similarly outperform A on tests involving ability 2. A similar analysis has revealed some ten perceptual abilities, and others surely remain to be uncovered. Some abilities, such as those of word fluency or verbal understanding, depend for their exercise on learned language, and so performance improves over much of the life-span. But others, such as space visualization, show little improvement in their use after the age of six to eight years; in fact, performance may actually decline. The case for inborn capacities, of particular degrees for each capacity in each person, is thus strong.

Is imagination some one or several of these separable abilities or some common "power factor" underlying them? The answer is not yet available, but it is within easy grasp when persons of outstanding talents of various sorts are measured by such standardized tests. Meanwhile, some interesting guesses may be made. At least four of Thurstone's factors might be involved in imagination, and one of these seems almost to define it. The I, or induction, factor is the ability to see logical patterns or relations (and so would be less related to imagination than to reason).

A convenient test for it is to have the subject supply the next item of a series. A very elementary series is: OXXOXXXOX?. A more severe demand is made by: 1, 7, 3, 6, 5, 5, 7, 4, 9,?. The K factor, measured by the Rohrschach "ink-blot" test, is almost at the other end of the mental spectrum and, far from impinging on logic, plumbs the unconscious. It is of the free completion type; the subject is given an amorphous stimulus and allowed to react with no restraints—as when a person gazes into the flames playing over a fire or at clouds drifting in the sky and "sees" castles or bears or witches acting out untold stories. It is suggestive that a group of successful executives performed (in richness, variety, etc., of responses to the ink blots) significantly above the average on this test.

Two other factors rather specifically deal with closure. The A factor is the ability to make a closure or complete a gestalt and is measured, for example, by having the subject identify partially erased pictures or words. The E factor is the ability to replace one closure by another and is tested by the Gottschalt figures, or by "hidden faces" in a picture of different manifest content. The two abilities, especially E, are rather precisely those considered earlier in defining the act of creative imagination. It is impressive that two independent factors can in fact be isolated for such intuitively equivalent actions as making or remaking a closure! When such primary abilities have been measured in our Einsteins, Edisons, Toscaninis, Van Goghs, Masefields, and Lincolns we shall be far along the way. From descriptions of Coleridge, for example, there is little doubt that he would have performed very well indeed on tests for K, S (space), W (word facility), M (memory), and I and A . . .

Brain Pathology and Imagination

It remains sadly true that most of our present understanding of mind would remain as valid and useful if, for all we knew, the cranium were stuffed with cotton wadding. In time, the detailed correlation of psychic phenomena and neural processes will surely come; but today we are hardly beyond the stage of unequivocal evidence that the correlation does exist. The neuro-anatomist and physiologist are still crudely deciphering the architecture and operation of the organ of mind; the psychologist and psychiatrist are concerned with nuances in the overtones it plays. Yet the gap is narrowing, and a primitive bridge is offered by the grosser disturbances of brain and mind. Perhaps most dramatic are the aphasias, a group of disturbances in the ability to handle "meaning," associated with more or less sharply delimited regions of brain damage. Since disease or accident rarely destroys an exact division of the cerebrum and since different divisions have unique functions, the symptoms are commonly mixed and vary from case to case; but such a diagrammatic instance as the following has been reported.

An educated man, proficient in several languages, suffered a "stroke" which left him aphasic. At one stage in his slow improvement he could converse freely and intelligently but could not read. His vision was not disturbed; he could copy a paragraph correctly, but it carried no meaning to him. He was able, in fact, to take dictation in one language, translate in his mind, and write the correct passage in another tongue. But having written it, he could not read his own writing; it was Chinese to him! One is reminded of the small boy who, called on to read aloud in class, was asked the meaning of what he had read and gave the startled and startling reply, "I don't know. I wasn't listening." Another type of case, with disturbance more on the motor than the sensory side, could not give the word for 7 but could say it, by counting aloud from one. Another, wanting to say "ruler" could not do so until he had made a sketch of one. Yet another could not say words but "knew" them. For example, "What is a baby cat?" No sound of kitten, but two fingers raised in response. Even when words remain, they are often inexact or roundabout, and the subject seems to be indulging in fancy speech or "overwriting," as shown by the following quotations from a patient during and subsequently to an aphasic episode: "I trust I am now learning to do my very best to secure the ideas to put myself carefully to operate the item to me which was seeming away when needed so much by me." And, later, describing his aphasic condition, "Personally I got dumb and could not remember things." (These cases are quoted from Weisenburg and McBride's *Aphasia*.) . . .

Thus meaning, in its widest sense, is imperiled by such brain insults, and the gestalt psychologists have not failed to point out that the very ability to create closures is damaged in aphasics. But, in man, language (with mathematics as one form of language) remains an especial index to the workings of mind; and Pick, combining philological study with his clinical observations, has formulated a series of stages in language use, which may be interrupted anywhere by the aphasic slash. On the sensory or receptive side there is, first, the perception of speech as distinct from mere sound. There follows the recognition of words as separate entities and then of the "musical" parts of speech, cadence, and intonation. Only then comes an awareness of meaning, followed by full understanding of sentences with their proper word relations and emphases. Turning now to the motor or expressive sides, the sequence is intuitive thought (also called verbalizing or inner speech), which becomes structured thought, and is then cast into the scheme of a sentence, only after which are the actual words chosen and the result articulated. Aphasia may thus prevent sensation from emerging into meaning, meaning from eventuating in behavior, or meaning itself from coming clear. The last would be a disturbance in closure or structuring. This represents, perhaps, the basic disintegration of imagination. Imagination may be the word for that all-important no man's land between the end of the receptive process and the start of the expressive one . . .

IMPLICATIONS

. . . The ideas tossed into consciousness by imagination are, we have seen, overwhelmingly bad—untrue or unbeautiful—and must be curbed and ruddered by reason. Here, surely, lies a difference between the more imaginative initiator and the more rational critic. Formal education is directed to our conscious reason, which can at least be supplied with content and practice; if the more intuitive and unconscious imagination can be cultivated we have yet to learn the secret. There is the danger of reason stifling imagination, that "enterprises of great pith and moment" will be "sicklied o'er with the pale cast of thought." From the young, the naive, the dreamings, the drug users, comes a great spate of fresh imaginings, overwhelmingly dross but with those rare grains of great insight yet more common than from the old, the critical, the staid, or the sophisticated. To teach rigor while preserving imagination is an unsolved challenge to education.

Again, each important advance in form, in structured truth or beauty, is the result of a new closure, of a fresh set of axioms; a better set, resulting from the greater knowledge and understanding built with the aid of those dying. The forming mind of the young can use the new as comfortably as the old, but the formed mind of the teacher cannot readily run along the new-gauge tracks. The concepts of infinity, relativity, indeterminism in the physical realm, as evolution in the biological, were difficult for the established generation, simple for the oncoming one. Yet unless we forever question the basic imaginative constructs of our predecessors we condemn ourselves to working at progressively more detailed and trivial levels, to filling in further digits past the decimal point. Recall Trotter's provocative statement:

When, therefore, we find ourselves entertaining an opinion about the basis of which there is a quality of feeling which tells us that to inquire into it would be absurd, obviously unnecessary, unprofitable, undesirable, bad form, or wicked, we may know that that opinion is a non-rational one, and probably, therefore, founded upon inadequate evidence. Opinions, on the other hand, which are acquired as the result of experience alone do not possess this quality of primary certitude. They are true in the sense of being verifiable, but they are unaccompanied by that profound feeling of truth which belief possesses, and, therefore, we have no sense of reluctance in admitting inquiry into them.

In ethical and religious attitudes, even more, the axioms are set at childhood; the re-education of a generation of "Hitler Youth" gives little promise of success. Why, even in aesthetics we learn our particular values; the dissonances of a mere generation ago are consonances to ears of today. To preserve openmindedness while teaching current systems is another unsolved problem of education.

A final word on creative imagination. Besides the intellectual factors, certain emotional ones are demanded. The unconscious work goes on only over problems that are important to the waking mind, only when the mind's possessor worries about them, only when he cares, passionately. As Pavlov wrote shortly before his death at 87, advising young men on the requisites for effective pursuit of science: "Third, Passion. Remember that science demands from a man all his life. If you had two lives that would not be enough for you. Be passionate in your work and your searchings." This is related to the conscious work recognized by Poincaré as preceding the unconscious work of imagination; another emotional factor is involved with the second period of conscious work which follows: courage. It takes courage to face the unfamiliar, to espouse the different; courage to fight one's own prejudices only less than those of others. Was it not a little child who first dared call the emperor naked? It took great fortitude for Kepler to adhere to his new notion of infinity (as the second focus of a parabola), for, as he said, "The idea seems absurd, but I can find no flaw in it"; just as it did for Galileo to murmur among his inquisitors, "Yet the world does move." Most of us will never achieve great imaginative insights; we might at least attempt to be tolerant of those offered us by others.

Somehow, "this power of human thinking . . . seems in times of emergency or conflict to leap ahead to new truth" (Dummer). Sometime, when research in this "constructive power of the unconscious" has increased our understanding of insight, man will more effectively guide his onward movement.

10. Creative Thought in Poets*

This investigation is one of a series of parallel studies of the creative process conducted by Patrick in several fields of creative endeavor. She relates her findings to certain previously held theoretical explanations of the creative process, particularly to the identification of a series of stages in the process of creative thought: preparation, incubation, illumination and verification. This study represents one of the first attempts to study the creative process under controlled conditions.

METHOD

The aim of this experiment was to study creative thought in poets. We wished to study the writing of poetry under laboratory conditions in order that we might watch the actual development of poems. In this way we felt that we could learn more of the essentials of the process than by relying on the analysis of written documents, biographies, and clinical evidence, as other investigators have done. The data thus obtained might then be compared with some of the theories that have been offered to see how far they substantiated them.

SELECTION OF SUBJECTS

One hundred and thirteen subjects took part in this experiment and were divided into two groups, an "experimental group" of fifty-five poets, and a "control group" of fifty-eight non-poets . . . The experimental group was composed of poets of ability whose work had appeared in the better poetry magazines . . . For the purpose of comparison with the group of poets there was a control group composed of fifty-eight persons who were not writing poetry and had never written any, except possibly as school assignments in their high school days . . .

The two groups were equated as to vocabulary ability, which is closely related to intelligence, sex, age, and race. They differed in that the experimental group was composed of poets of ability, while the control group was composed of those who had not written poetry, or had done so to a negligible degree . . .

* CATHARINE PATRICK. Abridged from *Archives of Psychology*, Vol. 26, No. 178, 1935, pp. 10–62.

For this type of experiment it was necessary to have an individual interview with each subject. The experimenter made a personal call on each poet at his or her home or place of business, although it was generally at the home . . .

The first part of the interview consisted of a preliminary conversation, the chief purpose of which was to enable the poet to become accustomed to talking out loud, while the experimenter took down what he said in shorthand. Also it served the purpose of getting some of the information for the questionnaire on methods of work . . .

When the poet had become accustomed to the situation he was presented with a picture of a landscape and asked to write a poem about it or whatever it suggested. The picture included a variety of objects. It depicted clouds and snow-capped mountains with waterfalls and pine forests further down. Below in the valley the stream could be seen running quietly among grassy banks, where people and animals could be distinguished. It was finished in tones of greens and blues, and gave a general impression of the vastness of nature . . .

The poet was presented with this picture and given the following instructions: "Write a poem about this picture or anything that you happen to feel like as you look at it, no matter how irrelevant it may seem. Take all the time that you want and write it at your leisure, for there is no time limit. The chief thing is to talk aloud constantly from the minute I present the picture, for I want to get everything you happen to think of, no matter how irrelevant it may seem. Talk about anything you want to as you look at it, and then eventually, when you feel like it, write the poem. The poems will all be treated anonymously, and no one will know them. Take all the time you want, for there is no time limit. Make it at least four lines longs and a complete poem."

The experimenter was seated a little distance from the subject, either at his side or behind him, depending on circumstances of furniture arrangement. It was necessary to remain close enough to hear any words that might be half whispered, and yet not too close to bother the subject . . . The time was recorded in five minute intervals, but great care was taken to conceal that fact from the subject . . .

A record was kept of everything that was spoken from the moment of presenting the picture until the subject announced that the poem was completely finished, and needed no more revision. The subject was then asked the remaining questions on the questionnaire about methods of work, which he had not answered in the preliminary conversation. The questionnaire consisted of the following questions:

1. Do you usually complete the essential structure of a poem at one sitting?

2. Do you have any special place where you write your poems?

3. When you get ready to write a poem do you incubate it a while first? If so, describe the process of incubation to me. How long does it usually last? What are its characteristics?

4. Was the method of writing the poem under the conditions of this experiment fairly representative of your usual method of working?

5. When you compose a poem does the content or the form seem to come first?

6. When you compose a poem, do you do it in a warm, stirred-up emotional state or in a cold, detached, objective state?

7. Do a few lines of a poem seem to compose themselves and come automatically and spontaneously, as though they could not be said in any other way?

8. Do you revise your work much?

9. Do you have regular hours for writing?

10. Do you write prose?

11. Do you consider writing poetry a vocation or an avocation?

12. Do you consider your poetry an important source of funds? . . .

Each of the one hundred thirteen subjects, both control and experimental, was given a private interview in the manner described. The procedure for the two groups was the same, except that the control subjects were not given the questionnaire about their usual habits of work.

ILLUSTRATIVE PROTOCOLS

. . . In the following report of poet A, we find each of the four stages represented. We find first the period of preparation, in which the associations are shifting rapidly. We likewise find incubation. The idea of Yosemite, which is the climax of the poem, is found in the first line of the report. The associations change and she talks of other things, scenes in Wyoming, Mt. Vesuvius, a glacier which she had visited, Boulder Dam, fresh water, and pine trees. The period of illumination follows, in which the lines are composed . . . The last stage is verification. We find elaboration of the thought in such a case as when "mountain stream" is changed to "gurgling stream." The checking up of the poem is seen in the critical re-reading of it . . .

Poet A

It looks like the Grand Canyon, but this is like Yosemite and
    this is like dual nature.
In the far distance it reminds me of Yosemite.
This in the bottom is like the Merced River.
This peak is like Wyoming or Vesuvius.
We were at the foot of that glacier.
It looks very inviting in summer, but not inviting in winter.
5 min. We visited Boulder Dam. That is a stupendous thing.
Doesn't this water here look like swift and pure, not stale water.
Lord, let my thoughts be as pure as this mountain stream. No,
    I want the idea of topsy turvy; in the stream the pine trees
    gleam.
Topsy turvy in the stream the pine trees gleam.
10 min. What to me is loveliest
The mountain stream,
The mountain crest
    What to me is loveliest
    The mountain stream
    The mountain crest
The cascade with its
Glistening mist,
The pine trees by
The sunset kist.
    What to me is loveliest
    The mountain stream
Change "mountain" to something else
    The cascade with its
    Glistening mist
    What to me is loveliest
    The _____ stream. Put "gurgling" stream.
    The mountain crest
    The cascade with its
    Glistening mist,
    The pine trees by

The sunset kissed.
   Put "kist" I guess.
Isn't this Yosemite?
   Now speak to me Yosemite
Change "speak to me."
   Now speak to me always Yosemite
   You speak to me always Yosemite
     Of grandeur undeniably.
      What to me is loveliest
      The gurgling stream,
      The mountain crest
      The cascade with its
      Glistening mist,
      The pine trees by
      The sunset kist.
      You speak always Yosemite,
      Of grandeur, undeniably.
15 min.   Of grandeur, undeniably.

. . . The next report illustrates how the poet may get the climax or last two lines first and build the rest of the poem up to that. This report is atypical in that it does not show much preparation and there is no evidence of incubation. In this case, the poet probably had the idea for a poem in mind and so started right off composing it, although the actual writing was done in the experiment. Revision overlaps with illumination.

Poet G

I might have a love poem. Comical if write it about one person I
   know. I will think.
Part of it is going to be. It may be the last part of it.
   The very small heart of a very young fool
   Is ____ ____ ____ of a very small pain.
   The very small heart of a very young fool
   Is aware of a very small pain.
   Is aware of a very small pain.
   There's a love as light as the little wind.
   Sounds sticky, crap.
   That shudders alone in the lane.
5 min.   Like Eddy Guest.
   Wind-blind. Never can rhyme that. Going to use "then" as rhyme.
   Only thing I can think of.

And when the afternoon has thinned
  Has thinned
To dusk and the smell of rain
Is upon the leaves
Is upon the leaves and the grass is cool
And a last lone leaf trembles against the pool
  And a lone leaf trembles
  And a lone leaf trembles upon the pool
Can't use "upon" because used it before.
  And a lone leaf trembles above the pool.
The very small heart of a very young fool
Is aware of a very small pain.

  There's a love as light as the little wind
  That shudders alone in the lane
  And when the afternoon has thinned
  To dusk and the smell of rain
  Is upon the leaves and the grass is cool
  And a lone leaf trembles above the pool
  The very small heart of a very young fool
  Is aware of a very small pain

  There's a love as light as the little wind
  That shudders alone in the lane,
  And when the afternoon has thinned
  To dusk, and the smell of rain
  Is upon the leaves and the grass is cool
  And a lone leaf trembles above the pool,
  The very small heart of a very young fool
10 min.   Is aware of a very small pain.

. . . We will now quote [one] of the protocols of the non-poets. We find the four stages represented in this report also. The following protocol of subject A shows this. Preparation, when the associations are shifting rapidly, is found here. Incubation also occurs. The first thing that he speaks of is where the water goes, and the fact that it cuts the bottom of the mountain to go that way in the stream. He then turns to other topics as the differences of the picture in two parts. Summer is below, yet the mountains have snow . . . Then the original idea of where the water goes recurs as the subject of the poem, typical incubation. Illumination follows. Then verification, with critical re-reading and elaboration of the thought, as changing "course" to "source."

Subject A [Non-poet]

The thing that bothers me is what happens when the water goes in circles. I do not notice where it goes. I see. It cuts the bottom of the mountain and the water goes that way in the stream. The picture is different in the two parts. It is summer time because of grass and the trees shed leaves. High mountains have snow on them and glaciers are in those mountains. That waterfall is spread out like a hair being blown by the wind, I should say. To the left are clouds that are low. They seem to be staying on the top of the mountain. According to the way the wind blows it may rain or clear up. If it blows from the black cloud forward it will rain, if it blows opposite it clears up. The coloring is good but I like warm coloring better in pictures. Though only a few stones there must be others there, for the water is very rough. Looking over the plain here where the cattle are I see shreds of water above the plain. Pleasant picture at that part. The sun comes up from where the clouds are darkest. Not make sense.

5 min.   I said spring, but from the color of leaves it must be autumn instead of spring. Dead trees are in the foreground. I wonder whether that fellow is shooting at something or what he is doing. I see he may be shooting at something. On the other side are a few animals. Few spots are suggestive of animals. Why shoot animals when there are cows there, or am I dreaming. There are some sort of animals. They look like sheep or cows or something. Another thing that seems peculiar is that the low mountain is white. The taller one is gray. That is like the color of rock. The thing is I don't know what to say or how to say it or anything.

10 min.   The water starts from its course
                 Rolling and spilling over rocks
                 Drops precipitously down a gorge
                 Then to the sea, it never stops.
                     I try to make "rocks" rhyme with "stops."
                         The water starts from its course
                         Rolling and spilling over rocks
                         Drops precipitously down a gorge
                         Then to the sea, it never stops.

                 I look at the picture again.
                 Change "course" to "source."
                 Change line 1.
                 The river in starting from its source
                 Change line 2.
                 Goes very rapidly from the start.

> The river in starting from its source
> Goes very rapidly from the start

Change "drops precipitously down a gorge" to "Then as it reaches the plains."

> Then as it reaches the plains

Change "Then to the sea it never stops" to "Slows down for the greater part."

> The river in starting from its source
> Goes very rapidly from the start
> Then as it reaches the plains
> Slows down for the greater part.

Third line is out of kilter.

> The river in starting from its source
> Goes very rapidly from the start
> Then as it reaches the plains
> Slows down for the greater part.

Put "level" in third line. Then as it reaches the level plains

> The river in starting from its source
> Goes very rapidly from the start,
> Then, as it reaches the level plains,
15 min.   Slows down for the greater part.

Discussion: Stages of Thought

As we examine the results of this experiment we find evidence of four stages of thought: . . . *preparation, incubation, illumination* and *verification*.

In order to investigate the first stage, *preparation,* when the subject is receiving various ideas, we have measured the number of thought changes that occur in each quarter. We find that over half of the thought changes occur in the first quarter for both groups . . .

To present evidence that this leads to *incubation,* or the second stage, we have noted those cases in which the idea of the poem appeared earlier in the report, after which the subject talked of various things, and then this original idea reappeared as the subject of the poem. This is the fact in over two-thirds of the cases in both groups . . .

The stage of *illumination,* in composing a lyric, would be the period at which the poem was first formulated. For both groups, we find that two-thirds of the poems were first formulated in the second and third quarters . . .

The fourth stage, *verification or revision,* is easily identified. We find that two-thirds of the instances of revision occur in the last quarter for both groups. Revision thus constitutes the final stage.

Our data show four stages of creative thought. We will now discuss their characteristics in more detail.

First comes preparation, when the subject is assembling or receiving new ideas. During this time the associations shift rapidly. One's ideas are not yet dominated by any coherent theme or formulation. It is a time when new thoughts seem to be "pressing in upon the mind," as one writer expressed it. A poet gazes at a landscape or sunset and receives various impressions of it. A mathematician, as Poincaré, starts to solve a problem and considers its various phases. Often this period is longer for the mathematician, who spends some time laboring over a problem, or for the writer of a historical novel, who collects much factual information, than for the poet, who often receives his impressions in a very short time. Preparation is a time when the creative thinker is receiving or gathering his raw material.

Incubation follows preparation, although it may accompany it . . . From the data of the questionnaire, we find that with the poets it is generally a mood which is incubated. This mood keeps recurring from time to time. It is often not formulated in words or is but vaguely expressed. Usually the stimulating situation sets up a mood which is incubated, although sometimes it results in a phrase or sentence which keeps recurring and in turn induces a mood . . .

Incubation can be defined as follows: A mood or idea is being incubated when it involuntarily repeats itself with more or less modification during a period when the subject is also thinking of other topics. It may be indefinitely related to an ultimate goal, as a poet while incubating a mood may have the ultimate goal of writing a poem about it later . . . As soon as the mood or idea becomes definitely related to a specific goal, we have the third stage of illumination or inspiration . . .

The results from the questionnaire and experiment point to a fact which has not received sufficient attention in previous accounts of incubation. The poets report that the *incubated idea or mood recurs from time to time* during the incubation period. When the idea recurs, there is a chance of some work being done upon it . . .

When we compare the incubation that occurs in the writing of a poem, the making of an invention, and the solving of a problem, we find that there are certain characteristics common to this stage of thought. In the first place, no active work is done on the idea or mood that is incubated. The subject thinks of other topics. In the second place, the idea or mood that is incubated recurs spontaneously. In the third place, the idea or mood is more clearly defined at the end of the stage than it was at the beginning, for it has been modified . . .

The length of the period of incubation varies from person to person, and also within the same individual from time to time. One person may have the habit of incubating a poem only a half hour or so, while another may require several years for incubation. More often this stage lasts several days or weeks or perhaps months. But the generalization can't be made that it will always last a certain time for a certain person, for under one set of circumstances the period may be only a half hour and under other conditions it may last several weeks . . . It is not surprising that there is such variation in the length of the period of incubation, for there are various factors which influence it. Some of these would be the nature of the original stimulating situation, the intensity of the emotional reaction set up, and the daily life of the individual, not to mention numerous other factors.

Illumination follows incubation. This is seen from the data of the questionnaire where the content or idea, which has been incubating, generally comes before the form . . .

If we summarize the data which we have on the third stage, or that of illumination, we find the following facts: Illumination occurs when the idea, which has been incubating, becomes definitely related to a specific goal. It is the period when a poem is composed. In this period the essential structure of the poem is completed. An emotional reaction does not necessarily accompany this period, although it generally does. A part of the poem seems to come automatically and spontaneously by itself . . .

We agree with Wallas (2) and Poincaré (1) then, that there are four stages of creative thought, preparation, incubation, illumination and verification, but we differ from them in the explanation of incubation. We believe that it can be explained in terms of changes of mental sets as well as in terms of the subconscious. We bring out the recurrence of the mood or idea during incubation, which he does not show.

Although these four stages can be distinguished in the thought process, yet it must be remembered that they may overlap. Incubation often occurs along with preparation, and revision may begin during the period of illumination. In the stage of preparation, while the subject is still receiving new ideas, one mood or idea may be incubated and recur from time to time. Also revision of the lines may start before they are completely formulated . . .

REFERENCES

1. POINCARÉ, H. *Science et Methode.* Paris: Flammarion, 1908.
2. WALLAS, G. *The Art of Thought.* New York: Harcourt, Brace, 1921.

11. Creative Processes in Painting*

The scant number of experimental studies of the nature of artistic creation led Eindhoven and Vinacke to question the *a priori* conception of four stages in the creative process identified by Patrick and others and to investigate the specific processes involved in painting under conditions believed to be more spontaneous and natural. The authors attempt to remedy some of the deficiencies in earlier studies by carefully recording the behavior of their subjects from the time they are presented with a task to the creation of a final artistic product. An analysis of their data leads the authors to question the interpretation of the creative process as a series of "stages."

THE PROBLEM

. . . [This experiment] is characterized by two principal differences from previous approaches. In the first place, it was designed to obtain samples of creation under as spontaneous conditions as possible. In the second place, the analysis was oriented as much as possible to actual requirements of the task and to the actual behavior of the subject, rather than formulated in keeping with advanced notions about the character of creation.

The specific problem was to observe and analyze the behavior of artists and non-artists during the painting of an illustration for a poem ["Night," by Charles Peguy, translated by Julian Green] . . .

SUMMARY OF PROCEDURE

This experiment was designed to investigate creative processes under conditions rendered as natural as possible while still meeting certain mini-

* JAN E. EINDHOVEN AND W. EDGAR VINACKE. Reprinted and abridged with permission of the authors and publisher from *The Journal of General Psychology,* 1952, 47:140–69.

mum requirements of standardization. The task given to a group of 13 artists and 14 non-artists was to paint an illustration for a poem which could be suitable for publication. The poem was selected to be suggestive and abstract rather than realistic or marked by definite imagery. Subjects were allowed to determine for themselves the length of time they wished to work on the problem, up to a maximum of four visits to the laboratory. At the end of each session, the subject discussed his day's work with the experimenter and a recapitulative account of the process was given. Four monochromatic mediums, pencil, poster paint, ink and charcoal were available, together with appropriate implements and an ample supply of paper. The experimenter observed the subjects, took notes, and recorded certain activities at five-minute intervals. In addition, the subjects were given notebooks and paper to use for records and sketching relevant to the project, if they wished, while out of the laboratory. The data were analyzed and the two groups compared with respect to time relationships, characteristics of the products, processes followed while painting, and individual patterns of creative thought . . .

Case Histories

Although quantitative analyses revealed important characteristics of the creative process for the subjects as a group, it proved exceedingly fruitful to assemble all available materials into "case-histories" of individual subjects. These materials include the notes taken by the experimenter, the series of sketches produced, and especially the recapitulative account given by each subject at the end of every session . . .

It was generally apparent that it is impossible to understand meaningfully the nature of creative processes without giving proper attention to individual differences . . . As an illustration of individual differences in creative activity, the cases for two artists are summarized below.

Case A. *An exploratory creative procedure*

This woman artist, age 38, had her art training in high school, two years of college, and a year in Paris. She had also studied in India. She came to the laboratory four times in the course of a week, making a total of six laboratory sketches and one home sketch. [Figures 1a, b, c represent her work.] The latter, she stated, would, with a little more work, constitute a publishable sketch [Fig. 1b] . . . Figure 1a is her work in the laboratory during the first period . . .

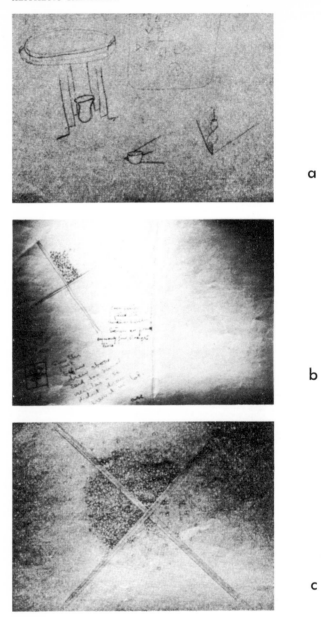

a

b

c

F<small>IG</small>. 1.

Between each sketch, she paused, closed her eyes, and tried to review new imagery. She stated that it was her custom to meditate before painting, probably reflecting her training in the East. To aid her imagery, she re-read the poem and re-touched some of her previous work between sketches.

During the second period, she made no new sketches. The cause, she explained, was that the house next door had been on fire as she left, and she could not get her mind on the painting. However, she showed the experimenter a sketch which she had jotted down at midnight one evening (Fig. 1b) and stated that this sketch would be best fitted for the publishable sketch. The idea had come as a visual image, suddenly, but more simplified.

[As] she worked on the publishable sketch (Fig. 1c) . . . elaboration and care of execution show that polishing is taking place. Thus, the preliminary, small, off-center sketches in pencil eventually terminated in the appearance of one of them, complete in itself, as a final product . . .

Case B. *A gradual evolutionary creative procedure*

This male artist, age 33, had his training in art school. He came to the laboratory three times within a week, and painted six sketches (Figures 2a, b, c, d, e, f). The last sketch (Fig. 2f) . . . was selected by the artist as the publishable sketch. At a later date, however, he was undecided, and thought that the first sketch (Fig. 2a) was perhaps superior.

The first three sketches (Figs. 2a, b, c) are similar in motif and subject matter, but the size and number of the figures change, and the picture becomes more stylized. A purposeful stylization was admitted by the artist, who felt that the abstract qualities of the poem demanded such treatment. He also remarked that he visualized easily and had a good preconception of the sketch before he began it. He painted extremely rapidly after first laying in the broad outlines of the sketch, either in pencil or paint.

During the second period, a single picture was made . . . (Fig. 2d). The artist said that he felt in "an abstract mood." . . . After having completed the abstraction, the artist stated that this sophisticated approach was not appropriate to the childlike qualities of the poem, and that he would revert to a more academic treatment . . .

The publishable sketch (Fig. 2f) appears to be a combination of the first sketches in motif and subject matter, the third sketch in number, size and style, and the penultimate sketch in its ovoid arrangement on the page. Thus, the final sketch evolved gradually from preceding work, and represents many small thought changes . . .

Discussion

The aim of this experiment was to study creative processes under conditions rendered as natural as possible . . .

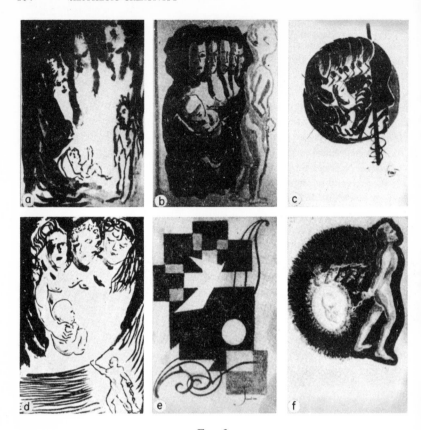

Fig. 2.

In the first place, it has been found that the creative process in painting a picture has certain general characteristics, regardless of whether the subject is an artist or a non-artist. Thus, it appears to be typical for creation to require a considerable period of time, during which there is a rather gradual evolution of the finished product. The subject tends to be variable at first, but increasingly concentrates on the sketching itself and on a particular sketch. Given the relatively free conditions of this experiment, it is typical for the individual to produce more than one sketch, the series ranging from an extreme in which each separate product is potentially a final one to an extreme in which earlier attempts are incomplete, hasty, simply exploratory, with a steady progression towards the final product.

Painting, as observed in this experiment, is marked by certain typical qualitative features. For example, it is likely that the motif will be established very early, whereas subject matter, composition, size and other aspects undergo many changes. Furthermore, more obviously, the earliest activities in painting a particular picture are usually those concerned with space delimitation and arrangement, whereas the working out of details comes later. With respect to medium usage, too, when a choice is available, a pattern emerges wherein the easy, rapid, readily altered medium (pencil) is employed for early small sketches (or for preliminary work on a single sketch) and a different medium is chosen for later work.

A second major finding of the present experiment has to do with differences between professional artists and non-artists. If the four stages usually cited for the creative process are accepted uncritically as typical, it might mistakenly be assumed that anyone in a creative situation behaves in about the same way, the only difference, perhaps, being that the artist produces a better result than the non-artist. Actually, this experiment demonstrates that the artist differs in three crucial ways from the non-artist: . . .

1. Artists have more control over their creative processes than do non-artists, whether because they have greater spontaneity, more practice, or other factors. Thus, the former are more variable in the qualitative aspects of painting, use more mediums, etc.

2. From their training, artists also appear to acquire a pattern of dealing with creative situations which differs from that of the non-artists . . . That is, they may be expected not only to produce a better work, but to do it in a different way.

3. Finally, this experiment shows that artists are more likely to evolve their products more gradually than do non-artists. Artists seem to experiment in early stages and little by little concentrate on certain features which are selected, modified, and reorganized for the final product.

The third major finding of the present experiment has to do with the four stages alleged of the creative process. It is our contention that previous studies have approached creative activity with a predetermined, logically defined conception of what goes on. In fact, because of the logical character of this formulation, there can be little argument with it. The present experiment, too, can be fitted into the framework. But we have attempted to go beyond previous experiments in two principal respects, on the one hand by establishing conditions conducive to spontaneity and by analyzing the data in terms of objective aspects of the subject and his work, rather than in terms of successive stages defined in advance . . .

It cannot be said that the present experiment refutes previous concepts of the creative process; rather, it is felt that two additional contributions have been made. The first is that we have striven to analyze what artists and non-artists actually do from the time they are presented with a problem to the creation of the final product. Thus, we have outlined, tentatively, a general pattern of activity, and shown differences within this pattern between artists and non-artists.

The second contribution bears more directly upon the proper formulation of stages in creative thought. From our results, it appears that successive activities are not sharply differentiated from each other. On the contrary, they blend together in an intricate manner. In short, although previous investigators have admitted overlapping between the stages, our results suggest that there is an interweaving of all the aspects subsumed under the successive stages. Thus, creativity might be thought of as one whole process consisting of all the various aspects participating concurrently. For example, it would be very difficult to define "illumination" by reference to our data, even though there was seemingly direct evidence of it in one case (Case A). On the other hand, if illumination is conceived to be, not a stage in itself, but a process leading to some definite idea or choice of object or reorganization of previous ideas, then it can readily be seen that it occurs throughout the creative process. In fact, at the very least, it would be desirable to think of a series of illuminations, beginning with the first sketch. Preparation, similarly, may be conceived as a process rather than a self-contained stage; thus, the subject unquestionably readied himself in the first session, by listening to the instructions, reading the poem, examining the mediums, etc. But, in effect, there was frequent recurrence of preparation up to the end of the experiment, as the subject started a new sketch or set to work in a new period, etc. In any case, there was certainly no sharply defined break between preparation and incubation or illumination. Incubation, itself, might be defined as thought about the problem, whether subconscious or not, and thus would constitute an aspect of creation which persisted throughout the experiment. It probably continues, for instance, even while the subject is finishing his final sketch, at which time it may influence the modification of detail (verification).

Thus, the "stages" are not stages at all, but processes which occur during creation. They blend together and go along concurrently . . . It is far more meaningful and in better agreement with the facts to regard these alleged "stages" of creativity as aspects, or processes, of the complete dynamic pattern into which they are interwoven.

REFERENCES

1. MURPHY, G. *Personality*. New York: Harper, 1947.
2. PATRICK, C. 1937. Creative thought in artists. *J. Psychol.* 4:35–73.
3. PATRICK, C. 1938. Scientific thought. *J. Psychol.* 5:55–83.

12. The Birth of a Poem*

As an illustration of the psychology of the creative mind, the poet Robert Nichols contributed to Harding's volume on the creative process, a detailed description of how he composed his "Sunrise Poem." While Nichols's first-hand account could hardly be considered experimental in nature, it is nevertheless an intimate and revealing description to consider in relation to the interpretation of creative processes by Patrick on the one hand, and by Eindhoven and Vinacke on the other.

SUNRISE POEM

The sun, a serene and ancient poet,
Stoops and writes on the sunrise sea
In softly undulant cyphers of gold
Words of Arabian charactery;
And the lovely riddle is lovingly rolled
With sound of slumberous, peaceful thunder
Around the sky and the sea thereunder
Toward my feet. What is here enscrolled?
Is it poem or a story?
I cannot command this charactery,
But I think it is both and that it reads
This glorious morning as of old
When the first sun rose above the first sea,
As read it will while there is sea
And sun to scribe with quill of gold.
It is both story and a poem,
A hymn as also a history
Concerning the mightiest of mages,

---

* ROBERT NICHOLS. Abridged with permission of the publisher from an appendix to R. E. M. Harding, *An Anatomy of Inspiration*, pp. 1–22. Cambridge: W. Heffer and Sons, Ltd., 1948.

The best that has been or shall be
Writ for any throughout the ages,
Writ for any, whoever he be
Or the most scholarly of sages
Or the most awkward of those who plod,
For Greek, Jew, Infidel and Turk—
As it was written too for me—
One page, two eternal sentences:
"The Heavens declare the Glory of God
And the Firmament showeth His Handiwork."

                                        Robert Nichols

. . . Five days before—was it?—I'd lost count of time!—I had gone ashore at Madeira and the "run" of poetry had started. Then we had touched at one of the Canary Islands—Teneriffe perhaps?—and now we were due at Las Palmas in the Grand Canaries. Talk about the lucid insanity of a fit of gambling! of following a rolling red ball or a dancing figure! Already I dared not lift eye from the notebook in which I scribbled, largely, alas, illegibly (as I was later to find) during my wanderings. These wanderings had little method. They were the zigzags of attraction and evasion. For the world had become an open Book, the seals of which had been broken, the pages of which blew this way and that as if fluttered by a wind whose passage I could not feel. And on every page a symbol clamoured to impart its significance . . . I remember a hummingbird, a flower, a silvery wall and a palladian tower above the wall. On which should I let my eye linger? Which would impart the most? Obviously a choice was imposed. For flesh, blood and faculties couldn't stand up to this incessant battering of significances . . .

I wished to get back to the ship and the isolation of the waters surrounding her. I pictured to myself the solitude and longed-for solidity of my little cabin with my dressing-gown sidling upon the wall and the loneliness of the pure, empty and perfect sky shining in the port-hole. Even that light, I reflected, could be partially shut out and, having screened it, I could lie in my demi-obscurity while I disentangled the web of scrawls in my notebook . . .

I made my way back to the road, found a broken-down fly, reached the ship and continued to be besieged by echoes from the shore. Things I'd seen but hadn't particularly noticed—or so I fancied—persisted in pestering me. I lunched in a state of dream, lay down in my cabin, dozed a little and uneasily, opened my eyes:

"There sparkled a fountain, glittered a tank;
  The shadows of leaves danced over the wall . . .

That had been found in Madeira. Glancing in my notebook I found the thing well on the way to completion. The impulse seemed unusually strong. Maybe it would keep further intimations off . . .

After doing what I could, worn out, I had dropped asleep, and here I was awake again . . .

At once I knew that further sleep was out of the question, that my business was to go on deck, if possible up into the bows by the anchor chains. Wasn't that, I told myself, the obvious thing to do on so glorious a morning? . . .

I took my time. Nonetheless within two minutes I was clambering up the iron stairs onto the fo'c'sle.

The ship was miraculously deserted. Upon the spick-and-span bridge the head of the officer of the watch could be descried behind the canvas. He lifted a hand and nodded me good morning.

It appeared we were once more on the move but so slowly that I shouldn't have known it had I not glanced over the side and observed the anchor snugged home and a noiseless ripple stealing about the stem . . .

I shoved my hands into the pockets of my silk dressing-gown—the notebook was there in the right-hand pocket—and drank in the superb chill blandness of the morning air. I was very well satisfied with existence. I felt extremely normal save for an unusual hollowness in my stomach where an unfortunate captive stirred, dreaming of bacon and eggs.

I stared for'ard. Not a sail. Nothing but the enormous tranquil, softly-heaving plain of the sea. Complete silence reigned, one of the most perfect I had ever known. And, what was better yet, there was silence within. I was merely "being." Very pleasant, very pleasant indeed! I turned about and lit a cigarette . . .

At that moment the newly-risen sun sent flickering over the long, low, smooth, glassy mounds of the rolling swells a series of elastic reflections which expanded and contracted and zigzagged and appeared and disappeared and reformed as they travelled in stately and regular motion toward me . . . I became aware of an extraordinary physical exhilaration. "Of course!" I said to myself—"Arabic" . . .

Had the reflections been merely blobs of light, had they been written in a script with which I was acquainted, had they for instance formed a succession of capital letters—such as RKP followed by LZO followed by NQT—they would, I fancy, have added little, if indeed anything, to my animal pleasure. But they were recognizable, though not decipherable, as units having the peculiarities of a cursive script, rightly or wrongly taken by me to be Arabic and Arabic, I instantly grasped, of a peculiar kind,— golden letters in a holy book, such a book as I knew I had once seen, a book with wooden covers, dated, so I was given to understand, about 1500. And as these units were so taken—that is to say as golden and written in a holy book (simply that and nothing more)—so I at the same or nearly the same instant apprehended that these figures *weren't* in a book but were, at that very moment, in the most literal sense *being written on the sea by the sun,* a being who was a poet . . . On an instant there was presented to my consciousness a favorite picture-postcard I had twice or thrice bought at the British Museum. Almost simultaneously there formed in my mouth the line

> "The sun an ancient, serene poet."

The picture on the postcard—that of a poet, possibly Persian, seated on the ground, wearing a rose-pink turban, a green caftan and a little pair of black slippers, and gazing to the spectator's left—and the line were indissoluble. They remain indissoluble to this day—in the sense that I cannot repeat the first line of the poem without seeing the picture on the postcard . . .

Nevertheless, no sooner was the line created, than I experienced a feeling of considerable satisfaction, first because there was as-it-were plenty of time (this being the first line) to supply that which would by elaboration give what had been stated adequacy and, second, because there seemed to me something very inclusive about the line's simplicity (that's to say, it promised well). I therefore repeated it to myself twice or thrice, partly for its own sake and partly because I was waiting for what would arrive next—obviously a verb of some sort.

As I repeated the line the personage I call the artificer in the poet drew my attention to the fact that the line

> "The sun an ancient, serene poet"

was lacking in the serenity it sought, among other things, to convey. It was too "jumpy." "Try shifting the order of the adjectives," said the artificer, "and inserting a conjunction between them. That ought to do it. Look—

> "The sun a serene and ancient poet."

No sooner had this change been effected than I recognized that the line had *set* in an order that no subsequent occurrence must be suffered to disturb . . .

The grandeur of the feeling induced by appreciating the word "ancient" assured me that this verb, the first word of the next line, would be of an emphatic nature. I was not surprised, then, to find it what it was when it arrived, bringing with it the rest of the line:

> "Stoops and writes on the sunrise sea."

Looking back, I now quite clearly perceive how this word "stoops" established itself and why its authority was so extraordinarily complete . . . The sun was now a handsbreadth above the sea. This implied that in order to write upon the sea, the sun would have to bend forward and downward. So, too, the Persian poet on the postcard, who, however, could only bend toward the left . . . And just as the bearded Persian poet is to be found on a postcard in the British Museum, so Blake's bearded ancient—the Ancient of Days—is to be found on a postcard at the Tate Gallery, copies of both of which I had at one time or another possessed . . . Blake's figure on the Tate Gallery postcard *stoops* forward and downward directly opposite the spectator (as the sun was opposite me) to divide the waters . . .

I had now, I perceived, the general framework of a "situation" and it was with a sense of tingling excitement that I turned to the artificer to find him smilingly confident that not only would the next line make its appearance with the utmost ease but that we should immediately enjoy it . . . We were not disappointed, for even as the line curtsied its way through my mind

> "In softly undulant cyphers of gold"

he nudged me, calling my attention to the softness of its motion while I remarked to him, "We shall have the core of the poem entire in a moment." And sure enough we did . . . The third line ran out into the fourth:

> "In softly undulant cyphers of gold
> Words of Arabian charactery"

Here the artificer rubbed his hands and said, "Listen to those open *a*'s associated with *r*. If that isn't nice to say, what is?" . . .

Meanwhile the tolling of the word "gold" (at the end of line three) continued in the inner ear and demanded satisfaction . . . Suffice to say that on this occasion I heard the syllable "gold" tolling at the same time that I was aware that a "pick-up" was needed. A sense of discomfort ensued and my "tactical instinct" instructed me to "surface" from the reverie within the poem (that is my constructional activity among words) to the reverie of the fo'c'sle . . . In point of fact I went even further and precipitated myself for a moment out of the world wherein poetry is composed into the world of conscious everyday aprehension . . .

The morning heat was already sufficient for me to notice the warmth of the metal plates beneath the soles of my thin slippers, to cause me to remark the crawling iridescence of the particles that composed the black paint upon that metal, and for me to smell the faint coaldusty odour of the air rising from those plates. On the bridge the officer of the watch had shifted not his position but his attitude, and was leaning his elbows upon the canvas. He had shoved his cap on to the back of his head and was scratching the hair above his ear. The tremor of the air over the funnels was more pronounced and its wanderings were more fluid. All around shone the expanse of the immense and rapidly whitening sea with, on my left, the island, now more of an island and less of a cloud, and, forward on my right, the disc of the sun still rolling characters of glittering liquidity toward me . . .

Meanwhile I was conscious that what I saw amounted to a statement of *isolation:* I stood on a moving ship and the shore hung stationary several miles away. No sooner had I gathered this information—and gathered it in a thoroughly matter of fact way—than I sank back into the workshop beside the artificer. The word "gold" was still tolling . . . and I whispered to him, "Look here—this is the trouble: I am on a ship and our viewer-of-the sunrise is obviously upon the shore. You're right, we haven't quite completed the arrangements necessary before we can proceed and make our 'pick-up.' We haven't all the 'situation,' for our topography isn't complete."

The artificer tactfully disappeared (he knows his job) and I inspected, coldly enough, the memory I had brought from my visit to the deck. Obviously our viewer was standing on a beach, a beach such as might exist yonder on the island . . .

I relaxed, sought the association of the glittering pebbles and found myself standing, as so often in past summers, upon Winchelsea beach. The sultry, lustreless sea, perfectly calm and as though half-stupefied by the heat, was rolling a few pebbles up and down the pebble-bank in a listless and perfunctory manner . . .

So there the rhyme was: "rolled."

Having discovered this, I perceived that the words which would follow "rolled" would give me the position of our viewer . . .

I read my lines over:

> "The sun, a serene and ancient poet,
>   Stoops and writes on the sunrise sea
>   In softly undulant cyphers of gold
>   Words of Arabian charactery" . . .

I read the lines again more slowly and perceived that it was the motion of the ship that had yielded them the rhythm they had . . .

> "And the lovely riddle is lovingly rolled
>   Toward my feet. What is here enscrolled?"

"For that's how it goes on, I'm sure. 'What is here enscrolled' is our 'pick-up.' It must be. Haven't we said the charactery is a 'riddle'? Isn't that what we've felt from the first? Isn't mystery what we're after?"

"Yes," he said, "but there's something missing. You do the feeling and I'll do the hearing, which is after all only the echo of your feeling" . . .

We remained silent and I descended into a deep drowse in which I could no longer . . . distinguish the slight roll of the ship from the welling of the water up and down Winchelsea beach. I became immersed in one of those long afternoons at the close of which one feels, rather than hears, afar off the reverberations of thunder . . .

> "With sound of slumberous peaceful thunder"—

"Is that it, artificer? Do you hear it?"

"Certainly I do. And very nice too" . . .

"Listen," I said . . . "Listen hard and you'll hear the love that is in the sky *talking* out of its loneliness to the loneliness on the beach."

"Is it '*in*' the sky?" he said.

"No," I said, "it's around the sky."

"Well, then," he said, "why not say so? 'Around the sky' . . . After which, of course, we've got to bring it back to 'Toward my feet' and that implies mention of the sea" . . .

We stood back and examined the affair:

> "And the lovely riddle is lovingly rolled
>   With sound of slumberous, peaceful thunder
>   Around the sea and the sky thereunder
>   Toward my feet."

"Must we have that 'toward my feet'?"

"Got to," I said. "Maybe we can carry it" . . .

"Toward my feet. What is here enscrolled?" murmured the artificer. And then suddenly in that jaunty manner he sometimes assumes and which I particularly detest, "And what precisely, guv'nor, on the square, *entre nous* and in strict confidence is enscrolled? I mean I've got to make my arrangements."

"I haven't the slightest idea," I returned coolly . . .

"Okay, guv'nor, okay; I get you. But to get the proper sort of lead up to the climax I've got to *have* that climax whatever it is. Two last lines I suppose it'll be, giving me two rhymes to play with on my climb. Come, guv'nor, is it two lines? I simply gotta know. Don't lose your nerve."

(He is confoundedly perspicacious. I was, in point of fact, becoming distinctly nervous. Well pleased with the opening of my poem, I trembled to think of so promising an affair coming to nought.)

"Take a turn," he said, "try the old dodge; forget you're writing a poem at all. And you needn't worry about the rhyme. We've nothing here save the 'gold' rhyme (if you need it), nothing, I mean, obligatory. There's a lot to come between what we have and the last two lines. So go ahead. We're out for something big. I feel just as enthusiastic about this poem as you do. So don't worry about the rhymes on the end of those last two lines. I'll fix 'em somehow!"

I thrust my notebook into my pocket and took a turn or two. The characters had almost entirely disappeared from the sea's surface. Light, peace, purity and splendor surrounded me. All was so beautiful that at that moment I no longer cared whether I finished my poem or not: enough to exist between that perfect sky and sea and feel their perfection!

I pulled out my notebook and scribbled hastily:

> "The Heavens declare the glory of God
> And the Firmament showeth His Handiwork."

I hadn't the faintest idea where this had come from or any doubt whatever but that this was the conclusion . . .

I handed it to the artificer.

"Pretty neat," he said, "pretty neat. But you've been and gone and done just what I was afraid you would. I had a notion that word 'God' was about—the content seemed to point to the likelihood of it turning up. And 'God'—it's the deuce of a word to rhyme to! . . . Whatever it is, the rhyme to 'God' nearly always looks what it usually is—dragged in."

"I'm sorry," I said, "but there's no option. We'll have to do what we can."

"And 'handiwork,'" he proceeded. "'Handiwork!' You've certainly set us a pretty problem this time and no mistake with your 'god' and 'handiwork.'"

"What about Turk?" I said lightly, "ever heard of 'Greek, Jew, Infidel and Turk'?"

"You're joking," he said, "surely you can't mean that?"

"Well, 'handiwork' ends our last line and we've got to rhyme to it. Stranger things have happened."

"Noted, guv'nor, noted. But I wish I shared your good spirits. Strikes me there's going to be a lot of—what d'you call it?—'artifact' about our penultimate line" . . .

"Don't fuss so;" I said, "this is going to be all right. I only need a run at it. Give me the notebook. Now I'm going to make my mind a blank and run through the stuff we've got" . . .

I ran through all we had and found I wasn't mistaken. It continued of itself—

> . . . "What is here enscrolled?
> Is it a poem or a story?
> I cannot command this charactery" . . .

I went to the ship's side and swept the horizon with my eye. "By Jove," I said, "Yes!—of course!

> 'When the first sun rose above the first sea'—

I say, artificer, think of that!—'*When the first sun rose above the first sea.*' What a picture!"

"Nice, guv'nor, nice. But don't stop to admire it or you may lose something. Continue. Keep it moving" . . .

"Yes, we sustain the feeling—

> 'As read it will while there is sea
> and the sun to scribe with'—

With what?"

"I'm holding 'gold' for you, guv'nor."

> "with reed of gold"

"Yes:

> 'As read it will while there is sea
> And sun to scribe with reed of gold.'"

"I don't like 'reed,' guv'nor. You've got the same sound with a different sense in the line before. Nothing doing. Can't stand for it" . . .

"Pity—I like the notion of a reed pen. But, after all, there was a sort of dagger-line brightness running down the center of what I saw early on. 'Quill'? Yes, it'll have to be 'quill.' I don't altogether like it. It will take some getting used to, but I suppose we've got to have it."

"And now your 'return,' guv'nor!" The artificer had become very energetic indeed. (He gets these fits of what I may call "muscular" energy. They have, I think something to do with the rhythmical side of his job. If we don't keep going in a situation of this sort the whole affair may "die on us" or not be found again for weeks.)

"It doubles back on itself," he said, "that's the structure of it—so doing, it gives us, you see, another run at the rhythm and helps the snowballing. See, guv'nor?" . . .

> "It is both story and a poem,
> A hymn, as also a history"— . . .

I said to myself. "That's emphatic, that's strophic. There's majesty here . . . It's beginning to broaden. And nothing like broadening for using one up."

I began to feel tired . . . I went and leaned against the rail. "Goethe would know," I said to myself. "What a pity one isn't Goethe. Evidently he had no trouble at all. Did this sort of thing almost without knowing he was doing it. But then he was a mage. Well?—of course!—

> 'as also a history
> Concerning the mightiest of mages.'"

I was becoming very tired indeed. I wrote that down. The artificer appeared.

" 'Ages,' 'ages,' 'ages,' " he said, "that's a nice rhyme for 'mages.' Get to that."

> "The best that has been or shall be
> Writ for any throughout the ages."

"That what you want?" I said, "I don't see it." I said, "I just don't see it."

"What about that 'Greek, Jew, Infidel and Turk' of yours?" he grinned. "Written *for* somebody and written *by* somebody" . . .

I seated myself on the bollard. I needed rest . . . He tiptoed away.

> "For Greek, Jew, Infidel and Turk"—

"Yes," I thought, "but why for them only? It is for all of us . . .

'As it was written, too, for me' " . . .

I looked once more on the glory about me. "The sky and the sea," I said to myself, "they are one, and yet they are two"—

"One page, two eternal sentences"—

"Yes, that's it"—

"One page, two eternal sentences!
The Heavens declare the glory of God,
And the Firmament showeth His Handiwork."

It was done. I handed it to the artificer, reached my cabin and lay down. My watch was lying on the counterpane. I glanced at it. Twenty minutes had passed.

When I woke it was eleven o'clock and I had missed my bacon and eggs.

CHAPTER : 4

Conceptual Learning

13. The Evolution of Concepts*

The series of early experimental studies of concept formation by Hull is often considered a landmark in a scientific approach to an analysis of this process. Hull was particularly concerned with the gathering of objective data, with its quantification, and with the manipulation of different conditions of learning to form concepts. His conclusions concerning the efficiency of various methods of learning to generalize have had far-reaching effects upon educational practice.

. . . The functional and quantitative aspects of the problem of the evolution of concepts remain almost untouched . . . This is true in spite of a very considerable activity on the part of experimenters in the field of higher mental process within recent years. The problem of generalizing abstraction has itself been directly attacked a number of times . . . but in every case the studies have been largely introspective in method, analytic in purpose, and qualitative in result.

The reason for such a condition is of course not far to seek. It lies in the great complexity of the process involved. Where many factors must be cooperating nearly or quite simultaneously within a single living process, it is not easy to keep all of them constant except one and at the same time to vary that one so as to make a direct quantitative comparison of the several phases of its variation. Difficulty or ease of solution of a problem

---

* CLARK L. HULL. Abridged from Quantitative aspects of the evolution of concepts. An experimental study, pp. 1–85. *Psychological Monographs,* Vol. 28, No. 2, Whole No. 124, 1920.

is, however, often largely an expression of the efficiency of the methods and technique available . . . The present study is an effort to elaborate such a technique and to apply it to a number of the characteristic quantitative problems concerned with the evolution of concepts . . .

THE EFFICIENCY OF EVOLVING CONCEPTS BY PROCEEDING FROM THE SIMPLE TO THE COMPLEX: EXPERIMENT A

Problem. The first problem which we shall consider arises from the familiar educational injunction to "proceed from the simple to the complex." We shall try to determine experimentally how far this method justifies its reputation when applied to the evolution of concepts . . .

Technique. . . . The basis for a series of visual experiences was supplied by the 144 Chinese characters shown in Plate I. These characters were taken from a Chinese dictionary, and freely adapted to the present purpose wherever deemed necessary. They were drawn with great care in black ink upon cards two inches long and one inch wide. The characters thus prepared were presented to the subject one after another by means of a specially constructed apparatus.

This device somewhat resembled the drum form of Wirth memory apparatus. The slips on the drum held twelve cards. The periodic movements of the drum were controlled automatically and exactly by a simple pendulum clockwork which was built into the apparatus. By means of a special form of cam this clockwork released the drum at periods varying anywhere from one to six seconds as desired. Throughout the present study a uniform exposure-time of five seconds was employed . . .

In addition there were three supplementary measures . . . The first and most important of these is based upon exactly the same principle as the main measure. At the first presentation of each succeeding "pack" of the evolution series . . . there arises the necessity of reacting to the respective characters during the two-and-one-half seconds before the prompting takes place. This obviously gives the required functional measure and at a point of peculiar interest as it takes place periodically throughout the entire evolution process . . .

The second supplementary measure came from the evolution series also. It was furnished by the number of promptings which were required to perfect the reactions to each of the first six "packs" . . .

A third supplementary measure of the stage of the evolution of concepts . . . is obtained by requiring the subject to define the concepts (by drawing them) at the end of the process . . .

PLATE I. SHOWING THE CHINESE CHARACTERS WHICH SERVED AS THE MATERIAL FOR THE EVOLUTION OF CONCEPTS.

Task. . . . The twelve characters of "pack" I are inserted in the twelve holders of the drum. The drum goes round and round without interruption, making successive exposures of each character of exactly five seconds.

The characters are stationary while being viewed. The experimenter pronounces the concept-name of each character at the middle of its exposure and the subject repeats it with care. After the first revolution of the drum the subject himself begins to react to the characters by pronouncing the name wherever possible, before being prompted. At length every character will be reacted to correctly at a single revolution of the drum. The characters are at once removed from the drum and replaced but in a *different* order. The prompting is then resumed as before until the subject has made a perfect score on each of two successive revolutions of the drum.

Subjects. The subjects in the immediate experiments . . . were university students. In most cases they had little or no training in psychology and were thoroughly naive. Ordinarily they regarded the work as a kind of memory experiment and were mainly interested in making a good score. It is safe to say that not one of the subjects used in this form of the experiment had the slightest suspicion that the ultimate purpose of the experiment was to compare this efficiency of two distinct modes of concept evolution. When informed of this at the end of the experiment they never failed to express more or less astonishment. For the above reason no form of suggestion arising from preconceived theoretical considerations could enter to distort the results . . .

Measures. . . . Only the first six "packs" of Characters (Plate I) were used for the purpose of evolving the concepts. The remaining six "packs" (VII to XII) were reserved exclusively for testing or measuring the concepts thus evolved. In making up the test "packs" the characters were rearranged from the order as they appear in Plate I in such a way that in a given "pack" or drum-full, two or even three characters of a given concept might be present and of course not any of certain others. This was to prevent subjects from determining the identity of characters by a process of elimination. Three exposures were given of each one of these test "packs" (of course without promptings) and the subjects were encouraged to "guess" at them very freely if any suggestion whatever of a possible identity came to mind . . . The three reactions to each of the six test-characters of a given concept gave eighteen measures for each concept and a total of 216 measures for all twelve concepts with a given subject. This was our main measure.

The "packs" II, III, IV, V, and VI which comprise the evolution "packs" are inserted and learned one after the other. In these cases, however, the "packs" are only learned in *one* order each, and to a perfect score on two successive revolutions of the drum.

In order to equalize any possible inequality of difficulty inherent in concepts A to F as compared with the concepts G to L, half of the subjects learned the reactions to the "packs" in the order of VI, V, IV, III, II, I. In this case "pack" VI was learned in two orders by these subjects just as "pack" I was by the first half of the subjects.

Lastly the six test "packs" are presented. They are inserted on the drum one after another and merely given three revolutions each, i.e., three exposures to each character. The subject reacts wherever possible, no promptings being given. Sometimes the subjects were then asked to draw on a specially prepared blank the characteristics which a character must contain in order to be called by its name.

Results. The results of the tests show a distinct advantage for the simple-to-complex method . . . This appears very clearly in Figure I where the

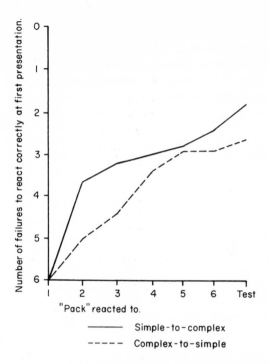

relation of the two sets of averages is shown graphically. These curves show not only a distinct superiority for the simple-to-complex method but at what an early stage in the process this superiority is established. Already at the beginning of the second "pack" it is greater than at any other time in the process. Indeed there is a distinct tendency for the curves to converge near "pack" VI. This however is doubtless due largely to the fact that the characters of the upper (simple-to-complex) curve are at their maximum difficulty at this point, thus tending to increase faulty reactions and so to make the curve fall. On the other hand the characters of the lower curve are at their minimum of difficulty which tends to make a minimum of faulty reactions and so to elevate artificially the curve at this point . . .

In the present experiment the time-element presented difficulties . . . An examination of the distribution of time among the various "packs" shows that about four times as much was given to the simple end of the simple-to-complex evolution series as the simple end of the other. Clearly this alone might account for the advantage obtained for the simple-to-complex method. That such is actually the case is strongly suggested by the fact that the entire advantage gained by the simple-to-complex method is secured on the first one or two "packs" (Figure I), where an excessive amount of time is spent upon the easy end of those series.

Accordingly, three new experiments were instituted. One (Experiment B) reduced the disproportion of time spent upon the simple ends of the respective series evolved by the two methods. In the other two (Experiments C and D) it was equalized entirely . . .

Summary and Conclusions

The results of Experiments A, B, C, and D may be briefly formulated as follows:

1. In the evolution of functional concepts simple experiences are more efficient than complex ones. This appears to be true regardless of whether the simple experiences take place at the beginning or end of the process of evolution.

2. Concrete experiences in the simple-to-complex order appear to be no more efficient in the evolution of functional concepts than when in the complex-to-simple order if inequalities of the time-factor are excluded.

3. But if each individual experience in the evolution series is continued until the reaction to it is just perfected before passing to the next, there is a distinct advantage in favor of the simple-to-complex method. This is due to the fact that under this method a greater amount of time is spent upon the simple or efficient end of the simple-to-complex series than upon the corresponding end of the complex-to-simple series.

The Efficiency of Receiving Concepts Without the Labor of Generalizing Abstraction: Experiment E

A second theory of essentially quantitative implications has long been held concerning the evolution of functional concepts. This theory is that to have functional value, concepts must be evolved from the concrete by each individual for himself. Practice has on the other hand very often striven to give the concept to the individual outright . . . Here then we find our problem: Is it more or less efficient to spend a given amount of time in perfecting the reaction to an abstract characteristic never seen in its concrete setting, or to spend the same amount of time perfecting reactions to a series of concrete situations with the incidental amount of generalizing abstraction?

The main features of the method utilized are the same as those employed in the experiments just described. It differed from them in having half of the characters of the evolution series replaced by their respective common elements. That is to say, the characters comprising the six members of each of the evolution series G to L say, would be replaced in every case by the common element shown in the first vertical column headed "concept" (Plate I). The other half of the evolution series (A to F) remains exactly as before in the simple-to-complex order. Thus in learning the evolution "packs" in the order I to VI, there would be a simultaneous comparison of (1) evolving concepts by the simple-to-complex method (Series A to F) with (2) receiving concepts in the abstract apart from their concrete setting (G to L) . . . Each "pack" was learned to a perfect score on two successive revolutions of the drum.

Ten subjects were used in the experiment. They were university students from a class in introductory psychology . . .

The results of the experiment may be briefly summarized as follows: Where the evolutionary process has reached an average efficiency of approximately 50 per cent,

1. Concepts given outright show a functional efficiency equal to concepts evolved by the subject himself from concrete cases in the simple-to-complex order.

2. The ability to define the concept by drawing is about twice as great where the concepts are given outright as where they are evolved from the concrete by the subjects themselves.

3. From (1) and (2) follows the corollary that ability to define is not necessarily a true index of the functional value of a concept . . .

THE EFFICIENCY OF EVOLVING CONCEPTS BY A COMBINED METHOD OF ABSTRACT PRESENTATION AND CONCRETE EXAMPLES: EXPERIMENT F

In the last experiment we found reason to suspect that mere abstract information is of rather doubtful efficiency in coping with new situations in the later stages of the process of generalizing abstraction. Where the process has been approximately half completed, its efficiency is about the same as by the simple-to-complex method. The problem accordingly arises: May not a combination of the two methods be more efficient than either alone? Specifically, is it more or less efficient to evolve functional concepts by first receiving the abstract characteristic and then a concrete case, or to have the subject evolve it entirely for himself by the simple-to-complex method?

The method of attacking the problem was very similar to that employed in Experiment E. Two changes were made to adapt it to the present problem: In the first place all the characters of evolution series G to L were reversed so that they stood normally in the simple-to-complex order in exactly the same sense as series A to F (Plate I). After being reversed the characters falling in "packs" I, III and V were replaced by the naked common elements used in Experiment E. Otherwise the learning was exactly as usual, to a perfect score on two successive revolutions of the drum. In this way series A to F would be experienced in the ordinary simple-to-complex order. But series G to L would be experienced as: first the "concept" given abstractly, second an example, third the "concept" given abstractly again, fourth another example, fifth the "concept" given abstractly once more and lastly another example. Thus series G to L was evolved from an alternation of abstract presentation and example, the examples being in the simple-to-complex order . . .

The results of the experiment may be formulated as follows:

1. A combination of abstract presentations and concrete examples is upon the whole distinctly more efficient in evolving functional concepts than either method alone.

2. The advantage of the combination method appears at the beginning of the process and probably continues to increase at a fairly uniform rate through the first two-thirds of the process, as far as it was carried in the present experiment. [See Fig. II.]

3. It may be that at certain stages of perfection, concepts evolved by the combination method are less efficient in coping with new situations of exceptional difficulty than when evolved by the simple-to-complex method . . .

The Efficiency of Evolving Concepts from a Series of Concrete Cases Where the Attention is Attracted to the Common Element in situ: Experiment G

Closely related to the method of concept evolution by abstract presentation, is that of demonstration. For our purpose demonstration consists essentially in the presentation of a series of concrete cases and directing the attention of the subject to the essential characteristic of each in its

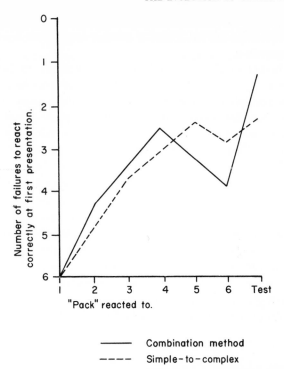

Fig. II. Showing the origin of the advantage of the combination over the simple-to-complex method, evolution series, experiment F.

concrete setting. The problem before us then is: What is the relative efficiency of evolving functional concepts from concrete cases in which the attention of the subject is continuously attracted to the significant common element as compared with the ordinary simple-to-complex method?

Only a slight modification of the technique of Experiment F was necessary in order to adapt it to the present problem. As there, *all twelve* of the evolution series were arranged in the simple-to-complex order with the simple end of the series at "pack" one. But with half of the evolution series, e.g., G to L, the characters were redrawn so the common element appeared in a saturated red, everything else being the same. The redrawing was done with great care and the new characters except for the color of the common element, were practically identical with the originals. It was assumed that the color would attract the attention of the subject mildly but continuously to the common element. Nothing whatever was said concerning the color however, the same instructions as usual being given. Ten university students were used as subjects . . .

The results of the present experiment may be briefly formulated as follows:

1. There is a distinct advantage in evolving concepts from concrete cases in the simple-to-complex order where the attention of the subject is attracted to the essential common element *in situ,* over the normal simple-to-complex method.

2. The advantage appears at the beginning of the process and increases continuously as far as it has been investigated.

3. There is a mild shrinkage in functional ability when the subject passes from the artificial material to normal experiences, but there still remains a substantial functional advantage in attracting attention to the common element while in its concrete setting . . . [See Fig. III.]

THE EFFICIENCY OF EVOLVING CONCEPTS AS A FUNCTION OF THE THOROUGHNESS OF FAMILIARITY WITH THE CONCRETE CASES: EXPERIMENT H

An important factor in all kinds of learning is the matter of thoroughness . . . There seems to be quite a general belief that a thorough mastery of each concrete case involved in the evolutionary process will be specially conducive to efficiency in coping with new situations. This accordingly determines our problem: In the evolution of functional concepts, is it more economical to have an evolution series made up of six concrete cases each experienced moderately well, or to have half as many concrete cases each experienced twice as well?

Only a moderate variation of the general method used in the previous experiments was required in the present problem. The characters of the evolution series were rearranged so that all the "packs" were of presumably equal difficulty. This at the same time largely eliminated the simple-to-complex arrangement shown in Plate I . . .

A second modification of the technique previously used was to make the characters in "packs" I, III and V do double service . . . That is, the characters normal to "pack" I would be used both in "packs" I and II, characters normal to "pack" III would be used both in "packs" III and

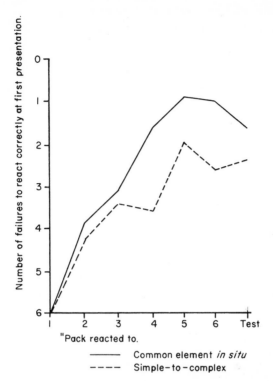

F<small>IG</small>. III. S<small>HOWING THE ORIGIN OF THE ADVANTAGE OF CALLING ATTENTION TO THE</small>
<small>COMMON ELEMENT IN SITU, EVOLUTION SERIES, EXPERIMENT G.</small>

IV, characters normal to "pack" V would appear both in "packs" V and
VI. The characters normal to "packs" II, IV and VI of course did not
appear at all. A uniform time of nine exposures was given to each
"pack." Thus in evolution series G to L, 54 exposures were equally divided
among six concrete cases while in series A to F, 54 exposures were equally
divided among three concrete cases. In the first case 9 exposures were
given to each concrete case which we shall regard as "moderate" familiarity, while in the second case 18 exposures or twice as many are given to
each concrete case, which is regarded as "thorough" familiarity . . .

The subjects in this experiment were scholarship students from the
University High School. They ranged from 13 to 18 years of age . . .

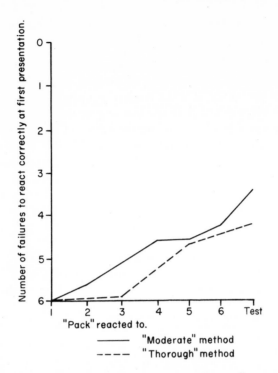

Fig. IV. Showing the origin of the advantage of the "moderate" method over the "thorough" method, evolution series, experiment H.

The results of Experiment H may be summarized as follows:

1. A moderate amount of time spent upon each of six concrete cases is perceptibly more efficient in the evolution of functional concepts than twice as much time spent upon each of three concrete cases.

2. This superiority appears at the outset and is maintained at least through the first third of the process, as far as investigated in the present experiment . . . [See Fig. IV.]

Of . . . importance is the question as to why the "thorough" method should prove less efficient? The reason seems to be that the eighteen exposures of the "thorough" method carried the process of generalizing abstraction as regards the individual concrete example, farther into the region of "diminishing returns" than the nine exposures of the "moderate" method . . .

QUALITATIVE ASPECTS OF THE EVOLUTION OF CONCEPTS: EXPERIMENT L

. . . In the first part of the present experiment the general experimental technique was followed. But instead of limiting the evolution series to six "packs" as previously, it was extended to include all twelve "packs" (Plate I). At the conclusion of the learning of the second "pack," the subject was given a blank containing the names of the various concepts and asked to draw with as much care as possible, the strokes which a character must have in order to be called by the respective names. Four university students served as subjects in this part of the experiment. A typical series of such drawings are shown in Plate II. Two other subjects repeated the experiment according to the general technique previously used. They were called on for drawings every six minutes throughout the process . . .

In examining the drawings obtained for all three methods perhaps the most striking characteristic is the *extremely gradual way in which the concepts come into existence*. This is particularly true of the concepts

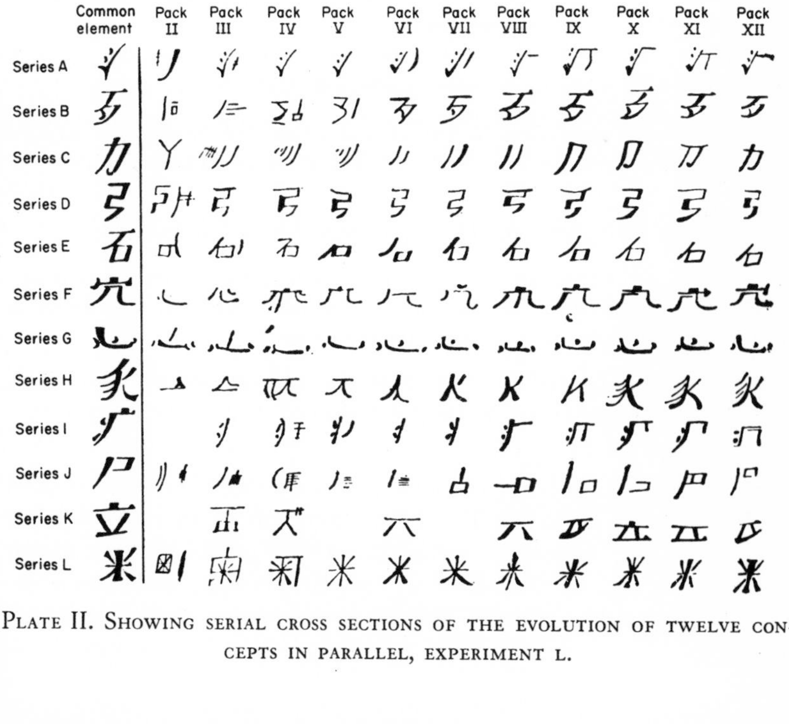

PLATE II. SHOWING SERIAL CROSS SECTIONS OF THE EVOLUTION OF TWELVE CONCEPTS IN PARALLEL, EXPERIMENT L.

evolved by the more natural methods (Plate II). It is true that in some cases (Series D) where the common element is very simple, it may be almost or quite perfect at its first appearance . . . But again where the common element is seemingly very simple it may come to consciousness only in the most halting and gradual manner (Series C). The evolution of a rather complicated concept is shown in Series F and perhaps even better, by Series H.

A second interesting characteristic shown by this investigation is *a tendency to transmute an essentially erroneous first notion of a concept by almost imperceptible degrees into its true form.* This also is admirably illustrated by Series H . . . The subsequent transformations are not unlike the transformations which the common philosophical and religious concepts have undergone in the history of thought.

The third and most important fact which emerges from the examination of the cross-sectional views of the concepts in the course of evolution is *the enormous role of "trial and error" in the process* . . . It is shown in an objective way by the continual appearance of false strokes which disappear again after a more or less protracted existence. This objective evidence is confirmed in a certain sense by introspective accounts given by the subjects at the conclusion of the process. The present writer is strongly of the opinion however, that this *conscious* trial and error so revealed is largely spurious. It is believed that this deliberate seeking of the common element is largely in artifact resulting from experimental technique, so far as the *spontaneous* process of generalizing abstraction is concerned . . . There thus appears a large element of trial and error in the process but not in the conscious or deliberate sense that this expression is often understood.

Summary

We may now briefly summarize the results obtained by the various experiments described in the preceding pages.

1. Evolving concepts by proceeding from the simple to the complex in the evolution series yields a substantial advantage over proceeding from the complex to the simple, where the activity in each succeeding case is continued until the reaction is just established. But by this method much more time is spent upon the simple cases of the simple-to-complex method than upon the corresponding cases of the complex-to-simple method. When the disproportion is partially reduced, the advantage of

the simple-to-complex method is somewhat decreased; and when the disproportion is completely eliminated, the advantage of the simple-to-complex method is completely eliminated also. This fact, together with the shape of the two curves throughout the evolutionary process, indicates that the simpler characters are much more efficient in the evolution of concepts than the complex ones. There appears to be no advantage in the simple-to-complex order merely as such.

2. Concepts given to the subject directly, the common element concerned never being experienced in its concrete setting, shows about the same functional efficiency as concepts evolved from the concrete. The ability to define however is about twice as great with the former method. The power to define is thus in some cases at least a very inadequate index of the functional value of a concept.

3. A combination of abstract presentation and concrete examples yields a distinctly greater functional efficiency than either method alone.

4. During the evolution of concepts, mildly attracting attention to the common element *in situ* considerably increases the efficiency of the process. The increase is continuous from the beginning of the process as far as it was investigated. But when the transition is made from the artificial evolution material to that of the normal test material the advantage is perceptibly decreased.

5. Moderate familiarity with each member of an evolution series comprising a number of concrete cases is perceptibly more efficient than twice as thorough familiarity with half as many cases. This advantage appears at the very beginning and persists at least through the first third of the process, i.e., as far as investigated . . .

6. The individual concepts usually come into consciousness very gradually. Erroneous first impressions are either discarded or transmuted into the correct form by a continuous development. Trial and error plays, if not a dominating, at least a very great role in the process . . .

REFERENCES

1. FISHER, S. C. 1916. The process of generalizing abstraction; and its product, the general concept. *Psychol. Rev. Mon. Supp.* 21:213.
2. HULL, C. L. 1917. The formation and retention of associations among the insane. *Amer. J. Psychol.* 28:419–35.
3. MOORE, T. V. 1910. The process of abstraction: an experimental study. *Univ. Calif. Pubs. in Psychol.* 1:124.

14. An Objective Study of Concept Formation*

The experimental task and procedures used by Smoke enabled him to study more than the purely analytical aspects of the process of concept formation. He raises questions as to what aspects of a complex stimulating situation the learner responds and the role of hypothesis seeking and formulation in this process. Smoke's findings also suggest several implications for the measurement of understanding and concepts.

The Task

. . . In this study . . . we count the subject as having learned a concept if he is able to go faultlessly through a test series of sixteen stimulus patterns, some of which fulfill the conditions of the concept in question and some of which do not. Let us suppose that the concept is "zum" and may be defined thus: "three straight red lines, two of which intersect the third, thereby trisecting it." When the subject has indicated his belief that he knows what a "zum" is, he is asked to go through a series of sixteen drawings (stimulus patterns), some of which are "zums" and some of which are not, writing "Yes" after the number of each drawing that is a "zum," "No" after the number of each drawing that is not a "zum." If no mistakes are made, we regard the subject as having learned the concept in question . . .

Because the discriminative responses involved in going through the test series were regarded as the crucial test of whether or not the subject had learned the concept, the construction of the test series was a matter of considerable importance. Such a series was developed for each of the ten concepts, a series consisting of sixteen figures, each drawn on a card that had been eyeleted so as to fit a standard office calendar file. About half of these sixteen figures were regular figures; the others were confusion figures. These two types of figures were mixed in "chance" order, and each card was numbered and placed in its position in the calendar file. The regular figures, like those used in learning, were drawn so as to differ greatly among themselves, though still being true representatives of the concept. The confusion figures . . . were also made unlike each other.

* KENNETH L. SMOKE. Adapted and abridged with permission of the author from *Psychological Monographs,* pp. 9–40. Vol. 42, No. 4, Whole No. 191, 1932.

Moreover, they were drawn according to two principles: (1) each confusion figure must violate one and only one condition essential to the concept; (2) every condition essential to the concept must be violated at least once. A glance at the responses made by the subject while going through the test series was therefore all that was needed to discover what he had failed to learn, if anything.

APPARATUS AND METHOD

. . . The (drum) mechanism or exposure apparatus is completely screened from the view of the subject by a framework on which black oil cloth has been stretched . . . The sequence looking from the position of the subject

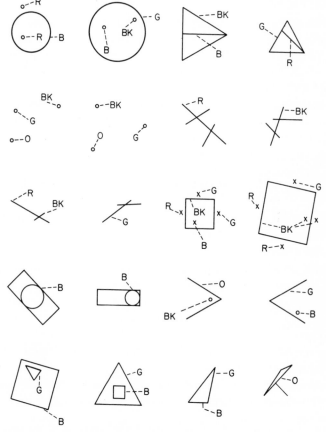

FIG. 1. SPECIMENS OF DESIGNS USED IN THE EXPERIMENTS.

towards the exposed card on the drum is as follows: (1) opening in screen framework; (2) vestibule three and one-quarter inches square leading into the window frame behind which the shutter moves; (3) hole two inches square in a piece of black wood fiber that is mounted on the shutter unit but as near to the drum as possible. Everything is therefore screened from the view of the subject except an area of the exposed card two inches square . . .

Ten concepts were used in this study. Each concept concerned a certain type of geometrical design. Each type of design was given a name . . . A specimen of each type of design is shown in Figure 1. Columns one and three, reading from left to right, contain these specimens. The letters refer to colors: "O" stands for orange, "R" for red, "G" for green, "B" for blue, and "BK" for black. Each design in these two columns is a "regular" figure; that is to say, it fulfills all of the conditions essential to the concept in question. To the right of each "regular" figure is a "confusion" figure; that is, a design that violates at least one of the conditions essential to the concept in question . . . The name and definition of each of the ten concepts follow:

A "dax" is a circle and two dots, the one dot being inside the circle and the other outside of it.

A "vec" is an equilateral triangle together with a line which is perpendicular to one side and which extends from that x side to the vertex of the opposite angle.

A "zif" is three dots, the distance between the two farthest dots being twice the distance between the two nearest ones.

A "zum" is three straight red lines, two of which intersect the third, thereby trisecting it.

A "mef" is two intersecting straight lines, the length of the shorter being equal to the distance from it to the nearer end of the longer line.

A "tov" is a square and four crosses, each side of the square having a cross that is nearer to it than to any other side.

A "pog" is a blue rectangle enclosing a blue circle that touches only the long side of the rectangle.

A "wez" is two straight lines of equal length that touch on end together with a dot equidistant from the free ends of the lines.

A "gid" is a green triangle and a blue square, the triangle being within the square but not touching it.

A "mib" is a triangle and a line extending at right angles from its shortest side . . .

The instructions and procedure varied somewhat from experiment to experiment, but the general methodology was the same throughout.

On entering the experimental room, the subject was invited to take a seat at a table on the other side of which . . . the exposure apparatus rested . . . When the subject indicated that he understood the instructions, the experimenter raised the window shade and at the same time started a stop watch. When the subject raised his hand, indicating that he thought he had learned the concept, the experimenter lowered the shade, stopped the stop watch, and recorded the time on a card . . .

The experimenter then handed the subject a sheet of paper and a pencil, and said, "I shall give you three tests. The first of these is that of definition. Please state what a '_____' is." After the subject had finished, the experimenter gave him another sheet of paper, saying, "The second test is a matter of drawing. Please draw two '_____s.'" In introducing the third test the experimenter handed the subject a sheet of paper . . . and said, "Here is a series of sixteen drawings. Some of these drawings are '_____s' and some of them are not. If the drawing is a '_____' write 'Yes' after its number. If it is not a '_____' write 'No.' If you should happen to change your mind as to what a '_____' is, be sure to stop and change your definition." If the subject made no mistakes in going through the test series, he was regarded as having formed the concept. The experimenter then moved the shutter unit over to the series of designs on the drum from which the next concept was to be learned. If the subject made mistakes, the experimenter said, "You know something about '_____' but you do not know everything. We shall try it again." . . . In Experiments III and IV the subject was instructed to do all of his thinking out loud and a permanent record was obtained of his comments with reference to each figure . . . The subjects used in these experiments were undergraduate and graduate students in psychology, with most of them being in the former classification.

EXPERIMENT I

. . . Once the choices in regard to underlying theory and learning material had been made, and the ten concepts developed, two questions immediately arose: (1) Are the designs in question suitable for studies of concept formation? (2) What is the relative difficulty of the concepts? These could be answered only by an appeal to experimentation. Experiment I was the result. It showed that most of the designs could be used as material for concept learning and that certain of the concepts were relatively difficult, whereas others were relatively easy. It also indicated that individuals who have learned concepts, in the sense of being able to make consistently correct discriminations while going through a crucial test series, frequently fail to define these concepts with accuracy. This occurred again and again in subsequent experiments.

Experiment II

All of the designs used in the first experiment had been positive instances of, i.e., true to, the concept in question. What would happen if negative instances of the concept, i.e., designs false to it, were introduced? Experiment II suggested that negative instances are not necessarily aids to rapid learning. Some subjects did appear to learn from them, it is true, but others seemed to find them a waste of time or even a source of confusion . . .

Experiment III

The negative instances in Experiment II had violated only one condition essential to the concept. What would happen if two or more conditions were violated? Experiment III was designed to throw some light on this question and at the same time to reveal something of the nature of the process of concept formation.

Negative instances that violate more than one condition essential to the concept do not make for either more or less rapid learning than those that violate only one essential condition, this experiment seemed to show. It also pointed to the presence of a number of factors in concept formation, the most significant being these: grouping, insightful behavior, and formulation, testing and acceptance or rejection of hypotheses.

. . . We came to the experiment supposing that concept formation ought to proceed more rapidly in cases in which the negative instances depart rather widely from the concept than in cases in which the negative instances violate only one condition essential to the concept. In the former, we reasoned, the negative instances ought to accentuate the positive ones by contrast, and therefore make for more speed in learning . . . The evidence at hand is against the above supposition, or at least fails to support it . . .

Our results seem to point clearly to the presence of grouping in the process of concept formation . . . The following quotations are presented as examples of this process of grouping:

With reference to designs in the "vec" series (one of the easiest):

"Another triangle with a straight line bisecting the angle." . . .
"Another triangle with angle bisected." . . .
"These three belong to the same class, for there is a line down the center of each." . . .

With reference to designs in the "mib" series (one of the hardest):

. . . "Triangle and line again.". . .
"Another triangle with line cutting side." . . .
"The others have all been perpendicular to the base." . . .

Another result of this experiment which seems to us to be of some importance is the evidence which it furnished of the presence of insightful behavior in the process of concept formation. Two instances will be cited.

Subject K spent two minutes and fifty-seven seconds examining a total of twelve figures in the "zum" series, and then raised her hand. As her definition of "zum" she wrote, "A 'zum' is three lines of different lengths two of which are bisected by the third." . . . The subject's drawings were defective, and she made a number of mistakes in going through the test series.

The subject spent three seconds re-examining the figure last seen, pressed the contact key for a new figure, and approximately fourteen seconds later advanced the idea that the one line was trisected. About ten seconds thereafter, having examined another figure, she stated the generalization, "Three red lines, two of them dividing another into three equal parts." After examining four more figures, apparently with the idea of testing her hypothesis, the subject raised her hand. Then she wrote, "A 'zum' is three red lines of different lengths, two of which divide the third into three equal lengths or segments." She then made several drawings of "zum" that were accurate, and went through the series of test cards faultlessly.

Subject P spent one minute and thirty-one seconds examining a total of sixteen figures in the "zum" series, and then raised his hand. He defined "zum" as "Three red lines which cross each other but do not form an enclosed figure." His drawings were inaccurate and he made errors in going through the test series.

Two minutes and fifty-one seconds were then spent by this subject in examining seventeen more designs. This time he defined "zum" thus: "Three red lines cross each other; the two shortest cross the longest." Again his drawings were defective, and his responses to the test series incorrect.

During the first fourteen seconds of the next learning period he re-examined the design last seen, remarking that the majority of the designs were red. Then he pressed the contact key for a new figure, and several seconds later came out with the observation, "Two short lines seem to cut one line into three equal parts." . . .

The formulation, testing and acceptance or rejection of hypotheses was seen again and again. Perhaps one instance will suffice. Subject S had been attempting to conceive of "zum" in terms of the relative length of the three lines. Then he took a new lead, for he made the observation, "The top angle is larger than the lower." He examined the next figure and said the same. He examined the following figure and said the same, adding, "That's promising." With his examination of the next figure came the remark, "Maybe it's the angles rather than the lines." This proved to be a blind alley, however, for not long thereafter, having examined several more figures, he confessed, "I'm lost." . . .

As in the previous experiments, subjects who could go through the test series without error were often quite incapable of defining the concepts accurately. Of the fifty-nine definitions that accompanied a faultless test performance, twenty-three were defective . . .

Experiment IV

This experiment was designed to attack the problem of the nature of concept formation, the approach being somewhat different from that employed in Experiment III . . . Only one concept was true to all those designs in a series that were marked plus and at the same time false to all the designs in that series that were marked minus . . .

As in Experiment III, a considerable number of quite varied expressions were used that seem to us to point clearly to the presence of grouping in concept learning. Quotations of comments of this sort, including at least one from each of eleven subjects follows: . . .

With reference to designs in the "dax" series (one of the easiest):

"Same geometrical pattern."
"Still a circle with two dots, one inside and one outside."

"Same as first and third." . . .

With reference to designs in the "zum" series (one of the hardest):

"Red again is the color of 'zum.' "
"They seem to be all the same thing." . . .
"Same thing in each case." . . .

A considerable number of instances of insightful behavior occurred in this experiment. [Two] of these will be cited here . . .

After approximately one minute and fifty seconds, during which time he had examined nine designs in the "mib" series, subject O said, "A short line attached to one side of a triangle, either on the inside or the outside." He then pressed the contact key. Twelve seconds later he pressed the key again, and about ten seconds thereafter stated that " 'mib' seems to be a triangle with a line extending on the shortest side of the triangle." Approximately twenty seconds later, while examining another design, he said, "The line seems to make a right angle." His subsequent definition, drawings, and test performances were satisfactory . . .

After examining the "zum" series for three minutes and forty-four seconds, subject F wrote, "A 'zum' is a figure consisting of one red line cut by two red transversals at points such that the end segments on the original line are equal." Mistakes were made in going through the test series. For two and one-half minutes after learning was resumed, she commented on the transversals, pointing out that they were sometimes parallel, perpendicular to the third line, etc. "Transversals aren't equal," she said toward the close of the period of time just mentioned, and then pressed the contact key. She spent only four seconds on the next design, but during that time she made this significant remark: "Divides it into three equal parts." She examined a few more figures, raised her hand, and then wrote, "A 'zum' is a figure consisting of a red line cut by two red transversals in such a way that the three resulting segments of the original line are equal." Her drawings and test performance were also satisfactory.

The conclusion reached in Experiment III to the effect that concept formation is to some extent a matter of the formulation, testing and acceptance or rejection of hypotheses found abundant support in this experiment. A large number of examples could be mentioned, but the comments of K while learning "mib" will perhaps suffice. (Quotation marks enclose the comments relative to separate but successive figures.) "Is a 'mib.' Obtuse triangle with line perpendicular to one side. Let's see now, that line is perpendicular to the short side and is inside." "This is a 'mib.' Line is perpendicular to short side." "Here's a 'mib.' Line is perpendicular to short side." "Not a 'mib.' Line is perpendicular to long side." . . . "Is a 'mib.' Line perpendicular to short side." "Same rule holds." "Same rule holds." "Same rule holds." "Same rule." "Same rule." While examining the next figure he raised his hand . . . to indicate that he thought he knew what the concept was . . .

As in the previous experiments, there were a number of instances wherein the subject's definition of the concept was defective, although his ability to go through the test series without error showed that he had learned the concept. Out of a possible forty-nine, eleven such cases were found in this experiment.

SUMMARY OF RESULTS

1. The process of concept formation appears to involve grouping. The learner tends to envisage certain stimulus patterns as constituting a group to which any given stimulus pattern does or does not belong.
2. Insightful behavior seems to be present in at least some instances of concept formation.
3. Concept formation, like most "thinking," appears to involve the formulation, testing, and acceptance or rejection of hypotheses . . .
4. One may have a concept and yet be quite unable to give an accurate verbal formulation of it . . .

REFERENCES

1. ENGLISH, H. B. 1922. An experimental study of certain initial phases of the process of abstraction. *Amer. J. Psychol.* 33:305–50.
2. GENGERELLI, J. A. 1927. Mutual interference in the evolution of concepts. *Amer. J. Psychol.* 38:639–46.
3. YERKES, R. M. 1916. A new method of studying ideational and allied forms of behavior in man and other animals. *Proc. Nat. Acad. Sci.* 2:631–34.

15. A Study of Concept Formation*

A major problem which confronts the investigator of the complexities of concept formation is the task of distinguishing between relevant aspects of the process and certain "pseudo-conceptual" opera-

* EUGENIA HANFMANN AND JACOB KASANIN. Reprinted and abridged with permission of the authors and the publisher from A method for the study of concept formation. *Journal of Psychology*, 1937, 3–4:521–40.

tions, such as those involved in memorizing and recall. The authors of this study endeavor to make this distinction through the use of an appropriate task and analysis thereof. Illustrative protocols of subjects lend concreteness to the analysis and interpretation of the data.

DESCRIPTION OF THE TEST

The experimental material consists of 22 wooden blocks varying in color, shape, height and size. There are five different colors: red, blue, yellow, green and white; six different shapes: circles, squares, triangles, trapezoids, hexagons and half-circles; two heights: tall blocks and flat blocks; . . . and two sizes of top or bottom area: large and small blocks . . . Figure 1

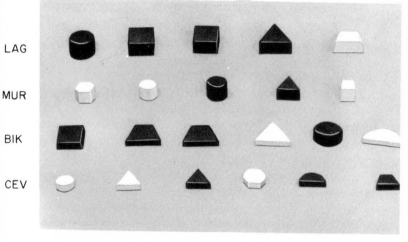

LAG

MUR

BIK

CEV

FIG. 1. ILLUSTRATION OF BLOCKS ARRANGED BY CLASSIFICATION GROUPS.

gives a representation of the experimental material. On the under side of each figure which is not seen by the subject, is written one of the following four nonsense words; *lag; bik, mur, cev*. Regardless of color and shape, *lag* is written on all large tall figures, *bik* on all large flat figures, *mur* on the small tall ones, and *cev* on the small flat ones. At the beginning of the experiment all blocks, well mixed as to color and size, are scattered over the central circular part of a square board, the rest of which is divided into four corner spaces (Figure 2). The subject is told that these are four different kinds of blocks, that each kind has a name and that his task is to find the four kinds, and to put each of them into a separate corner. The examiner then turns up one of the blocks, shows its name to the subject, and

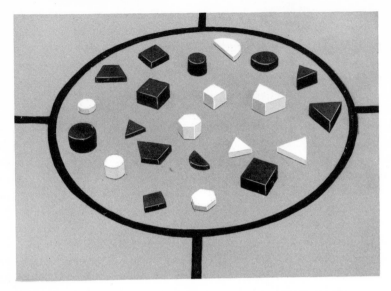

FIG. 2. ILLUSTRATION OF BOARD AND BLOCKS IN MIXED ARRAY.

putting it into one of the corner spaces, suggests that the subject start by picking out and putting in the same corner all blocks which he thinks might belong to the same kind. After he has done so, selecting, for instance, all blocks of the same color or all blocks of the same shape as the sample, the experimenter turns up one of the wrongly selected blocks, showing that this is a block of a different kind, and encourages the subject to continue trying. This he may do in any way he pleases, either by trying to match the first or the second sample, or by trying to organize the entire material simultaneously into four classes. After each new attempt one of the wrongly placed blocks is turned and the process continues until the subject discovers the principle of the classification, and organizes the blocks accordingly, or until the same result is achieved through all the blocks having been turned by the examiner in the process of correction. In either case the subject is asked to formulate the principle of the classification. After this the blocks are turned over and mixed up again and the subject is asked to put them in order once more, this time without any help from the examiner . . . Throughout the experiment, the subject is encouraged to "think aloud" and a detailed record is made of his and the experimenter's remarks, as well as of all selections made by the subject and of all corrections made by the examiner . . .

Two Test Records

Subject A is given standard instructions with a triangular *mur* (tall small) as a sample. He immediately counts the colors, says, "There are five, so it is not color." He organizes all the blocks into four groups according to shape, putting the trapezoids with the squares, and presents his classification, saying: "Circles and half-circles, triangles, quadrangles, hexagons; there are just two of these (hexagons) but I suppose it is all right." From the group of triangles which contains the *mur* sample a triangular *bik* is turned up. The subject exclaims, "Aha! So it is not shape!" Surveys the blocks, and says, "There are only two heights; how many sizes? I must find that out." Starts organizing blocks by sizes, presently discovers that there seem to be only two orders of size but carries the division through, as if to see if this is actually so. "No, I have the large and small ones—that makes only two kinds. Now, let's see . . . within each group . . . how could one subdivide each group: in round and angular? We'll try that . . . surely it will be wrong!" Organizes the blocks saying: "Large and round, large and angular; small and round, small and angular." Square *lag* (large and tall) is now turned up in the group containing the corrected *bik*. Subject says, "How mean! It was wrong then . . . But now at least I already have three determinants. If I had time I would make a list and describe all the blocks in detail." Subject is silent for a few seconds, then says, "Well, large and thick—small and thick, large and flat—small and flat; that also would make four groups." Reorganizes the blocks correctly. (Time: 8', corrections: 2, score: 18.)

This subject immediately understands the task as the search for a definite consistent classification, and in his procedure never once departs from this conception. He displays the conceptual thinking in all its aspects: the categorical attitude, demonstrated by his immediate reaction to correction, insight into the multiple possibilities of the choice, consideration of the total system. The principle of the double dichotomy is grasped even before the actual solution is found. The suggestions derived from the material itself are accepted and utilized only insofar as they fulfill the requirements of the system.

The record of the Subject B because of its length can be given only in parts. On being given the standard instructions and a triangular *mur* as a sample, the subject asks, "In other words, you want all blocks of the same shape." Examiner: "It is up to you to find out which blocks belong together; they must be similar in some way." Subject: "The ones that

I think are similar in shape?" Examiner: "I did not say shape." Subject: "Oh! It is color then?" Examiner: "I am not supposed to tell you." Subject: "All right!"

The subject adds to the triangular sample *mur* all triangles and two (out of four) trapezoids. When one of the triangles is shown to be a *bik*, he does *not* remove the other triangles from *mur*, in spite of the explicit explanation that he may do so. Even when two more triangles are turned up, and prove to belong to the third and fourth groups respectively, he continues to distribute the remaining triangles and the trapezoids between the four groups, and is for a long time reluctant to add blocks of dissimilar shape.

During further trials, he is led by similarities—probably in shape and color—for which he is often unable to account and which he never pursues consistently. Occasionally he tries to "fit" blocks together, so as to get some composite shape, or puts together blocks that seem to him dissimilar, "Get a set of different blocks." In doing so, however, he frequently chooses blocks of the same height, until finally, after prolonged and confused trials, he has two sets of tall and two sets of flat blocks, but undifferentiated by size. The subject declares that they look all right to him now, and in response to question says that they all go by height. He is not disturbed by the fact that the height is the same in each of the two pairs of groups. Even after the examiner turns up all of the wrongly placed blocks and the intended grouping is actually achieved, the subject does not yet discover the additional principles of size involved in it. When the examiner finally asks directly, "How are the *cev* (small flat) different from *bik* (large flat)?" the subject answers, "It is a different variety for one thing—more colors." Examiner: "What about size? Which one is larger?" Subject: "Size is all right—there are more pieces in this one . . . Oh, you mean piece by piece? This one (he points out one *cev*) is larger (than the other *cevs*)." In other words, he considers size as the characteristic of an individual, be it the whole group of blocks or a single block. It is only with great effort that the examiner makes him see that all *biks* are larger than *cevs*. But an attempt to make him define the four groups in terms of double dichotomy (*lag*—large and tall, etc.) fails, and in repeating the task the subject proceeds very slowly, occasionally putting the blocks together according to their shape, instead of their dimensions. (Time: 40', corrections: 11, score: 95.)

From beginning to end the task of classification is not grasped. The subject has no insight into the multiple possibilities of solution; he does not understand that his ignorance of the reason why certain blocks belong together is the core of the problem and not an accidental annoying handicap. He never actively applies definite categories to the material but is rather passively led by vaguely perceived similarities of the blocks which may become related to one another as individuals, with all the variety of their aspects. Even when the correct groups are effected, he is unable to see that differences of dimensions are essential for it, while differences of color or shape are not. In spite of all help and explanation, this subject at no time during the experiment reaches the level of conceptual thinking . . .

DISCUSSION OF TASK AND PROCESS

. . . In the version of this test here described, the subject from the outset is given a definite task, and information which is sufficient to suggest that the nonsense words refer to some characteristics of the blocks and that the discovery of what these characteristics are will enable him to carry out the task. This task does not involve memorizing, and the concepts to be found are not supported by already existing simple names which the subject may have ready at hand, nor is there any general name for the combination of height and size of the top surface. Thus it is impossible for the subject to reach the solution in a pseudo-conceptual way by merely operating with words. It is actually a classification problem and, as such, calls primarily for the exercise of systematic conceptual thinking. It might therefore be assumed that the optimal performance is achieved where the subject sets about establishing a consistent classification leading to a system of four mutually exclusive classes.

Of the various closely interconnected aspects of this general conceptual approach to the task, three major aspects have been found to be most important.

The first aspect, and the very core of conceptual thinking, is the *"categorical attitude"* . . . It consists, in our setting, of viewing the experimental objects not as individuals, but as bearers of certain general characteristics, representatives of certain categories, such as color or shape. A subject who has this attitude will, if he uses color as a basis of classification, include in one class *all* objects of one color and exclude *all* objects of a different color, regardless of all other similarities or dissimilarities of the objects. A subject who will include in his chosen class only part of the objects showing a definite characteristic, is not using this as a concept, even though he may give it as a reason for uniting the objects. The two subjects may even start in an exactly similar manner, by adding to the given sample *mur,* all blocks of the same color (red), but the first correction brings out the differences clearly. When one of the red blocks is shown to belong to the group *bik,* the subject who has proceeded conceptually will immediately discard the idea of color as a basis of classification and will remove the red blocks from the first group. The subject who lacks the categorical attitude may leave them there with no misgivings, and to the question whether he still thinks that they belong together, will answer, "Sure, they still have the same color." The categorical attitude also enables the subject to understand that there is a meaningful connection between the words and blocks, since the category in which the blocks are united gives meaning to the word and makes it the name of this given kind of block. Where the categorical attitude is absent, the subjects may insist that there is no way of finding out which blocks have the same name except turning them up and reading the names. For them the names of the blocks are comparable to proper names of individuals.

The second aspect, closely related to the first, we shall term the *insight into the multiple possibilities of the choice,* or into the arbitrariness of the classification. The subject realizes that he does not know the basis of classification, that this task consists precisely in finding it by trying different possibilities, and that *any* characteristic applicable to the blocks may prove to be the one sought. A subject who lacks this insight, whose horizon does not include the merely possible, may be able to organize the blocks according to some characteristics which to him appear fundamental. He may, for instance, see the blocks as squares, circles, triangles, but not realize that this is only one of the possible ways of seeing them: for him they *are* circles, squares and triangles. Consequently, he will not be able to find any other characteristic, or rather he will not be able to look for it . . .

The third aspect, and probably the highest stage in the development of conceptual thinking, is the consideration of the *total system* by the subject. This attitude prompts him to test every general characteristic to see whether or not it will yield four classes, and keeps him from establishing groups based on different principles and therefore not mutually exclusive, such as triangles, red blocks, large blocks, etc. . . . One of the effects of this attitude is the greater spontaneity of the subject, his greater independence of the examiner. Instead of placing the blocks with one given sample and then waiting passively for a correction, he will try to organize the whole material simultaneously, discarding all characteristics which do not yield four classes. His actions are regulated by the nature of the task much more than by the rules of the experiment . . .

REFERENCES

1. HEIDBREDER, E. F. 1934. A study of the evolution of concepts. *Psychol. Bull.* 31:673 (abstract).
2. KUO, Z. Y. 1923. A behavioristic experiment on inductive inference. *J. Exp. Psychol.* 6:247–93.

CHAPTER : 5

Skill Learning

16. The Psychology of Skill in Learning to Typewrite*

> This early study by Book is one of the most comprehensive investigations of skill learning process. It is a noteworthy attempt to describe the course of learning in a very complex skill area, typewriting. By combining data from objective records of progress in the form of learning curves, plus his subjects' self-reports and his own shrewd observations, Book suggests a generalized interpretation of the processes and stages involved in learning a complex skill.

THE PROBLEM AND AIM OF THE STUDY

In making this study of the acquisition of skill a double purpose was kept constantly in mind: (1) To obtain for each of the learners taking part in the study a practice or learning curve which should accurately represent his progress; and (2) to obtain from his self-observations and from objective records of his writing such data as would make possible the explanation of his curves . . .

METHODS EMPLOYED

APPARATUS AND LEARNERS

Apparatus. Since our aim was the getting of learning curves explicable in detail by checked introspections, we had need first of an accurate record

---

* WILLIAM F. BOOK. Abridged from *The Psychology of Skill*, pp. 7–100. University of Montana Publications in Psychology. Bull. No. 53, Psychological Series No. 1, 1908.

of what each learner did while at the typewriter, and second of a systematic procedure in making and recording his introspections. The first was obtained by means of electrical connections between the machine and three Deprez markers writing upon a kymograph drum in such a way that everything the subject did on the machine was recorded. Every time he struck a letter ("a", Fig. I), every time a word was finished ("b", Fig. I), or the carriage moved back for beginning a line ("c", Fig. I), the fact was recorded so that the time consumed in the performance as well as the manner of its execution could be determined from the record. By means of a switch key attached to one of the markers and controlled by the experimenter the number of times the learner had to look at the copy as well as the actual amount of time spent in fixing it in memory was likewise recorded ("d", Fig. I). All apparatus was placed on a separate table nine feet away and carefully screened from the learner's view.

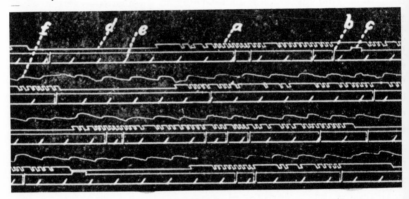

Fig. I.

But these records of the writing proved insufficient for supplementing and checking the learners' introspections. After some weeks of experimenting on X it was found by introspection that the amount of effort put into the work varied from day to day, even during the course of a single test. A maximum degree of effort could seemingly not be kept up. How hard and successfully a learner tried depended upon many factors, most of which were too subtle for observation. Some objective index of these variations in effort was obviously desirable.

It was thought that a pulse record, though not all that could be desired for such a purpose, might give a fairly reliable measure of whatever fluctuations in effort might occur. With the view of testing this hypothesis and with the hope of getting a reliable index of these variations in attention and effort, an apparatus was devised for getting a continuous pulse record from the learners as they worked. Two small tambours, made in the laboratory, with round cork points cemented to the centers of their rubber surfaces, were placed so as to receive the pulsations of the temporal artery in front of each ear ... These receiving tambours were connected by means of rubber and glass tubes to a third tambour which inscribed a pulse curve beside the record of the writing on the drum ("f" in Fig. I). With this apparatus writing and pulse records were taken at every subsequent test for all the learners.

To get a reliable norm for measuring the amount of variation in pulse caused by the work, the following method was employed: A careful count of the pulse was taken each day after the subject had seated himself ready for work and had been quiet long enough, supposedly, to reduce his heart beat to normal. In general five minutes were allowed. Enough counts were then taken (the pulse being counted by the experimenter at the wrist) to insure that the rate recorded as normal was really a normal pulse ...

The typewriter used throughout the experiment was an Underwood machine having the "universal keyboard" and visible writing. During the earlier experiments a No. 4 machine was used, later a No. 5. The slight differences between the machines were, for our purpose, unessential. With both machines it was necessary for making capital letters and certain marks of punctuation to press a "shift key" which slightly raised the carriage, a fact taken into account when measuring the amount of work done for any minute or test. No change of paper was required for any of the tests, the sheets receiving the writing being regularly lengthened as the learners' skill increased.

All regular tests were executed in the presence of an experimenter who looked after the apparatus and made, during the test, such notes of the learner's general behavior as seemed desirable or significant. For all the tests made on Y and Z and the tests made on all special subjects, the writer served in the role of experimenter; for all tests made upon the writer, Y acted as experimenter.

Learners. Eleven subjects took part in the experiment, three regular learners, X, Y and Z, three professional typists, four beginners and a typewriting expert. Of the regular learners X first learned to write by the sight method and afterwards by the touch method; Y, who could write at a slow amateur rate by the sight method when the experiment began, learned to write by touch; Z, who had never used a typewriter at all when his practice began, learned to write by the sight method. Y and Z were selected for regular learners because of their special psychological training and past drill in introspection, and because they were so situated that they could give all the time needed to the experiment. Four other subjects who knew nothing about typewriting were taken through the earlier stages of the learning (two for each method), after the experiment was well under way, with the view of determining still more accurately just how the earliest writing was done and how the first steps of improvement were made. Introspections and a number of records were also obtained from three professional typists (two sight writers and one touch writer), who possessed a greater degree of skill than that acquired by any of the regular learners. Careful introspections and a number of records were also gotten from Miss Carrington, a finished expert. By the help of the records and observations of these special subjects the history of the learning process was followed from the beginning to the most expert stage . . .

GENERAL PROCEDURE AND PROGRAM FOR INTROSPECTION

Experiments on the Sight Method. As already stated both methods of learning, the so-called Sight Method and the Touch Method were studied. In the S. M. learning two subjects, X and Z, neither of whom had ever used a typewriter before, co-operated. After a few general directions as to what they should do they were given their first practice and test. A half hour's test was taken each day. At the close of the first and second ten minutes of the test, "time" was called by the experimenter, the learner marking the close of the ten minute period by striking three times a certain key so that the amounts written in each third of the tests might be compared. These half hour sessions continued in the case of X through 174 consecutive days of practice . . . for Z through 86 actual practice days . . .

In addition to this general training there was started for each learner, soon after his regular writing tests began, the writing of a special "practice sentence,"—"A quick brown fox jumps over the lazy dog" . . . or "Pack my box with five dozen liquor jugs" . . . embodying all the letters of the alphabet, because this promised to give in miniature the whole story of the learning. Z wrote the first of these sentences ten minutes each day for 61 days, all his practice on it being in the form of a test of which a drum record was taken. X wrote the same sentence 120 times each day for 70 days or until a physiological limit was approached. At a regular time each day a drum record was taken of twenty executions of the sentence to test the progress and speed of writing, the other practice being taken at his convenience and at any rate of speed desired. The same conditions prevailed in Y's writing of the practice sentence. The general observations for determining how the writing was done were made during this general practice when there was no trial for speed.

This practice sentence writing together with the half hour daily tests and some three or four hours writing, at irregular intervals every eight or ten days, for purposes of special introspective analysis, constituted the total practice of the subjects learning to write by sight.

Experiments on the Touch Method. For the two subjects learning to write by the T. M., X and Y, the conditions were the same except that the regular daily tests lasted ten minutes only and the total daily practice amounted to one hour including the ten minute test. No special periods for introspection were required in this method since all necessary introspections could be made during the regular fifty minute practice period each day. The regular tests on Y . . . continued 130 days. With the exception of a break in the practice his practice was continuous. X began his T. M. practice Nov. 17, 1905, and continued uninterruptedly for 60 days. In addition to the regular practice Y wrote the practice sentence, "A quick brown fox jumps over the lazy dog," ten minutes each day for a period of 40 days, all his practice on it being in the form of a test the same as for the S. M. practice of Z. X wrote the sentence, "Pack my box with five dozen liquor jugs," 120 times a day until he could write it at the rate of 100 words per minute. This constituted the total practice of the T. M. learners.

During all the T. M. writing, for both kinds of practice, the keys were covered by a thin board fastened to a standard in such a manner that free movement of the hands was allowed while it shut out completely every part of the keyboard from the view of the learners . . .

Except for the "practice sentence" all writing for both methods of learning was from copy. Three plain articles in the *American Journal of Psychology* and Munsterberg's book, "Psychology and Life," furnished the material copied.

Program for Introspection. Two kinds of introspective data were gathered. At irregular intervals of from eight to ten days (in the first stages of learning much oftener) the learner was set to copying for the express purpose of observing how the writing at that stage was done. These periods, which, it will be remembered, were used only with the S. M. learners—the special fifty minute practice periods each day in the T. M. writing serving a similar purpose in that method—lasted from one to three hours at a sitting with short periods of rest taken whenever the subjects began to feel fatigued. Special care was always taken that all this writing be at a maximum rate as in the regular tests. In all these introspective sessions a specific point was focused upon and carefully worked out before another problem was taken up. For example the learner first determined how he located the keys or what sort of spelling he did before taking up some other point. If, however, when any special point was being worked out, another fact of interest was observed, it was immediately recorded whether it related to the particular problem considered at the time or not. No questions were asked the learners during these special practice periods though a schedule containing a list of the problems to be worked out, or topics with reference to which information was desired was kept before them. They were alone in the room and tried during these special introspective periods to get a complete analysis of the learning consciousness for that stage of advancement.

A second sort of introspective data gathered consisted of the notes written down at the close of each day's test. It was a part of the regular program to have each learner write down, immediately after finishing a test, any facts which he had observed during the course of the experiment, either on the manner of doing the work or on what had helped or hindered his progress that day. After this he was usually questioned about certain points which the writer had found from previous observations or from the objective records, to be important . . .

RESULTS

From what has been said it is clear that our results will include: (1) a group of individual tables and learning curves picturing more or less accurately the progress in learning made in both the regular learning and in the writing of a practice sentence. (2) The special introspective notes and records of the writing which show how the work was done in all stages of advancement, the analysis of the learning consciousness for all stages of practice . . . (3) The facts revealed by the daily notes which, with certain objective data, enable us to determine the phenomena which conditioned the learning and rate of work in our experiments . . .

THE LEARNING CURVES

In determining the progress made by our learners, the actual number of strokes made on the machine during a test was taken as the measure. To get a still more accurate measure of the amount of work done the following method of evaluating the strokes was used. Each letter and mark of punctuation, not requiring a shift of the carriage, was counted as one stroke; striking the word spacer was counted as half a stroke; making a capital or any mark requiring the use of the "shift key" was counted as two strokes; moving the carriage back to make a line was counted as three strokes. On the basis of the total number of strokes made in the several daily tests the learning curves were drawn. The result or progress made by the learners is graphically shown in Fig. II . . .

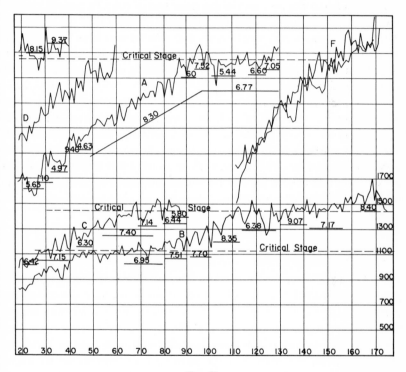

Fig. II.

To facilitate comparison the curves are all drawn on the same scale. The number of days of practice is shown on the horizontal axis, the amount of work done (in strokes) on the vertical axis, for curves "A," "D" and "E" to the left and for curves "B" and "C" to the right. The figures on the horizontal lines under the curves represent the average rise in pulse above the normal for the period of practice indicated by the length of the line on which the figures are placed. Curve "A" represents Y's

regular T. M. practice; "B" X's regular S. M. practice; "C" Z's regular
S. M. practice; "D" X's regular T. M. practice; "E" Y's writing of a
practice sentence (T. M.,) "F" X's regular T. M. curve (same as curve
"D") and the first part of Y's T. M. curve drawn to the same scale. To
show the individual features of these T. M. curves, X's regular T. M. curve
("D" Fig. II) had to be pushed higher up on the scale than it rightfully
belongs. Each point in this curve as measured by the vertical scale to the
left is just three hundred strokes higher than it should be. Because these
T. M. curves practically coincide (curves "F") for the first sixty days of
practice, curve "D" was started higher up on the scale.

It will be seen that these curves are in their main features similar to
those obtained by previous experimenters. There is in all a rapid and
continuous rise in the early stages of practice followed by a slower and
more gradual rise in the later stages. All show marked daily variations
picturing the fluctuations in the learner's ability to do what might be
assumed to be the same task under constant objective conditions. In
addition to these daily variations there are in all of the curves short periods
of non-improvement lasting from six to eight days, *"Breathing Places,"* as
it were, where the learners for a time made no determinable improvement,
often falling below their best records for previous days.

In addition to these more general features the curves reveal certain individual features not common to all. Two of the curves, . . . "B" and
"A," . . . show one or more distinct *plateaus,* periods of arrest longer
than the "breathing places" just mentioned, where the learners for stretches
of from 17 to 33 days made no measurable improvement, [but] . . . "D"
and "C" . . . show no plateaus. It is significant that these curves represent
shorter periods of practice, the former but 60, the latter 86 practice days,
while . . . [curves] . . . "B" and "A" . . . represent respectively 174 and
130 days.

It may also be observed that even the general features of the curves vary
with the different learners. There are more of the "breathing places" in
some cases than in others and they do not come at corresponding stages
of advancement while the plateaus, on the other hand, seem to belong to
rather definite levels of attainment. Again, the daily variations in the
S. M. . . . "B" curve . . . for instance, seem less pronounced and variable
than for the other subjects while his progress as a whole is much less
steady and continuous than that of the other subjects, notably that of
"C" . . .

The curves picture the general character of the progress made by each
learner and show his actual "ability to do" from day to day, week to week

and stage to stage of the practice. To explain them fully we must not only determine to what their general rise is due, but account for all their salient features and individual peculiarities. What do these curves mean psychologically? What associations and habits were formed making possible their general rise? How were these associations and habits developed and perfected in the course of the practice? What factors helped or hindered their formation and growth? To a consideration of these questions we now must turn . . .

DESCRIPTIVE ANALYSIS OF LEARNING TO WRITE BY TOUCH

THE LETTER ASSOCIATION STAGE*

The Writing in the Earliest Stage. Learning the Keyboard.—The first task of the subject was to learn the keyboard as a preliminary to the formation of an association between the letters in the copy and the corresponding keys of the machine. Y learned the keyboard . . . by committing it to memory. He learned it so well that he could draw it correctly from visual memory when he began his first test. The thought or inner pronunciation of any letter called up at once a visual image of its exact position on the keyboard. This gave him his cue for finding it with his fingers . . .

X, though a good visualizer, used a different method in learning the keyboard. After a twenty-minute attempt to get a workable visual image of the keyboard . . . he gave up trying to commit it to memory and made an actual map of it instead, which he kept before him in his practice as long as necessary. He at once began to write. If he did not know the location of the letter he would refer to his map moving his fingers to the desired key and striking it while looking at the map. An independent visual image was never used to locate the keys . . .

Locating the Keys.—The next task confronting the learner was to get his fingers to the proper keys. This was in the beginning of the T. M. a very difficult process, especially for all those letters situated near the center of the keyboard. The little fingers had to be kept constantly on the "a" and

---

* In describing the growth of skill in a complicated manipulation like typewriting it is necessary for the sake of clearness to mark off definite stages and to speak of them as though they were distinct and successive, while as a matter of fact this is only relatively true. Let it be understood, then, once for all, that while we shall speak of letter, word, and phrase stages, we are to conceive them not only as passing into one another by imperceptible gradation, but also as not exclusively successive. Certain simple and common phrases are handled as wholes at a time when certain rarely used letters still require individual attention.

";" keys. From these as reference points the key desired was located by the unseen fingers, if its position was known. To reach such a key it was first necessary to locate (by feeling) the row in which it was situated, then find the key itself by touching all the intermediate keys up to the one desired. If, for instance, the "t" was wanted, the learner would go to the row above his little finger and with the other three fingers of his left hand feel each key separately, noting as he raised his fingers, *q, w, e, r, t.* This method of literally "feeling his way" to each letter as wanted was the first regular procedure of all the subjects in getting their fingers to the keys. The final step required to make a letter in this earliest stage was a second inner speaking of it necessary to set off the final letter-making movement.

The earliest writing involved, therefore, (1) getting the copy, (2) an actual spelling or thinking of each letter to be made, (3) mentally locating it on the keyboard, (4) getting the proper finger to the key, (5) again pronouncing the letter or initiating the final letter-making movement . . .

Short Circuiting the Earliest Methods of Writing. Fusion of the First and Second Steps.—In the earliest writing the copy was memorized as in the S. M. learning and held in immediate memory until tapped off on the keys. The spelling of the words, i.e., the associations necessary for reading the letters composing them, was of course, something which the learners brought with them to the task and which they did not need to learn. It was a habit ready for use, but even in this most habitual part of the work an important change occurred. The learners unconsciously began to keep their eyes focused more and more on the copy because of the difficulty occasioned by holding the copy in memory. The spelling became more and more incipient and fugitive until the mere sight of the letter in the copy, which soon came to be closely attended to, set off at once all the processes, [mental] and physical, involved in striking that letter on the machine . . .

When letter associations are developed and fixating the letters with the eyes has taken the place of the former spelling, there is no difference, so far as getting the copy is concerned, between long and short words. The spelling occasions no difficulty because no real spelling is done. A foreign word can be as easily written as an English word. A very strange or long word may call a little extra attention to itself and so, like any distraction, cause slower work on the keyboard, but none of the troubles that come later from uncertain, nonautomatic spelling can occur here because the letters are taken directly from the page as a visual sensation.

Fusion of the Third and Fourth Steps.—The third and fourth steps required to make a letter, the dual process of first locating the keys mentally and then finding them with the fingers, went through a still more elaborate process of "short circuiting" as direct letter associations were formed. With practice the thought or sight of the letter in the copy came to call up ever more readily the visual image (for Y) or movement of attention (for X), which served as a guide for the fingers. But though continually changing in character and efficiency to meet better the learner's needs, these earlier ways of mentally locating the keys were very soon outgrown. The visual image which Y used to locate his letters very early began to give way to a higher, more economic form of direction for the fingers and hands. On the fifth day of his practice he wrote: "I have still a general visual image of the keyboard, but the keys are now located by making use of a sort of visual-motor image that tells me more readily and surely the direction and distance of the keys desired." The second and third steps in the work had already begun to fuse with the fourth. X, at about the same stage of advancement, described at length how the movement of attention to the exact position of each key came to follow always more naturally and easily upon the sight or spelling of the letters, and the movements necessary for getting the proper fingers to the keys more closely upon this movement of attention.

Abbreviating the Fourth of the Five Steps and Rise of Motor-tactual Image.—As might be inferred from the description of the earliest stage of learning . . . the greatest opportunity for saving was in the fourth of the five steps, in acquiring more economic methods of getting the right finger to the proper key. It marks a long step forward in the learning when the subject acquires the ability of going directly to any key desired merely by attending to the motor-tactual "feel" of that particular letter-making movement. Improvement in learning to make this movement directly is very gradual and slow . . .

In this part of the learning all sorts of temporary helps and devices were used, and shorter and more direct methods of getting the fingers to the keys were constantly *fallen* into. All sorts of connections between the successive letters of words were formed, by the learners, in feeling their way from one letter to another, and many short cuts across the keyboard were made. X observed that he was unconsciously letting the fingers of one hand rest on the letters last struck while working with the other hand. At first the fingers were always raised from the board as soon as a letter had been struck so that each letter had to be located from the little finger position as reference. This new procedure proved helpful because the next letter to be made with that hand could, as a rule, be located more easily from this position than via the little finger as a point of reference . . . Many other devices were employed in getting the fingers to the separate keys, such as learning to skip across the keyboard in all sorts of ways within the scope of a group of letters to be made by the same hand, e.g., learning to go directly from "i" to "o" and from the "o" to "n" when writing "ion" with the right hand or going from "d" to "e" direct when writing "dear." *But as direct letter associations developed these devices were all slowly discarded,* the one direct movement being more economic than any improvement of the earlier detailed method. *The tendency to use this better method and to strike for a letter directly instead of locating it by the older (and for a time) surer way was very strong in both subjects. They wanted to strike the keys directly long before they were able to do so.*

As time passed the learners came to rely with more justifiable confidence on the motor-tactual image of the direct lettermaking movements for guidance and became less and less conscious of the keys which lay between their little fingers and the keys to be struck. X developed his motor-tactual image by gradually eliminating the steps used in building it up and paying less and less attention to the keys that lay between his little fingers and the keys wanted. Y very early applied the "method of trial and error." As soon as he dared, he tried to make each letter directly and if wrong corrected himself by referring to the written sheet. In this way he soon developed a direct association for all the letters, and came to rely for guidance and a test of correctness on the motor-tactual image of his movements. X used the intermediate steps as guides until the direct associations were sufficiently developed for these helps to be discarded.

The most important element in this advance was improvement of motor-tactual discrimination or making clear the motor-tactual image for each letter-making movement. In the earliest writing such discrimination was very weak. The learners had to actually raise their fingers after each stroke in order to be able to count their way to the next key. The keys could not be distinguished if the fingers were not separately raised. The learner could not tell by touch alone whether he had his fingers correctly placed or not. After some days practice three fingers could be put down on as many keys and the keys recognized with one stroke of attention. Later a finger could be slowly moved across the keyboard and by close attention to the "feel" of the movement it could be correctly placed on the key desired. Still later the learners could go directly to any key wanted and recognize at once by *"touch"* alone whether or not the finger was rightly placed. Building up direct letter associations in the T. M., might, therefore, be defined as getting the right motor-tactual "feel" for the separate letter-making movements, or learning to attend to the motor-tactual image of the movements and making it guide the fingers.

The Advance from the Letter Association Stage. If, as soon as a letter is thought of (spelled) or visually attended to in the copy, the right movement for striking the corresponding key is called forth, and if this movement can be directed as made, a *letter association* has been formed; the association needs but to be further perfected to make possible the development of the next higher order of association (word association). When it has become rapid, easy and certain, the next stage has already been entered upon. The individual movement becomes so easy that less and less attention is required for its execution and attention is free to assume a higher form of direction, making possible the higher method of work.

The process of finally perfecting these simple associations is, however, very gradual and slow; it was necessary to make the direct movement a great many times with attention carefully focused on its "feel" before it became distinctly easier. At first the movement must be carefully attended to throughout its whole course. As practice continues its motor-tactual image comes to be attended to more and more generally; as the individual movement becomes fused with other letter-making movements in writing words, less and less attention needs to be given to its "feel." But some conscious guidance is required for months after it can be almost automatically made. Long after the subjects thought that these movements were no longer attended to they were often surprised to find that a little attentive direction to the individual movements was still given and required. A half conscious following of the individual movements for the last letters of the words occurred long after these words could be reacted to as a whole and after it was thought that these letters were being taken care of quite automatically. The complete direction of these movements was turned over to the fingers *very gradually* and conscious direction dropped out too gradually to be accurately described.

It was further observed that the motor-tactual "feel" for these letter-making movements was very easily forgotten. For weeks of the earlier practice it was lost over night and had to be built up each day anew. Moreover, it is not a simple motor image that is to be remembered; the hand is rarely in exactly the same position when a letter is made; the motor image is, therefore, not always the same. Much correct practice is required (the freer from mistakes the better) before one is certain of the correctness of his movements, and a still greater amount of careful practice and the development of a higher order of associations is required before the individual movements are perfected and made wholly automatic. A little attention and guidance is required for many months after the letter associations have been well established. *They are indeed perfected only in and through the formation of the word and phrase associations by which they are superseded.*

An interesting feature of the perfection of letter associations and the transition to the next stage was the way in which the motor-tactual images disappeared from consciousness. The motor-tactual image is needed as a guide for the movements for a short time only, and having served that purpose it soon drops out of consciousness altogether and only reappears when a mistake is made or when for any cause the learner drops down to a lower plane of writing. On April 9, Y wrote: "I now recognize by touch alone as soon as I have made a mistake." April 14 he wrote: "As soon as I get on the wrong row, a very misleading mistake, I notice it at once. When all is going well the feel of the movement does not come into consciousness any more at all." *Failing to recognize the correctness of the individual movements when going right is the first step in the automatization and the beginning of the formation of a habit of the next higher order where the syllable or word is made the unit of attention.*

Distribution of Attention in the Letter Association Stage. The attention of the learners in this stage was variously employed according to their grade of advancement. In the earliest writing the whole attention was focused successively on each of the five steps required to make any letter—first on getting the copy, then on spelling the letter or fixating it in the copy, then on mentally locating the corresponding key on the keyboard, next on the movement required for reaching that key with the proper finger, lastly on the initiation of the final letter-making movement. A number of cases were recorded where the letter was actually forgotten during this process of making it, so much attention had to be given to the separate steps. The last step, initiating the final letter-making movement, was rather easy; the major part of attention was given to guiding the fingers. Gradually, the four steps fuse into one continuous process which came to be attended to as a whole, the stress of attention being on the motor-tactual image of the final letter-making movement . . .

The way in which this motor-tactual image of the letter-making movement is attended to at different stages in the development of the letter association is important. When a letter association first becomes operative the letter-making movement is so difficult that it consumes the entire attention, which is distributed over every part of the movement and follows it guidingly throughout its whole course. Every turning point in its course must be zealously guarded which makes it necessary that the movement be made rather slowly. With practice the direct letter-making movements become easier and easier to make, as we have seen, which means that the movement as a whole does not need any longer to be so carefully directed.

At this point attention naturally tends to drift to outside interests or to be pushed too far ahead in the work. If kept as closely focused on the work as formerly, it goes to the invention of more advantageous methods of work and to the control of larger and larger units as fast as freed from the guidance of the individual movements. If this natural tendency to relaxation at this stage is not successfully met and attention pushed ahead to a higher form of direction as fast as naturally freed from the over-sight and guidance of these letter-making movements or if attention is pushed ahead too fast there will be an arrest of progress. The stage where these letter associations are being finally perfected, therefore, is a distinctly *"critical stage"* in the learning.

THE SYLLABLE AND WORD ASSOCIATION STAGE

Initiating the Movements. A distinguishing feature of the syllable and word association stage is the clear re-entrance of .inner speech. In the letter association stage when the copy was gotten letter by letter, the sequence of movements following immediately the focusing of each letter on the page, no actual spelling was required. Visually fixating the letters in quick succession initiated and controlled the sequence of the movements. When the word or syllable became the unit for attention the copy could not so be gotten and the movements had to be initiated and controlled by an actual or incipient mental "spelling."

Getting the Copy. The copy in the word association stage is taken as a syllable or as a word at a time and a little ahead of the hands. Attention as freed from the guidance of the individual movements goes more and more to getting the copy and to the unique mental spelling just mentioned. The copy is not actually learned; for the writers are never aware of the connected meaning of what they are writing . . .

The increase of speed itself naturally led to this change. When word associations were sufficiently developed for the movements in certain connections to be made faster than the letters could be focused individually by the eye, the copy had to be gotten further ahead and the succession of movements controlled in some other way. When word associations had approached perfection, the inner spelling or pronunciation gave a sort of specific mental adjustment for the required group of movements as a whole, and served to guide the fingers to the proper keys as well as to control the order or sequence of the movements . . .

Abbreviating the Spelling. That which takes the place of the visual fixation of the letter association stage is at first, for most words, a full mental enunciation of all the letters, but as time passes, it becomes more and more incipient and soon links itself closely with the process of locating the keys and yields to a characteristic pronunciation of the syllable or word as a whole. The spelling now constitutes a sort of mental attitude or preadjustment for the word in question . . .

Later, as the word and phrase associations became perfected, a higher form of "group spelling," where less and less attention had to be given to this succession of the individual movements, became slowly operative. But it went through many changes and developed more gradually than can be described. The lower and more detailed forms of mental "spelling" proved useful long after it was thought that they had been outgrown. And an actual or incipient spelling of the individual letters persisted and was useful long after it ceased to be consciously attended to. At the close of one of his last practice sentence tests when Y's writing was as automatic as it ever got to be, he wrote: "Just for an instant today, when my attention was half directed to it, I found myself, after all, incipiently pronouncing every letter as I wrote for several sentences. I had felt for a long time that no spelling was any more present." . . .

Locating the Keys. The group method of locating the keys, which in this stage of advancement gave direction to the fingers and which was developed in conjunction with the group spelling just treated, was described by Y as follows: . . . "I make my best speed, I think, when writing by groups, striking off the easy words and groups of letters very fast and then stopping somewhat, for an orientation for the next group. It seems that this anticipatory 'feel' or orientation for a word or group of letters is increasing considerably. I have not been able to analyze it much. I believe in these cases I always start with some sort of initial recognition of the position of my fingers; i.e., my orientation must be gotten at the start. With this much I approach such an easy word with an attitude of confidence. I feel certain that it can be run through with as a group. In writing it I am quite unconscious of the individual letters or strokes; the correctness or wrongness of such a group of movements is recognized as a whole. If an error occurs, I simply recognize that something is wrong but will not know what the error is until I stop to analyze or look at the writing." . . .

Another important factor in the development of this group method of locating the keys is the change which occurs in the growth of the motor-tactual image used in directing the fingers . . . As word and phrase associations are perfected the motor-tactual image, which formerly was attached to the individual movements for purposes of guidance, now, in this stage, changes and comes to be attached to the larger groups of movements representing phrases and words, and serves to guide the group of closely associated movements as a whole. All the learners described such an image* for the practice sentence as well as for many individual words and phrases . . .

Distribution of Attention in the Syllable and Word Association Stage. Attention in this state is, as we have seen, chiefly given to the mental "spelling" which controls the sequence of the movements and helps guide the fingers. As the individual movements become easier and easier of performance attention advances to a higher form of direction and control, coming at last to manage the group of movements representing a syllable or word, first by a detailed direction of its part members, later by a more general guidance of the group as a whole. Just here a great difficulty is encountered; *it is not easy to keep attention focused on the mental "spelling" and its motor accompaniments long enough to secure perfection in the word groups nor to cause it to assume the higher forms of direction and control as fast as it is set free from the oversight of the details.* Failure may take one or the other of two clearly marked directions. (1) As attention is gradually freed from the oversight of the former details it may desert the writing in a large degree and turn spontaneously to the many irrelevant associations that hover about the threshold of consciousness instead of pushing ahead to a new and better way of writing. *The learner at this stage is apt to be caught by the law of habit and continue the writing on a low plane when he should be forging ahead.* Or (2) the learner unconsciously assumes a freedom and

---

* It is psychologically important and significant that all the images which appeared in the different stages of the writing were first prominent and distinct, then hazy and indistinct, disappearing entirely soon after they had served their purpose in the learning.

skill which he does not possess, and pushes ahead to a higher form of direction *before* the associations have been made sufficiently automatic for this to be safely done. *The slight conscious direction needed for so long a time to properly perfect the associations is neglected and trouble and arrested development result.* The numerous mistakes in the regular writing at this stage and the "breakdown" in the practice sentence writing are evidence of the reality of this tendency and warrant our referring to this stage as a second "critical stage" in the learning.

THE EXPERT STAGE

In the expert stage word and phrase associations have been developed and perfected to such a degree that the writing is absolutely continuous. The word, phrase and clause have become the unit of attention. After describing his practice sentence writing, towards the last of his practice, Y wrote: "When I write several words in succession in this way they run more or less together. The movements no longer are separated into groups according to the words. I am no longer conscious of the words or groups of movements which they represent but have my attention on getting through with the sentence as a whole and on a general control of the successions of movements required to write it." . . .

One of the most serious difficulties encountered in the expert stage is caused by interference of associations . . . An association is soon built up for certain orders of words, and whole groups of words when coming in this order can be dashed off with much less attention than other arrangements of the same words. The possibilities of word combinations are, however, enormous, and the formation of perfect associations for all the combinations is impossible. A possibility of interference is therefore never absent and enough attention must always be given to the separate words and phrases to avoid such pitfalls . . .

Getting the Copy. The copy in this stage is gotten by reading it a word at a time, but, as has been said, a number of words ahead of the hands. The eyes were kept on the copy continuously. Each word is incipiently pronounced but in a peculiar way. For an easy word the pronunciation was incipient only and free from accents; for a long or difficult word the pronunciation was by syllables variously accented or emphasized. All this was brought out clearly by having the expert read her copy aloud as she wrote it . . .

Initiating and Directing the Movements . . . The incipient or actual pronunciation of the words somehow directed and controlled the sequence of the letter-making movements. The *former* group spelling and the psycho-physical processes involved in locating the keys in the previous stage have fused into this highest form of "group spelling," the reading of the copy. But the direction given to the letter-making movements as well as the control of their sequence is of a more general nature now . . .

Distribution of Attention. Attention in this stage is, as we have seen, largely on pronouncing the copy, the substitute for the mental "spelling" and locating processes of the previous page. But a little attention must still go to the control of the hands, keeping track of where they are and urging them forward. A part also goes to a sort of general control of the sequence of the movements . . .

The expert stage is normally not one of relaxation, but quite the opposite. Attention though, perhaps, more habitual is even more completely centered on the work than at any other stage of advancement. Especially is this true when the expert is at her own highest level. In discussing the writing of an international contest Miss Carrington remarked: "If, when I am in a contest, the thought ever flashes through my mind, 'I wonder how my rivals are getting along,' I know I have lost." . . .

Descriptive Analysis of Learning to Write by Sight

[The author at this point makes a detailed analysis of learning to write by the sight method which parallels the analysis made of the touch method. He concludes:] Similar psycho-physical habits to those developed by the "touch" method were developed in learning to write by the "sight" method with only such characteristic differences in the process of their formation as was occasioned by the fact that in this method the copy had to be learned and somehow held in mind until written and the further fact that there was as a result of this a constant shifting of attention from the writing to the process of learning the copy . . .

Order of Acquiring the Habits Which Constitute Typewriting Skill

Let us turn to our drum records which give an objective picture of the writing in every stage of advancement, and furnish, therefore, an index of how the special associations were developed. Figure III shows sections the special subjects who was learning to write by sight. He did not know from representative records. "A" is a portion of the first record of one of

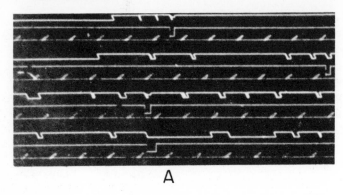

A

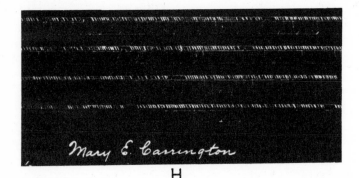

F

H

FIG. III.

the location of any of the keys, so that each of the steps required to make a letter in this early stage was more or less of a problem for him . . . Section "F" from the record of Miss A, who could copy at an average rate of fifty words per minute illustrates a semi-expert stage. Phrase associations are characteristic of the stage reached, and word and phrase associations need only to be further perfected to establish the supreme skill pictured in "H," a section of one of the regular writing tests of Miss Carrington, the finished expert. All word and phrase associations are now so far perfected that the writing is absolutely continuous. Seventy or eighty words per minute could be written from any sort of straight copy.

The above records are typical and with the introspective notes of the learners show clearly that in learning typewriting in the manner followed by our subjects there were no graded steps or stages in which habits now of this order and now of that were developed, but that all developed together. Throughout the practice there was a more or less general upward striving at once along many special and competing lines. Some of the earliest records showed some letter associations in the first stages of development, others well developed and joining to form syllable and word associations, while the easier words had already united to form phrase associations for the most common sequences of easy words.

A similar relation holds in the development of word associations. As the perfection of a letter association is dependent upon the order of letters. in words and the development of a method of reacting to the words as a whole, so word associations play an important role in the development of phrase associations long before the reactions to words as such is perfected. That is to say word associations are not perfected independently of phrase associations, or before the latter begin to develop. The associations which form between the words of connected discourse help to perfect word associations even while these partially developed word associations are making possible the more economic reactions to these groups of closely connected words. In learning typewriting by our methods the elemental habits were not finally perfected *before* higher-order habits began to form. The development of the higher and perfection of the lower went hand in hand throughout the practice. *The lower-order habits were perfected in and through the formation of the higher, as a further development of the higher was dependent upon the final perfection of the lower.* With it already described . . .

The "critical stages" in learning, where the plateaus appear, do, as a all went the simultaneous development of the more purely mental habits matter of fact, come in when certain lower-order habits or groups of such habits are approaching their maximum development, but these lower-order habits do not need to be perfected or further developed before attention can attack the higher-order habits. It normally attacks the higher-order habits long before these simpler habits even approach this stage of perfection and would continue to do so properly but for reasons later to be given . . . The length of a plateau, is, therefore, *not* a measure of the difficulty of making certain special associations automatic *preparatory for use as elements in the higher-order habits,* but a measure of the time and labor required to conquer certain difficulties encountered in the practice when these special habits are being finally perfected, difficulties which stop the development of *all* orders of habits in process of formation at the time. The elementary associations are *not* being developed, and *very rarely* further perfected during the plateau practices. *No real progress is being made* though changes important for future progress are taking place during a part of the plateau practice. The time is taken up with overcoming the special difficulties incident to that stage of advancement and to getting rid of the evil effects of the mistakes which the final perfection of the special associations naturally brings on. As soon as these are overcome and attention is again properly applied to the work *all orders of habits* begin again to develop . . .

How Special Typewriting Habits Normally Grow and Develop

While it is true as has just been shown, that habits of all orders develop simultaneously, it must not be inferred that all are making steady advance at the same instant. All learning curves that have been plotted, including our own, show that equal amounts of practice do not always give equal results as judged by the criterion "ability to do." In proportion as the measure of progress is accurate the amount of gain seems to be uneven and irregular. To what is this irregularity due? Was the development of each of the special habits involved in typewriting like the general progress of the learners, uneven and irregular, or once begun steadily continuous?

Our facts warrant an answer in favor of the first alternative. That is to say the special habits involved in the mastery of typewriting, though all developing together, are not actually driven abreast. Their manner of growth is something like the movement of a flock of sheep along a country road. The whole flock moves forward, now faster and now slower, while now this and now that particular sheep pushes ahead of the rest.

So in the development of these special associations, there is general improvement along many special lines at once; all associations involved are making progress almost from the first, but the gain is not steady, nor is it equal in various directions. It is in the matter of making new adaptations and short cuts in the line of each individual association that the irregularity comes in. There is what might be called a friendly rivalry among the various special associations developing at the moment. Progress is made along so many special lines that many opportunities for adaptation are presented. The learner's attention moves about over this array of improvement possibilities, causing an adaptation to be made, now in this, now in that department of the work as alternately focused on the different phases of the work. Now this, now that association is pushed ahead of the rest in its development, the ones not specially attended to being practiced on a lower and more automatic plane because they lack the considerable degree of attention needed to practice them in the highest way. It is, therefore, the particular distribution and use made of attention and the resultant adaptations secured that makes the development of the special habits, like the general progress in learning, uneven and irregular. One of the most common general observations revealed by the notes was the frequent relapses in the realm of the several special associations developing; there were many periods in the practice when the learner's skill in one or more special departments of the work seemed to go backward instead of forward because of the particular use made of attention at the time.

How New Adaptations or Forward Steps in Learning Are Made

Progress in typewriting is brought about (a) by the gradual perfection of . . . special habits, and (b) by the new adaptations or short cuts in method that are made as higher-order habits are formed. The special introspective notes of our learners, purporting to give a complete analysis of the learning consciousness in all stages of advancement, revealed two important facts about this "short circuiting." (1) That it was on the good days and during the good periods of writing, when the learners were fully warmed up, feeling good, and putting all available energy into the work, that they found themselves making new adaptations or taking a forward step in the learning. (2) That all new adaptations or short cuts in method were unconsciously made, i.e., fallen into by the learners quite unintentionally, on the good days, while practicing under strain.

ROLE PLAYED BY EFFORT IN LEARNING TYPEWRITING

. . . The present study shows that *less effort was actually put into the work at all those stages of practice where little or no improvement was made* . . . and has revealed the particular role which effort plays in learning typewriting. It was clearly determined that a learner must work with a "do-or-die" attitude to make new adaptations or take a forward step in the learning. Relaxation of attention or effort and fatigue not only keeps a learner from practicing the newest and most economical habits he has learned, but keeps him from making new adaptations because he is forced under such conditions to write in a more primitive way than he is capable of when in first class condition and doing his best. To prevent arrest and insure the most rapid progress, attention must be kept sharply focused on the details of the work and continually pushed out on the frontier where new adaptations in method can be laid hold of.

This fact will be made clearer by a . . . typical quotation from the notes. During one of his special practice periods, X wrote: "I am coming to believe that great effort is required to make the best progress in the work. The tendency to lag and revert to older and more primitive methods of writing is very strong and must be overcome. Only in moments of extreme effort am I able to make innovations or lay hold of higher and better ways of doing the work. I very suddenly catch myself doing the writing in a more economical way. In another week I find that I have improved on my method again and so it goes, but in no case have I found that the adjustment was purposely made. I was simply pushed into the better way by the strong desire to do my best." . . .

This brings us to the consideration of a second fact which shows more clearly still the specific role played by effort in learning. It was observed by the learners that the older and more elemental habits used in the earlier stages of writing tended strongly to persist and force themselves upon the learners long after they had been superseded by higher-order habits. At every lapse in attention or relaxation of effort, the older habits stepped forward, as it were, and assumed control, thereby tending to perpetuate themselves. Only when a high degree of efficient effort was being persistently applied, only when the learners were urging themselves forward so hard that these outgrown habits had no chance to be used was attention forced to lay hold of the higher and more economical methods of work . . .

PART PLAYED BY CONSCIOUSNESS IN LEARNING TYPEWRITING

A second significant fact about the learning is, as we have said, that all adaptations and short cuts in method were unconsciously made, that is, fallen into by the learners quite unintentionally on the good days while practicing under strain. The learners suddenly noticed that they were doing certain parts of the work in a new and better way, then purposely adopted it in the future. In learning to "short circuit" the first elaborate methods of making the letters, in developing syllable and word associations and associations between the words of compact phrases or clauses, in making improvements in mental spelling, in learning to get and hold the copy more economically, in learning to attend and economize effort, etc., the new adaptations or forward steps were all unconsciously made. It seemed to be the strong desire to write with the utmost speed, strengthened in some cases by the thought of the value or worth of the experiment, that pushed the learners into these new and more economical ways of writing . . .

We are now in position to see why little or no improvement is made when attention and effort are relaxed. A lapse in attention and effort means that fewer adaptations are made. The learner settles down to more primitive methods of work, writing on a low plane when closer attention and increased effort would mean new adaptations, rapid improvement, and the development of more advanced methods of work. The fact that these lapses in attention and effort were so largely beyond the learner's control, and the further fact that the learning was unconscious, the organism adapting itself to the conditions presented with so little help from consciousness, emphasize again the importance of hygiene for learning. It is not *what* the learner would like to do that determines his rate of progress in learning, but what his mental and physical conditions at the time will let him do . . .

How Special Typewriting Habits Are Perfected

The most obvious explanation of the general form of the learning curve for any complex process of learning like typewriting is, that it is really the summed result of a number of elemental habits all of which show the same typical rapid gain at the beginning, where there are many possibilities for "short circuiting," and slow gain at the end, where all progress must come from a further perfection of the habits as such. This our observations abundantly justify, but it is not the sole reason for the slow advance in the later stages of progress. Another is to be found in the fact, also sufficiently demonstrated by what has gone before, that gain in skill in typewriting is a process of progressive organization and co-ordination of simple activities, and there is every reason to think that such a process will itself go on more readily with simple than with more complex elements, so that in this respect also we should look for a regular decline in the rate of gain as practice continues. Still a third factor, and *one very important for learning,* is to be found in the relation of these nearly automatic processes to attention. As has already been pointed out . . . these processes need a minimum of oversight for a very long time even after they seem completely self-regulative. In other words habits are perfected . . . *very gradually.* If we might speak of their final perfection or dropping out of consciousness as dying, they die hard. At the same time they have become extremely hard to hold in attention because they are so nearly automatic. In the early stages of their development where many adaptations and short cuts in method were possible, they more naturally compelled attention because progress was rapid and easy. Later when most short cuts have been made, when advancement depends upon the perfection of the associations already formed, and when progress is slow and the chances for gain reduced to a minimum, attention tends *naturally* to drift to other things, making those stages in the learning where a particular association or group of special associations is being finally perfected distinctly "critical" in nature . . .

The General Course of the Learning Curves Explained

After what has been said our explanation of the general features of our curves can be brief. The first rapid and continuous rise is due to the fact that the learner is making progress along many different lines at once. Rapid strides of improvement are possible and made simultaneously in every department of the work. The learner is not only forming and perfecting letter associations but syllable, word and phrase associations as well. He is simultaneously improving his method of dealing with every problem that the writing presents; locating the keys, directing and controlling his fingers, "spelling" or initiating the movements, getting his copy, learning to deal with special difficulties, learning to keep attention more closely and economically applied to the work, etc. The curves will rise rapidly and continuously so long as many of these possibilities of improvement exist. As they grow less numerous the rate of gain will likewise decline until, as still more skill is acquired, a state is reached where most adaptations or short cuts in method have been made; fewer special habits remain to be developed; fewer adaptations are possible. Those possible have become harder and harder to make, because they must be made in the realm of higher habits where the learner has had less experience. Every man has had experience with the first stages of learning, but little with the later stages because most people touch lightly many things and are masters of nothing. There being now fewer adaptations to make and those possible being harder and harder to make, and the process of finally perfecting all the special associations being so gradual and slow, the learning curve becomes, as the expert stage is approached, almost horizontal. In the later stages of learning the sole gain must come from an occasional adaptation and from a further perfection of the present habits and methods of work . . .

17. Progressive Change in Skill Learning*

Longwell's elaborate study of "simple action" in skill learning suggests how complex is the behavior in learning presumably simple skills. A number of specific questions, including the perceptions of the task by the subjects and the effects of repetition upon action, are systematically examined in an effort to determine the essential changes occurring in skill learning processes. The broad range of phenomena reported in the study is derived in part from the reports of subjects trained in introspection and in part by highly trained observers.

It is our aim to study learning by way of a description of progressive changes in simple action. By "learning" we shall mean simply those modifications in course and in issue which appear under the continuation or repetition of a function or of a combination of functions . . . Acting we shall regard as a psychological function which includes in its successive stages a task, a prophetic forecasting of something-to-be-done-by-way-of-body-movement, and an appropriate resolution of the actional task by organic and other means.

* SARAH G. LONGWELL. Abridged with permission of the publisher from Progressive change in simple action: A study of learning. *American Journal of Psychology*, 1938, 51:261–82.

. . . The problems selected were novel chiefly in their recombination of well-known elements from many simple tasks. The devices used were (1) to capture rolling balls, (2) to duplicate "silhouette" figures, and (3) to trace reflected patterns. All of these devices provided occasions for describing the activity by stages and for setting varieties of task in the course of progressive functional modification. They differed among themselves in opportunities for appropriate occasional instruction and in the variety of psychological functions called forth.

From these problems, then, we seek answers to the following questions. (1) What tasks are set in the simpler forms of acting? How do the tasks arise? and How are they modified under repetition? (2) How does the "determination" develop? and How does it change as the acting is carried through time after time? (3) What are the inducing and guiding factors in the progress of such an action? and How are these factors modified in successive performances? (4) What are the antecedents and sequels of the motor phase? and How is the motor phase affected by repetition? (5) What is the entire, integrated, functional course of acting in its simpler forms? and, finally, What essential changes occur under repetition, changes which are commonly masked under the phrase "learning or perfecting the act?"

The Experiment Procedure

O was set a number of elementary problems which could be easily performed action-wise. Reports on the course of the functional operation were called for. The problems were repeated until performance became fixed or invariable. The number of repetitions naturally varied with the problem and with the observer.

Problem I. The capture of rolling balls. The task set was to roll four small steel balls into a wire cage set in an enclosed plane. The balls and cage were enclosed in a cardboard box 6 in. x 8 in. and 1 in. deep, all covered over by cellophane. The solution, by outside bimanual manipulation of the box, is possible to anyone without gross physical handicap who comprehends the task (cf. Fig. 1).

This preliminary problem was selected because (1) it provided divisible and describable stages in solution, (2) it gave ample scope for variations of task in terms of everchanging occasional instructions, and (3) it permitted, through repetition, a study of those progressive functional changes which are the essence of "learning."

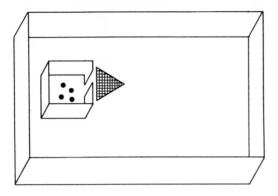

FIG. 1. APPARATUS USED IN PROBLEM I.

Formal instruction was as follows:

You are to manipulate the box until one ball is inside the cage, giving a full functional account as you proceed. Be sure to distinguish product from function and to report the temporal sequence of your operations. Try to differentiate the various periods of action. . . . Now cage the other balls, one at a time, reporting as before.

Problem II. Dissected "silhouette" figures. Ten filled black pictures representing animate objects in various poses were printed, each on a separate small white card. Seven irregularly shaped block pieces were provided with which O was to duplicate each figure (Fig. 2).

The first step in the presentation was designed to encourage a detailed report on the foreperiod of action. To this end O sat just out of reach of figure and blocks (arranged in haphazard order on a table) but with a clear view. After an exposure of 10 sec., the figure and blocks were covered and O was instructed to report. Then O sat close, the cover was removed and O continued the solution by manipulation.

After each of the ten silhouettes had been once solved, six of them were selected for repeated presentation. The procedure remained unchanged except for the fact that, as O became facile in finding the solution, the exposure-time was accordingly reduced. A maximal solving-time of 45 min. was allowed.

This problem was selected for its promise of (1) multiple and distinctive stages in learning, i.e. progressive functional changes, and (2) throwing into commission several functional aptitudes of the organism.

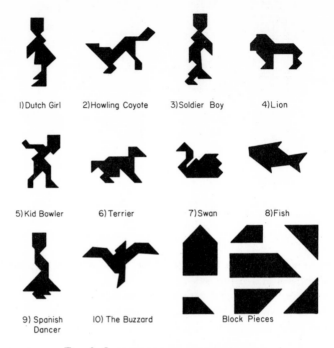

1) Dutch Girl   2) Howling Coyote   3) Soldier Boy   4) Lion

5) Kid Bowler   6) Terrier   7) Swan   8) Fish

9) Spanish Dancer   10) The Buzzard   Block Pieces

FIG. 2. SILHOUETTES USED IN PROBLEM II.
All illustrations © 1932 W & M.

The instructions follow:

Consider the objects to be shown here until I say "now." Then report in functional terms. . . . Carry out your task and report upon your procedure.

The formal instructions were not made explicit regarding the precise nature of the task in order that action might be set automatically by the occasion, i.e. by occasional instruction.

Problem III. Tracing reflected patterns. Three patterns were used, each more difficult than its predecessor. The first was a double line 3-in. square with a vertical dividing line down the middle (Fig. 3a). *O* was required merely to keep a moving pencil-point between the double lines. The second pattern was a square of the same size but single-lined. Here *O* was required to keep the moving pencil *on* the line. The dividing line was first placed vertically (b), then horizontally (c), through the middle of the square. The third pattern (d) was of the same size. The single

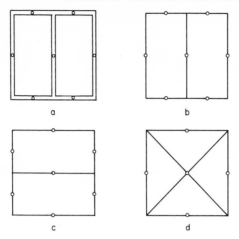

FIG. 3. APPARATUS AND PATTERNS USED IN PROBLEM III.

line made a square divided diagonally in both directions. Again *O* was to trace on the lines.

The pencil was placed in the middle of the figure to provide *O* with an initial choice in direction. The task was arbitrarily fractionated by holes in the line. Here *O* rested his pencil while reporting.

Each design was presented to *O* seated at a table. The pattern was screened from direct vision but clearly visible in a mirror. *O's* visual field was restricted to the pattern on its white background entirely surrounded by gray facings which eliminated visual apprehension of all other objects except the hand and fore-arm with which *O* worked. Each *O* used the right (preferred) hand.

The instructions follow:

Take the pencil. When I say "go," proceed between (on) the guide-lines (line) until you come to a hole in the track. Leave your pencil there and report fully your procedure step by step. . . . Now go on to the next hole . . . the next hole . . . the place of beginning.

THE RESULTS

(A) *The task*. We first consider the role of task in the simpler forms of acting, the varieties of task, their origination, and their change under repetition.

The initial task commonly falls within the anticipatory phase, the prophetic phase of "something-to-be-done" (balls rolled into cage, silhouette duplicated, or tracing followed from place to place). We consider her this initial task when formally set in verbal instruction or drawn from the occasion.

Problem I. Capturing rolling balls. The tasks are general, specific, and sec ondary.

(1) *General task.* The general task is an undetailed reference to a total an imminent problem. It may be definite or indefinite . . .

(2) *Specific task.* The specific task is a detailed reference to a phase of per formance. It is set before resolution-by-movement occurs . . .

(3) *Secondary task.* The secondary task is a sub-task which occurs as phase of the determination during the course of resolution . . .

It appears that definite and indefinite *general* tasks were set with about equa frequency (13, 12); that *specific* tasks were least frequently set (9), whil *secondary* tasks occurred most often (98) . . .

Problem II. Dissected silhouette figures. The same kinds of task appeared *i.e.,* general, specific, and secondary.

(1) *General task.* The general task rarely appeared in the strictly indefinit form, though it did come as "make whatever is there," or (infrequently) "t make (*e.g.*) the fish." All *Os* reported the general task, albeit with variabl frequency. It was unrestricted as to place in the series . . .

(2) *Specific task.* The specific task, detailed reference to a part of the com ing performance, appeared about as frequently as the general form . . .

(3) *Secondary task.* The secondary task, *i.e.* the task set as a phase of th determination during the course of resolution, appeared only in the early mem bers of a series . . . Just as soon as *O* had so stabilized his determination tha the method of duplicating any given block-pattern ran itself off from the ap prehension of the pattern-to-be-duplicated, he had no further need for sec ondary tasks. Since this series tended to a progressive stabilization of methoc and ligation of movements, there was finally a complete elimination of sec ondary tasks.

In this problem, foreperiod was definitely separated from the rest of th acting . . . One-third of all the tasks are set preliminarily while *O* is lookin at (but not handling) the material. About three-fourths of all (35) *genera* tasks are set here. In the early stages of the midperiod, the same fraction o *specific* tasks (27) are set under manipulation.

This problem illustrates more clearly than the others the tempora development of the task. The general task may be set as *O* enters th experimental room, while a very specific task sometimes appears as *O* draws his chair to the table at the completion of his preliminary report . . .

The distribution of times when the task emerges was reported in general by O to follow a given pattern. First, setting of the general task (to make whatever is there) [before the pattern was uncovered]. The next stage followed the apprehension of the uncovered pattern. Here the task was to "make the thing." The third stage may occur while O was still sitting out of reach of the blocks. This task was to "make it this way." The last stage appeared as O handled the blocks. It was the specific command 'to make the block-pattern by placing each block in a now determined precise relation to every other block." Although all of these steps were not always reportable, the account of a fairly fixed temporal ordering of the various kinds of task suggests that the common terms "attitude" and "set" may sometimes be explained by such a sequence of tasks.

Problem III. Tracing reflected patterns. Again the same three forms of task are reported; general, specific, and secondary.

(1) *General task.* The general task (undetailed reference to the total problem) occurs . . . in two forms, definite and indefinite.

(a) *Indefinite.* The most indefinite is, as before, a vaguely formulated demand (*e.g.* "do as told") or an unqualified statement that a general task is set. The same conditions appear to hold as were found before, *i.e.* task either appears early in the series . . . or later in the series . . .

(b) *Definite.* A more elaborate general task is to 'move around the square' or to "steer the pencil." This differs from the indefinite form in that it indicates in a general way what is to be done. Ordinarily it occurs late in the series . . .

(2) *Specific task.* The specific task, as already defined, is a task in which there is a detailed reference to a prospective phase of performance. It is set before resolution-by-movement occurs, . . .

(3) *Secondary task.* The secondary task was infrequent in this problem. It requires no further comment . . .

The problems compared. We have found that general, specific, and secondary tasks are set in all three problems. Let us examine them all together to discover the conditions for their arousal and the changes which they suffer under repetition.

In the first and third problems the task is approached by formal instruction. In the second it arises from an inspection of the materials and is set from the occasion or by a self-instruction. Revision, reinstatement, or fractionation of the task occurs . . .

In the silhouette problem is found the clearest example of a psychological product which serves in task-setting; the fruits of inspection leading to a task. Thus, the occasion calls out a task before the pieces are handled or movement induced. Fuller inspectional, comprehending, and imaginational operations forecast an arrangement of the blocks . . .

Over and beyond these functional specialties, called for by the broad use of the "occasion" in the silhouette study, the general forms of task were much the same in all three problems. Variety and lability, showing all through the process of "tasking," indicate the versatility and the resourcefulness of the organism making use of such outcomes to redirect, to modify, and to advance the actional course toward its final goal.

A fair scrutiny of the facts of report makes it evident that the bare account of bodily movement as "response" to a "stimulus" quite overlooks the essence of this rich variety in psychological performance. The notion of an unvarying "stimulus" as inducing an unvarying "response" leaves out of account the central and highly variable part played dexterously by the organism, where a repeated stimulus seems to the superficial observer merely to lead on to one and the same responsive type of movement of capturing balls, duplicating an outline figure, or retracing a linear pattern.

Our most important phase of the comparison still remains. It concerns the modifications of the task under repetition from the first to the last member of the series of actional performances. This progressive change has now to be described.

In capturing rolling balls the trend in modification was as follows. Either a general or a secondary task was set at first. After a few repetitions the general task dropped out and the secondary persisted. After many repetitions there is, as a rule, no task remaining. Rarely a general task may reappear or a secondary task persist. Excerpts from *Sh's* reports represent this trend. (They are taken from the 1st, 4th, 12th, and 16th reports.)

1st	balls outside are to be put inside	(general)
4th	task to keep three in and capture fourth	(secondary)
12th	same task as before	(secondary)
16th	to capture one and retain three	(secondary)

In duplicating the silhouette figures, the trend in modification was somewhat different. All three kinds of task may occur at first. After a few repetitions, general and specific drop out, while the secondary may persist. After more repetitions, there is ordinarily no task; rarely a general or a specific task may reappear. Excerpts from *Le's* reports are selected to illustrate this trend (first pattern in 1st, 3rd, 6th, and 8th presentations).

1st pieces are to be fitted into a pattern	(general)
3rd to make the skirt from these three pieces	(secondary)
6th to put the skirt together	(specific)
8th no task reported	

In tracing linear patterns the trend is almost the same as in the preceding problem. The difference lies in the fact that more specific than secondary tasks tend to survive the first few repetitions. Excerpts from Co's reports taken from the 1st, 2nd, 8th, and 14th presentations of the first pattern are typical:

1st do as told	(general)
2nd go same way	(general)
8th go to that hole	(specific)
14th specific task set [to follow previously determined direction]	(specific)

Although any given task may be set at any given point in a series, there is a tendency for a task to be set in the early members of a series, and for it to undergo change, abbreviation, and elimination under repetition . . .

(B) *The course of determination.* Beyond the task, acting demands a provision for appropriate resolution. That is to say that acting is "determined." The "determination" is the previsory stage of acting. Sometimes it is carried through in the form of physiological functions only; sometimes the psychological moments of searching, perceiving, imagining, and so on, appear. At times determining is directly provided for by [previously acquired modes of response]. In such a case there may be little that is reportable, a flashing task flowing rapidly to a neuromuscular resolution. But where the situation is novel, abrupt, or complex, the determination may be developed from the products of apprehending and other functions in course, search usually appearing and tending toward goal or outcome.

The determinational phase represents the going-on-ness of the operation. On those occasions when it does not directly affect psychological functioning, it may be announced indirectly through an accidental interruption, as when O overshoots the marks while capturing balls, "automatically" bringing back the ball to a prearranged starting point, or when a linear tracing takes the pencil beyond a turn.

In developing determination out of task, the organism employs much the same inducing and guiding factors as accompany the fully established performance. These will appear in [an] instance which follows.

Problem I. "Capturing." Evidence of determination sometimes appears in *O's* first report. *Sh* reports a flash "tip the box this way and the balls come to this end; tip it the other way and they go in." She elaborates this through anticipative comprehension that, with one ball captured, the tipping must be altered to prevent its escape. *Co* develops (comprehending) the most advantageous position for the balls, anticipating their movement to reach it and their subsequent movements to be rolled into the pen. *Le* begins in an exploratory manner to roll balls around in the box in order to ascertain how many go in with random movements, and then immediately refines the neuromuscular coordination to retain the captured balls. Setting of task is directly followed by movement accompanied by "apprehension of eye and hand coordinations necessary to accomplish this."

Each of these represents a prophetic anticipation of movement supplemented by comprehending, or by manipulative searching out, of the possibilities. The functional witnesses of determining tend to lapse under repetition . . .

The problems compared. We have found determination arising out of task in each of our problems. The course of its modification as the acting is carried through time after time is now to be considered.

With repetition the determination becomes a fixed and relatively invariable rule with little that is reportable. Where it is reported, it may be in symbolic form as "follow the system" or "always turn right." Hints, too, are gleaned from comments on how things are getting on.

In subsequent repetitions of ball capturing, *O* modified his performance in accord with exigencies of the occasion. These modifications, however, were incidental to an established procedure. In the following reports a typical determination is developed.

task to be resolved by aiming balls from opp end of box
edge balls in without using extra space
tap box to shoot ball in
edge them in from side [*i.e.* roll balls forward around cage and in] . . .

Determination was least reportable in the linear tracings. Evidence of it appeared when *O* began tracing with the "ready" signal instead of waiting for the "go." . . .

(C) Accessory factors. In addition to the directive agencies guiding the organism toward resolution, there are certain factors which are accessory. They appear as commentaries, in terms of (verbal) comment, or nonverbal flashes and functional incidents. They are not "determined" in the

sense of forecasting, but they are integral to the course and refer to the present phase of the acting. They appear throughout the problems and may or may not be modified under repetition. Again, these incidents may serve as occasional hints; i.e. they are ostensibly accessory and accompanying factors, yet they appear to induce turns in the operation. A few examples of these accessories may clarify their position in the actional course.

Problem I. Capturing. Every O reported accessory factors in this exercise. They appeared unchanged by repetition. Occasionally they indicated a slight emotional coloring to the performance, *e.g.* when the situation became predicamentive because O set an inappropriate task . . .

"balls not going in" . . . ["Am tense trying to lower my own time. Feel hurried and impatient because I am slow; could speed up if I could overcome this feeling"]. . .
"box-as-something-I-had-to-tilt" . . . "I'm sick of this" . . .
"ball is not rolling straight" . . .

Problem II. Silhouettes. Every O reported accessory factors which became minimized under repetition. Comments dropped out and the non-verbal flashes and functional incidents were reduced to a perceptive accompaniment of the resolution.

"it's the old woman" . . . "it looks like the red queen" . . .
"this block must be the head" . . . "this makes body" . . .

Problem III. Tracings. Accessory factors were reported by each O in this problem also and these incidents tended toward elimination and stabilization under repetition . . .

The problems compared. In each of the exercises these accessory factors appeared and became stabilized or largely eliminated under repetition. Finally they appeared almost entirely in the form of a perceptive accompaniment to the smooth resolution.

There were also self-instructions bearing upon the operation in terms of admonitions to do better, or to go more carefully or accurately. These were more plentiful in capturing the balls and tracing the lines than they were in duplicating the silhouettes.

More comments appeared than have been represented in the examples selected. They were indicative of the status of the performance at any given moment as, com ("one of the balls must have come out"), com ("are there enough pieces?"), and com ("it is better to keep moving than to go back") . . .

(D) The motor phase of acting. The displacement of balls, blocks, and pencil-point forms, in these three problems, a part of the resolutional

stage. These object-movements, their immediate antecedents, their sequels, and their remodelling under repetition, are now to be considered. Evidence has come in part from O and in part from E.

Problem I. Capturing. Early reports in the series include tipping, shaking and tapping the box, using both gross and fine movements. After more repetitions, the most effective means is settled upon, neuromuscular digressions eliminated, and the whole operation refined and stabilized . . .

As the performance was run through time after time, E observed an increase in $O's$ facility in manipulation. Gross movements became refined, more capturing of the balls was carried through to completion, balls seldom escaped, and posture and movement became invariable and prompt.

Problem II. Silhouettes. Every O reported two kinds of movement, directed-tentative and undirected.

(1) *Directed-tentative.* Tentative movements appeared from the first trial under antecedent determination. They were guided by OI [occasional instruction] and led to a change in position of a given block. Later the tentative movements became prompt and unequivocal. They are revealed by queries and the uncertainty of their antecedents and by the discarding or modifying of their sequels.

(2) *Undirected.* Undirected movements sometimes accompanied, then directed, search. They were reported as "random" or "just trying." O was baffled: productive functioning was at a standstill. O resorted to undirected movements in the hope (searching determination) that a chance combination might serve as OI to resolution. This disappeared after about five repetitions.

Fitting the blocks together to duplicate a pattern depends upon the fact that O comprehends that any given block stands in but one particular relation to every other block in any given pattern. The outcome of inspecting is "the position of that block is known" or "I will place the known blocks first" . . .

In attempting to duplicate the silhouettes, O shifted the blocks many times and made many combinations. Old combinations also reappeared after being discarded. By the last (8th) presentation of each silhouette, movements were direct and precise, ligated into a stabilized pattern.

The oft-repeated movements might have been observed and described by E as random or "trial and error" attempts, but $O's$ reports show that only a small number of them were really undirected and indeterminate. Besides, "trial and error" is not descriptive of $O's$ actional course. It is a theoretical explanation from $E's$ observation and needs the check of reported functional flow.

Problem III. Tracings. Separate, non-ligated movements with discrete antecedents and sequels were at first reported by every O on each of the four designs. Presently the movements became ligated. Digressions from the line never drop out entirely (except in one pattern) but become ligated into the movement-in-progress . . .

E observed at times an initial hesitancy and fumbling in starting early trials. Jerky movements marked indecision at corners, and inability to progress directly to the goal were also noted in early attempts to trace the patterns. With time, however, these characteristics were eliminated. After a few repetitions, *O* started promptly, digressed less, eliminated hesitancy at the corners, and finally drew a smooth line from beginning to end.

The problems compared. The ball-rolling supplied the clearest example of a movement-pattern. It was not so clear in the other two problems for the reason that more digressions were possible. Nevertheless, it was implied in the relatively frequent report of successive placement of blocks in an orderly fashion from head to foot. There was a tendency toward patterning in the two *Os* who made the rule always to trace the designs in the same direction, but the inevitable digressions in the course of tracing tended to keep the performance labile so that it approached a pattern only after several repetitions, when the digressions became included in the course of the movement.

The silhouettes brought out the distinction between tentatively directed and undirected movements. Although the undirected or indeterminate movements may have occurred in the other two problems, they were not so definitely reported. The final, unequivocal movement found in the silhouettes was not attained in the other problems because *O's* control of the situation was less complete. That is to say, there was always opportunity for balls to roll in a relatively unpredicted direction, and digressions of the pencil from the line were never entirely eliminated. But once position of a block in its precise relation to every other block in any given silhouette figure was "learned," placing the block was unequivocal.

Continuity of movement and function develops from discrete phases of object-movements with their antecedents and sequels in each problem, but perhaps it is most clearly observed in the linear tracings. Here the performance may be finally reported as "movement in one continuous sweep accompanied by perceiving the course of the line." . . .

SUMMARY OF RESULTS

The task, determination, accessory factors, and motor phase heretofore described in some detail must now be brought together into a consideration of the entire integrated functional course of the action. The essential changes found to occur under repetition must be summed up and briefly presented all together. The entire integrated course, which includes the prophetic anticipation of something-to-be-done, the forecasting of, and providing for, accomplishment through movement, has been described, phase by phase, in each of the three problems of this study. We recapitulate in order.

Problem I. Capturing. Appearance of the successive phases of acting was facilitated by the natural subdivision of the problem into the capture one by one of the individual balls. *O* sometimes established a general task covering the entire performance of caging all four balls: sometimes he set a specific task bearing upon the penning up of a single ball. It was possible for the determination to follow . . . directly from the task or to develop by degrees out of the demands of the task. Often no functional representation of determining was reported. There appeared also an intermediate stage wherein both task and determination were monophasic. The motor stage with its preceding and succeeding moments, forming the central part of the resolution, also came to be telescoped and abbreviated. Accessory factors were present throughout the early execution of a given performance, but after several repetitions these were usually reported in terms of a generalized and undetailed perceiving coincident with the movement . . .

Problem II. Silhouettes. The same phases appeared in this series and underwent by repetition similar modifications. Although *O* was provided with more freedom in setting this task, his formulations were nevertheless classifiable into general, specific and secondary. In the well-isolated preliminary period (when *O* considered, without handling, the blocks) the development of determination was most clearly demonstrated. That abbreviation or substitution of a part for the entire determining phase may occur was also demonstrated in this previsory period. Ligation and stabilization of the motor phase occurred unevenly. That is to say, the precise spatial relations of a few blocks in any given pattern were established more rapidly than the position of other blocks. But finally a complete ligation did appear. Accessory factors were present at all times. Under repetition they became fewer and fewer and the commentaries took the form of perceptive accompaniments to the main operation in course . . .

Problem III. Tracing. Tasking in this exercise appeared, as before, in general, specific, and secondary forms. Like the first problem, again, this had moments of task and determination combined in the same functional phase. Determination was less fully reported in this problem than in Problems I and II, but hints of its presence were plentiful. Antecedents and sequels of the motor phase were somewhat more frequently reported. Accessory factors were also numerous . . .

Repetition was found variously to affect each of the phases in course. Changes were in the direction of (1) elaboration and in the direction of (2) abbreviation, of (3) inclusion and of (4) elimination. (5) Ligation and (6) stabilization also marked the total course. Modifications were greater in some parts than in others and were also more clearly described in some problems than in others.

Elaboration of *task* occurred in the setting of secondary tasks during resolution. The general initial task especially called for subdivision and recasting to attain a satisfactory resolution. Elaboration was also apparent in the intermediate stage, when determination was released. Here new and detailed directions for resolution were profitable, *e.g.* "go around to the right carefully and keep the pencil-point on the line." Here task lasts over into the determining phase.

The task was at all times fairly well ligated to the rest of the performance in the first and third problems, while the second exercise brought out a progressive and developing ligation between the two parts. That is to say that, in the first presentations of the silhouettes, the developing determination—often incomplete—separated task from resolution in a manner not observed in later repetitions, when task "to make this thing" flowed directly into determination with every following movement forecast. Very early in the serial performance of each exercise the task became stable and fixed.

The *determination* went through a special form of elaboration in the silhouette series. Subsequent abbreviation appeared when, after a few repetitions, the reported determination provided the means for solving one part of the figure only. Elimination of the determining phase was only apparent. Often it went unreported, but its presence was announced in the travel of the pencil beyond the turn or the unannounced returning of stray balls . . . Progressive smoothing and stabilizing of this phase appear when searching was replaced by perceptive and inspectional moments.

Changes in the *motor phase,* with its antecedents and sequels, occurred after the first repetitions of a performance, where many slips, errors, or false movements came in. As these were eliminated, this aspect was abbreviated, consolidated, and made precise.

The *accessory* factors are rarely elaborated but sometimes condensed under repetition. Their ligation to the rest of the operation appears unaffected by repetition: they are parenthetical accompaniments tied into the operation at any point with little effect upon the main course. Where they do come in they appear as moments in, or comments upon, the determination.

A careful comparison of reports selected from various temporal places has revealed typical progressive changes from trial to trial and from week to week. The most salient of these functional modifications are (1) the elimination of task, (2) elaboration followed by abbreviation of determination, (3) gradual diminution of accessory factors, and (4) final ligation of the whole operation into a rapid and accurate performance. Such modifications in course under repetition we have regarded as "learning," a term which more commonly implies gain or accomplishment of a useful sort. In this more uncritical sense, learning is inferred from reduced times, decreased errors, increased skill, or performance without a model and pattern, as in "nonsense" learning. It therefore obviously deals with end-results and products. It does not attempt to describe the fundamental processes by which "acquisition" is made possible. This description has been our chief aim and concern . . .

Much remains to be done. The present investigation has improved our understanding of what goes on in one variety of simple acting. Complex actions, choices, resolves, and equivocal situations remain for study in this single mode of operation, and enough has been done in a preliminary way to suggest that in the other primary modes of psychological functioning, too, the same fundamental facts of progressive change may be found to underlie the perfected or "learned" performance.

CONCLUSIONS

This study has described the functional course of certain instances of acting and it has tried to demonstrate how this sort of performance changes under repetition.

The successive phases of acting have been found to evolve from, and to be describable in terms of, a wide variety of interrelated functional moments. The task variously appears, determination develops out of many factors, and the whole leads on to motor resolution and accomplishment.

Functional modifications brought about by repetition have taken the two general directions of expansion and reduction. The final result has been described as a unified, stable, and highly integrated performance.

18. Intellectual Processes in a Sensori-Motor Performance*

An important problem in motor learning has to do with the role played by the cognitive or intellectual processes. To examine this specific question, Vince exercises considerable care in the selection of a motor task in which some cognitive anticipation or formulation of the correct response pattern is possible. Differences in the ways in which successful and unsuccessful subjects apparently employed cognitive processes to guide their performance are then examined.

Problem

Little is known about the change in, and development of, intellectual processes in the course of learning sensori-motor tasks. Tasks of this kind are often treated in isolation from the "higher" mental processes; and there is, perhaps, a reason for this. It is difficult to record directly changes in perception and concept while learning a skill.

Changes in perception and concept can be investigated however by an indirect method which depends on assuming that they are revealed in the character of the record of movements and its relation to the objective situation. This evidence can be checked by introspections and by other means. The method also depends on relating changes in the intellectual processes to the motor response, since the interaction of the motor and intellectual processes is of primary importance.

It is known that learning cannot take place without activity, but not known how the intellectual changes occur in relation to this activity. It is this problem which is to be considered.

Task and Procedure

A task was devised which requires a simple response, but one which to be successful has to become anticipatory, thus allowing for the building up of the intellectual element, and providing some opportunity for detecting and assessing the intellectual activity at various stages in the subject's performance.

It will have to be assumed that the nature of the motor response (e.g.

---

* M. A. VINCE. Reprinted with permission of the author and publisher from The part played by intellectual processes in a sensori-motor performance. *Quarterly Journal of Experimental Psychology*, 1953, 5:75–86.

whether it is anticipatory or not) provides some clue as to the stage of learning. It will be necessary to look for changes in the performance which indicate what stage has been reached. The existence of these stages, inferred from changes in the response, can be checked by other means.

The subject sat facing a screen, in which was a 6-in. vertical slit, 7.5 mm. wide. Behind the slit could be seen a single small black circle, 2.5 mm. in diameter, drawn on white paper. The subject was given the following instructions:—

> "You look at this slit and you will see this one circle. When I switch on, the paper will move and the circle will cross the slit and disappear in this direction. The circle is the first of a series of circles, which will appear one at a time. They may appear in any position in the slit. You have to try to draw a pencil line through the circles. You hold the pencil point always against the right hand side of the slit and you can move it up and down. Try not to follow the circles as they move across the slit, but to be ready for each one when it appears."

The paper band on which the circles were drawn moved from right to left. The circles therefore appeared without any warning from the side of the slit against which the subject was told to hold his pencil point. In order to hit a circle at all he had to predict its position, and move the pencil point to the part of the slit where it would appear. It was left to the subjects themselves to find out how the circles were arranged, and they were not told that there was a repeating pattern to be learnt.

The circles were arranged on the paper band in a repeating pattern of twenty-four (Fig. 1). Spaced at equal time intervals of 1 second, they lay on

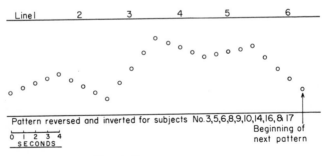

FIG. 1. PATTERN OF CIRCLES.

six straight lines, so that, not counting the first circle, there were always four, and then a change of direction. The lines were all at different angles from the vertical, in an irregular zig-zag. The slope of the line determined the rate of the required response, so that some parts of the pattern were "fast," and some "slow." The pattern was repeated just over four times in each record. There were in all eight records, and in each one the pattern began in a different place. At the end of the experiment subjects were asked to draw their idea of the pattern, and after each record they were asked for their introspections.

The subject's performance was scored by two methods. The first was simply to count the number of circles touched at any point by the pencil mark. The second was to go through each record, circle by circle, and decide from the tracing what the subject had been doing while waiting for the appearance of the next circle; had he, for example, made a "correct prediction" (a movement towards the circle), or an "incorrect prediction" (a movement away from the circle), or a "waiting response," in fact, no movement at all, leaving him in the position of the previous circle.

There were twenty subjects, of whom eleven were psychology students, six were research workers, two were air mechanics of the Fleet Air Arm, and one was a housewife.

Results

Scrutiny of the records revealed three stages in the learning of the skill.

First stage. At this stage the response was of the "waiting" type. This was made under two different conditions, first when the position of the next circle was not known, and secondly as a corrective movement when a mistake had been made. It was not a possible solution to the problem of hitting the circles, and had in fact to be abandoned before a successful prediction could be made.

Second stage. The response was now of the "predictive" type. Most subjects began to predict quite readily, and early in the experiment. After seeing one or two circles appear in line with one another, it was not difficult to predict another in the same line. This type of response led inevitably to overshooting at the points in the pattern where changes of direction occur, so that the pencil record often showed three correct predictions followed by an incorrect prediction (an overshoot), which was in line with the four preceding circles, although not with the whole pattern. This type marked an important stage in the learning because it emphasized the key points of the pattern—the corners which were continually overshot. It appeared that subjects who became conscious of these recurrent errors of overshooting, and who made some effort to avoid them, often managed to learn and predict correctly, usually by actually counting the circles, and turning the corner after the fourth. (A correct prediction at a corner will be referred to as a "correct anticipation," and a similar response, but made one circle too soon, as an "incorrect anticipation.")

Third stage. This stage, of correct anticipation of the corners, was the highest reached by any subject in this experiment. To predict all the circles it would be necessary to predict and respond accurately to the slope of each line. These stages were not often clearly separated from each other, although they sometimes were; it was usual for a record to contain isolated responses belonging to a higher stage, as well as some from a stage lower—some parts of the pattern were easier to learn than other parts. But with very few exceptions one type of response clearly predominated. These stages, which are illustrated in Figure 2, indicate re-

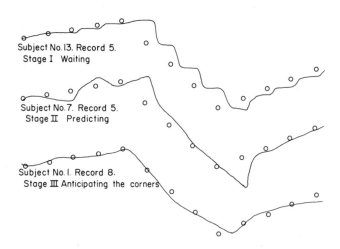

FIG. 2. LEARNING STAGES.

sponse first to single separate circles, then to parts of the pattern, and finally to the whole pattern.

The task given to the subjects was a fairly complex one, and the individual differences in achievement were considerable. This makes it difficult to state the results quantitatively. The intention is therefore to present them in a more general way, although no more than as hypotheses which may be tested in future experiments. A general picture of the results is given in Table I, in which subjects are ranked according to the number of correct predictions achieved in their best (which was not necessarily the last) record. Seventeen of the twenty subjects were ranked in this way, as

	PERFORMANCE			IDEA OF PATTERN					
Subject number	Max. number of correct predictions	Number of dots hit	In record number	Pattern repeats	Consists of six parts	Direction alternates	Rhythm (slow—quick—quick)	4 dots in each line	W or S
GROUP I									
1	96	48	8	R	—	R	R	R	—
2	95	49	7	R	R	R	R	R	S
3	93	37	8	R	—	R	—	R	S
4	92	56	6	R	R	R	R	R	S
5	88	17	8	R	R	R	R	R	—
GROUP II									
6	82	24	8	R	R	R	R	—	S, W
GROUP III									
7	77	12	8	—	—	—	R	—	W
8	76	14	7	R	R	R	R	—	S, W
9	75	29	4	—	—	R	—	—	—
10	75	20	5	—	—	R	—	R	W
GROUP IV									
11	71	24	8	R	R	R	R	—	—
12	69	40	7	—	—	R	—	R	—
13	69	22	8	R	R	R	R	—	W
14	68	20	6	—	—	R	—	—	—
15	67	13	8	—	—	R	—	R	W
16	50	15	8	—	—	R	—	—	—
17	27	12	7	—	—	—	—	—	—
GROUP V									
18	—	78	4	R	R	R	R	—	—
19	—	60	4	—	—	R	—	—	—
20	—	48	8	—	—	—	—	—	W

"R" indicates a correct idea.

In the last column "S" indicates a "step-like" distortion, and "W" a "wave-like" distortion.

Column 4 indicates the subject's best record; this being the one from which the scores in columns 2 and 3 are taken.

three performed the experiment in a way which prevented their records from being scored.

When subjects were thus ranked they seemed to fall into fairly well defined groups, the groups being distinguished in part by the stage of learning reached by the subjects. These groups will now be described. The appropriate figures are given in Table I.

Group I. The first group contains five subjects whose scores varied from 88 to 96 out of the possible total of 96, and who distinguished themselves by predicting correctly a whole pattern at least once in the course of the experiment, and by the clarity of their idea of the pattern as revealed in their drawings. They all assumed that there would be a pattern, and proceeded to build up an idea of it, putting in from the beginning a mixture of responses; waiting, predicting, overshooting and anticipating. Their introspections included much information about the pattern, and they appeared to be both formulating the problem and looking for solutions. The final solution to the problem depended on knowing the points at which changes of direction would occur. It involved therefore knowing and being able to make use of the information that there were four circles in each line. The way in which this information was obtained will be discussed later.

Example: Subject 1 (Research Worker). Began by predicting and overshooting, falling back on waiting when uncertain, or when expecting a change of direction. Began anticipating correctly and incorrectly in record 1, tried counting the circles in record 2 "to work out a rhythm." Learned line 3 in record 2, but had difficulty with lines 1 and 5. (Knew pairs of movements, but not how to join them.) She stated her difficulties: "I hit dots mainly on the quick ones, but sometimes move up too soon." She said she arrived at the solution to overshooting (the number of circles in each line) in record 5. Her drawing was correct except that it contained an extra peak. The learning curve rose steadily, having begun with 55 correct predictions in record 1.

Group II. The second group contains only one subject, who scored 82 correct predictions out of the possible total of 96, and who did not quite achieve one completely correct pattern. Her method appeared to be different in that she decided very quickly that the pattern of circles was a repeating one, and she worked all the time on this idea of the whole pattern.

Example: Subject 6 (Research Worker). In record 1 was waiting mostly and sometimes predicting and overshooting. Predictions increased in record 2, with some anticipations, mostly wrong. The number of correct anticipations increased gradually, mistakes occurring mostly in the same places. Introspections show that she was working on an idea of the whole pattern, conscious of repeating the same errors. Did not mention the number of circles (but when asked afterwards said: "They were more or less in units of four, I have just thought of that"). The drawing was mainly correct, but the number of circles wrong; and line 5 was drawn as wave-like. There were 28 correct predictions in record 1; then the learning curve rose fairly steeply.

Group III. In the third group there are four subjects, their maximum scores ranging from 75 to 77. They began well, but their learning curves rose little in the course of the experiment. Their introspections suggest that these subjects relied for learning mainly on "feel." With the exception of one subject who soon learnt the quicker parts of the pattern, there was little change in the nature of their responses; they remained throughout in the second stage of learning. Afterwards their idea of the pattern was much less clear than that of the subjects who ranked higher. Only one subject put in his drawing the main features of the pattern, and none put in the number of circles correctly, although one had stated the number correctly after his fifth record. These subjects did not appear to formulate the problem nor were they apparently worried by their repeated errors of overshooting. It is perhaps significant that all but one achieved a best record soon after the middle of the experiment, whereas most subjects were still learning on the seventh or eighth.

Example: Subject 10 (Student). Began predicting, sometimes wrongly, waiting occasionally, and anticipating changes of direction fairly often. His last record was much the same, with fewer anticipations. Knew the number of circles, stated after record 5: "I noticed they were in groups of four, so it will be easier to anticipate changes of direction." Did not formulate the difficulties; continued to overshoot. Introspections became more vague and general: "there is a subconscious patterning. I push the pencil one way without knowing why and sometimes hit a dot." Said afterwards was relying largely on feel. Drawing poor—including nine peaks of various sizes. Learning curve began with 66 correct predictions, fell slightly, then rose a little.

Group IV. With the lowest scores, ranging from 27 to 71, comes a group of seven subjects which is less homogeneous than the other groups, but which have in common the fact that they spent too long in the first learning stage, that of the waiting response. They either began with or fell back upon the waiting response, regarding it as a possible solution to the problem. It was the wrong solution and could never be successful, but some subjects were convinced that if they could move fast enough when a circle appeared they would succeed in hitting it. In their introspections these subjects emphasized the difficulties of the task, or the dangers of incorrect prediction. Five of them were unable to draw the pattern, although the other two knew the shape of the pattern, but not the number of circles. Most of them were still learning at the end of the experiment.

Example: Subject 12 (Research Worker). Spent about half of record 1 waiting, then fell into predicting and waiting at the corners. This method continued until the end of the experiment with only occasional anticipations, and occasional overshoots. Hit a large number of circles. Stressed the difficulties; worked out a "safe" method. After record 7 said: "It is necessary to be confident that one does one step properly and to continue to pay attention to that, rather than to try to leave that to be done automatically, and try to work out more complicated stages; if one does the latter, the former goes wrong." Knew the number of circles early; the drawing gave three series of four circles, on slightly different slopes, did not know the relationship between them. The learning curve began with 35 correct predictions, and rose unevenly.

Group V. The final group contains the three subjects whose records were not scorable because they used a different method. They concentrated mainly on the problem of hitting the circles and were highly successful in this respect.

Example: Subject 20 (Fleet Air Arm). Began with few predictions, often wrong. Then appeared to be waiting for each circle and shooting towards and past it when it appeared. Thus produced up and down movements, one for each circle. Was responding to the timing. After record 2 said: "It seems as if a certain number have the same interval between them, and if you timed the stroke, you could hit the dot." Continued in this method until the end; drawing very poor, including a horizontal line.

DISCUSSION

The results will be discussed in terms of the differences between groups. The discussion falls under four different, but related headings.

1. THE ORIGIN OF THE IDEA OF THE PATTERN.

The nature of the task made it essential for the subjects to anticipate; it was not possible to succeed by responding to each circle separately. It was necessary to build up a correct idea of the whole pattern. The subjects realized this, and all but one mentioned the pattern as important. The results showed that, in general, a good drawing of the pattern corresponded with the capacity to predict it well, although there were exceptions to this which will be considered later.

But, in addition to this, it was possible to relate the drawing of the pattern more closely with the motor record, by investigating the origin of distortions which occurred in the drawings. Half of the subjects introduced distortions into their drawings. These distortions are not readily explicable if considered only in relation to the actual pattern, but may be understood in relation to the mode of response.

One example of this was that five subjects (Nos. 6, 7, 8, 10 and 14) reproduced one or sometimes both of the slower parts of the pattern as a series of small waves. When their records were examined, it was found that their drawings corresponded well with their patterns of response. It is true that an uneven or wave-like response did occur in many records, including some where the subject drew the pattern as a series of straight lines. But when the single wave-like responses in the final record were counted, it was found that those subjects who reproduced the pattern as wave-like had produced far more of these irregular responses (between seven and eighteen) than the remainder, the number here varying from 0 to six only. Wave-like responses of this kind can be shown to be built up in the course of predicting the pattern of circles, and so not to result solely from an assumption that the line is a wavey one. They occur in the flatter (and consequently from the subject's point of view, the slower) parts of the pattern, such as lines 1 and 2 or 4 and 5 (Fig. 1). When a sub-

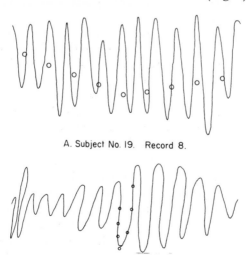

A. Subject No. 19.   Record 8.

FIG. 3. RELATION BETWEEN NATURE OF RESPONSE AND IDEA OF PATTERN.

ject overshoots at the end of line 3 or 6 (the quicker lines) he has to reverse the direction of his response on seeing the first circle in the next line, and often makes a rapid movement which takes him far beyond the second circle, and this causes him to reverse the direction of his response again, and so on. It is perhaps significant that three of these five subjects were members of Group III.

Again, six subjects (Nos. 2, 5, 6, 8, 11 and 15) revealed signs in their drawings of an error illustrated in Figure 3 from the records of subject 2. Line 1 or 4 in the pattern was begun with a rapid long movement which then flattened off (a "step-like" error in Table I). This is believed to be the effect of overshooting the previous lines so that the next movement in the opposite direction as far as the first circle is in fact larger than the subsequent movements. Something of this kind is described by subject 2 at the end of his second record: "Sometimes there has been a large step followed by smaller ones." He overshot very little after his third record, but the effect persists in his drawing. Although the overshooting which had given rise to this idea had long disappeared from the motor record, the idea of the pattern introduced a characteristic error into his responses (Fig. 3B). This was to begin line 4 with a quick downward movement at roughly the same speed as the previous quick line.

There were two atypical drawings which also illustrate this point. Subject 3, who was able to predict correctly, drew the pattern as a series of vertical rows of circles which suggest that the actual vertical response guided by the edge of the slit may have played a part in his reproduction of the pattern . . .

Distortions of this kind provide evidence of a concept affecting the response. They suggest further that this concept has its origin in the whole situation, including the subject's motor responses; that it is in fact based on experience rather than on the objective situation alone.

It is true that these examples are exclusively distortions of the pattern. This does not imply that the response distorts the idea. It merely means that in this particular situation it is only the evidence provided by distortions which is unambiguous in elucidating the origin of the idea.

It is not suggested that the motor response alone provides the basis for the idea of the pattern. As has been mentioned, success in the motor performance does correlate with a clear idea of the pattern, but by no means completely. In spite of their capacity to predict the pattern without any errors, subjects 1 and 3 in particular were uncertain when they came to draw it; while subjects 11 and 13 reproduced the pattern adequately, although they were unable to predict it correctly, and, in addition, subject

18 produced a general idea of the pattern which was correct, although his mode of response alone (a rapid "scanning") could not provide any simple basis for this. This feature of the results will be discussed further in Section 4.

The evidence suggests that the origin of the idea of the pattern is to be found only indirectly in the actual pattern. The actual pattern to which the subject responds may, from his point of view, be changed by his responses. The movements, although made in response to the actual circles, may sometimes explain distortions in the idea of the way in which they are placed.

Two similar experiments, using the same apparatus, but without the subject making an overt response, help to show what is meant by a response in this context. In the first, twenty subjects were instructed merely to watch the circles as they appeared in the slit, and to work out how they were arranged on the paper band. After seeing eight records they were asked to draw the pattern. No subject in this group made errors in his reproduction comparable to the "wave-like" and "step-like" errors of many subjects in the first experiment. A further group of ten subjects was given the same task, but in this case the instructions were to think of drawing a line through the circles. In this group two subjects made drawings which included both types of distortion. Both of these subjects said that they were following the circles with their eyes. "I am painting the line with my eyes," and "I was actually moving my eyes up and down to draw temperature charts."

2. THE SUBJECT'S FORMULATION OF THE PROBLEM.

Success in this task depended on developing an idea of the pattern of circles as a whole, but the conditions made this difficult; the subjects were, in fact, presented with a problem, and their success depended to a considerable extent on how they formulated it. They were given no guidance, and they differed markedly in their approach.

Some subjects considered their performance in relation to the external situation, their errors and the completeness of their idea of the pattern or worked out different methods of tackling the problem, while others did none of these things. The point which emerges is that the most successful subjects, those in Groups I and II, were those who formulated the problem in terms of the task itself and looked for solutions, while the third group relied on "feel" or on some kind of "subconscious patterning" (in the words of subject 10) and did not try to formulate the problem. The fourth and least successful group contained those subjects who formulated the problem, but incorrectly, by considering objections or difficulties which were irrelevant (such as reaction time), or which made the solution more difficult (an unwillingness to predict because of the confusion produced by an incorrect prediction, or the adoption of the waiting method as a possible solution). It might be concluded from this that a tendency to formulate the problem represents a danger only, as in this case it resulted in seven subjects (Group IV) failing to some extent, while only six (Groups I and II) benefited from it. The difference is however a clear one: the successful subjects formulated the problem correctly, on the basis of their experience; they followed the evidence and tried to correct tendencies to respond at variance with the pattern. The unsuccessful subjects either failed to make this correction (Group III) or brought in extraneous concepts which prevented them from following the evidence (Group IV).

An incorrect formulation was not a purely intellectual error but could prevent the subject from responding in a way which might lead to a more correct formulation.

On account of this kind of incorrect hypothesis, a number of subjects in Group IV in particular continued to respond in a way which failed to emphasize the key points of the pattern (waiting response as in Fig. 2); these key points were emphasized for those subjects who made straightforward predictive responses in line with the pattern (as in the early record of subject 2, Fig. 3, or subject 7 in Fig. 2). It is apparent that the formulation of the problem was not exclusively an intellectual process, but depended also on the nature of the performance. The problem could not be formulated until the subject had some idea of the pattern; and his idea of the pattern depended in part at least on the level of his activity, so that the successful subjects did in fact provide themselves with more information than the unsuccessful ones.

However, it is clear from the performance of subject 12, for example, that given enough time he might have constructed an idea of the pattern in a way which depended less on successful activity than on intellectual effort. The same is true of subject 18, although his approach was different. Again, this raises an apparent inconsistency which will be discussed in Section 4.

In building up a useful idea of what to do in this kind of situation, it may be a help to formulate the problem in terms of the whole situation. It may be a danger, however, if this formulation is one-sided, or if it is accepted too early, and not changed in the light of further activity.

3. THE TAKING OF A STEP FROM ONE STAGE OF LEARNING TO A HIGHER STAGE.

Bryan and Harter (1897, 1899), in their study of the telegraphic language, developed the concept of learning stages; skill depends on the building up of a hierarchy of habits; the elements must be learned first, and the advance to a higher stage depends on the elements becoming automatic; the learning of the elements is, however, only perfected at a higher stage; in each stage of learning the foundation is being laid for the advance to the higher stage, but the actual taking of this step depends on a strenuous and increasing effort. Book (1925) in his study of typewriting comes to similar conclusions.

In the present experiment the task is simpler than and rather different from telegraphy or typing, but here as well definite stages of learning can be distinguished. The stages exist as noticeably distinct modes of response in the graphic records, and so provide evidence of the idea of the pattern with which the subject was working. For example, the early record of subject 2 in Figure 3 shows that this subject understood the general trend of the pattern, but did not know when changes of direction would occur, while the waiting responses of subject 13, reproduced in Figure 2, show that he was probably uncertain even of the general trend.

There are three main factors which relate to the question of whether or not a subject would advance to a higher stage: (1) the nature of the responses, (2) the attitude of the subject towards his errors and (3) a tendency for the responses to become automatic.

The first factor has partly been dealt with in the preceding section, but the details need investigation. The crucial information in this case was the number of circles in each line; ability to utilize this information gave mastery over the key points of the pattern—the changes of direction. Three subjects in Group I counted the circles from the beginning and appeared to build an idea of the pattern round this information. The other two decided to count the circles as a solution to the problem of overshooting and as soon as they had counted correctly their performance improved. Of the subjects in the three other groups, only three mentioned the circles and these all counted them correctly. Subject 6 knew the number when asked afterwards, but had not thought of it before and had not made use of it. Subject 10 (Group III) said after record 5, "I noticed they were in groups of four, so it is easier to anticipate changes of direction," but did not go on to do so. The other subjects in Group III did not seem to be worried by their repeated errors of overshooting. In Group IV, subject 12 stated the number correctly after record 4, but this had no effect on his performance, and subject 16 grasped the number in record 7, confirming it in 8, but again made no use of the information.

This evidence is slight, but it raises an important point in connection with the relation between the motor and intellectual aspects of the task. It seems probable that the crucial information (which in this case could be grasped at any stage in the learning) could only be effectively utilized when the performance reached a certain level. In fact, this information was needed at a definite stage in the learning at the point when over-shooting arose and was recognized as a problem.

The ability to advance from stage II to stage III therefore appeared to depend on two factors: the possession of a fairly coherent idea of the pattern, based on effective responses, and also a determination to complete this idea with the information required to eliminate errors.

This leads on to the second factor: the attitude of the subjects towards their errors. It is clear that subjects who became aware of making repeated errors, and tried to correct them, improved, while those who were either not worried by overshooting or were so cautious that they did not make mistakes, did not. Errors followed inevitably from attempts to vary re-sponses away from the earlier and lower stages of learning. This point underlines that of Bryan and Harter, that the taking of a step towards a higher learning stage depends on strenuous effort on the part of the learner. A fairly universal feature of the learning is an increase in incor-rect anticipations which is either simultaneous with or precedes a rise in the number of correct anticipations. But the subjects were then affected differently. Whereas those in Group I solved the problem presented by this increase in errors, those members of the other groups who tried anticipating and made mistakes gave up the attempt. As a result of their errors, they either regressed to an earlier stage of learning, or remained in the same stage. The cautiousness of some subjects in Group IV was caused by an unwillingness to make mistakes. Subject 14 fell back on the waiting response in his eighth record because of dissatisfaction with his performance.

It seems that taking a step towards a higher stage of learning involves the hazarding of solutions which, if not quite correct, often result in errors; at this point success depends on whether or not the subject is able or willing to persist, and the situation is complicated further by the fact that success also depends on discarding incorrect "solutions."

The third factor, also referred to by Bryan and Harter, concerns the necessity for responses to become automatic before the step to a higher stage is possible. In the present less complex task there is little direct evidence for this. One or two introspections are interesting in this connection. At the end of the experiment, subject 16 remarked that he had been so busy in the early part of the experiment that he had not thought of the possibility of there being a pattern; and after record 3, having stated his difficulties, subject 2 said: "I shall have more time now and skill, I shall be able to think more as I go along."

4. SUMMARY: THE RELATION BETWEEN THE MOTOR AND INTELLECTUAL ASPECTS OF THE TASK.

There is a complex relation between the motor and intellectual aspects of this task. Its exact nature needs further investigation, but a number of points have arisen which provide some guidance.

In particular, the graphic record reveals something of the intellectual processes, even if this needs to be supplemented by introspections and the drawings of the pattern. But the actual situation alone is not sufficient to explain the motor record except at a very early stage in the learning. The pattern of circles alone could not produce the wave-like distortion in some drawings; but it was sufficient to provide for the wave-like responses which helped to determine the subject's perception, his idea of the pattern and so at a later stage could perpetuate the wave-like error.

It is important, therefore, to consider the subject's own view of the situation when his attention has been channelled by his activity; and in this task which requires predictive movements, his responses can reveal what he thinks the pattern is like. Whether objectively right or wrong they show what he is trying to do.

However, the experiment has raised some problems: it has been indicated that the intellectual activity is important in the learning; for example, in formulating the problem, in correcting errors and so on. At the same time it has been shown that this intellectual activity cannot be considered in separation from the motor activity: in that the subject's idea of the pattern is to some extent determined by it, and in that the development of the intellectual activity may depend very largely on the character of the motor response (as in seeking the final solution to the problem of hitting the circles).

But there were difficulties: in general, when the number of correct predictions was large, the drawing of the pattern was good, but there were cases where the drawing was a little better than the subject's predictions (e.g. subjects 11, 13 and 18). In addition, it was possible for subjects to predict the pattern correctly and afterwards make errors in their drawing. The inconsistency implied by this could be resolved by considering the intellectual activity as an abstraction from the whole situation, including the motor responses, in fact, from the subject's total experience in this task. As has been shown, subjects tended to take a one-sided view of the situation, some concentrating mainly on the "feel" of their responses, and those whose responses were not completely correct, but who nevertheless gained a good idea of the pattern were clearly attending more to the actual pattern of circles. It is not implied by this that a change in the motor response must be followed inevitably by a change in the intellectual activity; in fact, the conditions in which this occurs are what need investigating.

There is evidence that the responses played a part in the structuring of the pattern, but the details are not known. This experiment could be improved by changing the pattern to one requiring less stereotyped responses. If the pattern were more complex and subjects were allowed to choose a path, it is likely that their drawings of the pattern would vary more. It would then be possible to compare this with their final path, and to work backwards through their records to find out how the idea arose.

REFERENCES

1. BOOK, W. F. *The Psychology of Skill*. New York: Gregg Pub. Co., 1925.
2. BRYAN, W. L., HARTER, N. 1897. Studies in the physiology and psychology of the telegraphic language. *Psychol. Rev.* 4:27–53.
3. BRYAN, W. L., HARTER, N. 1899. Studies on the telegraphic language; the acquisition of a hierarchy of habits. *Psychol. Rev.* 6:345–75.

CHAPTER : 6

Attitudinal Learning

19. An Experimental Approach to the Study of Attitudes*

> Sherif's study is an excellent example of how a social psychologist
> may profitably use the resources and techniques of the psychological
> laboratory for the more precise investigation of certain social phe-
> nomena. He is here concerned with the effects of an attempt by one
> person to influence judgments by another toward a predetermined
> norm. How such suggestion affects the subsequent judgments of the
> naive subject in a series of judgments made individually is the crux
> of this investigation of one aspect of attitude formation.

. . . Taking the stimulus side of the problem into consideration, it will
be safe to say this: indefinite, unstructured fields of stimulation are especially useful in getting positive results in experiments dealing with the
influence of suggestion and kindred social influence. In such cases the
stimulus field more easily yields itself to organization in different ways.
In this paper our aim is to show how an indefinite stimulus field can be
organized or determined by one kind of social influence.

In our opinion autokinetic movement is a very convenient phenomenon
which can be utilized to investigate in the laboratory various kinds of
social influence. Experimentally it is easy to produce autokinetic movements. In a completely dark room a single point of light which is fixed
at some distance from us and which is physically stationary cannot be

* MUZAFER SHERIF. Abridged with permission of the author and publisher from
Sociometry, 1937, 1:90–98. J. L. Moreno, M.D., Editor. Beacon House, Inc., publishers.

209

localized at a fixed point in space. It moves, and may move in any direction, because there are no other visible points or objects in relation to which it can be localized.

The present experiment is an extension of the results of the previous experiments with the autokinetic movement. It will suffice in this paper to give the main findings of the previous experiments . . . For our present purposes the main findings may be summarized in a few sentences:

When an individual perceives autokinetic movement which lacks an objective standard of comparison, and is asked during repeated stimulation to report in terms of the extent of movement, he subjectively establishes a range of extent and a point (a standard or norm) within that range which is peculiar to himself, differing from the range and point (standard or norm) established by other individuals.

When individuals face the same unstable, unstructured situation as members of a group *for the first time,* a range and a norm (standard) within that range are established which are peculiar to the group. When a member of a group faces the same situation subsequently *alone,* after once the range and norm of his group have been established, he perceives the situation in terms of the range and norm that he brings from the group situation.

The ranges and norms established in the above cases are not prescribed arbitrarily by the experimenter or by any other agent. They are formed in the course of the experimental period and may vary from individual to individual, or from group to group, within certain limits.

Our concern being the study of social influence, we may go further and put the question: can we experimentally make the subject adopt a prescribed range and norm directed by specific social influences?

Different kinds of social influences may be experimentally utilized to define certain prescribed ranges and norms. Among many possible ones we took the following: (a) The influence of group situations on the individual as a member of the group. We have already mentioned the main conclusion of this previous work. (b) The influence of the direct suggestion of the experimenter in raising or lowering the reported extents of movement. (c) The influence of a fellow member with prestige (cooperating with the experimenter) on another ("naive") member of the group. (d) The influence of one naive member on the judgments of another. In this last case there is no prestige effect, because the subjects have not met each other prior to the experiment.

We shall say only a few words about the experiments under (b). If the subject is distributing his judgments, say, about three inches, without any socially introduced influence, the remark of the experimenter, "you are underestimating the distances" tends to raise the point round which the judgments are distributed to about five or six inches.

The following experiment under (c) shows how the autokinetic phenomenon can be utilized as a sensitive index of the prestige effect of one person on another:

Here we report verbatim the account of an experiment with prestige:

"Miss X and I (Assistant in Psychology, Columbia University) were subjects for Dr. Sherif. I was well acquainted with the experiment but Miss X knew nothing whatsoever about it. Since she was a close friend of mine, and I carried some prestige with her, Dr. Sherif suggested that it would be interesting to see if we could predetermine her judgments. It was agreed beforehand that I was to give no judgments until she had set her own standard. After a few stimulations it was quite clear that her judgments were going to vary around five inches. At the next appropriate stimulation, I made a judgment of twelve inches. Miss X's next judgment was eight inches. I varied my judgments around twelve inches and she did the same. Then I changed my judgment to three inches, suggesting to Dr. Sherif that he had changed it. She gradually came down to my standard, but not without some apparent resistance. When it was clear that she had accepted this new standard, Dr. Sherif suggested that I make no more judgments lest I might influence hers. He then informed her on a subsequent stimulation that she was underestimating the distance which the point moved. Immediately her judgments were made larger and she established a new standard. However, she was a little uneasy with it all, and before the experiment had progressed much farther, whispered to me, 'Get me out of here.'

"When we were again in my office, I told her that the point had not moved at all during the experiment. She seemed quite disturbed about it, and was very much embarrassed to know that we had been deceiving her. Noting her perturbation, I turned the conversation to other matters. However, several times during our conversation she came back to the subject, saying, 'I don't like that man' (referring to Dr. Sherif) and similar statements indicating her displeasure with the experience. It was not until some weeks later when she was again in my office that I discovered the full extent of her aversion. I asked her to serve as a subject for me in an experiment and immediately she exclaimed, 'Not down in *that* room,' pointing to Dr. Sherif's experimental room."

The experiment which will be given presently deals with the influence of a fellow member in the adoption of a prescribed norm. There were seven groups in this experiment, each group consisting of two members. In every group one subject cooperated with the experimenter, i.e., deliberately distributed his judgments within the range and around the norm assigned to him by the experimenter beforehand. The other subject was unaware of his predetermination. The degree of this "naive" subject's conformity to the norm and range of the cooperating subject may be taken as the index of the social influence. In all the groups the subject who was cooperating with the experimenter was the same person. This was done in order to keep the influencing member constant in all groups.

The range and norm prescribed for every group were different. For the first group, the prescribed range was 1–3 inches, 2 inches being the prescribed norm. For the second group, the prescribed range was 2–4, and 3 inches the norm, and so on to the eighth group for which the range and norm were 7–9 and 8 respectively. It will be observed that the prescribed range was rather narrow; consequently in the course of the experimental period the cooperating subject gave no judgments which deviated from the norm by more than one inch in either direction.

In the first experimental session, both subjects (the cooperating and the "naive") took part. After each exposure of the point of light for two seconds, the subjects spoke their judgments aloud one at a time and the experimenter recorded these on separate sheets of different colored pads. In order not to stress the factor of primacy, the cooperating subject was instructed to let the other subject utter his judgment first, at least half of the time. The social influence in our previous experiments with the autokinetic effect was found to be not so much a function of this and that separate judgments as of the temporal sequence of judgments. Fifty judgments were taken from each subject.

In the second session only the naive subject was present, so that we might see how much of the prescribed range and norm he carried from the first group session. In this individual session also, fifty judgments were taken . . .

In the presentation of results we give the prescribed range and norm, and the norm, and the number of judgments of the "naive" subject falling within the prescribed range, and his norms (as represented by the median of the distribution of his judgments) in the first (group) and second (individual) sessions. The means and medians of the distributions of the judgments given by the cooperating subject in the group sessions are not exactly identical with the prescribed norms, though the modes and ranges are the same. We did not think it necessary for him to memorize a perfectly normal distribution. Our aim is chiefly to show a fundamental psychological tendency related to norm-formation.

GROUP 1

Prescribed	Experimentally obtained (from "naive" S)	
	Session I (in group)	Session II (alone)
Range 1–3 inches	1–5	1–4
Norm 2	3.36	2.62
No. of the 50 judgments falling within the prescribed range ...	41	47

At the end of the second (individual) session the subject was asked to answer in writing four questions related to the problem. The answers to two of the questions further verify our former results. We shall therefore confine ourselves to the introspections given to the other two questions which are important for our present paper. These questions were: (1) What was the distance that the light most frequently moved? (This was formulated to find out whether the subjects became conscious of the norm formed in the course of the experiment); (2) Were you influenced by the judgments of the other person who was present during the first session? (This question was formulated in order to find out whether the subjects were conscious of the fact that they were being influenced by the cooperating subject).

The introspections of the subject in Group 1 are important for any theory of suggestion and norm formation:

1. "Most frequent distance was 2 inches. Seemed to be more consistently 2 inches second day than on first day.

2. "Yes, they were despite my efforts to be impartial. Probably many of my judgments were inordinately large because of small distances given by other subject. I think this was an attempt at avoiding suggestion and in so doing going to the other extreme. I do not think I was influenced by first day's judgments on the second day. I tried to be impartial in my judgments the first day. I felt resentment toward the other subject the first day because of the successive equal judgments by him. I tried to be objective toward this feeling: that is to banish the thought. But I feel that this

resentment caused my judgments to differ from his by a greater amount than they would have if the judgments had been kept separate; that is if I had not heard his judgments. The second day I felt more independence in my judgments and I believe that these judgments were therefore more accurate."

GROUP 2

Prescribed	Experimentally obtained (from "naïve" S)	
	Session I (in group)	Session II (alone)
Range 2–4 inches	1–10	1–5
Norm 3 inches	4.25	3.77
No. of the 50 judgments falling within the prescribed range ...	30	43

The introspections to the two questions were:

1. "Three or four inches were the most frequent estimates.

2. "No, I was not influenced by the other person. This I believe was because I stated my estimates first for the most part."

GROUP 3

Prescribed	Experimentally obtained (from "naïve" S)	
	Session I (in group)	Session II (alone)
Range 3–5	2–8	3–6
Norm 4	4.61	4.57
No. of the 50 judgments falling within the prescribed range ...	43	49

The introspections follow:

1. "(a) 4 inches yesterday.
   "(b) 5 inches today.

2. "Yes, my first judgments are much higher than those following. In a way I scaled them down to ranges nearer to his. The majority of times I gave my judgments first. The same distance seemed shorter after a few trials. My judgments were influenced by yesterday's. I measured them by the same scale both days."

GROUP 4

Prescribed	*Experimentally obtained (from "naive" S)*	
	Session I (in group)	Session II (alone)
Range 4–6	3–6	3–6
Norm 5	5.20	5.21
No. of the 50 judgments falling within the prescribed range ...	47	46

The introspections:

1. "5 inches.
2. "For the first three or four times. After that, no."

GROUP 5

Prescribed	*Experimentally obtained (from "naive" S)*	
	Session I (in group)	Session II (alone)
Range 5–7	3–7	3–7
Norm 6	5.50	5.42
No. of the 50 judgments falling within the prescribed range ...	34	35

The introspections:

1. "Five inches both days.
2. "No. I was not influenced by the presence of another person. But I sincerely believe that my partner was exaggerating the distance when he made his estimate. I say this because it seemed to me that he hesitated several seconds after I gave my estimate . . ."

GROUP 6

Prescribed	*Experimentally obtained (from "naive" S)*	
	Session I (in group)	Session II (alone)
Range 6–8	3–8	4–8
Norm 7	5.94	6.18
No. of the 50 judgments falling within the prescribed range ...	24	27

The introspections:

1. "7 most frequent, 5 next frequent.
2. "No, I was not influenced."

GROUP 7

Prescribed	Experimentally obtained (from "naive" S)	
	Session I (in group)	Session II (alone)
Range 7–9	4–12	6–9
Norm 8	7.40	7.83
No. of the 50 judgments falling within the prescribed range ...	17	40

The introspections:

1. "The most frequent distance was about 8 inches. The next most frequent was about 7 inches.

2. "I think it did make a difference when somebody else was with me. When I gave my judgment first, there was no difference, of course, but when he was with me I sometimes, though not all the time, modified my judgment when it was very far from his, and when I thought that I might easily have been mistaken. Of course, this did not occur frequently, but I cannot deny that it happened sometimes."

GENERAL CONCLUSION

From these results we may conclude that the subjects may be influenced to perceive an indefinite stimulus field in terms of an experimentally introduced norm. The degree of the influence may be different in different subjects. It may be great as is the case of the subject of group 4. It may not be so striking as is the case of the subject of group 5. It may be negligible as is the case with the subject of group 6. Even in this last mentioned case, an influence on the norm (not in the range) is evident.

The introspections reveal that the subjects become conscious of the norm which develops in the course of the experiment. However, they need not be conscious of the fact that they are being influenced toward that norm by the other members of the group. (See introspections of the subjects in groups 1, 2 and 4.) In connection with this point, it is interesting to note that in some cases, the *conformity* to the prescribed range and norm when the *influencing* person is no longer present (Session II) is closer than the *conformity* produced by his actual presence. (See the results of groups 2, 3, 6, 7.)

It seems to us that the psychological process embodied in these facts may be basic to the daily phenomena of suggestion, especially to the role of suggestion in the formation of attitudes. It is not a rare occurrence in everyday life to react negatively or hesitatingly to suggestion on some topic raised by an acquaintance while in his presence, but to respond positively after leaving him (perhaps there is a disinclination to accept suggestions readily unless there is some strong prestige or pressing demand; to appear easily yielding is not so pleasant for an "ego").

Attitudes, whatever else they may be, imply *characteristic modes of readiness in reacting* to definite objects, situations and persons. Our experiment has demonstrated in a simple way how a *characteristic* kind of readiness may be experimentally obtained in relation to an indefinite stimulus field . . .

REFERENCES

1. GUILFORD, J. P., DALLENBACH, K. M. 1928. A study of the autokinetic sensation. *Amer. J. Psychol.* 40:83–91.
2. RICE, S. A. 1926. Stereotypes. A source of error in judging human character. *J. Person. Res.* 5:267–76.
3. SHERIF, M. 1935. A study of some social factors in perception. *Arch. Psychol.* 27: No. 187.

20. Attitude Change Through Modification of Attitude Structure*

One of the more interesting characteristics of human behavior is the disposition to accept a situation or happening if it is compatible with one's own goals, and to reject the situation if it is not. Carlson describes a controlled experiment designed to change the liking or affective aspects of an attitude toward a social problem in the light of highly valued goals of the subjects. He reports his findings of the relationships between attitude affect and valued goals and considers these with respect to the strength of the initial attitude.

* EARL R. CARLSON. Reprinted and abridged with permission of the author and publisher from the *Journal of Abnormal and Social Psychology*, 1956, 52:256–61.

There is wide agreement that "attitudes" are complex, in that they are composed of a number of components, characteristics, or dimensions. Psychologists generally agree, also that changes in attitudes may come through the operation of different processes . . . There have been few studies, however, which attempted to differentiate either components of attitudes or the processes of change experimentally. The present study is of this nature—an investigation of the importance of two independent sources of *affect* (the liking or favorableness-unfavorableness aspect) of an attitude . . .

Attitude change . . . should result from changes in either the expected satisfaction from goals, or in the instrumental relationship perceived between the attitude object and the goal. The present study was designed to test this latter hypothesis—that changes in attitude (affect) result from altering perceptions of the attitude object (situation or event) as leading to the attainment of valued goals . . .

Method

The experimental procedure of the study was designed to increase the subjects' perception that "allowing Negroes to move into White neighborhoods" would be a means for attaining four specified goals, or values. The attitude issue of Negro housing segregation was selected as the vehicle for studying attitude and attitude structure change. Since the subjects varied widely in attitude on the issue, the attitude was relatively stable, yet some change could be produced using a limited experimental procedure. Attitudes on five related issues were also measured in order to test for generalization of attitude change.

The four values discussed in the experimental communication were (*a*) American prestige in other countries, (*b*) protection of property values, (*c*) equal opportunity for personal development, and (*d*) being experienced, broad-minded and worldly-wise. These values were selected on the basis of their probable importance for this issue.

The data were collected in three major stages. Early in the semester experimental and control *S*s were given attitude and value measures during regular class periods. Code numbers were used to maintain anonymity for the *S*s. The experimental change procedure was administered to the experimental *S*s in two parts: the first consisted of an assignment given by the instructor to be completed outside of class, one to two weeks after the initial measures were obtained; the second, five to ten days later, consisted of a prepared discussion given orally by the experimenter. After a further interval of three weeks the attitude and value measures were readministered to both experimental and control Ss . . .

In order to minimize the Ss' awareness of the nature of the study, the change procedure was presented as a separate experiment by a person not involved in the measurement of attitudes and value . . .

Attitude measures. The measures of attitude toward the primary issue of study, Negro housing segregation, and the five related attitude issues required the S to rank six alternatives (ranging from "I am completely opposed to allowing Negroes into White neighborhoods" to "I am completely in favor of allowing Negroes into White neighborhoods") in terms of the degree to which they represented the person's own opinion. The measure of the person's attitude position used in the analysis was coded directly from the S's first choice of the six alternatives. The measure of attitude change was obtained through coding the first three ranks given of the six alternative positions; using only transitive rankings, the three ranks gave a 16-point scale, ranging from position 1 (subject choosing alternatives in the order ABC), to position 2 (BAC), position 3 (BCA), and on to position 16 (FED). The Negro housing segregation measure had an uncorrected reliability of .67 for the control group . . .

Value measures. The measures of "value satisfaction" and "perceived instrumentality" required the Ss to rate each of the 25 value items given in Table 1. Two items, using different words but identical in meaning, were used within the set to measure each of the four areas selected for experimental change. The four sets of experimental items were items 5 and 19, items 8 and 11, items 10 and 22, and items 6 and 17. The remaining 17 values were selected to cover the broad range of further general goals in life that individuals regard as important in some degree. The items were presented on cards in random order, with a randomly assigned number on the card being used to record judgments of the value.

The value satisfaction index was obtained from Ss' ratings of the extent to which each value represented goals from which the S gets, or would get, satisfaction. Each value was judged independently in terms of 11 categories on a graphic rating scale. The scale of positively-valued goals was defined by three descriptive phrases: "No satisfaction from the goal" (Category 0), "Medium satisfaction from the goal" (Category 5), and "Maximum satisfaction from the goal" (Category 10). One further category was for judgments of "Dissatisfaction from the goal." The index of value satisfaction for the four experimental values was then obtained through arithmetic summation of the ratings of the eight items, coding

TABLE 1

Value Items Used in the Satisfaction and Instrumentality Ratings

---

Value Item

---

1. Everyone being assured of a good standard of living.
2. People sticking to their own groups.
3. People looking out for the welfare of others.
4. Being looked up to by others.
5. America having high prestige in other countries.
6. Being well-rounded, enlightened and sophisticated about life.
7. Serving the interests of the group to which one belongs.
8. Security of the value of one's real estate.
9. Having power and authority over people.
10. All persons having the chance to realize their potentialities.
11. Having the value of property well-protected.
12. Self-discipline—overcoming my irrational emotions and desires.
13. All human beings having equal rights.
14. Complying with the wishes of persons in authority.
15. Being like others in general; having the same interests, opinions and ways of behaving as other people have.
16. People having strict moral standards.
17. Being a person who is experienced, broad-minded, and worldly-wise.
18. The open expression of disagreement between people.
19. People in other nations respecting our principles and standards.
20. Being allowed to maintain the privacy of one's opinions and beliefs.
21. Being with other people; socializing.
22. Everyone having opportunity to develop himself and his capacities.
23. Letting others make their own decisions.
24. People being strongly patriotic.
25. Not being ashamed of one's own feelings and behavior.

"dissatisfaction" ratings minus 5. This index yielded an uncorrected test-retest reliability of .79.

The measure of "perceived instrumentality" required the Ss to judge each value in terms of the "probability that the goals will be attained by allowing Negroes to move into White neighborhoods." The judgments were made on an 11-point graphic rating scale defined by three descriptive phrases: "Maximum probability that the goal will be blocked by allowing Negroes to move into White neighborhoods" (Category −5), "Allowing Negroes to move into White neighborhoods is irrelevant to achieving the goal" (Category 0), and "Maximum probability that the goal will be achieved by allowing Negroes to move into White neighborhoods" (Category $+5$). The index of perceived instrumentality was a summation of the ratings of the eight experimental value items, and had an uncorrected test-retest reliability of .66.

An index of "affective loading" . . . was computed separately for the total set of 25 value items, the eight experimental items, and the 17 non-experimental value items . . .

Change in the value satisfaction ratings was not predicted, since the experimental procedure was directed only toward change in perceived instrumentalities, and no change was found. A significant proportion of experimental Ss, however, changed on the indices of affective loading based upon the eight experimental items . . . and on the total set of 25 items . . . Although not predicted, this change is consistent with the theory and with the rationale of the index, which is a direct function of instrumentality ratings as well as value satisfaction ratings. No systematic change was observed for the control group on the Negro segregation attitude scale or on any of the attitude structure measures.

It was anticipated prior to analyzing the data that Ss with different initial attitudes toward Negro housing segregation would react differently to the experimental procedure, but specific predictions were not made concerning the form of the relationships. No systematic differences were

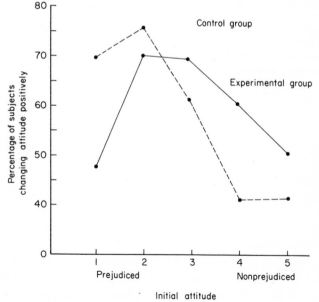

FIG. 1. RELATIONSHIP BETWEEN INITIAL ATTITUDE AND ATTITUDE CHANGE.

found for attitude structure changes, but the data clearly indicated a curvilinear relationship between initial attitude and attitude change for the experimental Ss, as shown in Figure 1. Tests comparing positive changes against the combination of no-change and negative-change Ss indicated that a significantly smaller proportion of Ss at position 1 (extreme prejudice) changed positively than Ss at positions 2 . . . and 3 . . . ; at position 4 the difference was at the .10 level. Similarly a significantly smaller proportion of Ss at position 5 changed positively than at positions 2 . . . and 4 . . . The Ss at the moderate positions (positions 2, 3, and 4) were found to be significantly influenced by the experimental procedure, while extremely prejudiced (position 1) and extremely non-prejudiced (positions 5 and 6) persons were not found to change systematically. An analysis of change in the control group is not meaningful as a result of the small number of Ss at each initial attitude position . . .

What accounts for this curvilinear relationship between initial attitude and change? The smaller proportion of positive changes at the non-prejudiced positions can be explained by the fact that the Ss already largely agreed with the change communication, and by the ceiling placed on change by the measuring instrument itself. The finding for experimental Ss of fewer positive changes in attitude for prejudiced Ss than for those at intermediate positions can be accounted for in terms of the possible wide range on the attitude continuum over which Ss at this extreme position may be spread. Some prejudiced Ss may have actual attitudinal positions far below the cutting-point between positions 1 and 2, and the same amount of actual positive change would result in fewer position changes than for Ss initially at other positions.

These findings indicate the importance of considering the possible interaction of initial attitude on effects of attitude change techniques. In the present study the absence of attitude change for Ss at the extreme positions prevented tests of the major hypotheses for these Ss. Consequently the analysis of relationships between attitude structure change and attitude change, and the generalizations from the findings, must be restricted to persons with moderate initial attitudes toward the issue.

RELATIONSHIPS OF ATTITUDE RANGE TO ATTITUDE STRUCTURE CHANGE

The hypothesis that Ss who changed in perceived instrumental relationships would also change in attitude was clearly supported by the data. Experimental Ss with moderate initial attitudes (positions 2, 3, and 4) who altered their perception of the relation of segregation to the values discussed also tended to change their attitude toward Negro housing seg-regation, this difference being significant at the .01 level . . .

Changes in the value satisfaction measures, if occurring, should covary with changes in attitude, but the amount of value satisfaction change was too slight to enable an adequate test of this relationship. Changes in atti-tude, however, were significantly related to the indices of affective load-ing, which reflected both instrumentality and value satisfaction changes. The relationship for the total set of 25 value items was significant at the .02 level . . . and the relationship for the eight experimental items was significant at the .05 level, measured in terms of a correlation coefficient . . . but not significant tested by chi-square analysis . . . A relationship found between attitude change and change in the index of affective load-ing for the 17 nonexperimental values . . . is also consistent with the theory, since the basic relationship between perceived instrumentality and attitude should hold for all values, whether experimentally manipulated or not.

What are the implications of these findings? This test does not account for all of the variance of attitude-affect change, certainly, but it has tested experimentally the significance of *one* important source of affect of an attitude. The role of perceived instrumental relations was demonstrated for Ss with non-extreme attitudes, but was not tested for persons ex-tremely prejudiced or extremely nonprejudiced . . .

Summary

This experiment was designed to test the hypothesis that attitudes toward an object, or situation, may be changed through altering the person's per-ception of the significance of the object as a means for attaining valued goals . . .

One hundred eighty-three experimental Ss responded to three sets of measures before and after a change procedure: (a) measures of attitude toward "allowing Negroes to move into White neighborhoods" and five related issues, (b) a measure requiring ratings of 25 general values in terms of the expected satisfaction from each, and (c) a rating measure of the 25 values in terms of the probability that "allowing Negroes to move into White neighborhoods" would lead to, or block, the attainment of each of the values. Thirty-nine control Ss took the same measures but did not receive the change procedure. The change procedure was designed to increase the Ss' awareness that nonsegregation would lead to the attain-ment of each of four important values.

The experimental procedure changed perceptions of the role of Negro housing segregation in attaining the four values, and changed attitude toward Negro housing segregation for Ss with moderate initial attitude on the issue. Insufficient attitude change was produced in extremely prejudiced and extremely nonprejudiced subjects to permit tests of the hypotheses for these Ss. Satisfaction ratings were not affected by the change procedure.

Changes in attitude were related significantly to changes in perceived instrumental relationships, and to changes in an index based upon both satisfaction and instrumentality ratings . . .

REFERENCES

1. ROSENBERG, M. J. *The Experimental Investigation of a Value Theory of Attitude Structure.* University of Michigan: Unpublished doctoral dissertation, 1953.
2. SARNOFF, I., KATZ, D. 1954. The motivational bases of attitude change. *J. Abnorm. Soc. Psychol.* 49:115–24.
3. SMITH, M. B. 1949. Personal values as determinants of a political attitude. *J. Psychol.* 28:477–86.
4. WOODRUFF, A. D., DiVESTA, F. J. 1948. The relationship between values, concepts, and attitudes. *Educ. Psychol. Measmt.* 8:645–59.

21. The Transmission of Authority Patterns in the Family*

The relationship between current attitudes of subjects toward authority and previous familial experience is the focus of this study. Family history documents are used by Ingersoll to classify family attitudes toward authority and to examine the process of the transmission of these attitudes to the subjects of the study. Excerpts from these documents illustrate concretely the patterns of change found.

PURPOSES OF THE STUDY

. . . The author's interest in changing authority patterns prompted the setting up of this research with the following purposes in mind: (*a*) *to*

* HAZEL L. INGERSOLL. Reprinted with permission of the author and publisher from A study of the transmission of authority patterns in the family. *Genetic Psychology Monographs,* 1948, 38:225–302.

establish a classification of authority patterns as found in the data, and *to describe each class* for purposes of differentiation; (*b*) to use these classes in *tracing the processes of authority transmission* from one generation to the next, and to attempt a scientific explanation of the transmission process as well as to account for some of the modifications and variations that result; and (*c*) *to illustrate the transmission* processes by using "ideal typical" cases from each authority classification.

DEFINITION OF CONCEPTS

. . . An authority pattern may be defined as a consistent organization of (*a*) leadership or control relative to family activity, and (*b*) accommodation of interpersonal relationships involving dominance and subordination. That authority of one member refers to the relative control he exercises over the other members of the family and over spheres of family activity. This control may be exercised in a variety of ways ranging from repressive or forceful means based on "respect, love, reverence or some emotional acceptance by other members of the family of the dominant member's claim to power." This authority becomes a pattern when interaction involving control becomes established in a fairly consistent organization of reciprocal behavior. It is assumed that these authority patterns can be described and classified.

Each authority pattern has its antecedence in the marriage relationship from the early authority interaction of husband and wife to the present control situation. Moreover, the partners have contributed to the authority pattern from their experiences before marriage and outside of marriage. The authority organization of each marriage partner, then, may include the origin of *all* the perceptions regarding authority he has acquired from childhood to the present. Each partner brings a latent self-other pattern derived from interaction with his parents into the present marriage where it influences the evolving control-relationship. The authority pattern which results from the husband-wife relationship is dependent upon (*a*) each partner's concept of his own authority role in the marriage, (*b*) his expectation of his partner's response to his role, and (*c*) the interaction of the two authority roles. Moreover, the authority pattern emerging from this interaction, although peculiar to the marriage of which it is a part, has characteristics in common with those of the same classification. It is on the basis of these common characteristics that the patterns can be described and classified . . .

Basic Assumptions

In addition to the concepts regarding authority relations, the investigator wishes to present the following as basic assumptions: (*a*) that authority in the family takes various forms ranging from autocracy through democracy to *laissez-faire;* (*b*) that the authority in a given sample of families may be exercised: by husband and wife jointly; by one partner controlling the other partner and the family members; or by each controlling his specified area in accordance with a division-of-labor in the family; (*c*) that patterns of authority found in a representative sample would range from the extreme father-controlled pattern through equalitarian or balanced patterns to those of extreme mother-control; (*d*) that authority may be exercised in a variety of ways, some overt, some covert, and irrespective of the accepted institutional pattern of masculine dominance, and therefore, control must be studied in its psychological context as well as in its behavioral manifestations; and (*e*) that the authority pattern developed in the family is related *first* to the internalized self-other patterns introjected from the authority roles of the parents; *second,* the accommodations of the partners (as the result of interaction) in the marriage relationship; *third,* so-called "personality" factors, as compulsive drives, emotional disturbances; and *fourth,* environmental circumstances.

Sources of Data and Methodology

The investigation used data from personal documents called *Family Histories* written by 37 senior students in a Family Relationships class. These histories were written according to a questionnaire-guide constructed by the investigator to bring out specific characteristics in the background, interpersonal relationships, and social-personal roles that may be associated with the authority patterns in the parental and grandparental families of the students. It covered the cultural milieu, family background, school adjustment, vocational history of both the present family's members and of their immediate ancestors. Particular emphasis was placed on revealing as much of the control practices, interaction, and accommodation with regard to authority as was possible for the students to supply. The information gained from the personal documents and from the interviews which followed was of three kinds: *factual,* as age and sex of family members, time and place of marriage, economic status, etc.; *illustrative,* as descriptions of family-interaction; and *interpretive,* as student insight into, and evaluation of, the family situation. No effort was made to select a sample with well-defined limits as this was a study of *process* (transmission) . . . It was deemed advisable, however, to use the family histories of students who were reared in non-farm areas because it is believed that due to urbanization, greater mobility, and the decline of familism, changes in authority patterns are more pronounced in the urban areas . . . All families are white and all reside in non-farm areas of western and central New York State. They are of the upper-lower and middle socioeconomic classes . . .

To insure completeness of the data as nearly as possible, the investigator interviewed each student to clarify the student's presentation of the case and to get what additional information she might volunteer. This interview served to verify many of the students' statements for reliability because it furnished the investigator with a check of her previous writing.

Treatment of Data and Procedure

The data were treated from two points of reference, one centering in the authority patterns expressed in the *present* family relationships, and the other in the patterns which formed the husbands' and wives' earliest conceptions of authority role in their *parental* families. Consideration was given first to the classification and description of the existing authority patterns as described in the family histories. Then attention was directed to the *combinations* of parental authority patterns (paternal and maternal) from which similar and modified patterns of authority have been transmitted to the present generation.

The classification and description of the cases proceeded according to the following plan:

Each family history was read and the detailed material tabulated. Before attempting to classify the authority patterns of the present family relationships as presented in the case studies, a tabulation of excerpts from each case was made according to the following organization: (*a*) the accommodation and conflict of the marriage partners; (*b*) influence or control of one over the other and of each over the children; (*c*) the affectional relationship and polarization within the family group; (*d*) the division and sharing of family work; (*e*) the acceptance and rejection of own and opposite sex roles; and (*f*) any other statements that could be related to, or associated with, the authority pattern in each specific case.

A study of these organized excerpts together with the investigator's interpretation of each case *as a whole*, led to a classification of the authority patterns under one of the following headings: Equalitarian,

Father-controlled, Mother-controlled, Conflicting-control, and *Laissez-faire*. The excerpt analysis also yielded a like classification of the authority patterns in the paternal and maternal family backgrounds of the students' parents . . .

Attention was then directed to an analysis of families of the present generation under each major classification. For example, the matricentric cases were re-read and grouped according to common characteristics. First, they appeared to fall into two classes, one of distinct mother-control, and the other of mother-leadership. Second, the parent-child relationship in the first group appeared to be autocratic; in that of the second, democratic. This group was verified by a checking of each case against a variety of characteristics to determine whether the differences between the groups were real or imagined. In order to distinguish them, the two groups illustrated were named "Mother-controlled"-Autocratic, and "Mother-led"-Democratic. The patricentric and balanced cases were handled similarly . . .

TABLE 1

CLASSIFICATION OF THE SAMPLE

	No.	Total
A. *Matricentric:* Authority patterns in which the mother has the greater control		
1. Mother-controlled-Autocratic*	4	4
B. *Patricentric:* Authority patterns in which the father has the greater control		
1. Father-controlled-Autocratic	3	
2. "Pseudo" Father-controlled-Autocratic	3	6
C. *Balanced:* Authority patterns based on balanced husband-wife control		
1. Equalitarian-Democratic	7	
2. Equalitarian-Indulgent	2	
3. *Laissez-faire-Laissez-faire*	2	
4. Conflicting-control-Inconsistent	2	13
D. *Intermediate:* Authority patterns indicating a mid-point between balance and inequality in husband-wife control		
1. "Mother-led"-Democratic	5	
2. "Father-led"-Democratic	7	
3. "Father-led"-Autocratic	2	14
		37

* The words *democratic, autocratic, laissez-faire, indulgent,* and *inconsistent* describe the parent-child relationships as they are presented in the family histories.

A complete classification of the sample . . . is given in Table 1 . . .

The second point of emphasis in the treatment of the data was on the *process of transmission and modification* of the authority patterns. In other words, attention was now turned from the classification of the families *in the present sample* to the patterns *in the past generation* from which these were derived. Five such combinations of parental authority patterns (formed by the marriage of a wife from one authority background and a husband from a similar or a dissimilar one) were found to exist in this sample. These were designated for brevity as Types *A, B, C, D,* and *E.* Cases in which *both* husband and wife had grown up in matricentric homes were grouped and designated as Type *A* authority-background derivatives. Those in which the wife had been reared in a mother-controlled home and the husband in a father-controlled home were referred to as Type *B* derivatives. Type *C* represented the authority background of husbands and wives whose parental authority patterns had both been balanced, and Type *D* those in which the husband's background had been patricentric and his wife's matricentric. Cases in which both husband and wife had grown up in patricentric homes were designated as derivatives of the Type *E,* homogamous authority background . . .

The transmission and modification process itself was the next problem for explanation and illustration. In order to facilitate the explanation, a continuum was constructed which consisted of cases in the present fam-

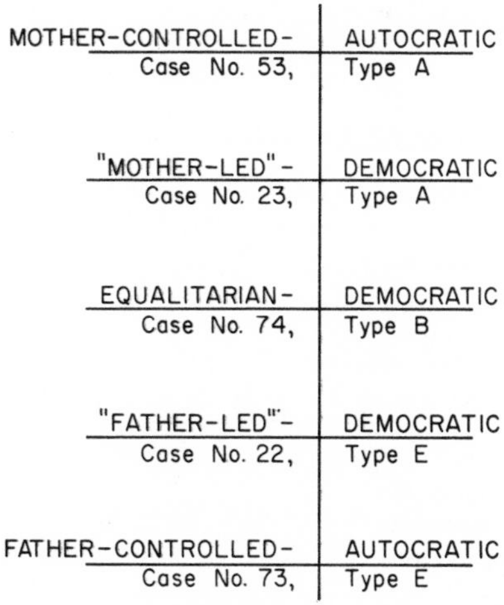

MOTHER—CONTROLLED—	AUTOCRATIC
Case No. 53,	Type A
"MOTHER—LED"—	DEMOCRATIC
Case No. 23,	Type A
EQUALITARIAN—	DEMOCRATIC
Case No. 74,	Type B
"FATHER—LED"—	DEMOCRATIC
Case No. 22,	Type E
FATHER—CONTROLLED—	AUTOCRATIC
Case No. 73,	Type E

FIG. 2. THE "IDEAL" CASES AND THEIR APPROXIMATE POSITIONS ON THE CONTINUUM OF CONTROL ACCOMMODATION.

ilies whose authority patterns ranged from extreme father-control through the balanced and equalitarian patterns to the extreme mother-control patterns . . . The investigator placed the cases on a control continuum using only interpretative judgment as a measure of the authority accommodations. When this was done five cases were selected, one from each end of the continuum, one from the center, and one from each of the midpoints between the center and ends (Figure 2). When this was done, five points along this continuum were chosen to form the range of "ideal" types—the case studies at these points forming "classical" illustrations of Mother-controlled, Equalitarian or Balanced, and Father-controlled authority relationships; and two intermediate types of control —one designated as "Father-led," to represent a less autocratic type of authority between Father-controlled and the Balanced patterns (Table 1) and the other "Mother-led," to represent a form of authority between Mother-controlled and Balanced (Figure 2).

Each combination of parental authority patterns, Types *A, B, C, D,* and *E,* was treated separately to describe its transmission to an "ideal" authority type in the present generation, i.e., to a case placed at some point on the continuum . . .

THE TRANSMISSION AND MODIFICATION OF AUTHORITY PATTERNS

DESCRIPTION AND ILLUSTRATIONS OF THE TRANSMISSION AND MODIFICATION PROCESS

Transmission from the Type A (homogamous) parental control patterns to the matricentric patterns of the sample . . .

General. Both husband and wife, representative of these matricentric families, were reared in mother-controlled homes. The authority of the maternal grandmothers represented in the group ranged from rigid, demanding, dominance to leadership from possible necessity precipitated by the illness, death, irresponsibility or drunkenness of the grandfather.

Generally speaking, the husband from these matricentric backgrounds had spent a happy childhood under a mother-controlled pattern of authority. As a child he had responded with compliance to a "strong" mother who controlled the household. Thus he incorporated a self-other pattern with regard to the authority role that conditioned him to wife-control or leadership in his own marriage relationship. In the first place he chose a wife who would take the initiative in decision-making (that being a part of *her* introjected authority role). When she assumed the leadership in authority, he responded to her control of him in family activities as he had to his ascendant mother. Moreover, his interpretation of the wife-mother role carried with it the conception of mother-control of the children, as he had experienced it in his relationship to his own mother. These two functions, child-rearing and authority over the family activities, became a part of his expectations of the wife-mother role.

The wife came from a matricentric background and was conditioned by her early family experience to fulfill such expectations as her husband held. She had obeyed, although not altogether happily, with the directions of an authoritative mother, this interaction pattern having formed the basis for her self-other pattern of child-compliance to mother-control. At the same time she incorporated the other functions of her mother's role into her own behavior. That is, she learned the wife-mother role, as exemplified in her mother, through association and observation of the husband-wife interaction of her parents. Thus she was prepared to re-enact the dominant wife and mother role as it has been transmitted to her in her family experience. Her expectations of a husband were, likewise, conditioned by her contacts with a father who accepted or expected wife-control. These expectations influenced both her choice of a husband and her adjustment to him in the control relationship . . .

Illustration of the transmission from the Type A (homogamous) parental control patterns to the Mother-controlled-Autocratic pattern.

Mr. D.'s father "was kind, honest, and friendly to everyone," and "well-spoken of in the community." He and his wife were agreeable toward each other. Neither was as strict with the children as was the custom of the times.

Mr. D.'s education terminated in the third year of high school when he became angry with a teacher and quit school. He attempted a business course later which he gave up when he contracted measles. Because his mother wanted to keep him near her on the farm, she encouraged him to remain at home until after his marriage. Then his parents bought the young couple a farm and stocked it with a purebred dairy herd.

Mrs. D.'s mother was the pampered daughter of a well-to-do merchant before she married. She was very proud of her English heritage and her "cultural attainments in music and art." She collected antique furniture as a hobby. Mrs. D.'s father was a successful farmer of considerable means and held a position of status in the community. He was "stimulating and very intelligent. He enjoyed reading Byron and Keats." Both he and his wife were "high strung" and "nervous" people, a characteristic also attributed to Mrs. D. by the student.

Mrs. D., the eldest child, had a strong affectional attachment to her father. She was a "tomboy" and decidedly preferred her father's companionship to her mother's. Her mother favored the second daughter and compared Mrs. D. unfavorably with the younger girl. Mrs. D. was always protector of her brother, the youngest child, when he was teased at school. In the student's words, "She thinks the world of him."

Mrs. D. reportedly stood in awe of her mother. She was afraid of her "biting tongue." She angered easily when her will was contested. The student reported, "Grandmother was really the dominant person in the family. . . . She didn't want you to think she was boss and yet she wanted to be the boss. . . . She had fixed ideas and was very peculiar in some ways."

Both the mother and Mrs. D.'s sister spoke of the father disparagingly. Mrs. D. spoke often of "the bitter experience of being torn from her father's companionship by her mother." She believes the mother was jealous of the children's affection for him.

Mrs. D.'s introduction to school was delayed until she could take her sister, who was two years younger, with her. The younger sister was supposedly brilliant and surpassed Mrs. D. in some school subjects. A strong sense of rivalry which still persists sprang up between the sisters. She finished high school with honors, however, and became a teacher, a profession she left at marriage but returned to, when her husband lost his farm during the depression.

Mr. D. was never satisfied as a dairy farmer, and was glad to seek a position in the city. However, he has never been able to find or keep a position that his wife considered adequate to support the family. She secured a teaching position in the city to which Mr. D.'s stepfather had retired. He accepted her and the children as a part of his household and that has been their home since that time.

In the meantime, Mr. D. held various jobs, most of them away from home. He gradually became incidental to his family's welfare, Mrs. D. taking over both parent and provider functions. The student writes: "My father is hurt by neglecting to be recognized as part of the home or of the situation that arises—even though he sends you to Mother for the final check on a command," and "he has seemed quite satisfied with letting Mother earn money to support us." He has had a position where he can stay at home for the past five years. His earnings are his own except that he pays room and board to his wife. He is completely disregarded by Mrs. D. in all matters pertaining to family policy. Only the student, his youngest daughter, appears to have any appreciation for him. She is apparently rather fond of him. With regard to family control, the student writes:

"She [Mother] is the one who tells us what to do and the one we go to for the answers," and "My mother is the recognized head of our home. . . . The home we live in belongs to my step-grandfather but my mother drew the designs for it and has planned the furnishings. The bedrooms are furnished by the inhabitants, however. Dad has had very little to say about any of it. It is Mother's money that we spent. Now that Dad is home he pays her his room and board, and she is the one who keeps the budget, figures the income tax, 'and hands out the money."

This assumption of control of the family by the student's mother seems to have paralleled the family's financial crisis. The older sisters reported to the student that the authority relationship between the parents was more nearly "fifty-fifty" in their childhood on the farm.

The student has suffered by comparison to her three older sisters who are, she feels, more adequate than she. They lived up to their mother's high standards of intellectual attainment and became successful school teachers. The student thinks she is like her father—content to let come what may. She shows ambivalence toward her mother who has attempted to hold her to standards beyond her ability. She tends to identify with her father whose way of life is less demanding, more passive, and therefore easier for her to emulate.

Interpretation. Mrs. D. grew up under the control of a demanding obdurate mother whom she feared but obeyed. She was fond of her father and sought his companionship to escape her mother's biting tongue. Her "tomboy" behavior and her preference for the so-called "masculine" role would suggest that she rejected her mother's role and identified with her father.

Nevertheless, when a crisis situation arose in her marriage which called for forceful action, she took the responsibility for the family into her own hands. She became both parent and provider for the children, thereby assuming control of the family activities. In spite of her dislike for the mother, she had internalized her energetic, "managing" behavior through her childhood response to the mother's control. When the situation appeared to her to demand it, she could and did re-enact the incorporated "other" pattern of her mother, i.e., the role of the "managing" wife and mother.

According to her interpretation of their strained financial situation, Mr. D. had failed to live up to her expectations in his provider role. The father in her childhood home had played a secondary role in the authority pattern but he had been a good provider. Mr. D.'s inability to earn a good living for his family probably caused his wife anxiety to which she responded by taking over the management of home, children, and finances herself.

The former accommodation of control relationships was thrown into disequilibrium until Mr. D. came home to live as a boarder without influence in his own family. He has accepted the passive, submissive role his wife assigned to him.

The secondary role is acceptable to Mr. D. because it allows him to maintain the position of subordination to a mother-person that prevailed in his childhood. Also he may have introjected the passive role of his father where control of the children was concerned. Neither of his parents set a pattern for strict control of the children, although his mother assumed the major responsibility for his upbringing. His "other" pattern in its reproduction, therefore, results in lenient, "happy-go-lucky" fatherhood.

This case has illustrated how authority patterns are transmitted from the parental families to the present marriage by way of self-other patterns developed in the childhood experience of the husband and wife. Some of the factors that have modified the authority pattern are also given, notably Mr. D.'s affectional attachment to his mother, which may account for some of his passivity toward his wife, and the financial crisis in the marriage which was accompanied by his loss of status and control in the family.

Transmission from the Type A (homogamous) parental control patterns to the "Mother-led"-Democratic patterns of the sample . . .

General. The "Mother-led"-Democratic class is intermediate between the mother-controlled and the equalitarian families. The case chosen to illustrate this type of control has the general characteristics of all of the mother-led families. These are given briefly in the following paragraphs.

Each husband in the families classed as "mother-led" had a happy childhood in an affectionate family. The father was in an occupation that took him out of the home weeks or months at a time. This arrangement required the mother to assume control of the home and children. Her management of the children was so relaxed as to produce no resentment.

Although the culturally determined role of the period supported father dominance in the family, this man apparently had no such pattern to follow. Each husband grew up under the control of his mother who assumed leadership in home and family affairs. He acquired a self-other pattern that predisposed him to follow the wife's leadership in shaping family policy and in child control. He not only played the secondary role as his father had done in relation to the authority of his mother, but he was conditioned by his early response to his mother's easy control to follow her leadership. This was the direct expression of a self-other pattern of authority learned in childhood which is being repeated in a like situation in the present marriage. It is probable that he chose his wife in part because of her leadership qualities which resembled those of his mother.

Each of the wives in the "mother-led" families also had internalized the mother-controlled authority interact in her early family experience. Therefore, each had expected to manage home and children while the husband followed her leadership. This accommodation was acceptable to both partners because it met their expectations of each other in accordance with their previous perception of the husband-father and wife-mother roles. In other words, each brought into the marriage an expectation of mother-leadership and father-cooperation in family affairs. This has become the authority pattern in which they feel most comfortable because it incorporates the self-other patterns that were persistent and pervasive in each partner's perception of family living.

The specific case chosen to illustrate the "ideal" intermediate type of control is that of Mr. and Mrs. B. which is presented in brief below.

Illustration of transmission from the Type A (homogamous) parental control patterns to the "Mother-led"-Democratic pattern. Mr. B.'s parents married in their late thirties. Mr. B. was their much-wanted and only son. Mr. B.'s father's work as a mining engineer took him to many parts of the country. The arrival of a child resulted in Mr. B.'s mother building a home on a small farm where she and the son could live while the father traveled. His mother was an "austere English woman" who took over the authority in the home. When Mr. B.'s father retired from engineering and came home to live, the control of the mother had become firmly established. The student writes that Mr. B.'s mother was often impatient with his father and never appeared sentimental or affectionate towards him. Mining had impaired his hearing, "so she often shouted at him in a cross voice."

Mr. B. preferred his father to his mother. "For," reports the student,

"Grandfather was always a pal and would drop what he was doing to be of help to my father. Grandma was the disciplinarian but my father was free when he was out in the fields with grandpa." In spite of the annoyance of keeping out of his mother's way, Mr. B. reports a happy childhood in a home where, basically, he was wanted and loved.

The student gives the following information about the father's friendships:

As a young man, my father had many friends his own age. His friends were of both sexes for he attended a co-educational school. However, he courted only my mother.

Mrs. B, the student's mother, was the youngest child in a mother-controlled home. Her father was a farmer who had become ill and was forced to turn over the management of the farm to his wife and the hired hands. The student writes:

Grandmother was the "school-teacher type" and always had the run of things . . . Since Grandfather was sick Grandmother had all the more reason to take over the running of the house . . . She was a domineering person under her outside sweet appearance. She ran the household and kept the books and accounts . . . Grandmother is a great "pusher" to this day for she always pushes her plans.

Mrs. B.'s older brother was the mother's favorite. This brother was a source of annoyance to Mrs. B. because "he was a big tease and always bossed her around." The student believes her mother is sensitive to teasing and to "being bossed" even now because of this relationship with her older brother.

Mr. B.'s education at O——— College was interrupted by World War I. He married Mrs. B. before he went to camp and she continued her teaching-training course in his absence. When he returned they set up housekeeping in a new residential district of B———. Mr. B. did not complete his college education but took a short business course and became "a white collar worker" with a small firm. He has had periods of "hard times" about which the student comments, "We have not always been financially secure, which has caused us worry at times." During the depression, Mrs. B. took in boarders, and during World War II she took a 4:00 A.M. to 12:00 shift in a war industry. The student states that her mother's working has not affected the relationship between the parents. The student described the leadership of her mother in these words:

I believe mother has exercised the greater amount of authority in our family. She is home all day figuring ways to solve a difficulty and so when night comes she lays down the solution to my father. If he doesn't agree, he will bring forth his counterpart to the issue. . . . In the end they may both compromise after the subject has been hashed over enough. They often come to a decision that will solve the problem just by discussing it together. This seems to be the pattern most used with Mother in the lead and Father in the end, using some of her suggestions.

The family interaction is polarized around one dominant head which is Mother . . . This is not a strong position, however . . . If Mother has discussed her plans with us before (ahead of time) we are likely to side with her.

Mrs. B. also leads in allowing the children a part in family planning. These children are becoming independent and responsible young adults under her guidance.

Interpretation. Mr. B.'s family background fostered mother control because of his father's long absences from home. In spite of the close contact with his mother, Mr. B. preferred his father's company, and as he grew up identified with him. In so doing he probably introjected his husband and father role as he perceived it in his interaction with his parents.

Mr. B. married a woman who had grown up under a capable, dominant mother and whose father's illness placed the management of farm, home, and children in her hands. She has learned her mother's leadership techniques but has modified them to encourage participation by her husband in shaping of family policy. She values the emotional satisfaction derived from working with him for successful family life. This may have some relation to the fact that her need for affection and companionship was met largely by her father when she was a child. She may have transferred that love to her husband who plays a similar role toward her as her father played toward her mother (at least in the authority accommodation).

This transmission of the leadership role, presumably, came about through the self-other pattern of authority which Mrs. B. incorporated in response to her mother's control. This is perpetuated in the present authority pattern in its reversed form. That is, Mrs. B. has learned her mother's leadership through responding to it and incorporating it in her response. Now, when she is in a similar situation with a compliant husband and dependent children, she reproduces several aspects of her mother's role, especially that of leadership in home and family life.

*Modification in transmission from the Type B (heterogamous) paren-
tal control patterns to the authority patterns of the sample . . .*

General. The husbands of these equalitarian families have been middle
children in mother-controlled homes; their wives were middle children
in strict father-controlled families. The fathers of the wives were respected
and regarded as "heads-of-the-family," but the mothers were more loved
and admired by their daughters.

The fathers of the three husbands in this classification apparently had
little contact with their sons, as one died, another was divorced, and the
third was "easy-going" and content to let his wife rear the children.

None of the husbands is a favorite child, although one must resist the
efforts of a possessive mother who covets his attention and affection.

The husband who is typical of this equalitarian group apparently has
introjected an authority pattern that does not demand the submission of
his wife and children. The wife, however, comes into the marriage expecting her husband to be family head (if we are to judge from the authority
pattern she reacted to in her childhood home). This woman is warmly
affectionate toward husband and children alike. To the extent that she is
content with her feminine role she encourages her husband to adopt the
masculine role as she saw it in her father. He is not prepared to do this,
having introjected a "feminized" version from his own father. Nor is *she*
prepared to meet his expectations of aggressive womanhood such as he
experienced with his own mother. Neither apparently feels the compul-
sion to challenge the masculinity or femininity of the other, but rather to
encourage the other to complement his own role. This leads to an interaction process which results in the new accommodation to be discussed in
the next few pages.

The fact that both husband and wife were middle children may have
some bearing on their ability to adjust to a partner whose introjected
authority role differs from his own. They have played descendant roles
to their older sibling(s) and possibly have been ascendant in their relation
to the younger one(s). These situations may have produced several role
tendencies, which together with the self-other patterns developed in the
parent-child relationships gives them a choice of roles with which to meet
the control-demands of the marriage.

An outstanding characteristic of this marriage, also, is the strong affection between husband and wife. The attainment of an equalitarian relationship has probably called for an adjustment by each partner to the
expectations of the other. The deep affection between them may have been

a motivating factor in this interaction. They both *want* to make a successful adjustment of their differences.

Supposedly this has been the process which brought about the equalitarian accommodation: The husband married, expecting of his wife approximately the same control role as his mother had played. The wife expected to "look up to" her husband and to be the lovable but firm, calm mother-type, such as her own mother had been. One conveys to the other his expectations by his responses. *Neither one* conforms to the other's expectations. In accordance with the concept of interaction each redirects his behavior in the direction of the partner's expectations. He calls upon his past experience and learning for this new (or modified) response. In the same way each modification becomes a stimulus to a new (or modified) response from the other partner. Thus a new authority accommodation evolves by way of interaction which may have elements of the original expectations of both.

The children of these parents as they mature become a part of this equalitarian relationship. They are treated as individuals in their own right and, learning to respond to the equalitarian control-pattern, they take their places in a democratic family.

Illustration of a modification in transmission from Type B (homogamous) parental control patterns to the Equalitarian-Democratic pattern. Mr. S. grew up in a suburb of a large eastern city where he and his five brothers and sisters spent a happy childhood. Mr. S. was the third child and second son of German Lutheran parents. His father was a policeman who was stationed at intersections where school children crossed. He was a favorite of the children. Mr. S. describes him as an "easy-going" father who left it up to the mother to put the final word on matters concerning finances, social contacts, and religious participation . . . "He had a sense of humor and was more lovable" than the mother. She "liked things her way" and directed the family activities. Mr. S. says his parents had no favorites among their children. He expresses no resentment of his mother's desire to run things, and he definitely respects his father. He has maintained good relationships with his parents through the years. Family reunions are traditional and the brothers and sisters all like to reminisce about the fun they had as children.

Mrs. S.'s father came to America from Germany at the age of 19. Her mother was of German parentage but American born. She had a jovial nature and was always doing things for people. Mrs. S. "found her mother much more lovable than her father." He was a stern patriarch whose

German cultural pattern condoned his domination of the family. The student reports:

My grandfather played the dominant role in the family. He managed all the finances (he used the "dole" system. Grandmother had to justify every want before she got any money). He controlled the children when he was home (they had to obey; they couldn't talk back). He chose the place of residence . . . and saw that the children kept up with their religion—going to church, catechism, confirmation, etc.

Mrs. S. liked friends and social groups. She was popular with young people and still likes the outdoor activities she and Mr. S. share with their friends.

Mr. and Mrs. S. have always expressed their affection openly and share it freely with their children. They like to tease each other, and many conflicts are resolved in good-humored "kidding."

It is evident from the student's description that her mother enjoys homemaking and accepts the functions of the feminine role as prescribed by our culture. "She thinks home-making education is wonderful and is always interested in what I have to tell her about it," writes her daughter.

Mr. S. helped care for the children when they were small and shared in family work such as "in large house cleaning jobs, painting and papering, and odd jobs such as repair of screens and storm windows, and general upkeep of the house."

Mr. S. always had his masculine friends who enjoyed outdoor sports with him but both he and his wife prefer "mixed couples" for cards in the winter and summer vacation at the lake-shore cottage.

The family history gives evidence of the equalitarian relationship between husband and wife in such quotations as these:

Mother and Father talk over bills, keep track of expenses, and consult on big purchases. They have a joint checking account and are very conscientious about reporting purchases to each other and in justifying their individual purchasing.

And:

The authority in our family always seemed to be equally shared. I can seldom remember one doing anything without the consent of the other. Discipline problems were always talked over between them. . . . Sometimes it annoys me a little when you ask one something . . . they say, "I'll have to see what your father (or mother) has to say."

During the depression period, from 1929 to 1931, Mr. S. was unemployed except for occasional odd-jobs. Mrs. S. did dress-making to help upport the family. When he *did* get steady employment he worked nights for eight years. This was the period of his youngest daughter's early childhood. She is at present a "demanding" young adolescent whose adjustment, the student believes, was thrown off-balance by the suppression she endured, and the bribes she was offered, to keep quiet during the day while the father was sleeping.

The parent-child relationships in the S. family have been less democratic than those in some of the other cases. In the student's early childhood control was fairly autocratic. But the children were encouraged to assume responsibilities and allowed to become independent as they matured, so that a near-democratic relationship between parents and children has evolved. The student describes their family life in the present state of adjustment as active and generally cooperative:

> We all have such good times together. Arguments and disagreements are had but are so easily patched. Everyone helps with jobs and there seems to be a unity in which everyone is pulling together for a common goal. We are all very honest with each other and everyone can take criticism. . . . Everyone has a great sense of humor and an awfully lot of fooling and kidding is done. When an emergency, illness, death, or other crisis arises everyone pulls together, working just as hard as they can.

Interpretation. This case shows the accommodation that may result when husband and wife have internalized conflicting interaction patterns of authority in their early childhood experience. We would expect Mr. S. to attempt to play a secondary control role, while expecting his wife to be the dominant member of the marriage, if we accept the proposition that self-other patterns are formed in early family life contacts and that the reciprocating role (in this case, the *parents' authority* role) will be reproduced when he himself becomes a parent.

For the same reason his wife could be expected to want a dominant husband and to play a secondary role herself. A surface evaluation of the conflicting situation would lead one to predict unresolved conflict but instead, an integration of the two expectancy patterns presumedly takes place. This accommodation is a result of interaction when two persons are motivated to adjust their differences . . .

Transmission from the Type E (homogamous) parental control patterns to the patricentric patterns of the sample . . .

General. Both husband and wife of this patriarchal classification spent their childhoods in homes that were under the supervision of a strong father-head. Their mothers took a secondary position in the control pat tern and taught their children to respect the father's authority.

According to the hypothesis, the dominant father role was transmitte in the following manner: The husband, as a child, obeyed his father commands and followed his leadership. In so doing, he incorporated h father's behavior with his own response. That is, the interaction betwee father and son became internalized as a self-other pattern and, therefor it is reproducible either in its original or in its reversed form. In othe words, when a son of an authoritative father himself becomes a fathe he can assume the position of authority with his child because such be havior is the reciprocal of his childhood response. In the same way, th secondary authority role of the wife was transmitted by way of inte nalized interacts involving mother-daughter relationships . . .

In the husband-wife relationship each would meet the authority e pectations of the other because each would conceive the husband and wi roles as embodying this authority arrangement. The respective roles (i. dominant husband, submissive wife) would have been learned so ear in life and learned so thoroughly that each partner would be able re-enact in response to the other his interpretation of the parental ro of the like-sex parent. Thus each would be meeting the expectations the other and a father-controlled pattern of authority would be establishe in their marriage relationship . . .

Illustration of transmission from the Type E (*homogamous*) *parent control patterns to the Father-controlled-Autocratic pattern.* The elde Mr. F., the student's paternal grandfather, was a German-American wh exercised his authority as head-of-the-family in the traditional patriarch manner. He laid down the rules for his wife's and children's conduct an was strict in enforcing his wishes. He himself did as he chose but h wife's behavior had to conform to his demands. She "put up with hin because she had to," according to the student's report. However, she wa by nature a very loving and considerate woman who gained satisfactio from serving others. Her house was always open to visitors and friend

The elder Mr. F. was definite in his policy regarding saving and spend ing of the family income. *He* did the family's shopping, general an grocery buying during his time off from work. When he gave his wif money she was obliged to use it according to his directions.

The elder Mrs. F. was the influential person in the children's religiou training. She cooperated with her husband in social participation. She wa a protective and motherly person to her children, and especially to M F., the student's father. He was her favorite child. "She waited on hin hand and foot"—a situation which his wife perpetuates. The student reports:

Our family life is very similar to my grandparents'. Father is just like grandfather, and mother and grandmother understand each other very well. . . . My father's mother always waited on him. . . . Although he is fully capable of doing things himself, he is just used to having others do for him and he just sits back and lets them. We do things for him from tying his shoes to running his bath.

Mrs. F., the student's mother, grew up believing that woman's place was in the home. She believes without reservation that a husband should be the head-of-the-family, as her father played that role during her childhood. Her mother died when Mrs. F. was three and her oldest sister became the mother-surrogate under the father's direction. He was a German-American workman who was "never idle a moment." He felt it was a man's duty to work and earn money for his family, and then he supervised its spending. He was "definite in his ways," and "His way was always right," according to the student's mother.

But he was not harsh in his discipline. Concerning this the student writes:

Mother never spoke of any punishments that were unfair and only speaks of how nice he was and how kind. He was very understanding of the children.

Both Mr. and Mrs. F. report happy childhoods and satisfactory relationships with all members of their families. They are equally content with their marriage relationship. This was evidenced in:

One of my father's first expectations of his wife was that she stay by him, help him, and encourage him through the difficult spots. This my mother has accomplished.

And:

Mother has often said that he has fulfilled every quality that she expected of him as a husband.

Mr. F. is a successful professional man while his wife has a ninth grade education. Mrs. F. was raised in the Catholic faith but considered it her duty to change to the faith of her husband. The children have been confirmed in the Lutheran faith through the insistence of their father.

Mrs. F. has accepted the authoritative role of her husband as natural and right. In doing so, she has probably made the major adjustments in the marriage relationship. She considers this a part of her duty also. That she has been able to instill in her daughters the same respect for her husband's authority as she has, is evident in the statement below:

In most things my father "lays down the law" or has the final say. However, his authority is exercised in such a nonoffensive way that we want to accept it. We respect my father's opinion very much and have found him to be right in his attitude. . . . We accept his commands and askings because we know that the purpose behind them is for our benefit and welfare. . . .

Mr. F. gives Mrs. F. an allowance to meet the household expenses. Most purchasing within this allowance is left up to her judgment. The major saving and investments are Mr. F.'s responsibility.

If Mr. F.'s decisions are contested—an infrequent occurrence—he may demand compliance.

Then it becomes a case where the rest of the family must give in. This doesn't occur often but when it does we usually give him his way because if we don't he argues and sulks until he gets it.

He punishes his wife and children by periods of "not speaking" which the student considers unfair. Mrs. F. seldom argues with Mr. F. and when she does her feelings are expressed frankly and she quickly forgets about the conflict. Mr. F., however, may resort to not speaking and sulking when *he* is in an irritated mood. The family lets him alone until the mood wears off.

Family interaction polarized around Mr. F. He has been very reluctant to let his older daughter (the student) enjoy normal friendships. She says he is over-protective and almost jealous of her interests outside the family. She writes: "Up until college years I was never allowed to stay over night at anyone's house although they were welcome at mine. Too, I couldn't accept food or money from friends."

The student attributes this careful supervision of her activities to the fact that her parents lost their second child at the age of four and have been overly concerned about their other children since. She thinks she is gradually gaining her independence, however, although her dating has been closely supervised.

Time was when he didn't want me to date despite the fact that I was going through the dating age. . . . When I did go I almost felt like a criminal passing through the line-up! "Where are you going, what are you going to do, when will you get in?" I'm glad to say that this attitude is one of the past.

During the last couple of years I have made great advancement in gaining esponsibility for my own conduct. . . . Before long I expect to be on my own. However, living at home requires certain ties and certain things that are expected of you—things that can't be broken while you remain there.

The younger daughter is being held to the same strict standards of conduct. In spite of the repressive nature of the control pattern in this family, the integration is good because each member accepts father control as normal. Wife and children love and respect Mr. F. and he is protective and (usually) benevolent in return.

Interpretation. Both Mr. and Mrs. F. as children responded to father control with compliance. Mr. F. probably identified with his father in the masculine role of a family-head. When he became a husband and a father he reproduced the patriarchal role with facility because he had internalized his father's dominant behavior with his own submissive response. Now he is able to play the role of his father, as he has conceived it, when he is in the situation which calls for such father-behavior. The husband role which he has also introjected from his father presumes an expectancy-response from his wife which corresponds to that of his mother. In Mr. F.'s childhood his physical needs were foreseen and met by a mother who "waited on him hand and foot." His wife and daughters, likewise, see that his home-life is made pleasant and easy by catering to his wishes. His wife and his mother are in full accord as to its being his due as husband and father of the family. Mrs. F. experienced father control in her childhood, her own mother and sisters being subordinate to the control of *her* father. In her marriage she is merely repeating the response pattern learned in her obedience to her father when she adjusts to the authority of her husband. Because both Mr. and Mrs. F. have experienced patriarchal patterns of authority, and because both were happy in these situations, they "feel right" in a control situation that follows a similar pattern. Also, the culturally determined role of their German heritage condones this authority pattern, and it is still supported in some sectors of the American culture. It is interesting to note that his form of control is inflexible for the adolescent and that it is gradually breaking down to allow the student independence. Had there been a son in this family, his reaction to father control leaves room for speculation. It is probable that he would have been the favorite child, as his father was, and would have perpetuated the father-control pattern. Or he may have rebelled against parental authority and rejected the "strong father" role.

Transmission from the Types D and E parental control patterns to the "Father-led"-Democratic patterns of the sample . . .

General. . . . The husband-wife relationship which is typical of the "Father-led"-Democratic group appears to be based on a specialization and division of labor. Each plays his prescribed part but the husband is recognized head-of-the-family. Child guidance and housekeeping duties are the wife's responsibility while control of family finances is considered the husband's obligation. Unity of purpose is achieved by joint planning and decisions made under the husband's leadership, with wife and children taking an active part. These families are stable and well integrated. The husband and wife typical of this group are happy, well-adjusted persons. Their childhoods were either difficult due to limited means, deaths or other crises, or were normal. All reported happy childhoods and satisfying relationships with parents and siblings.

Father control is not only the culturally accepted authority pattern of both husband and wife in the Type *E* derivation but also it is the type of control each has incorporated in his self-other pattern as a child. The presence of a "Father-led" authority pattern in the Type *E* transmission is not surprising under these circumstances. The question for clarification is how this group came to be as nearly equalitarian as it is, and why are these father-headed families democratic in the parent-child relationship considering that their authority derivation is similar to those of the strictly father controlled group? In other words, where does the wife of a "Father-led" family *get* her tendency to share the control with her husband? And how does it develop that he *accepts* her on a near-equalitarian basis? Discussions of, and explanations for, such relationships are presented in the interpretation of the case used for illustration . . .

Illustration of transmission from the Type E parental patterns to the "Father-led"-Democratic pattern. Mr. H. was the oldest of a large Czech family. He grew up on a farm in Europe where the difficulties of making a living were acute. He came to America at 18, found a job in a steel mill at B, and began to send money home to his family in "the old country."

Mr. H. looks back to a frugal but happy childhood in a close family group. The children worked with their parents to make their peasant life profitable. The student writes of her father's childhood:

The relations between the children in the family were very friendly. They played and worked together to benefit the whole family. . . .

When Dad was growing up he was equally attached to both parents. However, he had more contact with his Dad since he helped with the farm work.

while the girls helped Grandmother in the home. Dad had no resentment for either parent. He loved them equally and would do anything to make them happy. He did not leave his paternal home just to get away, but to try to better his standard of living and make a good place for himself in the United States.

From all Dad has told me concerning his childhood, I can be sure that he had a happy childhood. The entire family worked together and were secure in their own circle. They were all intent on making each other happy because in those days there was very little offered to them.

The parents of Mr. H. were strict with their children but they seldom punished them. "The children knew what they were expected to do," reports the student. ". . . In those days children catered to their parents' wishes or demands with no come-backs. They took for granted that they should do the things their parents wished."

Mr. H.'s father apparently took the lead in control of the family. The student states, "My father remembers his father as the dominant parent. It was assumed that Grandfather was head of the family." And:

My Dad's father exercised major control in respect to control of children, management of finances, family earning, and choice of residence. Both grandparents were concerned with social and religious participation and both had their say about these matters.

Mr. H.'s emigration from Europe to America was approved by his parents. He felt it his filial duty to send money home to his people, an obligation which he carried for several years after his arrival in the United States.

He married Mrs. H. when he was 25 and she was 18. Mrs. H., the middle child of three girls, was the daughter of Czech immigrants living in the industrial suburb of B. The control pattern in this immigrant family was not unlike that of Mrs. H.'s husband's family, i.e., a modification of the European patriarchal pattern. Mrs. H.'s father was family-head and "all worked together and were happy to do their part to benefit the entire family." The student reported that "Grandpa was the leader while he was living. It was understood that the family did what Grandfather wanted done" and, "Grandad had the major control where finances, control of children, etc., were concerned. Both grandparents had their say about the social and religious life of the family but there was much similarity in opinions because of similarity in backgrounds."

Mrs. H.'s parents owned and ran a restaurant business. Her father died when Mrs. H. was nine, leaving the care of the children and the management of the business in her mother's hands. When her mother died six years later, Mrs. H. quit school and went to live with her eldest sister, 11 years her senior. She met Mr. H. when she was 17 and married him two years later.

The restaurant business belonged to the three sisters, and when Mrs. H. married Mr. H. they allowed him to assume its management. The business is in Mr. H.'s name as he manages all the finances. The student gave the following information about the business arrangement, and the division of labor centering around it:

> Mother and Dad have always worked together in the store. Mother does the bookkeeping, collects the rents from the flats, and figures the income tax. Dad delivers while Mother stays in the store. Dad does all the purchasing and manages the finances. Mother has access to the cash in the bank. Bonds and savings are in both their names. All business is in Dad's name. She (Mother) consults him when she needs money. He says, "Everything that is mine is yours."

During the years when the children were growing up, Mrs. H. worked in the store. She had a part-time maid for housecleaning but aside from that she did the housework and had most of the care of the children. Mr. H. did none of the housework unless Mrs. H. was ill and could not do it. Mr. H. managed the business and attended to financial transactions. Each parent had his responsibility in accordance with his sex role and his capabilities. With regard to the meeting of problems, the student writes:

> My parents always consult each other when problems arise. They discuss them "pro" and "con" and decide. The leader in the discussion depends upon the topic (e.g., business-Dad; house-Mom).

Evidence of the father's influence on the children's behavior and his wife's function as arbitrator is shown in the following excerpt:

> Both parents exercise about the same control but when it comes to some things, Dad has the greater amount of authority. When my parents think C. and I have been going out too much Mother may say something to us about it but it is Dad who tells us to stay home at certain times. Mother is more lenient but she quietly complies with Dad's wishes and demands. If the demands do not seem just, Mother talks it over with Dad and together they decide what C. and I can do.

There is considerable evidence in this case that Mr. and Mrs. H. are near-equalitarian in their authority accommodation, and that they are establishing a democratic family. Mr. H., however, is accorded the status and some of the privileges of the recognized head-of-the-family. We read in the family history:

As we were growing up in the family Dad was the head-of-the-family in most respects but when it came to . . . (various area of home and family life) he and Mother discussed all the aspects of the situations, aired their viewpoints and then after much thought decided between them, what was best for the family. Now that we are grown, the decisions are made by all of us as a group. We discuss and present our ideas and thoughts and finally decide on what we, as a group, think is best. Dad still has the upper hand, but we have our say and when we show Mother and Dad that we are trying to do what is best for all of us, we can usually have some of our ideas used also.

Interpretation. The authority pattern in Mr. H.'s childhood home was probably typical of the European peasant family. Making a living on the land unified the family in their efforts toward the achievement of one fundamental goal. The status of head-of-the-family has been accorded to the father by the pattern of European peasant culture. Note that farming was a joint enterprise in which every member had a place. And, although Mr. H.'s father was the recognized "head" he was more the leader than the master of the household.

This description of a joint autocratic control pattern in which each parent operates more or less in his own field of specialization yet both work in unity for the good of the family probably explains the husband's authority role in the present family. He expects to head the family business, which he does, even though it is his wife's estate. *His* mother and the children cooperated in the business of earning a living. He assumes that his wife and children will do likewise by doing their part in the store. Their worth is recognized and rewarded by his sharing the joint earnings with them and by according them a "say" in family plans.

Disregarding the difference in the family's enterprise, the authority pattern of this case is not unlike that of the generation preceding on the paternal side. The father's role, which approximates status of head-of-the-family more than that of dominance, was transmitted to the son by way of an internalized self-other pattern which embodied these characteristics. The concept of familism appears to be associated with the role's interpretation. Mr. H. expects his wife to support his leadership and to promote this familistic feeling as his mother had done. This is clearly another instance in which the self-other pattern learned by the husband in the interaction with his father is being reproduced in its "other" form.

His experience with his mother evidently shaped his expectations of the wife and mother role. Mrs. H. has fulfilled these expectations in the way she has become a partner in the business, a support for his status of family-head; and in the way she has fostered a familistic feeling which unifies the family under his leadership.

Because we are concerned primarily with the authority roles and their transmission and modification, we must attempt some explanation of how Mrs. H. developed the partnership role dove-tails with Mr. H.'s head-of-the-family position. First, we observe that Mr. H. grew up in an immigrant family whose first generation in America approximated the cultural and economic status of the H. family of this generation. That is, the patriarchal pattern of the European culture had presumably established the father as head-of-the-family and director of a family enterprise. (In this case, a restaurant.) Although Mrs. H.'s father died when she was nine, and her mother became the center of control for the six years before her death, Mrs. H. apparently maintained the first-established self-other pattern of helpmate and follower rather than the role of mother control. The former role which had been latent was manifested in Mrs. H.'s response to Mr. H. as head-of-the-family. She became a partner in the business, regarding him as the director and manager, at the same time assuming responsibility for making decisions in realms considered hers to administer . . .

SUMMARY OF REGULAR TRANSMISSION

Illustrative cases from the family histories together with a description of the regular transmission and modification process present the bases for the following conclusions: That in this sample there is a tendency for children of matriarchal families, if they marry children of matriarchal families, to form matricentric authority patterns in their own family relationships; and for children from patriarchal families who marry children from patriarchal families to have patricentric control in their present authority interaction. Likewise, although the evidence is limited to one case in this sample, it is logical to assume that there is a tendency for children of equalitarian parents who marry children from equalitarian families to, themselves, form an equalitarian relationship.

The children from either father-controlled or mother-controlled families who marry children from the opposite pattern, that is, those from father-controlled homes marrying those from mother-controlled families and the converse, tend to modify their introjected authority roles to form an equalitarian relationship . . .

The findings of this study lend support to the proposition that the individual tends to express his introjected authority role, either in its "self" or in its "other" form, when he meets a situation (in this case, his own marriage) which he perceives as requiring a role similar to that learned under parental control in his childhood experience. However, if expected response to his role is not forthcoming from his marriage partner, and the partner's expectations of "self" and "other" behavior with regard to authority in family living differs from his, then an interaction may take place which modifies the introjected authority roles of both partners, and a different pattern of control is evolved in the family relationship . . .

RESULTS AND CONCLUSIONS

An examination of the authority patterns in the parental family of each husband and wife revealed three homogamous authority patterns in the childhood families of husbands and wives, and two heterogamous parental patterns. The homogamous parental backgrounds are those in which (a) both husband and wife grew up in matricentric families; (b) both were reared in patricentric homes; and (c) both experienced balanced control in their parental homes. The heterogamous patterns were matricentric and their wives' were patricentric, and those in which the husband's parental control patterns were patricentric and the wives' were matricentric. The principal tendency in the homogamous marriages was toward the reproduction of the parental authority patterns. The tendency in the heterogamous marriages was to modify the introjected parental authority roles of each partner through interaction with the result that a new authority pattern emerged. Thus matricentric patterns in the parental families of both husband and wife tend to produce matricentric patterns in their marriage relationship; patricentric parental backgrounds to produce patricentric patterns; conflicting authority backgrounds to result in modified types of authority accommodations (in this sample largely equalitarian): balanced, to produce equalitarian or balanced patterns. Deviations from these trends are also evident.

This transmission and modification of the authority patterns from one generation to the next is apparently related to the authority roles each husband and wife learned in his or her childhood contact with the parental control patterns. These roles, presumably, were incorporated in the personality of each as self-other patterns which, when projected into the new marriage, tend either to be reenacted, or to be produced in their "other" form. The husband tends to reproduce his father's authority role;

the wife, her mother's control behavior; or either may carry his childhood role into the marriage relationship.

When the expectations of one partner do not complement those of the other, an accommodation or conflict in authority roles becomes imminent; the former tending to produce an interaction which produces an equalitarian authority pattern and the latter an authority pattern dependent upon a balance-of-power relationship . . .

CHAPTER : 7

Group Learning Processes

22. Group Decision and Social Change*

Lewin infused new life into the study of group processes by his
ability to utilize relatively simple experimental tasks to explore and
illustrate a very complicated theoretical conception of social forces and
their interaction. This article reports several investigations of the
process of group decision versus decisions made by individuals in
effecting social change. He discusses the motivational factors involved
in group decision and action, the role of the leader, and the question
of the permanency of social change resulting from group decision.

The following experiments on group decision . . . are not in a state that
permits definite conclusions. But they show the nature of the problems
and the main factors concerned . . .

Scientifically the question of group decision lies at the intersection of
many basic problems of group life and individual psychology. It concerns
the relation of motivation to action and the effect of a group setting on
the individual's readiness to change or to keep certain standards . . . It
is in this wider setting of social processes and social management that
group decision should be viewed as one means of social change . . .

---

* KURT LEWIN. Reprinted and abridged with permission of the publisher from T. M.
Newcomb and E. L. Hartley (Eds.) *Readings in Social Psychology*. New York: Henry Holt
and Co., 1947, pp. 330–44.

253

PLANNING, FACT-FINDING, AND EXECUTION

Planning usually starts with something like a general idea. For one reason or another it seems desirable to reach a certain objective. Exactly how to circumscribe this objective and how to reach it is frequently not too clear. The first step, then, is to examine the idea carefully in the light of the means available. Frequently more fact-finding about the situation is required. If this first period of planning is successful, two items emerge: an "over-all plan" of how to reach the objective and a decision in regard to the first step of action. Usually this planning has also somewhat modified the original idea.

The next period is devoted to executing the first step of the over-all plan. In highly developed fields of social management, such as modern factory management or the execution of a war, this second step is followed by certain fact-findings. For example, . . . the bombing of . . . a certain factory may have been chosen as the first target after careful consideration of various priorities and of the best means and ways of dealing with this target. The attack is pressed home and immediately a reconnaissance plane follows with the one objective of determining as accurately and objectively as possible the new situation (Fig. 1).

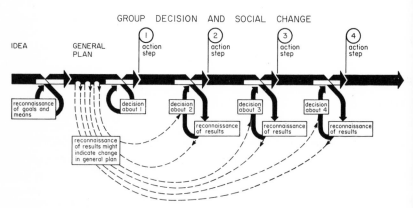

FIG. 1. PLANNING, FACT-FINDING, AND EXECUTION.

This reconnaissance or fact-finding has four functions: It should evaluate the action by showing whether what has been achieved is above or below expectation. It should serve as a basis for correctly planning the next step. It should serve as a basis for modifying the "over-all plan." Finally, it gives the planners a chance to learn, that is, to gather new general insight, for instance, regarding the strength and weakness of certain weapons or techniques of action.

The next step again is composed of a circle of planning, executing, and reconnaissance or fact-finding for the purpose of evaluating the results of the second step, for preparing the rational basis for planning the third step, and for perhaps modifying again the over-all plan.

Rational social management, therefore, proceeds in a spiral of steps each of which is composed of a circle of planning, action, and fact-finding about the result of the action.

In most social areas of management and self-management of groups, such as conducting a conference and committee meeting, family life, or the improvement of intergroup relations within and between nations, we are still lacking objective standards of achievement. This has two severe effects: (1) People responsible for social management are frequently deprived of their legitimate desire for reconnaissance on a realistic basis. Under these circumstances, satisfaction or dissatisfaction with achievement becomes mainly a question of temperament. (2) In a field that lacks objective standards of achievement, no learning can take place. If we cannot judge whether an action has led forward or backward, if we have no criteria for evaluating the relation between effort and achievement, there is nothing to prevent us from coming to the wrong conclusions and encouraging the wrong work habits. Realistic fact-finding and evaluation is a prerequisite for any learning . . .

Group Decision

LECTURE COMPARED WITH GROUP DECISION (RED CROSS GROUPS)

A preliminary experiment in changing food habits was conducted with six Red Cross groups of volunteers organized for home nursing. Groups ranged in size from 13 to 17 members. The objective was to increase the use of beef hearts, sweetbreads, and kidneys . . . There were . . . only 45 minutes available.

In three of the groups attractive lectures were given which linked the problem of nutrition with the war effort, emphasized the vitamin and mineral value of the three meats, giving detailed explanations with the aid of charts. Both the health and economic aspects were stressed. The preparation of these meats was discussed in detail as well as techniques for avoiding those characteristics to which aversions were oriented (odor, texture, appearance, etc.). Mimeographed recipes were distributed. The lecturer was able to arouse the interest of the groups by giving hints of her own methods for preparing these "delicious dishes," and her success with her own family.

For the other three groups Mr. Alex Bavelas developed the following procedure of group decision. Again the problem of nutrition was linked with that of the war effort and general health. After a few minutes, a discussion was started to see whether housewives could be induced to participate in a program of change without attempting any high pressure salesmanship. The group discussion about "housewives like themselves" led to an elaboration of the obstacles which a change in general and particularly change toward sweetbreads, beef hearts, and kidneys would encounter, such as the dislike of the husband, the smell during cooking, etc. The nutrition expert offered the same remedies and recipes for preparation which were presented in the lectures to the other groups. But in these groups preparation techniques were offered after the groups had become sufficiently involved to be interested in knowing whether certain obstacles could be removed.

In the earlier part of the meeting a census was taken on how many women had served any of these foods in the past. At the end of the meeting, the women were asked by a showing of hands who was willing to try one of these meats within the next week.

A follow-up showed that only 3 percent of the women who heard the lectures served one of the meats never served before, whereas after group decision 32 percent served one of them (Fig. 2).

If one is to understand the basis of this striking difference, several factors may have to be considered.

Degree of Involvement. Lecturing is a procedure by which the audience is chiefly passive. The discussion, if conducted correctly, is likely to lead to a much higher degree of involvement. The procedure of group decision in

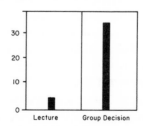

Fig. 2. Percentage of individuals serving type of food never served before, after lecture and after group decision.

this experiment follows a step-by-step method designed (*a*) to secure high involvement and (*b*) not to impede freedom of decision. The problem of food changes was discussed in regard to "housewives like yourselves" rather than in regard to themselves. This minimized resistance to considering the problems and possibilities in an objective, unprejudiced manner, in much the same way as such resistance has been minimized in interviews which use projective techniques, or in a socio-drama which uses an assumed situation of role playing rather than a real situation.

Motivation and Decision. The prevalent theory in psychology assumes action to be the direct result of motivation. I am inclined to think that we will have to modify this theory. We will have to study the particular conditions under which a motivating constellation leads or does not lead to a decision or to an equivalent process through which a state of "considerations" (indecisiveness) is changed into a state where the individual has "made up his mind" and is ready for action, although he may not act at that moment.

The act of decision is one of those transitions. A change from a situation of undecided conflict to decision does not mean merely that the forces toward one alternative become stronger than those toward the other alternative. If this were the case, the resultant force should frequently be extremely small. A decision rather means that the potency of one alternative has become zero or is so decidedly diminished that the other alternative and the corresponding forces dominate the situation. This alternative itself might be a compromise. After the decision people may feel sorry and change their decision. We cannot speak of a real decision, however, before one alternative has become dominant so far as action is concerned. If the opposing forces in a conflict merely change so that the forces in one direction become slightly greater than in the other direction, a state of blockage or extremely inhibited action results rather than that clear one-sided action which follows a real decision.

Lecturing may lead to a high degree of interest. It may affect the motivation of the listener. But it seldom brings about a definite decision on the part of the listener to take a certain action at a specific time. A lecture is not often conducive to decision.

Evidence from everyday experience and from some preliminary experiments by Bavelas in a factory indicate that even group discussions, although usually leading to a higher degree of involvement, as a rule do not lead to a decision. It is very important to emphasize this point. Although group discussion is in many respects different from lectures, it shows no fundamental difference on this point.

Of course, there is a great difference in asking for a decision after a lecture or after a discussion. Since discussion involves active participation of the audience and a chance to express motivations corresponding to different alternatives, the audience might be more ready to "make up its mind," that is, to make a decision after a group discussion than after a lecture. A group discussion gives the leader a better indication of where the audience stands and what particular obstacles have to be overcome.

In the experiment on hand, we are dealing with a group decision after discussion. The decision, itself, takes but a minute or two. (It was done through raising of hands as an answer to the question: Who would like to serve kidney, sweetbreads, beef hearts next week?) The act of decision, however, should be viewed as a very important process of giving dominance to one of the alternatives, serving or not serving. It has an effect of freezing this motivational constellation for action . . .

Individual versus Group. The experiment does not try to bring about a change of food habits by an approach to the individual, as such. Nor does it use the "mass approach" characteristic of radio and newspaper propaganda. Closer scrutiny shows that both the mass approach and the individual approach place the individual in a quasi-private, psychologically isolated situation with himself and his own ideas. Although he may, physically, be part of a group listening to a lecture, for example, he finds himself, psychologically speaking, in an "individual situation."

The present experiment approaches the individual as a member of a face-to-face group. We know . . . that goal setting is strongly dependent on group standards. Experience in leadership training and in many areas of re-education, such as re-education regarding alcoholism or delinquency, indicates that it is easier to change the ideology and social practice of a small group handled together than of single individuals. One of the reasons why "group carried changes" are more readily brought about seems to be the unwillingness of the individual to depart too far from group standards; he is likely to change only if the group changes. We will return to this problem.

One may try to link the greater effectiveness of group decision procedures to the fact that the lecture reaches the individual in a more individualistic fashion than group discussion. If a change of sentiment of the group becomes apparent during the discussion, the individual will be more ready to come along.

It should be stressed that in our case the decision which follows the group discussion does not have the character of a decision in regard to a group goal; it is rather a decision about individual goals in a group setting.

Expectation. The difference between the results of the lectures and the group decision may be due to the fact that only after group decision did the discussion leader mention that an inquiry would be made later as to whether a new food was introduced into the family diet.

Leader Personality. The difference in effectiveness may be due to differences in leader personality. The nutritionist and the housewife who did the lecturing were persons of recognized ability, experience, and success. Still, Mr. Bavelas, who led the discussion and subsequent decision, is an experienced group worker and doubtless of unusual ability in this field.

To determine which of these or other factors are important, a number of systematic variations have to be carried out. To determine, for instance, the role of the decision as such, one can compare the effect of group discussion with and without decision. To study the role of group involvement and the possibility of sensing the changing group sentiment, one could introduce decisions after both, lecture and discussion, and compare their effects.

The following experiments represent partly analytical variations, partly repetitions with somewhat different material.

LECTURE VERSUS GROUP DECISION (NEIGHBORHOOD GROUPS)

Dana Klisurich, under the direction of Marian Radke, conducted experiments with 6 groups of housewives composed of 6–9 members per group. She compared the effect of a lecture with that of group decision. The topic for these groups was increasing home consumption of milk, in the form of fresh or evaporated milk or both . . .

This experiment permits the following conclusions:

1. It shows that the greater effectiveness of the group decision in the first experiment is not merely the result of the personality or training of the leader. The leader was a lively person, interested in people, but she did not have particular training in group work. She had been carefully advised and had had a try-out in the group decision procedure. As mentioned above, the leader in lecture and group decision was the same person.

2. The experiment shows that the different effectiveness of the two procedures is not limited to the foods considered in the first experiment.

3. It is interesting that the greater effectiveness of group decision was observable not only after one week but after two and four weeks. Consumption after group decision kept constant during that period. After the lecture it showed an insignificant increase from the second to the fourth week. The degree of permanency is obviously a very important aspect of any changes in group life . . .

4. As in the first experiment, the subjects were informed about a future check-up after group decision but not after the lecture. After the second week, however, both groups knew that a check-up had been made and neither of them was informed that a second check-up would follow.

5. It is important to know whether group decision is effective only with tightly knit groups. It should be noticed that in the second experiment the groups were composed of housewives who either lived in the same neighborhood or visited the nutrition information service of the community center. They were not members of a club meeting regularly as were the Red Cross groups in the first experiment. On the other hand, a good proportion of these housewives knew each other. This indicates that decision in a group setting seems to be effective even if the group is not a permanent organization.

INDIVIDUAL INSTRUCTION VERSUS GROUP DECISION

For a number of years, the state hospital in Iowa City has given advice to mothers on feeding of their babies. Under this program farm mothers who have their first child at the hospital meet with a nutritionist for from 20–25 minutes before discharge from the hospital to discuss feeding. The mother receives printed advice on the composition of the formula and is instructed on the importance of orange juice and cod liver oil.

There had been indication that the effect of this nutrition program was not very satisfactory. An experiment was carried out by Dana Klisurich under the direction of Marian Radke to compare the effectiveness of this procedure with that of group decision.

With some mothers individual instruction was used as before. Others were divided into groups of six for instruction on and discussion of baby feeding. The manner of reaching a decision at the end of this group meeting was similar to that used in the previous experiments. The time for the six mothers together was the same as for one individual, about 25 minutes.

After two weeks and after four weeks, a check was made on the degree to which each mother followed the advice on cod liver oil and orange juice . . . The group decision method proved far superior to the individual instruction. After four weeks every mother who participated in group decision followed exactly the prescribed diet in regard to orange juice.

The following specific results might be mentioned:

1. The greater effect of group decision in this experiment is particularly interesting. Individual instruction is a setting in which the individual gets more attention from the instructor. Therefore, one might expect the individual to become more deeply involved and the instruction to be fitted more adequately to the need and sentiment of each individual. After all, the instructor devotes the same amount of time to one individual as he does to six in group decision. The result can be interpreted to mean either that the amount of individual involvement is greater in group decision or that the decision in the group setting is itself the decisive factor.

2. Most of the mothers were not acquainted with each other. They returned to farms which were widely separated. Most of them had no contact with each other during the following four weeks. The previous experiment had already indicated that the effectiveness of group decision did not seem to be limited to well-established groups. In this experiment the absence of social relations among the mothers before and after the group meeting is even more clearcut . . .

3. The change after lectures is in all cases smaller than after group decision. However, the rank order of the percentage of change after lectures follows the rank order after group decision, namely (from low to high), glandular meat, fresh milk, cod liver oil for the baby, evaporated milk for the family, orange juice for the baby.

The constancy of this rank order may be interpreted to mean that one can ascribe to each of these foods—under the given circumstances and for these particular populations—a specific degree of "resistance to change." The "force toward change" resulting from group decision is greater than the force resulting from lecture. This leads to a difference in the amount (or frequency) of change for the same food without changing the rank order of the various foods. The rank order is determined by the relative strength of their resistance to change.

4. Comparing the second and the fourth week, we notice that the level of consumption remains the same or increases insignificantly after group decision and lecture regarding evaporated or fresh milk. A pronounced increase occurs after group decision and after individual instruction on

cod liver oil and orange juice, that is, in all cases regarding infant feeding . . .

The Objective of Change. The objective of social change might concern the nutritional standard of consumption, the economic standard of living, the type of group relation, the output of a factory, the productivity of an educational team. It is important that a social standard to be changed does not have the nature of a "thing" but of a "process.". . . In other words, the "level" of consumption, of friendliness, or of productivity is to be characterized as the aspect of an ongoing social process.

Any planned social change will have to consider a multitude of factors characteristic for the particular case. The change may require a more or less unique combination of educational and organizational measures; it may depend upon quite different treatments or ideology, expectation and organization . . .

Social Habits and Group Standards. Viewing a social stationary process as the result of a quasi-stationary equilibrium, one may expect that any added force will change the level of the process. The idea of "social habit" seems to imply that, in spite of the application of a force, the level of the social process will not change because of some type of "inner resistance" to change. To overcome this inner resistance, an additional force seems to be required, a force sufficient to "break the habit," to "unfreeze" the custom.

Many social habits are anchored in the relation between the individuals and certain group standards. An individual . . . may differ in his personal level of conduct . . . from the level which represents group standards . . . by a certain amount. If the individual should try to diverge "too much" from group standards, he would find himself in increasing difficulties. He would be ridiculed, treated severely and finally ousted from the group. Most individuals, therefore, stay pretty close to the standard of the groups they belong to or wish to belong to. In other words, the group level itself acquires value . . .

INDIVIDUAL PROCEDURES AND GROUP PROCEDURES OF CHANGING SOCIAL CONDUCT

If the resistance to change depends partly on the value which the group standard has for the individual, the resistance to change should diminish if one diminishes the strength of the value of the group standard or changes the level perceived by the individual as having social value.

This second point is one of the reasons for the effectiveness of "group carried" changes resulting from procedures which approach the individuals as part of face-to-face groups. Perhaps one might expect single individuals to be more pliable than groups of like-minded individuals. However, experience in leadership training, in changing of food habits, work production, criminality, alcoholism, prejudices, all indicate that it is usually easier to change individuals formed into a group than to change any one of them separately. As long as group standards are unchanged, the individual will resist changes more strongly the farther he is to depart from group standards. If the group standard itself is changed, the resistance which is due to the relation between individual and group standard is eliminated.

Changing as a Three-Step Procedure . . . A change toward a higher level of group performance is frequently short lived: after a "shot in the arm," group life soon returns to the previous level. This indicates that it does not suffice to define the objective of a planned change in group performance as the reaching of a different level. Permanency of the new level, or permanency for a desired period, should be included in the objective. A successful change includes therefore three aspects: unfreezing (if necessary) the present level . . . moving to the new level . . . and freezing group life on the new level . . .

23. Phases in Group Problem Solving*

The first attempt to develop a comprehensive set of scaled categories for analyzing the process of social interaction was formulated by the senior author of this article. Bales and Strodtbeck here re-examine the application of this set of categories to several studies in a test of the hypothesis that groups involved in problem-solving tasks tend to move through a definite sequence of phases in the social interaction process. They discuss their findings in terms of the frequency of acts by type and phase predicted by the hypothesis under examination.

. . . . This paper presents a method of testing for the empirical existence of differentiated phases in group process and some evidence that under

* ROBERT F. BALES AND FRED L. STRODTBECK. Reprinted and abridged with permission of the authors and the publisher from the *Journal of Abnormal and Social Psychology*, 1951, 46:485-95.

certain particular conditions a certain type of phase movement does tend to appear. The type of phase movement described is *not* held to be universal in an empirical sense. Whether it appears empirically depends upon a large number of conditions . . .

By "phases" in the hypothesis presented below, we mean qualitatively different sub-periods within a total continuous period of interaction in which a group proceeds from initiation to completion of a problem involving group decision. Both the hypothesis and the empirical test of the hypothesis presented are to be understood in terms of the standard observation categories briefly defined and presented in Figure 1. These categories constitute a classificatory system into which each single act of each specific individual, whether spoken or gestured, can be placed with an acceptable degree of reliability by trained observers.

A Phase Hypothesis for Full-Fledged Problems

The present phase hypothesis is restricted to instances in which groups work toward the goal of a group decision on a full-fledged problem. Briefly stated, the phase hypothesis is the proposition that under these conditions groups tend to move in their interaction from a relative emphasis upon problems of *orientation,* to problems of *evaluation,* and subsequently to problems of *control,* and that concurrent with these transitions, the relative frequencies of both *negative reactions* and *positive reactions* tend to increase. The terms used in the statement of the hypothesis have as their operational referents the acts which are briefly defined in Figure 1. There are twelve categories on the observation list. The present hypothesis is stated in terms of five groups of these categories, identified by the brackets on the left and right of the list. Categories 6 and 7 are grouped as dealing with problems of orientation; 5 and 8 deal with problems of evaluation; 4 and 9 with problems of control; 10, 11, and 12 with negative reactions; and 1, 2, and 3 with positive reactions. This is a relatively crude grouping, and it seems likely that further experience will enable us to state the hypothesis in a way which treats each category separately.

This particular phase hypothesis is expected to hold only under *certain conditions,* which we try to identify and state below. In general, we believe that the rates of activity we observe in each of the categories, and the way these rates move, over time, vary with changes in the conditions under which the interaction takes place. A major distinction can be drawn between those conditions which may be regarded as constituted prior to

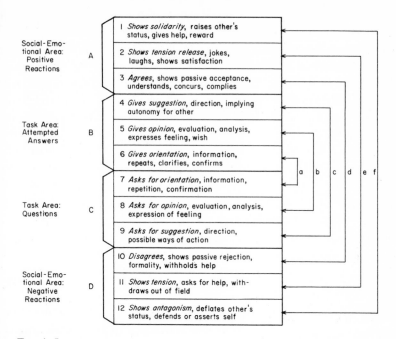

FIG. 1. INTERACTION PROCESS CATEGORIES DEFINED AND GROUPED BY TYPES.

Key: a, problems of orientation, *b,* problems of evaluation, *c,* problems of control, *d,* problems of decision, *e,* problems of tension-management, and *f,* problems of integration.

the period of observation, and those which arise and change during the actual period of observation.

Under prior conditions we tend to think of three broad classes of variables: (1) the personalities of the individual members in their idiosyncratic aspects; (2) those characteristics the members have in common, as a part of their parent culture, as well as of the sub-culture of the particular group under observation; and (3) the organization of the group, that is, the expectations the members have established concerning their social relationships with each other and their different positions in this total constellation of expectations.

In addition to these prior conditions we recognize (4) a series of conditions arising from the nature of the problems faced during the specific period of observation, which change as the group interaction moves through time.

Obviously, we are not able to specify the content of these four classes of conditions with the degree of refinement we should like but as a first approximation we sketch the following requirements as the conditions under which the present phase hypothesis is expected to hold. Whenever the group or the problem does not meet the requirements, the particular phase movement described above is not expected to appear.

1. We have no experimental evidence as to the effects of variations in personality composition of the group on phase movement. Our data are all obtained from groups of persons assumed to be "normal." There are more or less obvious reasons for supposing that the hypothesis should not be expected to apply to groups involving persons of sub-normal intelligence or seriously disturbed personalities.

2. We assume the participants will be adult, or near-adult, members of our own culture. This gives us some expectation that they will speak English, have some formal education, etc. As to the particular subculture of the groups, if the group has met before, it seems possible that special procedural customs, training in group discussion methods, etc., might directly affect the phase movement. Hence, it may be that certain groups could deliberately evolve procedures to circumvent the expected movement, or to follow it in spite of conditions which would otherwise prevent it. Obviously, it is necessary to exclude cases of this type.

3. We require a group in which there is some minimum pressure to maintain its solidarity so that joint decision will have some binding power over the members after the sequence observed, and so that the presence of disagreement, tension, and antagonism will be negatively valued. The status differences among members of the group should not be so great as to deny each member the right to participate and influence the choice of the ultimate decision. It appears likely that serious status struggles within the group may modify the phase movement, although this has not yet been explored. The group size may vary from two to twenty, or may be even larger perhaps, if there is the possibility of face-to-face interaction among the participants over a common problem.

4. As to the duration of the period of observation itself, we require the selection for analysis of a single complete "topical cycle of operations," from the recognition of a topical problem to its disposition by the group. We do not mean this requirement to exclude periods in which a group considers several topics involved in a single major decision, but we do require that when topical problems are considered serially as items on an agenda, the period of discussion on each topic be analyzed separately. Thus, an entire meeting in some cases may be an appropriate period for analysis; in other cases, discussion of a single agenda item may be appro-

priate. In addition, we exclude groups not concerned with a fairly specific problem of group planning and decision. For example, we exclude groups in which the aim or main emphasis is on expressive personal interaction, such as therapeutic interviews, play groups, meetings of friends at a cocktail party, and the like.

Finally, we require a task in which it may be assumed that the functional problems of *orientation, evaluation,* and *control* are each to a major degree unsolved at the beginning of observation and are solved in some degree during the period of observation. More specifically:

a) With regard to *orientation,* members of the group must have some degree of ignorance and uncertainty about the relevant facts, but individually possess facts relevant to decision. A clear example of a group which meets this requirement is a diagnostic council, where the members have seen the patient separately and have made different tests relevant to a decision as to what to do with the patient.

b) With regard to problems of *evaluation,* we require that the problem not be what is sometimes called an "open and shut" case. We need to be able to assume that the members possess somewhat different values or interests and that the problem is such that it involves several different values and interests as criteria by which the facts of the situation and the proposed course of action are to be judged.

c) With regard to problems of *control* (of the members over each other and over the common environment), we require that there be both pressure for a group decision and the expectation of further joint action. It is also assumed that there are a number of possible alternatives with different, and perhaps uncertain, degrees of potential frustration or satisfaction associated with various choices.

When problems lack or greatly minimize any of these three characteristics, we speak of them as being "truncated." When the three characteristics are present, we speak of the problem as being "full-fledged." We do not expect the particular phase hypothesis stated above to hold for truncated problems. Presumably, it may be possible to formulate other phase hypotheses which will describe the phase movement for particular kinds of truncated problems . . .

In order to test the hypothesis empirically, it is necessary to specify the length of a phase. In the absence of any compelling rationale, we have adopted a simple convention: After the observations have been recorded on a moving tape . . . we divide into thirds the cycle of operations which constitutes the total period to be analyzed, producing the *first, middle,* and *final* phases. The total period is divided so that each phase includes one-third of the acts of the total set. (This is approximately equivalent to a time division into thirds, though not quite, since we have observed that there is some tendency for the interaction to speed up toward the latter part of topical cycles.) Since we have no basis for predicting the absolute number of acts by type for each phase, we implement the hypothesis by designating the phase in which we expect the number of acts of a particular type to be high, intermediate, or low when rank-ordered.

We have drawn Figure 2 on the basis of the summary data for all group

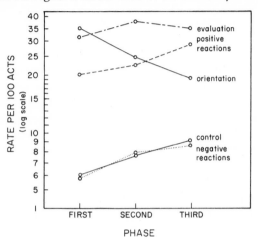

FIG. 2. RELATIVE FREQUENCY OF ACTS BY TYPE AND PHASE, BASED UPON 22 SESSIONS.

sessions examined in the present study in order to illustrate something of the magnitude of the variation which may be expected. It should be emphasized that when we say there is a shift in relative emphasis from problems of orientation in the first phase, to problems of evaluation in the second phase, to problems of control in the third phase, we do not mean that the absolute magnitude for the selected activity is greater than all others in that phase—we mean, rather, that the rate of the selected activity is at its own high point in the designated phase . . .

RATIONALE FOR THE HYPOTHESIS

The present rationale is based directly on conditions present in the overt process of social interaction between individuals through an appreciable lapse of time, and it may be compatible with any number of theories regarding the mental processes of individual problem solving.

In the most general rationale of the whole set of categories, 3 and 10 are thought of as dealing with problems of *decision,* 2 and 11 with problems of *tension management,* and 1 and 12 with problems of *integration* or *reintegration* of the group (See Fig. 1). For the present phase hypothesis, these categories have been grouped, not according to the type of functional problem with which they deal, but according to their implication, positive or negative, for the solution of these types of problems. These problems we call social-emotional problems, to distinguish them from those which are more directly task-connected (See Fig. 1, brackets on left).

It is our assumption that efforts to solve problems of orientation, evaluation, and control—that is, attempts to accomplish the task—tend to lead to differentiation of the roles of the participants, both as to the functions they perform and their gross amounts of participation. This assumption will be tested empirically as a separate hypothesis and reported later. Both types of differentiation tend to carry status implications which may threaten or disturb the existing order or balance of status relations among members and impair the basic solidarity of the group.

This impairment, we assume, tends to grow more marked as the group passes from emphasis on problems of orientation to problems of evaluation, and still more acute as it passes on to its heaviest emphasis on problems of control . . .

Thus, as we conceive the process, a series of changes in the social-emotional relations of the members tend to be set in motion by pressures arising initially from the demands of the external problem or outer situation. These social-emotional problems, as well as the task problems, as they grow more acute, tend to be expressed or dealt with in overt interaction. These, in brief, are the theoretical reasons for expecting that with our crude division of the cycle of operations into three phases, rates in Categories 10, 11, and 12 will be lowest in the initial period and highest in the final period, moving concomitantly with the emphasis on problems of control.

However, at the extreme end of the final period, assuming that the members' attempts at control over the outer situation and over each other are successful and a final decision is reached, we expect the rates in Categories 1, 2 and 3 also to rise to their peak. In other words, the group tends to confirm its agreement and to release in diffuse ways the tensions built up in its prior task-efforts, repairing the damage done to its state of consensus and social integration. We note joking and laughter so frequently at the end of meetings that they might almost be taken as a signal that the group has completed what it considers to be a task effort, and is ready for disbandment or a new problem. This last-minute activity completes the hypothetical cycle of operations both for the task problems and social-emotional problems. The apparent incongruity of predicting a peak for both negative and positive reactions in the third phase is thus explained. Negative and positive reactions tend to be successive emphases within the crudely defined third phase.

TESTING THE PHASE HYPOTHESIS

To test the phase hypothesis, we have considered *all* the protocols available in our files which had been scored in a form appropriate for this investigation. The number is small, only 22 cases. Some of these cases represent several hours of sustained interaction by one group, while others represent the discussion of single topics taken from longer sessions. The groups involved were originally observed for a number of different purposes. Some were experimentally formed groups with assigned tasks. Some were operating groups that allowed us to sit in and observe . . .

The writers have separately judged each of the 22 cases and have agreed that 8 of the 22 satisfactorily fulfill the conditions outlined in earlier paragraphs. The distinction between cases which meet and cases which fail to meet the conditions can be illustrated by discussion of a few concrete cases . . .

Cases 8, 10, 11, and 15 were chess problem-solving groups in which the participants were well oriented to the factual aspects of the problem before beginning interaction. Chess problems are almost uniquely "full information" problems, and the participants were skilled chess players. The profile of scores generated in these sessions was uniformly below the expected limit on giving information and orientation . . . On this basis the writers classified this problem as being "truncated"; it was assumed not to have the necessary requirement for orientation.

An interesting and partially parallel instance is Case 1. Here, again, a chess problem which the group solves cooperatively is involved, but the participants are novices who have just been instructed for one hour in the rules of the game. They have their instruction manuals with them and they are still uncertain about the identity of the pieces and the best mode of attack. The phase sequence of their interaction up to their decision as to their first move is in complete accord with the hypothesis. In the planning of their second move, however, they were able to draw upon their earlier discussion in which they had discussed future moves as well, and the problem was truncated for them in terms of the reduced emphasis on orientation, just as it had been for the previous chess group described above . . .

To test the conformity between the observed orderings and the orderings predicted by our original theoretical analysis, we have employed a model based upon the occurrence of the maxima and minima in the predicted phase rather than a model in which absolute magnitudes were considered. Table 1 presents the hypothesis in a form appropriate for this type of test. Table 1 may be compared with Figure 2 to clarify its meaning . . .

TABLE 1

EXPECTED PHASE IN WHICH FREQUENCIES OF ACTS BY TYPE WILL BE HIGH, INTERMEDIATE, AND LOW UNDER CONDITIONS OF THE FULL-FLEDGED PROBLEM

Type of Act	High	Intermediate	Low
Orientation	First	Middle	Final
Evaluation	Middle	Final	First
Control	Final	Middle	First
Negative	Final	Middle	First
Positive	Final	Middle	First

DISCUSSION OF RESULTS

When all of the acts of the 22 cases are summed together by type of act and phase, the values for each type of act have maxima and minima which correspond exactly with the particular phase movement under discussion. These data are presented in Table 2, and earlier, graphically, in Figure 2. How is this paradoxical finding to be interpreted? . . .

We suggest that parts of the interaction process itself tend to affect other parts in such a way that at the time of any given act, the acts which have gone before, or which have not yet occurred but are expected to come, constitute a set of "internal" conditions which operate in addition to whatever "external" conditions there may be of the sorts specified in the statement of the hypothesis. We know that in the more microscopic act-to-act sequences this is the case. Questions tend to be followed by attempted answers, and these in turn tend to be followed by positive or negative reactions or more questions . . . These are "internal tendencies"

TABLE 2

ACTS BY TYPE AND PHASE, TOTAL FOR 22 CASES

Type of Act	Phase			Total
	First	Middle	Final	
Orientation	1,668	1,170	916	3,574
Evaluation	1,550	1,792	1,656	4,998
Control	285	364	429	1,078
Negative	275	374	408	1,057
Positive	984	1,058	1,361	3,403
Total*	4,762	4,758	4,770	14,290

* The totals in phases are not quite equal due to the fact that no systematic technique was employed to distribute the extra acts when the total acts of a session were not divisible by three.

of the process itself on a microscopic time span. It may be that similar internal tendencies operate on the more molar level of longer chains of sequences leading to group decision.

It can now be pointed out that the rationale of the phase hypothesis presented earlier is essentially an argument based on an assumption that there are internal tendencies of interaction considered as a system distributed between persons and through time. If one starts with the assumption that interaction does constitute a social system and that it will tend to exhibit certain systematic properties on that account, how would he go about demonstrating this empirically? The critical logical difficulty would seem to be that the system he is trying to investigate never operates apart from external conditions which are expected to influence the behavior which actually occurs. The effects of the external conditions are always compounded with, or confounded with, the effects of the internal conditions . . .

The . . . approach which suggests itself is an attempt to randomize in some fashion the kinds of external conditions involved, and to deal with large aggregates of cases. If there are internal tendencies characteristic of interaction as a systematic process or social system, the similarity of these tendencies from case to case, in spite of the differences due to external conditions, would be expected to exert a constant "biasing" effect away from randomness. In aggregates of cases, then, where the external conditions of individual cases are varied enough to average out, one would expect the effects of the internal-system tendencies to become apparent . . .

SUMMARY

A set of categories for the first-hand observation of group process has been presented. A set of conditions has been described which we believe to be characteristic of many staff conferences, committees, and similar groups dealing with problems of analysis and planning with the goal of group decision. We have presented an hypothesis which states that under these specified conditions the process tends to move through time from a relative emphasis upon problems of *orientation,* to problems of *evaluation,* and subsequently to problems of *control,* and that concurrent with these transitions, the relative frequencies of both *negative reactions* and *positive reactions* tend to increase.

It has been shown that all 22 sessions available to the experimenters from prior observations, when considered as an aggregate, show a significant departure from a random distribution of acts between phases. It has further been shown that the observed significance is attributable to the inclusion of cases which meet the specified conditions. Individual cases which do not meet the conditions do not show a significant departure from a random distribution of phase movements.

However, when all of the acts of the 22 cases are summed together by type of act and phase, the values for each type of act have maxima and minima which correspond exactly with the particular phase movement postulated for individual cases under the specified full-fledged conditions. This finding may be accidental. The suggestion is offered, however, that in addition to the external conditions specified, the interaction process should be considered as a system, with internal tendencies which make each part of the process a condition to other parts. These "internal" conditions are assumed to be similar to some degree from case to case and to exert a constant "biasing" effect. This biasing effect becomes apparent either in individual cases under full-fledged external conditions or in aggregates of cases in which differences in external conditions average out . . .

REFERENCES

1. BALES, R. F. 1950. A set of categories for the analysis of small group interaction. *Amer. Social. Rev.* 15:257–63.
2. ELLIOTT, H. S. *The Process of Group Thinking.* New York: Association Press, 1928.
3. GUETZKOW, H., HENRY, W. *Group Projective Sketches,* Ann Arbor, Mich.: Univ. Mich. Press, 1949.
4. LIPPITT, R. 1940. An experimental study of authoritarian and democratic group atmosphere. *Stud. Topol. Vector Psychol.* No. 1, U. Iowa Stud. Child Welf., Vol. 16.

24. Case Study of a Basic Skill Training Group*

Recent interest in group processes has stimulated not only investigations of several characteristics of group interaction, but also studies of the effects of training by means of techniques emphasizing group dynamics and group values. Barron and Krulee describe in detail the course of such a training procedure reported by experienced observers and by the trainees themselves. Particular emphasis is given to evidence of the effects of training upon responsibility toward the group accepted by group members and to the nature of changes which take place in individuals as such responsibility develops.

. . . This article gives a picture of a training group in action. It shows what the faculty hoped to accomplish, how they hoped to accomplish it, and what they saw as key problems in making it a valuable learning experience. It gives a picture of the behavior of the faculty member, the behavior of individual delegates and their interactions with one another, and the content of the discussions. Emphasis in the article is primarily on how the group operated from day to day, with only incidental consideration of the actual curriculum covered by the group. The material has been organized to bring into clearer focus two major dynamic trends that seem to be important characteristics of the development of a training group. These are:

(1) The major dimensions of group growth and development as indicated by increase in responsibility of the members for the operation of the group, with a corresponding change in the role taken by the faculty member;

(2) The self development of individuals in the group as shown by their changing perceptions of their roles in relation to the group, by changes in the behavior of individual members, and by the increased participation of the members in the group's discussion.

The article concludes with a summary of the major outcomes from this group experience and a comparison of the actual outcomes with the outcomes desired by the faculty and with the expectations of the members of the group.

* MARGARET E. BARRON AND GILBERT K. KRULEE. Reprinted and abridged with permission of the authors from J. R. P. French and L. P. Bradford (Eds.). The dynamics of the discussion group. *Journal of Social Issues,* 1948, Vol. 4, No. 2, pp. 10–30.

SOURCES OF DATA

All delegates were assigned to one of five similar Basic Skill Training Groups. The delegates and the faculty member assigned to a given group worked together for fourteen meetings, each of which lasted about three hours. This case study is based on the experience of one of the groups. All five groups were quite similar, yet each had some unique characteristics. The data used are taken from the records of the "anecdotal" observer and the "group content" observer.

The duty of the group content observer was to keep as complete a record as possible of what was actually said while the group was in session. The content record was designed to give an objective account of the behavior of the individuals in the group. This observer was specifically directed not to interpret in any way the behavior of the group. There were five group content observers who rotated among the five training groups. From their records we can study the behavior and the activities of the group from the viewpoint of an observer who was not a permanent member of the group and who was seeing it in relation to four other similar groups.

The anecdotal observer met with the same group for the entire laboratory period. It was his function to observe the way in which the group operated, the relationships between individuals, and how the group and the members changed or developed during the laboratory period. The anecdotal observer was directed to attempt to interpret what he saw so as to reach insights into why members behaved as they did and what was behind the changes that took place. During so-called "evaluation sessions" he used these observations to help the group look at itself more objectively and improve its functioning . . .

GOALS OF THE DELEGATES

In a general sense the goals of the training staff and of the delegates were complementary. The faculty wanted to help the delegates develop as much skill as possible in handling human relations and the delegates wanted to be helped. However in terms of how the training group should operate in order to reach this goal, there were initially significant differences between the faculty and the delegates.

Many of the delegates defined learning in terms of acquiring additional information about techniques for handling specific situations. They thought that the ability to write down or talk about new techniques was equivalent to being able to use them. Many of the delegates, also, were oriented towards human relations for specific situations rather than towards a general basic skills framework suitable for work in industry, school, or community. Each person tended to think that his situation was unique and therefore that his goals were unique. Many of them, consequently, expected to spend most of the time talking about and developing definite answers to specific problems.

GOALS OF THE FACULTY

The faculty agreed that the training goal was to help improve the delegates' ability to handle human relations situations. They saw this general goal as differentiated into the following areas which had to be approached simultaneously:

(1) Increased understanding on a verbal level of underlying principles of dealing with people.

(2) Increased sensitivity to and awareness of those dynamic interactions between people in groups that are relevant to the diagnosis of human relations situations.

(3) Skill in actually using this understanding. The faculty believed that the ability to act correctly or wisely in a situation involved more than a set of principles and diagnostic ability.

(4) Increased understanding of one's own motivation and increased self-awareness. The faculty felt that self-understanding was essential in working with others . . .

To reach these goals of bringing about understandings and skills in human relations, certain methods were agreed upon by the faculty. These were:

(1) The use of skill practice techniques to supplement discussion. For example, role playing was used extensively both to increase member insight into a problem and to give practice in skills.

(2) The use of periodic evaluation sessions in which the group analyzed its previous operations. In this way, each group became its own laboratory example of the phases of group development and the skills required to facilitate such development.

(3) The encouragement of group experimentation in making changes in its own operation.

(4) The attempt to operate as much as possible at the level of basic

skills; because at this level the problems of the delegates were essentially similar.

The faculty members also had some personal goals: to improve their skills in working with groups and to increase their understanding of how to help people develop insight and how to help groups operate more efficiently and productively.

CONFLICT AREAS IN THE OPERATION OF THE GROUP

In general, the outcomes desired by both faculty and delegates were in complete agreement. Initially, however, there was some disagreement over how the group should operate in order to reach these goals as rapidly as possible. As has been pointed out, the training experience was at variance with the expectations of some of the members, and certain resistances developed. This had been expected. Conflict and resistance had been anticipated because of the following differences which the staff felt would appear:

(1) The delegates would tend to feel that there was information on a verbal level which could readily be communicated and which would be sufficient for handling problems. This would conflict with the faculty's emphasis on the need for *studying the skill of using information* and *the skill of operating in terms of the change-agent framework.*

(2) The faculty would emphasize the learning value of trying out or practicing a skill, whereas many members would feel that skills had been mastered as soon as they could be verbally communicated.

(3) The delegates would tend to think of problems in terms of their work situations, in which case each delegate would think that he had nothing in common with other delegates. Also, it might be difficult for some delegates to accept the change-agent framework as something useful for their particular situations.

(4) Many of the delegates would expect to be given answers; they might not understand at first why they were expected to participate to such a degree and why the major responsibilities were being delegated to them.

(5) The whole notion of examining their own operation through evaluation sessions might be strange to many delegates, and initially they might not see how such a study would be of any use to them in reaching those goals which motivated them to come to Bethel.

The resistances listed above did actually develop in the training groups. How they were expressed in one of the groups is shown in the following picture of a group in action. In this picture, the series of fourteen meetings is divided into four sections, each of which seems to represent a significant phase of group development. As will be noted, a major part of the first two periods was spent in reconciling the differences in expectations and viewpoints of delegates and faculty, in reaching an acceptance of a method of operation, and in creating an integrated work group. This was accomplished superficially during the first period (meetings 1-3), but the process continued actively throughout the second period (meetings 4-7), during which the group attempted to formulate its goals more clearly and develop a satisfactory method of operation. Marked development and progress occurred in period three (meetings 8-12), with increasing responsibility on the part of the delegates and a change in the role of the faculty member. This trend continued in period four (meetings 13-14), with the addition of greater member insight and understanding.

A Basic Skill Training Group in Action

INITIAL PERIOD (MEETINGS 1-3)

Meeting 1. The faculty member, whom we shall call Ray Andrews, opened the first meeting by talking briefly about what makes a group: common goals, common interests, emotional belongingness. He set a style of easy informality and asked the delegates to think through with him what should happen to them in order for them to become a group. Out of this discussion a framework developed for the introduction of members, what they would like to know about each other which would contribute to their establishment as a group. Major emphasis was focused on discovering common interests, experience, and ability, and common responsibilities for improving human relationships.

The leader . . . started by introducing himself, telling about his experience, training, and interests in the terms in which he wanted the group to think and operate, emphasizing particularly what he had in common with various members. The members used the same framework, but generally talked somewhat more in terms of the content of their own jobs. Some members expressed very specific interests and goals. Lou wanted "to attack the gap which exists between thought and action," and "to change attitudes and points of view." Helen was concerned with changing and improving food habits, and Pete with getting acceptance and understanding of improved administrative procedures. There was a good level of interest as indicated by active questioning of the member who was introducing himself at the time, and the members discovered much more in common than they had previously anticipated. They were interested in learning about the people with whom they would be working for the next three weeks; they were also interested in the process of getting a group acquainted and started, for this was a problem they had all faced in other groups. The tempo of the meeting was slow at first, with an increase in participation and interest as the meeting advanced.

During the discussion various questions arose which members wanted to consider, as for example whether a group needs to have a common enemy. It was agreed that such items be listed for consideration later, a procedure which seemed acceptable at the time. Continuing additions to the list, however, proved to be a source of frustration at some of the later meetings.

Meeting 2. The next day the level of morale in the laboratory was definitely lower. The differences between the expectations of the delegates and the way the laboratory was actually starting to operate were too great for comfort. The testing phase of the research program . . . was still receiving major attention and there was a rather general feeling that even now, after three days, the training had not yet really started. Aggression toward the research program was freely expressed. There was complete group agreement that the tests were requiring time which the members would prefer to spend in other ways. At this meeting, however, introductions were completed, and through them the feeling of homogeneity of interests among the members was further strengthened.

In his introduction Lou mentioned role playing as a technique in which he was greatly interested. A lively discussion ensued.

"I don't see how we can use role playing with rural people," said Jack.

"But it has been used there and in many other settings," replied Lou.

"I think it could be used in teaching people how to work with groups," said Pete.

"I think you could cover more ground through discussion," suggested Ann.

It was obviously a "hot" issue. After a few minutes Ray proposed that it be deferred to the list of items that were being postponed for later consideration. The group accepted this direction from the faculty member, but with it came a marked drop in interest. Ray was the authority, they would do as he said, but at the same time there was an increasing feeling of frustration in postponing things that were of interest.

As will be noted particularly in meeting 6 . . . strong resistance to role playing developed during the second period of the group's growth. The cutting off of discussion at a time when the group's interest was high and when the subject had arisen spontaneously may well have increased the strength of the subsequent resistance.

Reaction to the many new or unusual words which were being used in the laboratory, "Bethelesque" as they came to be called, began to be expressed in a way that persisted throughout the laboratory program. "Change-agent," "involvement," "out-group," and the like proved good for a laugh and served as effective tension relievers.

In spite of the resistance that appeared and the problems that might be developing, there was an easy, relaxed, permissive atmosphere, and good progress was made in strengthening group feeling.

Meeting 3. The leader's goals for the third meeting were: (1) to improve feelings about the research program; (2) to finish the testing; (3) to help the group look at how it is doing; and (4) to give the delegates information and a feeling of getting started in actual training.

The group eased into action with informal leaderless conversation. Ray gradually got more involved in this, began speaking a little louder, and in a few minutes established himself in the leader role. This was in definite contrast to the two previous meetings in which the members looked to the leader expectantly to open the meeting.

Ray first gave a brief explanation of the purpose of the research. "These are the pre-training measures. We want to find out how you people act before and after the training. That is all part of what goes on in a training laboratory and is important in helping evaluate the effectiveness of training and the usefulness of various training methods."

Then they were given the "productivity test" which required that they work together as a group in a job of conference planning. After the test Pete asked: "How do you think we did, Mr. Andrews?"

"Well, how do you feel about that?" replied Ray. "We might look at ourselves and see what we have been doing." This started the first period of real self-evaluation. The test provided some protection. Members were doing an assigned task and were not behaving as they would under "normal" conditions. This made it somewhat easier to be critical of each other than it might have been otherwise. Initial comments related specifically to the test.

Pete said: "I felt Jack, as chairman, spent too much time discussing what we already had in written form on the test material that was given us."

Later self-criticism developed, often with explanations for the behavior. Peg commented: "I think I did a lot of railroading. A group like this is too big for a planning job such as we were given unless somebody pushes things along."

Ray: "How did the rest of you feel about that? Did you resent railroading?"

Harry: "I resented it. I felt what we did was very arbitrary."

Peg: "But we had only an hour and we had to get something done."

After further active discussion Jack observed: "It is interesting that in this fake test situation we've held to our points of view even after the test was over. We were much more excited than normally."

Ray helped members to think about what had been happening in the evaluation by asking: "I wonder how you feel about this looking at ourselves. Sometimes it is helpful, and sometimes it is pretty annoying." It was a new experience for most of them and they were not yet ready to comment.

The leader then started working on what was seen by the delegates as actual training, and presented the set of ideas which would serve as a common denominator for the group during the laboratory period. He said, in brief, that they were concerned with effecting change in three possible areas: people's feelings, how people think, and how people act. He then developed a framework for listing skills which are needed by a person who wants to effect change in others, the "change-agent framework" as it came to be called. This curriculum set the direction for the work of the group . . .

A wide variety of examples were used as illustrations, and the group agreed verbally that all their problems of effecting change fitted into this outline. The presentation was largely a lecture. As such, it was in accord with the pre-laboratory expectations of the members and was well accepted. Pete commented: "I felt we were ready for a factual type of presentation." This expectation was jarred somewhat, however, when Ray asked the group: "What procedures do you see for making use of this framework?" It would have been more comfortable if Ray had told them how to use it.

At this meeting there was a definite indication of emerging leadership on the part of several group members, particularly Jack, Pete, and Peg. A trend started which became quite common at later meetings for one member to take over the leadership role for a while and then pass the ball to someone else. Progress was made in bringing into the group several members who had been very much on the side-lines. The meeting closed with the feeling that the birth of the group was about completed. There was a perception of common needs and an awareness of common goals, but the members were just beginning to recognize their share of responsibility for the operation of the group.

PROGRESS TOWARD GROUP GOALS (MEETINGS 4-7)

Meeting 4. At the end of the third meeting there had been a sense of direction and a feeling that "now we can move ahead." The fourth meeting, however, failed to sustain this. Problems of operation still assumed major importance and not much real progress was achieved.

Immediately obvious was a marked change in the seating arrangement, a change which was interpreted by one member as "a cleavage between the practical men and the educational people." The pattern of leadership in the meeting was different, too. Previously Jack and Pete had seemed to be vying for the leadership role. Today they were united against Peg and Ann, and this further emphasized the feeling of impending split in the group.

Discussion continued on how the change-agent framework might be used. Ray refused to answer this for them, and there was a growing uncertainty as to his role, what might be expected of him, and where the group was going and at what speed. There also seemed to be a growing irritation because of the time certain group members were taking. Some members knew more than others, were more sophisticated in the concepts of the laboratory, and there was a feeling of impatience in waiting for some of the slower ones to catch up.

At this meeting there was the first evidence of between-meeting planning by members in order to accomplish their personal objectives. This was revealed in the evaluation, when Harry commented: "A little politicking ahead of time is good. Jack and I did it today. We wanted a discussion of the various skills and we came out with pretty much that." Further light was shed on this after the meeting when Pete commented: "I'm going to do some politicking, too. Those guys, Jack and Harry, want to take a strong hand and not have any role playing. I want to use role playing and I'm going to see what I can stir up."

The meeting received an average rating of "good" by the members (on the rating scale of *no good, mediocre, all right, good,* and *swell*), but the leader sensed the impending split and rated it at the midpoint.

Meeting 5. For the fifth meeting the leader had five specific goals:

1. Diagnose and mend any possible split in the group.
2. Improve evaluation procedures.
3. Reduce group's expectation that leader is expert.
4. Explore best method of procedure in making use of skill area outline.
5. Warm up one member (Harry) who had held himself quite apart from the group.

Progress was made particularly in improving evaluation procedures, and a franker, more forthright evaluation helped in the partial attainment of goals 1, 3, and 5.

The split that had begun to be evident at the fourth meeting came out much more clearly. The leader distributed a revised and expanded list of skill areas pertinent to effecting change in other persons or groups, and attempted to give the group a feeling of success from its part in developing it as the result of work in previous meetings. There was considerable uncertainty, however, as to what the list was for and how to use it.

Pete said: "My feeling is that this is a road map showing things we could do. We'll study it and then go back and take some trips. Each trip would be a skill we ought to have."

Ann objected somewhat to this concept: "We're building pigeon holes in which to put our tools."

"I don't want to put the tools in pigeon holes," countered Pete. "I want to learn to use them."

The discussion pointed up a definite cleavage between the action people, those who wanted to learn *how,* and those who were more interested in classifying skills precisely, arranging them in carefully worked out categories, and talking about them on the theoretical level.

There was another interesting development. The whole group displayed some uncertainty as to the role of the faculty member. They had expected him to give them information, and he was not quite coming across. He had given out the list, but he would not tell them what to do with it. The responsibility rested with the group, and it took some change in orientation before they were able to accept it.

A large part of the change seemed to have been accomplished through the evaluation which took place at this session. It marked a painful step in group growth. Immediately after the mid-morning break in the meeting Ray suggested that the group make use of its own laboratory experience in attempting to solve the problem of how to begin. He called on Karen, the "anecdotal observer," to give her impressions of the group so far. Previously she had commented only on the group as a whole and on the leader. At this meeting, for the first time, she commented also on individual members. "At first we weren't a group. But the feeling of having common interests and goals, of being a team that is working together, became much stronger after the second meeting. At the last meeting and again today there seems to have been a drop in our cohesiveness. There is less feeling of solidarity as a group. I wonder whether there is a relation between this and shifts in the leadership role. First Peg and Pete were the main participants. Then Jack became much more active, and I seemed to sense some competition between him and Pete. Today Pete has been quite active and Jack has played ball with him. They were working together. Ann now seems to be on the other side of the fence, taking issue with Pete on various points."

Jack whispered aside: "This is very interesting."

Karen continued: "I wonder what Harry is thinking. Is he watching us to see whether he can find what he wants in the group? He was very active last meeting, but is not so active today. It's a problem to strike a pace that fits the group as a whole. Some of us are interested in by-passes. Some of us have clear-cut goals that we want to pursue. Some have a lot of faith in getting words down. Others feel that our concern must be with much more than words. . . . Dick has not been so active the last couple of days. I wonder what he is thinking. And Helen said nothing last time, but I felt she followed everything. One group problem is defining what we mean by participation. Does it have to be verbal? . . . We all have questions about how the group is operating. Some of us seem to be waiting for things to get going. How introspective should we be in looking at ourselves as members of the group?" There was a pause.

Ray helped the delegates to consider what the observer had said: "What are the causes of personality differences in the group? We've had splits of different types; all have to be compromised. What do you think of what Karen has said? I'm interested in why Jack's participation increased so much."

Jack: "Isn't it possible to grow without much verbal participation? I think a person can grow without taking an active part."

Helen: "Yes, I don't verbalize easily. But I feel my concepts are changing. I'm getting a lot out of it. It is selfish I know. I wasn't conscious that I wasn't taking part the first day."

Jack: "That first day I could have been over in one of the corners just watching the various people and their motivations for taking part."

Peg contrasted her own behavior: "I just have to get into it. It is very easy for me to try to get into the swim and to take the time of the group unnecessarily."

Others commented on what they had been doing. Ray summarized: "Some of us feel secure to participate. Some of us feel obligated to jump in. Others are just watching. That is hindering us in becoming a group. But many are participating more. I'm never sure of what Harry is thinking."

Pete: "I think he is running us from behind the scenes."

Lou: "He's probably taking it all in, but rather aloof."

Sarah: "I think our digressing bothers him."

Peg: "He's frowning on us."

Ann: "Perhaps he's just shy and shouldn't be probed."

Ray: "I hope you'll excuse us for using you as an example of a group member. What are your feelings?"

Harry: "Our bickering about words is very distasteful to me because I used to have a boss who did that. Sarah had me right when she said I wanted to move."

About an hour was spent in this self-evaluation, and members found that there was much to see. The leader concluded this part of the session by emphasizing that this is not looking in terms of goods and bads, but in terms of the factors that must be recognized in reaching the goals of the group.

This was a new type of group experience. Members had been amazingly frank in expressing feelings about themselves and each other. Everyone took it, but it made several people pretty sore, and the group was moved into an evaluation of the evaluation by Pete's comment: "I think it was a lousy evaluation. We dealt in terms of personality and not of group interaction."

In all of this, however, there was a permissive atmosphere, with good thinking by the members, freedom to express opinions, and a good degree of self-discipline by the group. The leader was throwing the responsibility on members and they were taking it. But the evaluation part of the meeting was definitely a form of shock treatment for some. The meeting received the lowest average rating to date, and the leader commented on the post-meeting rating form: "Catharsis occurred, but there was little chance for soothing any hurt feelings."

Meeting 6. Today the group expelled the leader from the head of the table by filling in the end seats before he got there, an overt expression of their changed perception of his role. The agenda for the session was developed by the group, their first experience in agenda setting. The first item was a discussion of how to go about learning in the various skill areas, and the leader pointed out three possible directions that might be followed.

The split between those who wanted action and those who wanted to talk about it became wider.

Pete suggested: "We should set up a common situation that we can role play. Then we would get the feeling of the thing. If we role play any situation the same skills will be used."

Harry and Jack objected. Ann supported them: "I want to clear up my questions and put things on the shelves."

Pete objected again: "That's where I disagree. I don't want it on the shelves. I want it inside me."

The conflict was more active than at any previous meeting. It was finally agreed that both discussion and role playing would be used in the meetings, and the role playing supporters had a definite sense of achievement.

After the meeting the observer learned that Pete and Lou had role played what they called the "big push" the night before in order to improve their own skills in putting across the idea of role playing, and they felt quite satisfied with their accomplishment. In this controversy the leader had taken a very neutral stand. Whether or not role playing would be used was a matter for group decision and not something to be imposed by the leader.

Both in the meeting itself and in the evaluation members expressed a lot of aggression against each other and the leadership. It received the lowest rating of any of the meetings, but it cleared the way to move ahead.

Meeting 7. As was suggested in the meeting itself and brought out more clearly in the evaluation, there had been a great deal of activity since meeting 6 which influenced the seventh session. In the afternoon program there had been a panel discussion on role playing, followed by the first session of the role playing clinic, both of which were attended by some of the members of this training group. On the informal side one of the members had had a long talk with the leader, and Harry, Jack, and Dick had had dinner together and discussed the problems of the group. They decided to experiment with whether Harry and Jack could focus on Dick and get the group as a whole to accept him as leader, displacing Pete.

Jack commented that they had it all cooked up, even to the seating arrangement, placing themselves in the form of a triangle around the table. The plan worked, with no awareness of the collusion on the part of faculty member, observers, or other members. This incident and others like it may have contributed to the growing concern of members of the laboratory that skills in effecting change in others might be used for undemocratic ends. A special group was formed to study this problem.

At this meeting further questions about role playing were raised and clarified. Role playing was not a substitute for discussion, but was an integral part of the discussion method. It was valuable in stimulating more active interest and involvement on the part of the members of a group, in facilitating communication about behavior where words alone often prove inadequate, and in helping make discussions concrete.

The group then explored possibilities in which they might try some action and selected a situation in which they would be making a sociological study of a small town. They assumed that there was great resistance in the community, suspicion of strangers, fear of hurting business, resistance to any change. They also assumed that there were three main interests among persons in their own group who would make the survey: scientists, welfare workers, and businessmen. Details were developed in the discussion and the situation became quite vivid. "This is a real set-up," was the comment.

The role playing at this meeting, the first that had been tried in the group, was very revealing. In the evaluation it was agreed that it had brought out feelings and increased sensitivity to problems which members would not have been aware of if they had just talked about the situations. "It helps you see the other side of the story." "You remember more about a situation than when you just talk about it." "The emotional aspects are better portrayed." By the end of the meeting the factions and conflict had largely cleared away and the group gave this the highest rating of any meeting except the final session.

INCREASING MEMBER RESPONSIBILITY AND CHANGING FACULTY ROLE (MEETINGS 8-12)

The plan for a survey, developed at the previous meeting, supplied material for role playing and discussion for most of the remaining sessions. As seen by the members, the first job of the eighth meeting was to select roles for themselves and to develop a plan of action. Ray suggested that the group choose one of its own members to serve as chairman. He took a rather active part in structuring the situation in this way and in placing more responsibility on the members. It was done smoothly and there was no sense of being pushed in a particular direction. There seemed, indeed, to be some feeling of relief in having a direction in which to go and a procedure under which to operate.

A different member led each of the meetings during this period. This was useful, both through the practice which it gave and the increased sensitivity it produced to various kinds of leadership techniques. Members learned that there was a great difference between understanding the principles of democratic leadership on the verbal level and actually being a democratic leader. One leader monopolized much of the time of the group by expressing her opinions to them. One felt that it was his responsibility to determine the agenda for the meeting, and another seemed compelled to try to answer all questions that were raised rather than use the potentialities of the other members. But the chairmen were not permitted to get away with such behavior. The members knew what democratic leadership was and they were not going to take autocracy. One leader commented later: "I felt I was wrestling with a healthy bull."

Through these meetings work continued on the basic skills, largely by means of role playing various aspects of the community survey, planned in the seventh meeting. Members divided themselves into scientists, welfare workers, and businessmen and developed individual roles within these sub-groups. The action opened with a situation in which the social scientists of the group attempted to convince the other members of the value of a survey of the town. From time to time role playing was interrupted for brief comments, followed by a more extended analysis in terms of change-agent skills that had been used.

Now that the chairmen were being drawn from the group it was necessary to give further consideration to the role of the faculty member . . . This was clarified gradually as the meetings advanced. Ray came to be recognized in two major capacities. First he was seen as the conscience or superego of the group, helping them to progress toward the expressed group goal of learning the basic skills. Part of this job was to help members look at themselves more objectively and develop clearer insights into their roles in the group. He was also seen as a resource person, someone who had a great deal to give, but who was not essential to group functioning.

There was an interesting change during meetings 9, 10, and 11 in the group's attitude toward Ray. In the ninth meeting there was some evidence of frustration because the group, rather than the faculty member, was compelled to make decisions and run things, though by the end of the meeting the group was accepting its responsibility more willingly. At the tenth meeting there was further discussion of the appropriate role of the faculty member when someone else was serving as leader. In the evaluation session it was brought out that the delegate-leader tried to have Ray function as a member of the group, believing that this would be a good way to use him as a resource person. The discussion of what he had tried to do resulted in a somewhat clearer understanding of how to use a resource person.

During this meeting Ray was called out of the room to an alleged emergency faulty meeting. This was the "leader-out" test, planned as a measure of the growth and development of all five groups. In his absence there was no change in the method of operation. The group no longer depended on him for direction or for strength to continue its operation. When his absence was discussed later, the major question that was raised was how much the group had missed that he might have contributed had he been present.

By the eleventh meeting the attitude toward Ray had undergone a complete shift from what it had been in the earlier meetings. At the request of the group he had brought to the meeting information on observation instruments and he presented this material largely in the form of a lecture. This procedure was definitely criticized in the evaluation. "There was too much lecture today. We were bleeding the leader without bleeding ourselves." This contrasted sharply with earlier meetings where the lack of lecture material resulted in resistance from the group.

There was also a change in the way members looked at themselves. Role playing was used extensively, and behind the partial projection of the role members became quite frank in expressing their perceptions of other members of the group. Gradually there was developed the use of soliloquy in which members expressed out loud their feelings about how they saw themselves. And if another member of the group felt that this was not the real feeling or that the person speaking had not gone deep enough or needed help in self-expression, he would come in as "alter-ego," attempting to put himself in the place of the member who was soliloquizing and express his perceptions. Members became more sensitive to the needs of others and positive efforts were made to understand and help their associates.

At the beginning of the eleventh meeting Harry told the group: "Peg is playing my role today so that I can see what a person who is not a member of the group looks like."

When the meeting was more than half over the observer noticed that

Peg had been sitting with her head in her hands for some time and had participated very little. She was in the role of Harry sitting in a somewhat withdrawn fashion and doodling. A minute later she said in Harry's role: "Don't tell me that you are going to get into role playing." Harry seemed amused, but later commented that that was not what he would have said.

After the meeting Peg reported: "I have made a wonderful discovery. What Harry does to make him seem out of the group is that he never contributes anything from his own experience. When I sat here and couldn't give anything to the group, it just about killed me."

Through these five sessions (meetings 8-12) the group continued to work on the various skill areas and improve abilities in them. Members showed greater skill than previously in diagnosing situations, in keeping a discussion on the track, in getting people to cooperate, and in being sensitive to the other person's point of view. Members gained both skills and information. They also gained more insight into their own roles and those of others. Many of the blocks had been cleared away and productivity was increasing. There was a definite sense of structure and goal orientation in the group that had not been present the week before.

THE FINAL DAY (MEETINGS 13-14)

On the last day of the laboratory two meetings of the group were held. As members assembled that morning there was an atmosphere that might be described as a combination of the last day in school plus some elements of the morning after. Members were late in arriving, and there was a good deal of kidding, horseplay, and friendly aggression. Several tried to postpone the meeting by suggesting adjournment for coffee. The group was faced again with the "productivity test," but seemed unable to get down to business. After much random activity, the voice of the group conscience was heard when Jack said: "We have a job to do. Let's do it." About half the time allotted to the test had already been wasted, but when the group started to work it did an amazing job. The job was divided and different parts of it went forward concurrently through four sub-committees, with free communications between these sub-groups. On the surface it appeared chaotic, but closer inspection revealed a well organized, purposeful group that knew where it was going and how to get there.

In accordance with the wishes of the group the rest of the meeting was spent on problems of skill areas 5 and 6, "carrying out the plan successfully and productively," and "evaluation and assessment of changee's progress, methods of working and human relations." In this discussion the group made extensive use of itself and its operations, evaluating its own progress and methods.

The final session (meeting 14) was devoted almost entirely to the self-evaluation of the role of each member in the group. The form of this self-evaluation was proposed by Harry, who remarked: "I don't want the group to drop dead, but I would like to have an alter-ego work with us as we evaluate ourselves." It was decided that each member would attempt to soliloquize about his role in the group as he saw it. During his soliloquy other members, as "alter-egos," would be free to make comments that might contribute to greater understanding.

Members looked at themselves in turn. After several others had finished, Harry said: "I don't know just what my role was in the group. I was pretty confused for the first several days. I just sat back and watched. I didn't want to make any mistakes. Karen sort of brought the issue to a head. She said I wasn't a member of the group. I thought I would try to work on her suggestion. I don't know whether I came into the group after that. I tried hard."

Peg (as alter-ego): "I think the last several days I really have come in."

Harry: "I guess I have. Maybe it was getting Peg's suggestion about what I was doing. She helped out by playing my role. I watched her pretty closely."

Ray (as alter-ego): "I really was interested in the group, but people didn't know I was."

Peg (as alter-ego): "Some of my gestures made them think I was out of it."

Harry: "Peg brought that out when she role-played me. After this I will look physically present at least."

Ann (as alter-ego): "I am really sort of sensitive and want approval, but I am shy about making contacts that will get it. In this group I couldn't help banging up against other personalities and coming out of my shell."

Harry objected: "But I don't think I have a shell."

Ray (as alter-ego): "But I do like to know how things stand."

Harry: "If the content level gets somewhat low it gets interesting to try a few experiments."

Pete (as alter-ego): "It is easy to push a group around."

Harry: "I was never aware of how easy it was to push a group."

Ray (as alter-ego): "That was quite a point that Peg picked up in role playing."

Harry: "That was a good use of role playing. I think there were a lot of feelings in that, my own and hers. They were both changed."

Peg then started to soliloquize about herself: "In the beginning of the laboratory I had a tendency to be tense. I sat with clenched fists. What I expected to get was so different from what I got that I had to be awakened to the idea that there was something happening to me inside, not on paper."

Ray (as alter-ego): "I'm glad that I believe in participating."

Peg: "I have a fear of taking too much time of the group, but at the same time I have a feeling of responsibility for the group."

Lou (as alter-ego): "But if I had taken too much time the group would let me know."

Peg: "The group did let me know. I found toward the end that no group member asked me to contribute while almost every other member of the group had special references made to them. They felt when it was my turn I would contribute. I felt I had taken too much time which was my fault."

Harry (as alter-ego): "I have more skill than any of the others. I had a real contribution to make."

Peg: "I think my alter-ego misses the point. I think it is a desire to be a contributor rather than a belief that I could contribute. I feel that what I said took more time than it was worth."

Ray (as alter-ego): "I learn by moving in on things and participating."

Peg: "I learned that you could have a completely erroneous picture of someone, and by role playing his part get a different picture. My feelings toward Harry before role playing were completely emotional and after that I have some sort of intelligent insight into him. I felt at first that he was doing it on purpose and that he didn't want the group to achieve, until I discovered by role playing that I had been entirely wrong."

* * * * *

Part of the assessment went far beyond the group and their roles in it. Lou commented: "It's a matter of putting aside your immediate aims and your own little world. Being thrust into the group here does something to us, bringing together these people from all over the place who have their own separate worlds and aims. If we can put them all together we will have one big world. But you've got to be patient. I found myself sitting and waiting until a guy would get warmed up. You can't hurry them. You may use the wrong tone in trying to cut it short. You can't build democracy in a day. It takes a long time to get the skills needed to permeate our society. I wonder if we realize that what goes on here is the same as what goes on in the broader community. We are similar to the outside world."

The members did not want to close the session and leave, and several commented afterwards that it was almost a spiritual experience. They had examined the changes which had taken place in themselves individually and as a group at Bethel. They saw themselves through new eyes, they shared and refined their feelings through the group process, and they came to a reluctant close with a higher level of insight and goal orientation than most of the members had ever previously experienced.

Summary and Evaluation

This article has presented a picture of a Basic Skill Training Group as it appeared to trained observers. The discussion has centered on two aspects of the group's behavior: first, the activities entered into by the group, and second, how the group organized itself and how the members interacted with one another during these activities. This picture of the group brings into focus certain major trends of group development. It also suggests the value of such group experience as a means of improving the human relations skills of the members.

1. The group was willing to accept and make extensive use of the methods of operation that had been considered important by the faculty members, namely, the curriculum framework, skill practice by means of role playing, evaluation sessions, and the utilization of the group itself in the study of groups.

2. In terms of the training rationale and philosophy of the faculty the changes in the functioning of the group were good in that: (a) the members became more cooperative towards one another; (b) they became more willing to accept responsibility for directing their own activity; (c) the leader was gradually placed in the role of a resource persons; and (d) the functioning of the group became more efficient.

3. The content records indicate that the members, with only the guidance of a brief curriculum outline, selected, discussed, and reached a fairly basic understanding of important human relations problems.

4. Group growth seemed to follow a definite pattern: initial resistance to accepting responsibility and to the method of operation, gradual understanding and acceptance of the method of operation, and finally a period of well-organized and productive meetings. It seems probable that

the resistance was a result of the demands which the methods used placed on the individuals. The methods were unfamiliar, they were at variance with the expectations of many of the delegates, and they required rather significant behavioral changes in many members before a cooperative and responsible group could develop. This period of resistance helped to focus the attention of the members on their behavior as it contributed to or hindered the functioning of the group. Such focusing was probably necessary if the group was to develop, in addition to verbal understanding, actual skills and increased sensitivity to the functioning of groups.

5. Observational data and examination of the evaluation sessions indicate desirable changes in the behavior of various individuals. Participation of many members who were quiet at first increased considerably; participation of the members became more problem-oriented, more cooperative, and less competitive. Material from the evaluation sessions and the role playing sessions brings out the development of increased self-insight and of improvement in skills . . .

6. Changes produced in a three-week training laboratory may not be maintained after the individual has left the training environment. A follow-up study is being undertaken to evaluate the long-term effects of the experience. However, the faculty of the Training Laboratory has had fairly extensive informal contacts with a large percentage of the delegates during the nine months that have elapsed since the conclusion of the Laboratory. These contacts indicate that the delegates have been able to use with considerable success the skills that were practiced at Bethel, and that many of the behavioral changes that were observed in members have been maintained up to the present.

Thus there are important reasons for concluding that the experience in the Basic Skill Training Group was an extremely valuable one for the delegates. They appear to have gained significant insights into their own behavior, to have acquired important new skills for understanding groups, and to have developed greater ability to help groups work more productively, more effectively, and more independently.

PART : 3

Learning Functions and Problems

A useful way to study the learning process is to examine certain critical functions that appear to be involved in the process. Such *learning functions* as motivation, retention and transfer are in reality theoretical concepts used to identify key aspects of this process. While these and other functions in themselves do not explain learning, and thus provide us with a theory of learning, it is commonly held that an adequate theory of learning must, among other things, account for the operation of such functions within the learning process.

The great amount of research oriented in recent years toward learning functions likewise suggests the importance of this approach to an understanding of the learning process. As research has progressed, it has become increasingly clear that some learning functions, such as transfer and retention, which were formerly sharply differentiated, are now seen as interrelated, if not intermingled, aspects of the learning process. An acquaintance with the nature and role of some of the important learning functions contributes materially to an understanding of how we learn and to the development of constructive teaching principles for the implementation of that process.

The term *learning problem* as used here refers to two broad types of instructional problem areas that depend for their effective resolution upon an understanding of their relationship to the learning process. One of the persistent types of learning problems which the teacher faces is that of the developmental level of the student. Since developmental level varies from student to student, and since the several aspects of development frequently vary within the student, an understanding of how developmental level affects the learning process is of paramount importance to the teacher.

A second major problem with which the teacher constantly works is that of evaluation. It is commonly asserted that teaching and learning involve a continuous process of evaluation by the teacher and the student. Insofar as this is true, it suggests that evaluation of the learning process as well as learning outcomes is important. It would also appear that an understanding of how the processes and outcomes of various types of learning may be evaluated is needed. Indeed, if the work of the teacher is to be effective, the importance of a high degree of professional competence in evaluating those aspects of the learning process which determine success or failure in learning cannot be underestimated.

Separate chapters in Part 3 are thus devoted to Functional Aspects, Developmental Aspects, and Evaluative Aspects of Learning.

CHAPTER : 8

Functional Aspects of Learning

25. A Classroom Experiment in School Motivation*

> Every teacher becomes aware, though perhaps vaguely at first, of the effects which his comments have upon student motivation. Page here reports an extensive classroom experiment upon the effects of written comments on student papers in high school classes in several subject-matter areas. He examines the apparent results of several intentionally directed types of comments, including no comments, upon classroom performance and upon teachers' judgments of student responsiveness to comments.

The present experiment investigated the questions: 1. Do teacher comments cause a significant improvement in student performance? 2. If comments have an effect, which comments have more than others, and what are the conditions, in students and class, conducive to such effect? The questions are obviously important for secondary education, educational psychology, learning theory, and the pressing concern of how a teacher can most effectively spend his time.

PREVIOUS RELATED WORK

Previous investigations of "praise" and "blame," however fruitful for the general psychologist, have for the educator been encumbered by certain weaknesses: Treatments have been administered by persons who were

* ELLIS B. PAGE. Reprinted and abridged with permission of the author and publisher from Teacher comments and student performance: a seventy-four classroom experiment in school motivation. *Journal of Educational Psychology,* 1958, Vol. 49, No. 4, pp. 173–81.

extraneous to the normal class situation. Tests have been of a contrived nature in order to keep students (unrealistically) ignorant of the true comparative quality of their work. Comments of praise or blame have been administered on a random basis, unlike the classroom where their administration is not at all random. Subjects have often lacked any independent measures of their performance, unlike students in the classroom. Areas of training have often been those considered so fresh that the students would have little previous history of related success or failure, an assumption impossible to make in the classroom. There have furthermore been certain statistical errors: tests of significance have been conducted as if students were totally independent of one another, when in truth they were interacting members of a small number of groups with, very probably, some group effects upon the experimental outcome.

For the educator such experimental deviations from ordinary classroom conditions have some grave implications . . . Where the conditions are highly contrived, no matter how tight the *controls,* efforts to apply the findings to the ordinary teacher-pupil relationship are at best rather tenuous. This study was therefore intended to fill both a psychological and methodological lack by *leaving the total classroom procedures exactly what they would have been without the experiment,* except for the written comments themselves.

METHOD

Assigning the subjects. Seventy-four teachers, randomly selected from among the secondary teachers of three districts, followed detailed printed instructions in conducting the experiment. By random procedures each teacher chose one class to be subject from among his available classes . . . As one might expect, these classes represented about equally all secondary grades from seventh through twelfth, and most of the secondary subject-matter fields. They contained 2,139 individual students.

First the teacher administered whatever objective test would ordinarily come next in his course of study; it might be arithmetic, spelling, civics, or whatever. He collected and marked these tests in his usual way, so that each paper exhibited a numerical score and, on the basis of the score, the appropriate letter grade A, B, C, D, or F, each teacher following his usual policy of grade distribution. Next, the teacher placed the papers in numerical rank order, with the best paper on top. He rolled a specially marked die to assign the top paper to the *No Comment, Free Comment,* or *Specified Comment* group. He rolled again, assigning the second-best paper to one of the two remaining groups. He automatically assigned the third-best paper to the one treatment group remaining. He then repeated the process of rolling and assigning with the next three papers in the class, and so on until all students were assigned.

Administering treatments. The teacher returned *all* test papers with the numerical score and letter grade, as earned. No Comment students received nothing else. Free Comment students received, in addition, whatever comment the teacher might feel it desirable to make. Teachers were instructed: "Write anything that occurs to you in the circumstances. There is not any 'right' or 'wrong' comment for this study. A comment is 'right' for the study if it conforms with your own feelings and practices." Specified Comment students, regardless of teacher or student differences, all received comments designated in advance for each letter grade, as follows:

> A: Excellent! Keep it up.
> B: Good work. Keep at it.
> C: Perhaps try to do still better?
> D: Let's bring this up.
> F: Let's raise this grade!

Teachers were instructed to administer the comments "rapidly and automatically, trying not even to notice who the students are." This instruction was to prevent any extra attention to the Specified Comment students, in class or out, which might confound the experimental results. After the comments were written on each paper and recorded on the special sheet for the experimenter, the test papers were returned to the students in the teacher's customary way.

It is interesting to note that the student subjects were totally naive. In other psychological experiments, while often not aware of precisely what is being tested, subjects are almost always sure that something unusual is underway. In 69 of the present classes there was no discussion by teacher or student of the comments being returned. In the remaining five the teachers gave ordinary brief instructions to "notice comments" and "profit by them," or similar remarks. In none of the classes were students reported to seem aware or suspicious that they were experimental subjects.

Criterion. Comment effects were judged by the scores achieved on the very next objective test given in the class, regardless of the nature of that test. Since the 74 testing instruments would naturally differ sharply from each other in subject matter, length, difficulty, and every other testing variable, they obviously presented some rather unusual problems. When the tests were regarded primarily as *ranking* instruments, however, some of the difficulties disappeared.

A class with 30 useful students, for example, formed just 10 levels on the basis of scores from the first test. Each level consisted of three students, with each student receiving a different treatment: No Comment, Free Comment, or Specified Comment. Students then achieved new scores on the second (criterion) test, as might be illustrated in Table 1, Part A. On the basis of such scores, they were assigned rankings within levels, as illustrated in Table 1, Part B.

TABLE 1

ILLUSTRATION OF RANKED DATA

Level	Part A (Raw scores on second test)			Part B (Rank-within-levels on second test)		
	N	F	S	N	F	S
1	33	31	34	2	1	3
2	30	25	32	2	1	3
3	29	33	23	2	3	1
...	...	...	...	...	...	...
...	...	...	...	...	...	...
...	...	...	...	...	...	...
10	14	25	21	1	3	2
Sum:				19	21	20

Note.—N is No Comment; F is Free Comment; S is Specified Comment.

If the comments had no effects, the sums of ranks of Part B would not differ except by chance, and the two-way analysis of variance by ranks would be used to determine whether such differences exceeded chance . . . Then the *sums* of ranks themselves could be ranked. (In Part B the rankings would be 1, 3, and 2 for Groups N, F, and S; the highest score is ranked 3 throughout the study.) And a new test, of the same type, could be made of all such rankings from the 74 experimental classrooms . . . Still a third way remained to use these rankings. The summation of each column could be divided by the number of levels in the class, and the result was *a mean rank within treatment within class* . . .

Results

Comment vs. no comment. The over-all significance of the comment effects, as measured by the analysis of variance by ranks, is indicated in Table 2. The first row shows results obtained when students were con-

TABLE 2
THE FRIEDMAN TEST OF THE OVER-ALL TREATMENT EFFECTS

Units considered	N	F	S	df	Xr^2	p
Individual Subjects	1363	1488	1427	2	10.9593	<.01
Class-group Subjects	129.5	170.0	144.5	2	11.3310	<.01

sidered as matched independently from one common population. The second row shows results when treatment groups within classes were regarded as intact groups. In either case the conclusions were the same. The Specified Comment group, which received automatic impersonal comments according to the letter grade received, achieved higher scores than the No Comment group. The Free Comment group, which received individualized comments from the teachers, achieved the highest scores of all. Not once in a hundred times would such differences have occurred by chance if scores were drawn from a common population. Therefore it may be held that the comments had a real and beneficial effect upon the students' mastery of subject matter in the various experimental classes . . .

The various tests are summarized in Tables 3 and 4 . . . All differences were significant except that between Free Comment and Specified Comment. It was plain that comments, especially the individualized comments, had a marked effect upon student performance.

TABLE 3

ANALYSIS OF VARIANCE OF MAIN TREATMENT EFFECTS
(Based on Mean Ranks)

Source	Sum of Squares	df	Mean Square	F	Probability
Between Treatments: N,F,S	1.23	2	.615	5.69	<.01
Between Class-groups	0.00	73	.000	. . .	
Interaction: T X Class	15.78	146	.108		
Total	17.01	221			

TABLE 4

DIFFERENCES BETWEEN MEANS OF THE TREATMENT GROUPS

Comparison	Difference	S. E. of Diff.	t	Probability
Between N and F	.182	.052	3.500	<.001
Between N and S	.103	.054	1.907	<.05
Between F and S	.079	.056	1.411	<.10(n.s.)

Note.—The *t* tests presented are those for matched pairs, consisting of the paired mean ranks of the treatment groups within the different classes. Probabilities quoted assume that one-tailed tests were appropriate.

Comments and schools. One might question whether comment effects would vary from school to school, and even whether the school might not be the more appropriate unit of analysis. Since as it happened the study had 12 junior or senior high schools which had three or more experimental classes, these schools were arranged in a treatments-by-replications design. Results of the analysis are shown in Table 5. Schools apparently had little measurable influence over treatment effect.

Comments and school years. It was conceivable that students, with increasing age and grade-placement, might become increasingly independent of comments and other personal attentions from their teachers. To test such a belief, 66 class-groups, drawn from the experimental classes, were stratified into six school years (Grades 7-12) with 11 class-groups in each school year . . . When the data were tested for interaction of school year and comment effect . . . school year did not exhibit a significant influence upon comment effect . . .

TABLE 5

The Influence of the School Upon the Treatment Effect

Source	Sum of Squares	df	Mean Square	F	Proba- bility
Between Treatments: N, F, S	.172	2	.086	. . .[a]	. . .
Between Schools	.000	11	.000		
Between Classes Within Schools (pooled)	.000	24	.000		
Interaction: T X Schools	1.937	22	.088	. . .	. . .
Interaction: T X Cl. W. Sch. (pooled)	4.781	48	.099		
Total	6.890	107			

[a] Absence of an important main treatment effect is probably caused by necessary restriction of sample for school year (N is 36, as compared with Total N of 74), and by some chance biasing.

Comments and letter grades. In a questionnaire made out before the experiment, each teacher rated each student in his class with a number from 1 to 5, according to the student's *guessed responsiveness* to comments made by that teacher. Top rating, for example, was paired with the description: "Seems to respond quite unusually well to suggestions or comments made by the teacher of this class. Is quite apt to be influenced by praise, correction, etc." Bottom rating, on the other hand, implied: "Seems rather negativistic about suggestions made by the teacher. May be inclined more than most students to do the opposite from what the teacher urges." In daily practice, many teachers comment on some papers and not on others. Since teachers would presumably be more likely to comment on papers of those students they believed would respond positively, such ratings were an important experimental variable.

Whether teachers *were* able to predict responsiveness is a complicated question, not to be reported here. It was thought, however, that teachers might tend to believe their able students, their high achievers, were also their responsive students. A contingency table was therefore made, testing the relationship between *guessed* responsiveness and letter grade achieved on the first test. The results were as predicted. More "A" students were regarded as highly responsive to comments than were other letter grades; more "F" students were regarded as negativistic and unresponsive to comments than were other letter grades; and grades in between followed the same trend . . . Plainly teachers believed that their *better* students were also their more *responsive* students.

If teachers were correct in their belief, one would expect in the present experiment greater comment effect for the better students than for the poorer ones. In fact, one might not be surprised if, among the "F" students, the No Comment group were even superior to the two comment groups.

The various letter grades achieved mean scores as shown in Table 6, and the analysis of variance resulted as shown in Table 7. There was

TABLE 6

MEAN OF MEAN RANKS FOR DIFFERENT LETTER GRADES

Letter Grade	N	F	S
A	1.93	2.04	2.03
B	1.91	2.11	1.98
C	1.90	2.06	2.04
D	2.05	1.99	1.96
F	1.57	2.55	1.88

TABLE 7

THE RELATION BETWEEN LETTER GRADE AND TREATMENT EFFECT

Source	Sum of Squares	df	Mean Square	F	Probability
Between Treatments: N, F, S	2.77	2	1.385	5.41	$< .01$
Between Letter Grades	0.00	4	0.000		
Between Blocks Within L. Gr. (pooled)	0.00	65	0.000		
Interaction: T X Letter Grades	4.88	8	.610	2.40	$.05 > p > .01$
Residual (error term)	32.99	130	.254		
Total	40.64	209			

considerable interaction between letter grade and treatment effect, but it was caused almost entirely by the remarkable effect which comments appeared to have *on the "F" students.* None of the other differences, including the partial reversal of the "D" students, exceeded chance expectation . . .

. . . The experiment provided strong evidence against the teacher-myth about responsiveness and letter grades. The experimental teachers appeared plainly mistaken in their faith that their "A" students respond relatively brightly, and their "F" students only sluggishly or negatively to whatever encouragement they administer.

SUMMARY

Seventy-four randomly selected secondary teachers, using 2,139 unknowing students in their daily classes, performed the following experiment: They administered to all students whatever objective test would occur in the usual course of instruction. After scoring and grading the test papers in their customary way, and matching the students by performance, they randomly assigned the papers to one of three treatment groups. The No Comment group received no marks beyond those for grading. The Free Comment group received whatever comments the teachers felt were appropriate for the particular students and tests concerned. The Specified Comment Group received certain uniform comments designated beforehand by the experimenter for all similar letter grades, and thought to be generally "encouraging." Teachers returned tests to students without any unusual attention. Then teachers reported scores achieved on the next objective test given in the class, and these scores became the criterion of comment effect, with the following results:

1. Free Comment students achieved higher scores than Specified Comment students, and Specified Comments did better than No Comments. All differences were significant except that between Free Comments and Specified Comments.

2. When samplings from 12 different schools were compared, no significant differences of comment effect appeared between schools.

3. When the class-groups from six different school years (grades 7-12) were compared, no *conclusive* differences of comment effect appeared between the years, but if anything senior high was more responsive than junior high. It would appear logical to generalize the experimental results, concerning the effectiveness of comment, at least to the early college years.

4. Although teachers believed that their better students were also much more responsive to teacher comments than their poorer students, there was no experimental support for this belief.

When the average secondary teacher takes the time and trouble to write comments (believed to be "encouraging") on student papers, these apparently have a measurable and potent effect upon student effort, or attention, or attitude, or whatever it is which causes learning to improve, and this effect does not appear dependent on school building, school year, or student ability. Such a finding would seem very important for the studies of classroom learning and teaching method.

*

26. The Effects of a Motor Handicap on Level of Aspiration*

> The concept of level of aspiration refers to the level of goal attainment which the subject sets for himself in the light of his previous experience. In Wenar's study the functioning of the level of aspiration is explored in non-handicapped, somewhat handicapped, and severely handicapped children of comparable chronological and mental ages. The study illustrates the importance of appropriate methods of analysis of such data and examines some of the possible theoretical interpretations of the experimental findings.

STATEMENT OF THE PROBLEM

. . . The present study was designed to test the hypothesis that the goals which a handicapped child sets for himself differ significantly from those of a non-handicapped child. Neither theoretical nor clinical observation is refined enough, however, to enable one to predict specifically what the difference will be: e.g., whether he will set unrealistically high goals in order to compensate for his handicap, unrealistically low goals in order to protect himself from failure, or whether he will adopt some other pattern of goal setting which differs from that of the non-handicapped child.

METHOD

Subjects. The subjects were 12 children with no motor handicap, 12 with a mild motor handicap, and 12 with a severe motor handicap. All were pupils in the Chicago public school system, between the ages of 8 and 10, of average or above intelligence, with no other severe physical handicap. The age range was chosen as representing a particularly stable period in the child's development, since the transition from a life centering around the home to one centering around both school and home has usually been made, and the difficulties of early adolescence have not yet started. The reason for equating the groups for intelligence and limiting the experimental groups to a single handicap was to see the effects of the motor handicap uncomplicated by such factors as mental retardation and

* CHARLES WENAR. Reprinted and abridged with permission of the author and publisher from The effects of a motor handicap on personality: I. The effects on level of aspiration. *Child Development,* 1953, 24:123–30.

other types of physical defects, both of which could have a significant effect on personality.

In all cases the handicapped children were suffering from different kinds of cerebral palsy and the motor handicap had been present from birth. Two criteria were used to determine degree of handicap: first, a rating by the examiner based on observing the child's gross motor coordination in class and on the way to the testing room, and observing his finer motor coordination in handling the test material; second, an objective criterion in terms of the number of pegs the child could place in a pegboard in a 20-second interval. It should also be noted that there were two criteria for the moderately handicapped group: a moderate or mild case of spasticity or athetosis affecting all limbs, or a severe spasticity which affected only two limbs, leaving the other two relatively intact. The only practical limitation for the severely handicapped group was that the child could not be so crippled as to be unable to handle the material used for testing.

It is important to emphasize that the control group was made up of non-handicapped children, and no attempt was made to get normal, well adjusted individuals. Since the handicapped children were selected with a complete disregard to the type of adjustment they were making, it would be erroneous to compare them with a special segment of the non-handicapped children whose adjustment was outstandingly good.

Procedure. The experiment consisted of a slightly modified form of the level of aspiration technique. The subject was seated at a table upon which there were two pegboards, each 36 x 5 x 1 inches. Each board contained 20 square holes ⅜ inch in diameter. The board the subject was to use had a square peg 4 inches long and ⅜ inch in diameter in front of each hole. Instructions were as follows: "This is a game to see how many of these pegs you can put in the holes before I say *Stop*. You see, they go in like this (illustrates with three pegs). Now you try a few. (Subject places three.) Fine. Now, when I say *Go,* you start and put in as many as you can till I call *Stop*."

For this and each of the subsequent trials, the subject was given 20 seconds. At the end of each trial the number of pegs was counted and recorded, and the board was left in the subject's view. The other board was placed in front of him and he was asked, "How many do you think you can put in this time? You will have the same amount of time before I call *Stop*."

There were five such trials, each of 20 seconds duration. For each trial both the achievement score (number of pegs placed in the 20-second interval) and the level of aspiration (the number of pegs the child said he could place on the following trial) were recorded. The wording of the instructions and the technique of leaving the board with the previous performance in full view of the subject were designed so as to obtain the child's realistic evaluation of what he could do, rather than a wishful estimate of what he would like to do.

Results

The initial problem was to determine whether there was a significant difference between the three groups in the over-all height of their level of aspiration. The measure used was the discrepancy score which was obtained by subtracting the number of pegs placed on a given trial from the subsequent estimate of the number the subject thought he could place—i.e., subtracting the achievement score from the subsequent level of aspiration. Since there were five trials, each subject had five discrepancy scores. The mean discrepancy scores for all five trials for each of the three groups ($N = 12$) are as follows:

Non-Handicapped	Moderately Handicapped	Severely Handicapped
1.93	1.98	1.18

An analysis of variance was done and an F of 1.43 was obtained. Since an F of 3.30 is necessary for significance at the .05 level of confidence one can conclude that there is no significant difference between the mean discrepancy scores for the three groups. This means that there is no general tendency for handicapped children to set consistently higher or lower goals for themselves than non-handicapped children.

However, inspection of the data indicated that the pattern of change in discrepancy scores from the first to the fifth trial might be different for the three groups. Therefore the mean discrepancy score for each of the five trials was obtained and were plotted on Figure 1.

A trend analysis was run and an F of 2.31 was obtained, which is significant at the .03 level of confidence. Thus there is a significant difference between non-handicapped and handicapped children in the goals they set for themselves as they continue working at a task. The non-handicapped group starts with high goals relative to achievement and gradually decreases this discrepancy as the task is repeated. The

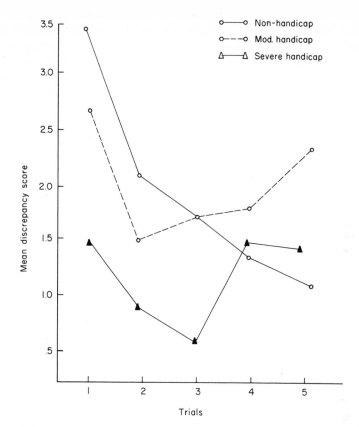

FIG. 1. MEAN DISCREPANCY SCORE ON EACH TRIAL FOR NON-HANDICAPPED, MODER-
ATELY HANDICAPPED, AND SEVERELY HANDICAPPED GROUPS.

handicapped groups are characterized by (a) a systematic decrease in
the initial height of the goal as the handicap becomes more severe, and
(b) after an initial decrease in the discrepancy between achievement and
performance, a reversal of the trend toward setting higher goals as the
task is repeated.

Before discussing the meaning of these results and how realistic such
goal setting behavior is, the actual achievement scores for the three
groups must be examined since there is no reason to assume equal
facility in performing the task. In order to obtain a general measure of
improvement with practice, the number of pegs on the first trial was

subtracted from the number on the last trial and group means were calculated. These means are as follows:

Non-Handicapped	Moderately Handicapped	Severely Handicapped
2.58	0.67	0.58

An analysis of variance yielded an F of 16.06, which is significant at the .01 level of confidence. Thus, non-handicapped children improve with practice to a significantly greater degree than handicapped children, whose over-all improvement is relatively small.

In order to obtain a picture of change in performance from trial to trial the mean achievement score on each trial was calculated for each of the three groups. These means are presented in Table 1.

TABLE 1

MEAN ACHIEVEMENT SCORES FOR TRIALS 1 THROUGH 5 FOR NON-HANDICAPPED, MODERATELY HANDICAPPED AND SEVERELY HANDICAPPED GROUPS

Trials	Non-Handicapped	Moderately Handicapped	Severely Handicapped
1	13.50	9.16	2.83
2	15.41	9.41	3.16
3	15.41	9.75	3.66
4	16.08	9.83	2.91
5	16.00	9.83	3.41

The pattern of achievement is quite different for the three groups. For the non-handicapped children there is a dramatic initial improvement followed by a rapid deceleration. For the moderately handicapped children the improvement is very slow and difficult. For the severely handicapped children the achievement pattern is erratic and unpredictable, with improvement followed by poor performance.

DISCUSSION

The two aspects of the present findings which will be discussed are (a) the initial difference in discrepancy scores of the three groups reflecting the fact that the level of aspiration was progressively lowered as the severity of handicap increased; and (b) the progressive lowering of the discrepancy score on the part of the non-handicapped group as the task was repeated, in contrast to the initial lowering and subsequent raising of the discrepancy scores on the part of the handicapped groups. The primary emphasis will be on the question of how realistic such patterns of goal setting are. In general, the discussion will follow Lewin, Dembo, Festinger, and Sears (1) . . . who regard level of aspiration as the product of the desires to seek success and avoid failure, plus such factors as the subject's evaluation of his abilities, the nature of the task itself, group standards of performance, etc. The desires to seek success and avoid failure can be considered as motivational factors, while the remaining can be considered cognitive factors.

In regard to (a), it is not necessary to assume a difference in motivation in the three groups. This is because there is an important cognitive difference resulting from the difference in abilities of the groups. An improvement of two pegs is well within the realm of possibility for the non-handicapped child, but would be extremely difficult or impossible for the handicapped one. Experimental evidence . . . indicates that, when faced with a difficulty continuum, the individual will set up goals near the boundaries of his abilities. Since such boundaries are much more limited for the handicapped child, it is reasonable for him to lower his initial level of aspiration. Expressed in another way, it would be highly unrealistic for the handicapped child, with his limited abilities, to aspire to achieve to the same degree as the non-handicapped child. Thus, the initial lowering of discrepancy scores with increased handicap can be accounted for in terms of a realistic limiting of goals in keeping with diminished ability to achieve.

In regard to (b), the progressive lowering of the discrepancy scores on the part of the non-handicapped child indicates a realistic adjustment to a task in which improved performance becomes progressively more difficult. However, the handicapped children seem to be able to maintain the realistic lowering of discrepancy scores only for a limited time, after which there is an increased disparity between what they actually achieve and what they aspire to do. This finding is all the more striking when one considers that, in reality, they can improve very little and, on this basis, should become more conservative in their estimates of future performance. There is experimental evidence (2) that such a phenomenon is seen in the case of children who in their daily lives are often unsuccessful in achieving what they set out to do. According to Lewin *et al.,* such repeated failure leads to emotionality and unrealistic attitudes. In the present study, the handicapped children not only failed to attain their initial goals but, unlike the non-handicapped children, failed to improve the level of their performance significantly. One can speculate that it is the frustration of slow, minimal improvement or erratic, unpredictable performance which increases the emotional tension and gives rise to a more unrealistic attitude. It is also possible that the handicapped children bring to the task a longer history of past failures and performance under the pressure of cumulated frustrations. In this regard a level of aspiration study using a non-motor task would make an interesting comparison study.

Although there is good reason for describing the increase in discrepancy scores on the part of the handicapped children as unrealistic, it is impossible to determine what psychological attitude accompanies this change. With non-handicapped children it has been shown that such behavior goes along with feelings of dissatisfaction with status and lower self-confidence. Whether this is true of handicapped children can be determined only by further investigation. Perhaps the most conservative speculation is that the change is from a realistic to a wishful attitude. Initially the handicapped child can maintain the realistic attitude of trying to keep his goal in line with his achievement; but, under frustration of his limited or unpredictable achievement he comes to think in terms of how well he would like to do.

Summary

In order to determine the effect of a motor handicap on setting goals of achievement, 12 non-handicapped, 12 moderately handicapped, and 12 severely handicapped children were given a level of aspiration task involving five trials of putting pegs in a pegboard. There was no significant tendency for the handicapped groups to set higher or lower goals for themselves when all five trials were combined. However, there was a significant change in pattern of goal setting from trial to trial, the non-handicapped group progressively lowered their level of aspiration, in contrast to an initial lowering followed by a reversal toward setting higher goals as the task was continued on the the part of the handicapped groups. This was interpreted as meaning that, when faced with a motor task, the handicapped child can maintain a realistic attitude toward his capabilities for only a limited period of time; then, under the pressure of the frustrations of limited or unpredictable achievement, his attitude changes to a wishful one of what he would like to be able to do rather than what he is capable of doing.

REFERENCES

. LEWIN, K., DEMBO, T., FESTINGER, L., SEARS, P. S. Level of aspiration. In *Personality and the Behavior Disorders*. J. McV. Hunt (Ed.). New York: Ronald Press, 1944.

. SEARS, P. S. 1940. Levels of aspiration in academically successful and unsuccessful children. *J. Abnorm. Soc. Psychol.* 35:498–536.

7. Value and Need as Organizing Factors in Perception*

Is the individual to a certain extent a determiner of his interpretation of a stimulus situation, or is one's perceptual organization merely a function of the properties of the stimulus situation? The experiment by Bruner and Goodman is an excellent illustration of one type of research which attempts to discover how needs and values affect perceptual organization. The fact that the authors worked with two distinct socio-economic groups of children—"rich" and "poor"—makes this study one of particular interest to teachers who are concerned with social values.

Empirical Hypotheses

. . Three general hypotheses . . . are under consideration.

1. *The greater the social value of an object, the more will it be susceptible to organization by behavioral determinants.* It will be *selected* perceptually from among alternative perceptual objects, will become *fixated* as perceptual response tendency, and will become perceptually *accentuated*.

2. *The greater the individual need for a socially valued object, the more marked will be the operation of behavioral determinants.*

3. *Perceptual equivocality will facilitate the operation of behavioral determinants only in so far as equivocality reduces the operation of autochthonous[1] determinants without reducing the effectiveness of behavioral determinants.*

In the experiments reported here, only one aspect of behavioral determination will be treated, what we have called *accentuation*—the tendency for sought-after perceptual objects to become more vivid . . .

---

* JEROME S. BRUNER and CECILE C. GOODMAN. Reprinted and abridged with permission of the authors and the publisher from the *Journal of Abnormal and Social Psychology*, 1947, 42:33–43.

[1] independent of experience.

THE SUBJECTS AND THE APPARATUS

The subjects were 30 ten-year-old children of normal intelligence, divisible according to certain characteristics to be discussed shortly into three groups, two experimental and one control. The apparatus consisted of a rectangular wooden box (9″ x 9″ x 18″) at one end of which was a 5″ square ground-glass screen and a knob at its lower right-hand corner. At the center of the ground-glass screen was an almost circular patch of light (16.2 app. ft. cdls.) cast upon the back of the screen by a 60-watt incandescent light shining through an iris diaphragm which could be varied in diameter from ⅛″ to 2″ by turning the knob on the front end of the box. All that was visible to the subject was the box with its ground glass screen and the circle of light whose diameter he could change by turning the knob . . .

Subjects individually sat in a chair in front of the screen on the box with the light circle slightly below eye level. The box rested on a table behind which sat the experimenter. The child was told that this was a game, and that he was to make the circle of light on the box the same size as various objects he was shown or told about. Before beginning judgments, each child, with no urging, was encouraged to see how large and small the circle of light could be made.

The two experimental groups received the same treatment. Two series were run for these groups, comprising 20 of the children in all. First the child was asked to estimate the sizes of coins from a penny through a half dollar from memory. He did the first in ascending order of value then in descending order, always making two judgments for each coin named, one from the open, the other from the closed position of the iris diaphragm. Four judgments were made for each coin by each child. No inkling was given the child as to how "close" he had come.

Following the memory series, and using the same order of presentation a similar series was then run with coins present. Coins, individually, were held close to the center of the palm of the left hand, at a level with the light circle and six inches to its left. The subjects took as much time as suited them.

A control group of ten subjects followed a procedure identical with the one just described. Instead of coins, medium gray cardboard discs of identical size were employed. No mention of money was made to this group.

RESULTS

Let us compare the difference between judgments of size of coins and identically sized cardboard discs. Two things can be noted in Figure 1,

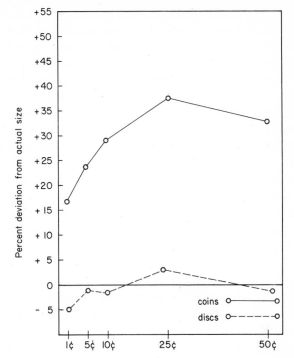

FIG. 1. SIZE ESTIMATIONS OF COINS AND DISCS OF SAME SIZE MADE BY TEN-YEAR-OLDS. (Method of average error)

which presents judgments of experimentals and controls with coins present. First off, coins, socially valued objects, are judged larger in size than gray discs. Secondly, the greater the value of the coin, the greater is the deviation of *apparent* size from *actual* size. The exception to this generalization is the half dollar, overestimation of which falls off below that of a quarter. By way of the sheerest guess one might explain this reversal of the curve in terms of the lesser reality-value of a half dollar as compared with a quarter for the ten-year-old . . .

The difference between experimentals and controls is, of course, highly significant. The variance in overestimation in the experimental groups introduced by using coins of different value is similarly significant . . .

So much for the first hypothesis, that socially valued objects are susceptible to behavioral determinants in proportion to their value. Consider now the second hypothesis, that the greater the subjective need for a socially valued object, the greater will be the role of behavioral determinants of perception. In the second experimental variation, the experimental group was divided into two component groups. One we call the *rich* group, the other the *poor* group, each comprising ten subjects. Well-to-do subjects were drawn from a progressive school in the Boston area, catering to the sons and daughters of prosperous business and professional people. The poor subjects came from a settlement house in one of Boston's slum areas. The reasonable assumption is made that poor children have a greater subjective need for money than rich ones. When the figures presented in Figure 1 are broken down into scores for rich and poor groups, a striking difference will be noted (Figure 2). The poor group overestimates the size of coins considerably more than does the

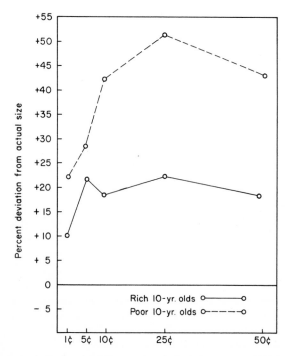

FIG. 2. SIZE ESTIMATIONS OF COINS MADE BY WELL-TO-DO AND POOR TEN-YEAR-OLDS. (Method of average error)

rich. Again there are some irregularities in the curves. The drop-off for the half dollar we have already sought to explain. As for the dip in the rich group's curve at a dime, the explanation is problematical. All curves which we have plotted for adults . . . show this dip. Perhaps it is due to the discrepancy between the relative size and value of the dime, perhaps to some inherent characteristic of the coin itself.[1]

The difference between rich and poor is highly significant . . . Our second hypothesis cannot, then, be rejected . . .

What of ambiguity or perceptual equivocality? We have arbitrarily assumed that a situation in which one is judging size from memory is more "equivocal" than one in which the object being judged is in clear view six inches away from the test patch. The assumption is open to

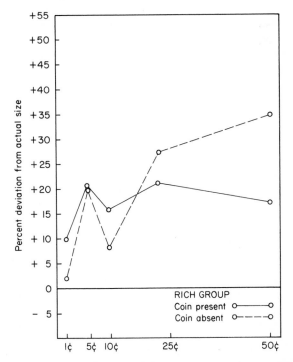

FIG. 3. SIZE ESTIMATIONS OF COINS WITH COINS PRESENT AND FROM MEMORY BY WELL-TO-DO TEN-YEAR-OLDS. (Method of average error)

---

[1] If the reader is a smoker, let him ask himself whether a dime will cover the hump on the camel which appears as a trademark on Camel cigarettes. Hold the two six inches apart. In spite of the apparently small size of the coin, it will cover the camel's hump with margin to spare.

serious question, but let us examine what follows from it experimentally. Compare first the judgments of the rich group under conditions like those described: with coin present as compared with coin as a mere memory image. The curves are in Figure 3. It would seem that, for all values below a quarter, equivocality has the effect of making judgments

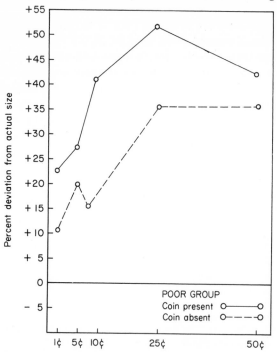

FIG. 4. SIZE ESTIMATIONS OF COINS WITH COINS PRESENT AND FROM MEMORY BY POOR TEN-YEAR-OLDS. (Method of average errȯr)

conform more to actual size . . . For values over a quarter, equivocality favors behavioral factors, making apparent size diverge still more from actual size. For the rich group, with coin *present,* a half dollar is over-judged by 17.4 per cent; with coin *absent,* by 34.7 per cent.

This finding is difficult to interpret by itself. Consider now Figure 4, showing the discrepancy in "absent" and "present" judgments for the poor group. Here there is no crossing. Equivocality seems, in this group, to have the exclusive effect of bringing judgments down toward actual size. Equivocality even brings out the "dime dip" in the poor group. How account for the difference? Why does equivocality liberate behavioral determinants among the rich children for higher values, and depress these factors for poor children? We can offer nothing but a guess, one which needs confirmation by further research . . . In the case of the poor children, judging coin size from memory, a weakened fantasy is substituted for the compelling presence of a valued coin, while among rich children equivocality has the effect of liberating strong and active fantasy . . .

In conclusion, only one point need be reiterated. For too long now, perception has been virtually the exclusive domain of the Experimental psychologists with a capital E. If we are to reach an understanding of the way in which perception works in everyday life, we social psychologists and students of personality will have to join with the experimental psychologists and re-explore much of this ancient field of perception whose laws for too long have been taken for granted . . .

REFERENCES

1. BRALY, K. W. 1933. The influence of past experience in visual perception. *J. Exp. Psychol.* 16:613–43.
2. FEHRER, E. V. 1935. An investigation of the learning of visually perceived forms. *Amer. J. Psychol.* 47:187–221.
3. KRECHAVSKY, I. 1932. "Hypothesis" versus "chance" in the presolution period in sensory discrimination learning. *Calif. Pub. Psychol.* 6:27–44.
4. LEEPER, R. 1935. A study of a neglected portion of the field of learning—the development of sensory organization. *J. Genet. Psychol.* 46:41–75.
5. PROSHANSKY, H., MURPHY, G. 1942. The effects of reward and punishment on perception. *J. Psychol.* 13:295–305.
6. SANFORD, R. N. 1937. The effect of abstinence from food upon imaginal processes: a further experiment. *J. Psychol.* 3:145–59.

28. Retention of Meaningful Material*

Numerous studies have shown the advantages which meaningful materials have in initial learning and in retention over non-meaningful materials. English, Wellborn, and Killian examine the comparative retention of two types of meaningful materials—verbatim passages and paraphrases of the substance of the same passages. Certain

* HORACE B. ENGLISH, E. L. WELLBORN, AND C. D. KILLIAN. Reprinted and abridged with permission of the authors and the publisher from Studies in substance memorization. *Journal of General Psychology*, 1934, 11:233–60.

aspects of the study, as the use of a series of classroom experiments and the different types of appraisal employed, have practical as well as theoretical implications for the teacher.

I. INTRODUCTION

. . . It is by no means easy . . . to isolate "substance memory" for experimental study. Apprehension of significance seems always accompanied by the more mechanical learning described as association by contiguity and apparently every effort to tie learning down to objectively measurable responses results in emphasizing the mechanical or rote aspects at the expense of the meaningful . . . We may, of course, discern the effects of meaning by contrasting the learning of the relatively meaningless with that of the relatively meaningful . . . But when we use learning tasks of differing degrees of meaningful organization, we thereby inevitably introduce uncontrollable variables which may or may not be corollary with the major variable to be studied. This difficulty has, we believe, infected all previous comparative studies of substance memory.

We propose to avoid it by comparing, not two different learning tasks, but the relative facility of the substance and the rote learnings to be found in a single task. Our actual procedure implies, what will probably be easily granted, that verbatim memory is more largely a matter of linking together "neutral" items than is memory for the ideas in a passage. Our procedure, then, in the first investigations reported is to compare verbatim and substance memorizing for the same passage by the same persons under varied conditions of learning and retention. Thus we inquire whether the conditions for effective learning are the same when one learns the "substance" of a prose passage as when one learns the passage verbatim. In Section II the main variable considered is the effect of varied spacings in the learning period upon the two tasks, in Section III the main variable is the effect of the number of repetitions . . .

General Procedure. From ten to three hundred college students were assembled and caused, under fairly well-controlled conditions, to study a passage of moderately difficult prose. A modification of the true-false test was used to measure recognition-memory. Some of the test items reproduced verbatim the words of the passage, while others stated the substance or meaning in entirely different language. The first kind of item could be answered correctly if the subject remembered either the meaning or the mere words, though almost certainly, under the conditions of the experiments, both factors were involved. With the second kind of item, the rigorous and systematic alteration of the wording gave primary effect to the subject's memory for the meaning. The two kinds of items thus permitted comparison of memory for the substance with verbatim memory of the same passage. Furthermore, in the several experiments there were systematic variations in the second type of test items; some of them tested memory for small "thought units," others for relatively large "thought units." The effects of the subjects' reorganization of the learning material were thus brought out. The technique was such, as will be shown later, that the differences to be discussed can not be attributed to any cause other than certain differences in the way the learner reacted to the task.

II. Verbatim and Substance Memorization with Varied Spacings of Readings

PRELIMINARY EXPERIMENTS

Specially prepared articles averaging 1100 words in length on topics in psychology were read twice by groups of college students. Two tests, each of which consisted of eighteen true-false items, were used. One test dealt with specific facts, the other with comprehension of thought. The subjects were arranged in paired groups. Both groups of a pair studied the same two articles; one took a fact-test on one article and a comprehension-test on the other, while the other group reversed this arrangement. About one-third of the subjects were tested immediately after reading, another third at the end of twenty-four hours, and the remainder at the end of forty-eight hours. Somewhat more than 600 test records were obtained . . .

Retention in case of the two kinds of tests at the end of the various intervals is shown by Table 1.

TABLE 1

Ranges and Median Scores in the Preliminary Series

	Fact-tests			Comprehension-tests		
Groups	Number of subjects	Range of score	Median score	Number of subjects	Range of score	Median score
Immediate test	73	0–15	9.04	75	3–15	9.33
24–hour test	66	0–15	7.62	67	3–15	9.33
48–hour test	73	1–15	6.36	70	1.5–16.5	9.25

The loss in memory for facts was 15.7% in twenty-four hours, and 29.6% in forty-eight hours, but in memory for thought (or meaning) there was no loss worthy of mention . . .

These results on retention and correlation were not sufficiently reliable to justify positive conclusions, but their consistency warranted the belief that reliable differences between the two contrasting learning tasks used could be obtained by a more careful use of the same or similar techniques.

SECOND SERIES OF EXPERIMENTS

Learning material and tests. The material consisted of three articles, averaging 1500 words in length and consisting of adaptations of published material on psychological topics. Two tests of the true-false type were prepared on each article. Fifty statements, hereafter called "verbatims," were prepared on each article. The verbatims were practically perfect reproductions of statements from the article; the vocabulary of the passage was used throughout. Then fifty statements, hereafter called "paraphrases," were made by rewriting the verbatims, using synonyms for the original words. Certain key words, however, were treated as common words and used in both kinds of statements, though never in such a way as to give a clue to the correct answer. The two lists of items were then divided in half, items being drawn alternately for each half. Then two tests were made by combining twenty-five items from each list so that each verbatim in one test corresponded with a paraphrase in the other and vice-versa.

A sample of the material will be given. A typical paragraph from one of the articles is the following:

If pupils were not endowed with the tendency to organize and to systematize their knowledge and to make number meaningful, or the power of generalization, the task in arithmetic would be utterly hopeless. Manifestly it is impossible to teach arithmetic in such a way as to cover all number combinations. The advocates of specific drill are driven to admit that pupils can learn how to deal with many number combinations without specific drill upon them. This is equivalent to admitting that transfer of training plays an important part in learning arithmetic. Specific drill makes no provision for transfer of training.

Corresponding items in the two forms of the test are given in parallel columns below.

1. Children are naturally inclined to classify facts. (Paraphrase; true)

1. Pupils are endowed with the tendency to organize knowledge. (Verbatim; true)

2. The teacher of arithmetic can not hope to deal with all number facts. (Paraphrase; true)

2. It is impossible to teach arithmetic so as to cover all number combinations. (Verbatim; true)

3. Advocates of specific drill deny that pupils can learn how to deal with number combinations without specific drill upon them. (Verbatim; false)

3. Proponents of definite repetition believe that it is necessary to have definite repetition of every number fact. (Paraphrase; false)

4. Specific drill makes no provision for transfer. (Verbatim; true)

4. There is no place for transfer of training under the method of definite repetition of each number fact. (Paraphrase; true) . . .

Learning groups and procedure. The learning groups were made up of classes in educational psychology at the Ohio State University. A special study of these groups showed that they were approximately equal in the sorts of learning ability utilized in these experiments. Furthermore, each group was divided into approximately equal halves on the basis of percentile rank on the Ohio State University Psychological Examination and one half of each group was tested with one test form, and the other half with the second form.

Four readings were provided for learning. To regulate the rate of presentation, the method of silent reading by the learners accompanied by oral reading by the experimenter was used. Each learning group was given three articles, with different spacing of reading on each. The spacings were:

1. Four consecutive readings.
2. Four readings at three-hour intervals.
3. Four readings at twenty-four-hour intervals.
4. Four readings at three-day intervals.

The plan, which has been described, equalized all factors in the situation except the two contrasting recognition tasks under varied spacings of readings. For each of the variables mentioned the number of test records obtained was between seventy-five and one hundred. Altogether somewhat over 1000 records were obtained.

Several groups were given an interpolated test at the end of the second reading, while the others were not. All groups were tested immediately after the fourth reading and again four weeks later. In two special groups an additional test was given at the end of eight weeks . . .

Comparison of verbatim and paraphrase memory. The principal results are given in Table 2.

TABLE 2

MEDIANS, STANDARD DEVIATIONS, DIFFERENCES BETWEEN MEDIANS, AND CRITICAL RATIOS OF DIFFERENCES OF THE FOUR SPACINGS OF READING

Groups	Medians V.	P.	S.D.'s V.	P.	Diff. between medians of V. P.	Diff./P.E. *Diff.*
			Test 1 (immediate)			
Unspaced	18.5	16	3.0	3.6	2.5	4.5
3–hr. spacing	20.1	17.4	2.9	3.3	2.7	5.0
1–day "	19.1	16.7	2.8	3.3	2.4	4.7
3–day "	17.4	16.4	2.9	2.2	1.0	2.3
			Test 2 (after four weeks)			
Unspaced	16	14.7	3.5	3.3	1.3	2.2
3–hr. spacing	17.4	16	3.5	3.9	1.4	2.3
1–day "	18	15.4	3.4	3.2	2.6	4.5
3–day "	15.9	15	2.7	2.7	0.9	1.9

V = Verbatim
P = Paraphrase

These data indicate that in all distributions the scores on verbatims were higher than on paraphrases in the same tests. In two spacings the forgetting of verbatims was noticeably greater in four weeks than that of paraphrases,[1] while in the other two spacings forgetting was practically the same in case of the two kinds of items. For the most part the differences may be regarded as statistically significant . . .

Comparison of results on various spacings of readings. Table 2 gives the principal results. A comparison of the results of each spacing with those on all the others indicates that, for our material and procedure, the results on both learning and retention are consistent in showing that there is an optimal spacing somewhere between unspaced readings and readings three days apart. Readings at three-hour intervals gave best results in all tests with one exception, and in the latter case daily readings were slightly better. The learning scores on verbatims yielded critical ratios

---

[1] As shown by differences between corresponding medians of Test 1 and Test 2.

above three between the optimal spacing and both unspaced readings and three-day spacing, and the retention scores yielded parallel critical ratios slightly below three. The critical ratios yielded by paraphrase scores on learning and retention were somewhat more than two . . .

Retention at the end of eight weeks. The learning groups available for this more extended period were too small for satisfactory comparison of verbatim and paraphrase retention, but the results are of special interest, because they show that the rate of loss was about the same the second four weeks as the first four.

THIRD SERIES OF EXPERIMENTS

There were two special purposes in carrying out this new series of experiments: (1) To compare the results of learning when the tasks differ to a greater degree than those of the Second Series; and (2) to increase the reliability of the tests used for comparison.

Learning material. Two of the passages previously used were rewritten and extended in length by about 75%. One test upon each passage, composed of eighty items instead of fifty, as in the preceding Series, was prepared. Fifty of the items were verbatims exactly like those previously used. Twenty-five were like the former paraphrases in the use of a vocabulary different from that of the passage, but they differed in scope. They were summaries or topic sentences covering sections of varying length in the passage. Furthermore, five items not covered by the passages were included, solely to provide a third alternative for the learner in marking the test items. The instructions were to mark each item as agreeing with passage, not agreeing, not derived, or not remembered. The score was the number of items correctly marked as agreeing or disagreeing.

A sample paragraph from one passage follows:

The accumulation of knowledge concerning the feeble-minded by the dawn of the 20th century had led to the clearly formulated conclusion that the feeble-minded are incapable of self-directed lives. Since then the advance in diagnostic methods has resulted in the detection of higher grades of feeble-mindedness; this, in turn, aroused hope on the part of many investigators that the high-grade feeble-minded at least may be capable of being educated sufficiently to meet the demands of society. On the other hand it has been shown that only a pitifully small percentage of feeble-minded make good when they are replaced in the community after being in an institution for the feeble-minded.

The summary based on this passage was as follows:

"Views as to the educability of mental defectives were less harmonious about 1900 than they have been since that time." (False)

The sample verbatims given in the Second Series will serve also for this Series.

Learning groups and procedure. Several classes in educational psychology at the Ohio State University, having a total of 218 students, were used. None of them had been used in either of the preceding series.

The mode of presentation was the same as that of the Second Series, except that it was necessary to reduce the number of readings to two. Half of the learners were given unspaced readings of the first passage and readings four days apart of the second passage while the other half were given readings of the first passage four days apart and unspaced readings of the second passage. This was done to eliminate any effect on scores due to difference in difficulty of the passages. Tests were given on each passage immediately after the second reading, again at the end of twenty-four hours, and again at the end of four weeks. Somewhat more than 900 test records were obtained . . .

Comparison of results of learning in case of summaries and verbatims. Table 3 gives the results on the complete data for all subjects. The same results are shown graphically in Figure 1.

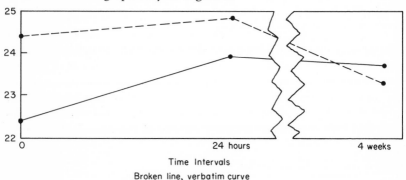

Time Intervals

Broken line, verbatim curve
Solid line, summary curve

FIG. 1. RETENTION CURVES FOR VERBATIMS AND SUMMARIES.

TABLE 3

Medians, Their Differences, and Standard Deviations for Summary and Verbatim Tests, Both Spacings Combined, 261 Cases

Kind of items	Test 1	Test 2	Test 3
Medians			
Verbatim	24.4	24.9	23.4
Summary	22.4	24.1	23.9
Difference	−2.0	−0.8	0.5
Standard deviations			
Verbatim	5.4	5.5	
Summary	6.6	6.8	
Difference	−1.2	−1.3	

It should be noted that, in Test 1, the scores on verbatims were higher than those on summaries. The critical ratio of the difference was found to be 4.53, and accordingly the difference is to be regarded as significant. The curves for both kinds of items rise between Tests 1 and 2, the rise in the curve of summaries being relatively greater. Between Tests 2 and 3 the curve for summaries shows practically no loss, but the curve for verbatims drops enough to fall below the other by the end of four weeks. The critical ratio of the difference between the two distributions on Test 2 is 3.73, thus indicating a significant difference. Though the difference in Test 3 is very small, it should be remembered that it is in the opposite direction from the differences in the preceding tests . . .

The two types of comparison of verbatim and summary learning give results that warrant the conclusion that there are important differences between the two kinds of learning.

Spacing of readings. No important differences were found between the results of the two spacings used. In only one comparison out of six was there a difference having a critical ratio as large as three. These results are consistent with those on spacing in Series II. In that Series it was found that unspaced reading and three-day spacing gave very similar results, and both spacings were clearly inferior to three-hour spacing.

FOURTH SERIES OF EXPERIMENTS

One of the passages used in the Third Series was studied three times (instead of two) by a different group of 85 college students. Figure 2 shows

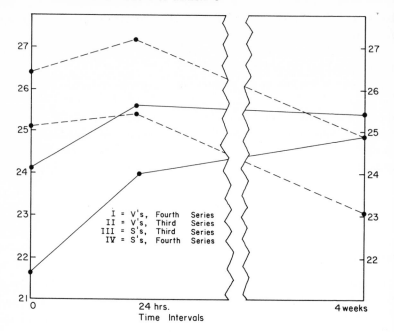

FIG. 2. RETENTION CURVES FOR THIRD AND FOURTH SERIES.

the results of the Fourth Series and also the portion of the results of the Third Series derived from the same passage. In the Fourth Series there was a somewhat greater difference than in the Third Series between verbatim and summary scores on the initial tests, possibly due to the extra reading. The more important result is that, as before, the verbatim scores showed a significant loss after four weeks, while the summary scores showed a small but noticeable gain. Similar curves in the two series are practically identical in form. The differential effect of the lapse of time on the two tasks is most evident.

SUMMARY

1. In the Second Series differences, for the most part reliable, among various spacings were clearly favorable to an inter-practice interval of from three to twenty-four hours. In the Third Series the results, though not clear-cut, were consistent with those of the Second. There were no reliable differences between the two kinds of recognition-task, the Ver-

batim and the Non-Verbatim. The effect of moderate spacing is greater for immediate than for delayed recognition.

2. Immediate recognition was inferior with both kinds of items to recognition after twenty-four hours.

3. There is less loss in the recognition of paraphrase items than of verbatim items based on the same passage and studied under the same conditions (Series II). There is an even larger difference of the same sort when the comparison is between summary items and verbatims. In fact in one case (Series IV), there is no apparent forgetting but even actual gain in summaries scores after four weeks without intervening study.

III. THE EFFECT OF THE NUMBER OF READINGS UPON SUBSTANCE AND VERBATIM MEMORY OF THE SAME MATERIAL

FIFTH SERIES OF EXPERIMENTS

The test prepared paralleled very closely that described in the Second Series. Two parallel test forms were thus constructed, each of 25 V- and 25 P-items. One half of each experimental group took one form of the test, the other half the other form. The subjects were 134 students in an elementary course in educational psychology. They were assembled to hear the passage read to them, and were divided by a random selection into five groups. One group heard the passage read once; another group heard it read twice, another three, another four, and one group heard it read five times. Speed of reading, expression, loudness, and such factors were fairly constant. The motivation of the subjects was in general good. After each reading the students who were to constitute that experimental group went to another room and after about 10 minutes took a test on the material they had just heard.

They were retested at intervals of 1, 8, and 71 days, each student taking the same form of the test on the later occasions as on the first. All the later tests were unannounced. Of the original 134, 91 students completed all three tests. Unless otherwise stated, data are given in what follows only for these latter . . .

Table 4 shows the results for immediate memory of the differing numbers of repetitions. From this table it can be seen that in the case of V-learning an increase in the number of readings beyond two certainly does not bring an increase in score. As many as two readings do seem to be of value. In the case of P-learning there are no significant differences.

TABLE 4

THE MEDIAN SCORES FOR THE VARIOUS READING GROUPS—
TESTED 10 MINUTES AFTER STUDY

| | Number of readings | | | | |
	1	2	3	4	5
V–score	17.5	19.33	19.33	18.0	19.08
P–score	17.13	17.5	18.0	18.9	17.38

$N = 124$. (All persons taking the first test are included.)
Possible score $= 25$.

The facts bearing on retention are shown in Figure 3. Recognition for
the V-items falls off consistently from the first to the seventy-first day.
On the other hand, recognition of the P-items shows a consistent rise.
Starting materially lower, the curves cross the retention curve for V-items
at about the eighth day. By the seventy-first day, the difference between
the two medians is 4.8 times the probable error of the difference.

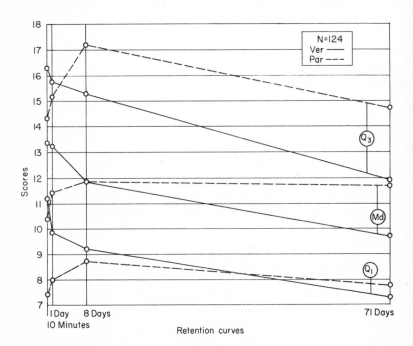

FIG. 3. RETENTION CURVES IN TERMS OF QUARTILES.
Series I

SIXTH SERIES OF EXPERIMENTS

In the fifth series of experiments no differential effect of number of repetitions was found on the two types of test-item. A possible explanation of this is that we had not departed far enough from verbatim learning in our paraphrase items. We decided therefore to make statements which should summarize the thought of a whole paragraph.

Due to the nature of the items only one test form was used. There were twenty summary items (called S-items) similar to those used in the Third Series, sixty verbatim items (V-items), and twenty items which were statements of such similar general tenor that they might reasonably be thought to have been in the passage, but were not (N-items). The subjects were instructed (before being tested but *after* study of the passage) as follows: "If a statement below conveys the same idea, whether or not in the same words, as is conveyed in the passage, mark it A for agrees. If it conveys an idea which is not in the passage at all mark it N." In comparisons, unless otherwise noted, the S-scores were multiplied by three in order to make them equivalent to the V-scores.

Three hundred and ninety-one elementary psychology students took part in this series of experiments, which were conducted during the spring and summer quarters of 1932. A prose passage of 2150 words was read to them as they followed along reading silently. They were divided on a random basis into four reading groups, studying the passage respectively one, two, three and four times. The test was given immediately after the reading and at intervals of 1, 14 and 30 days. The same test was used on the later occasions and the tests were unannounced . . .

In this series we have shown data separately for number of readings and also for all groups combined. The former are presented in Figure 4 and the latter in Figure 5. The S-items are much harder than the P-items of Series V, hence a greater initial difference between V and S. But the same phenomena appear as before: loss in one, gain in the other type of item with the passage of time . . .

It makes practically no difference how many repetitions (up to 4) one has if we consider the ability to recognize the general drift of the passage; it does make a difference if we consider ability to recognize correctly sentences which reproduce the original, verbatim. As we get further away from the learning period, however, the influence of the exact verbatim wording decreases and accordingly the value of additional repetitions is less.

Another approach is the correlational. If the verbatim and summary tests were measuring the same process we should expect the correlations between them to be as high as the split-half reliability coefficients. If, on the other hand, we find a high reliability coefficient and a low correlation between V- and S-scores it would be indicative that these two tests are measuring different processes. The correlation between V- and S-scores on the first 117 cases was .39. The reliability coefficient on the same group was .69. The difference is .30 ± .055, its critical ratio 5.45, which according to the usual criterion is ample. Here then we have two measures of the same *identical* material studied under *identical* conditions, yet yielding markedly different results. The inference that distinct factors are operative is clear.

SEVENTH SERIES

It is well known that recitation is a considerable factor in learning. It is quite clear that each testing period is in effect such a recitation. It was

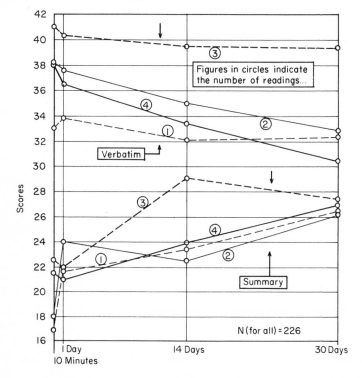

FIG. 4. RETENTION CURVES IN SUCCESSIVE TESTS.
Series II

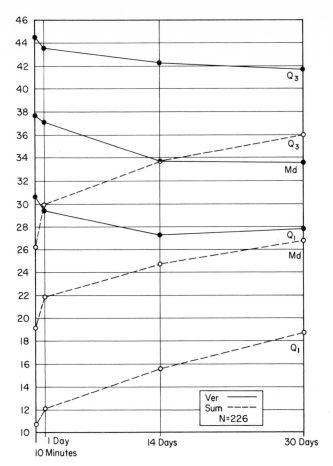

FIG. 5. RETENTION CURVES IN TERMS OF QUARTILES.
Series II

thought that this might account for the actual increase in score of the S-items, though one would still have to account for the fact that the V-items showed a loss. In any case, using the technique of Series VI we administered the test to 152 students directly after reading the passage 1, 2, or 3 times. No further test was given for 55 days. We find the same decline in V-items and the same increase in S-items . . . These results also confirm the conclusion of Series VI respecting number of repetitions . . .

SUMMARY

1. Repetition within the limits of the conditions of our experiments, favorably affects immediate and delayed recognition-memory of verbatim items. It seems to have little or no effect upon the recognition of summary items . . .

2. Retention curves for the two sorts of items, V and S, consistently show opposed trends. Those for V-items show a typical Ebbinghaus decline; those for S-items do not look like forgetting curves at all but like learning curves. This rise, however, takes place without intervening study or (in Series VII) recitation.

IV. GENERAL CONCLUSIONS AND DISCUSSION

1. The first conclusion which we draw is methodological: the learning parameter is a function not only of the external conditions imposed and of the motivation of the subject, but also and very distinctly of the technique of measurement. The identical bit of learning . . . may be made to show a rising or falling curve of retention by a shift in the measuring technique. The point, however obvious it may seem, is almost universally ignored in interpreting experimental data.

2. Certain practical implications deserve emphasis. Working with a kind of learning which resembles actual academic study fairly closely, we confirm previous investigations which favor at least a moderate spacing of "practice." Closely connected with this is the evidence that tests such as those used by us are themselves teaching devices of much merit when given at short intervals after a given unit of learning has been completed.

The outstanding differences between the Verbatim and the Summary test items lead also to a practical conclusion. There is a widespread opinion, implicit in most school and college examinations (by no means confined to the so-called new-type examination), that tests of verbatim learning are adequate tests of substance learning. Our results flatly deny this implication. Examination techniques must directly measure the kind of learning desired—and the Summary-items seem to us examples of one way to measure objectively a highly desirable form of learning . . .

3. Finally, we invite attention to the implications of this study for learning theory. Traditionally, learning has been conceived as the formation and fixation of routine, rote responses. Experimental literature is full of investigations which seem to validate this conception . . .

Our data, on the other hand, strongly suggest that our Verbatim-items measure predominantly just such rote associative-synthesis in learning while our Summary-items reflect a greater predominance of another factor which it is premature to delimit exactly or to name without further experimentation, but which is tied up with the organized or coherent or meaningful in experience or behavior. This comes out most clearly in the curves of retention. The same subjects, learning the same material at the same time and under the same conditions, on the one hand forget rapidly, or on the other retain what is learned, depending upon whether our criterion of learning is a fixed routine response or a grasp of the meaning or substance. The differential effect of frequency points in the same direction. Successive repetitions seem to yield new and deeper meanings rather than to fixate those already comprehended, but additional repetitions seem to fixate verbatim responses somewhat as asserted by associationism . . .

REFERENCES

1. JONES, M. G., ENGLISH, H. B. 1926. Notional vs. rote memory. *Amer. J. Psychol.* 37:602–3.
2. McDOUGALL, W., SMITH, M. 1920. Some experiments in learning and retention. *Brit. J. Psychol.* 10:199–210.
3. MEUMANN, E. *The Psychology of Learning. An Experimental Investigation of the Economy and Technique of Memory* (Trans. by D. Baird). New York: Appleton, 1913.

29. The Transfer Value of Given and Individually Derived Principles*

Does independently learning to derive a principle for the solution of a problem have greater transfer value than being given the principle at the outset of the learning task? After reviewing the evidence from previous studies, Haslerud and Meyers describe an experiment in coding which attempts to answer this question under controlled conditions. Their findings lead the authors to conclude that a new interpretation or theory of transfer is needed in educational psychology.

While there is general recognition of the value of organized learning for memory and transfer, differences on how that organization should be taught and attained lead to quite different theories of transfer. On the

* GEORGE M. HASLERUD and SHIRLEY MEYERS. Reprinted and abridged with permission of the authors and the publisher from the *Journal of Educational Psychology*, 1958, Vol. 49, No. 6, 293–8.

one hand are those who decry outside direction of learning when one is interested in transfer. Katona (6) using card and geometric puzzles found that his memorization group was significantly poorer on invention and transfer to new problems than his "Help" group that had only examples. He concluded ". . . that formulating the general principle in words is not indispensable for achieving application," but he was unwilling to say that learning of principle in words is always less efficient than by example. He put teaching the result as the worst method, teaching by stating the principle as intermediate, and teaching by example as best. However, Hendrix (5) found that with a mathematical principle those groups that discovered the principle independently and left it unverbalized exceeded those who discovered and then verbalized, and both exceeded in transfer those who had the principle stated for them and then illustrated.

Opposed to Katona and Hendrix are those like Craig who concluded: "The more guidance a learner receives, the more efficient his discovery will be; the more efficient discovery is, the more learning and transfer will occur" (1). In a further study with college groups and with the same method of having the S pick out that alternative among five which does not fit a principle (2) he verified that significantly more such problems were solved when the principle was stated above it than when the S was given only the instruction that one of the five items did not belong. One should note, however, that he found no difference between his groups on transfer to new principles nor was there any difference in retention after 3 or 17 days, although at 31 days the difference favored the directed group.

While Craig's experimental results actually gave little or no support to his claim that guidance is desirable for transfer, more serious opposition to Hendrix and Katona came from Kittell (7). He found that "intermediate direction" (stating a principle) was significantly superior to both the "minimal direction" (told only that one of five alternatives would not fit) and "maximal direction" (E told the principle and worked out the answer for S), with minimal direction definitely the inferior method. His subjects were sixth graders while Craig's were college students. That difference in age and educational level may explain the contrast in results. Also Kittell's low number of successful solutions (means only 4.59 for intermediate direction and 1.93 for minimal direction out of 15 principles) suggests that the problems based on linguistic arrangements and meanings may have been too difficult for the Ss. If that were the case, then following directions in the stated principle was about the only way to solve the problem when unprovided with sufficient apperceptive mass and experience. Haslerud (4) found that while naive rats transferred anticipatively from forced turns near the goal into prior free units of a maze just as well as when those goal turnings had been established by trial and error, only active trial and error cul-de-sac elimination in the goal region could readjust an established pattern in the prior free units. If a similar limitation on effectiveness of guidance is present in human Ss, then one might expect any advantage primarily in young Ss and that mainly on their initial learning but none for memory and transfer where Ss have sufficient background to derive a solution themselves.

While the Katona and Hendrix concept of how to get maximal transfer seems to have face validity, at least for adults, their controls and statistical supports are unsatisfactory. When one draws his conclusions on the basis of one principle, e.g., the sum of the first n numbers, a question remains of how much of the conclusion is a function of the particular problem used or the selection of individuals for the various groups. More convincing differentiation of principle given from principle derived would seem to require homogeneously varied problems posed in quantity to the same individuals. A likely material has been found in an extension of the familiar cryptogram "Come to London" in the Stanford-Binet. An unpublished pilot study by the junior author under the senior author's supervision indicated an advantage for memory of the independent solving of such coding principles. The present study extends a similar method to transfer. The hypothesis tested is that principles derived by the learner solely from concrete instances will be more readily used in a new situation than those given to him in the form of a statement of principle and an instance.

PROCEDURE

Subjects for the experimental group were 76 members, ranging from freshmen to seniors, of two general psychology classes at the University of New Hampshire. The control group of 24 students in another psychology class ranged from sophomores to seniors.

The experimental groups were each given two coding tests, the second being administered one week after the first. The control group was given only the second test. All tests were administered by the senior author.

The first test composed of 20 coding problems was designed to give the students two types of experience: (*a*) problem solving with specific directions for deciphering the code printed above each problem, and (*b*) problem solving with no directions given. The first part of each problem was the four-word sentence "They need more time," followed by the same sentence in code. A different code was used in each problem. The second part of each problem was the four-word sentence "Give them five more," which the *Ss* were asked to translate into the code for that problem. The given and derived problems were alternated so that the *S* would solve approximately equal numbers of each kind. As a control for differences between the codes, there were two test forms, A and B. The same codes were used in both, but those for which directions were given in form A had to be deciphered by the *S* in form B, and vice-versa. The problems were arranged in approximately the apparent order of difficulty. Examples of moderately easy coding rules are: "For each letter of the sentence write the letter that follows it in the alphabet." "Write the first two letters of each word and then the last two letters of each word." To introduce the test the senior author told the *Ss* that the test was an experiment in cryptography. He wrote an illustrative code on the blackboard and purposely worked it out partly incorrectly to encourage remonstrances from the group that a system or principle was possible. *Ss* were asked to solve the problems in the order they appeared on the test and to do as many as they could in the time allotted. Since the 45 minutes allotted was ample time for all but one or two students in each group, the test was essentially a power rather than a speed test. The *Ss* were not told that they would be retested on the same material.

The second test printed only in one form was given to both the experimental and control groups. Again, the 20 codes used in the first test were used, but instead of the common sentence of Test 1, there were 20 different English sentences 14 to 18 letters in length followed by four translations into code. Only one translation was correct, and the *Ss* were asked to check it. They were told that the other three were simply letters arranged in random order. They were not told that numbers had been assigned to letters of the alphabet and that letters for two of the four codes had been selected according to the order in which those numbers appeared in a list of random numbers. The third false code was composed of letters of the English sentence arranged according to random numbers. The order in which the four codes followed the sentence and the order in which the problems were arranged on the test were also random. No mention was made of the previous test, nor was the purpose of the test told until both tests had been given and the results compiled.

RESULTS

The data for each individual in the experimental group consisted of four scores: (*a*) Number of correct codings on Test 1 problems where the rule was given, hereafter called G_1 scores. (*b*) Number of correct codings on Test 1 problems where the coding principle had to be derived by the *S*, hereafter called D_1 scores. (*c*) Correct alternatives for those codes in Test 2 that had been G type in Test 1. (*d*) Correct alternatives for those codes in Test 2 that had been D type in Test 1. In the control group the score was the total number of correct alternatives on Test 2. Any coding was considered correct if no more than 1 of the 16 letters was wrong, since carelessness rather than lack of understanding of the principle was probably responsible for the lone error.

Since there was no difference between their results, the two experimental classes were combined. The analysis of results, however, was carried through separately for Forms A and B of Test 1 because a difference significant at the .05 level indicated that the 10 odd and the 10 even problems had not been exactly equated for difficulty. Nevertheless, the direction of results for both A and B groups showed equally high differentiation of G and D situations.

Test 2 performance of the experimental group was significantly different from that of the control group. The means, 15.74 and 10.75 respectively, differ beyond the .001 level. Apparently something is transferred from the Test 1 experience.

The crucial comparisons are between the G and D kinds of problems. For both Forms A and B on Test 1, significantly more G problems were correctly coded: 8.86 and 8.36 against 5.86 and 4.88 for G and D respectively . . . Since each individual was his own control for both G and D problems on Tests 1 and 2, it is legitimate to use the subtraction method to find the standard error of the difference for paired observations. The correct identification of those codes which had been D type on Test 1 increased 46% while those which had been G decreased 10%. Both changes are significant, at the .001 and .05 to .01 levels respectively. There is reason to think that both curtailing time to make Test 2 a speed test and increasing time to greater than a week between the learning of the codes on Test 1 and the transfer on Test 2 would accentuate the differences.

Discussion

This experiment has added strong support to the contention of Katona and Hendrix that independently derived principles are more transferable than those where the principle is given to the student. Even though Ss produced more correct codings on the original learning when the principle was stated for them, on the "pay-off," or "applying" to use Katona's term, the advantage definitely passed to those principles derived by the student himself. Fast and accurate learning or performance under immediate guidance is no guarantee of transfer to new problems without such support. From Craig's and our experiments the conclusions just stated are supported by results on college students, but testing of grammar level students by principles of a more suitable level of difficulty than used by Kittell might show a wider application. Our coding method could be easily adapted for that purpose.

The obtained results of this experiment do not follow from inadequate controls. The alternate Forms A and B allowed each principle to be given (G) and derived (D). Individual differences with respect to problem solving in the Ss were ruled out since each person responded to 10 G and 10 D problems on Test 1 and the follow-up of each of these on the transfer Test 2. The control group's much poorer performance on Test 2 indicated that a genuine transfer function was present. Making time on each test practically unlimited pushed the G and D types of presentation to their limit as power tests . . .

The theories of transfer found in current educational psychologies are inadequate to explain the present experiment. The senior author plans to develop in another place a theory that transfer is fundamentally an anticipative rather than a perseverative function and that to get transfer one must always counteract the finality of a goal . . . A stated principle to some extent, and even more Kittell's "maximum guidance" of E doing the problems for S after giving him the principle, practically stops transfer, like other goals. Hendrix . . . states from Thorndike that only 5% of high school students have language ability sufficient to receive a ready-made sentence and find readily illustrations in their own background to provide the prerequisite to meaning. If the results of the present experiment can be verified for a wider range of ages and apperceptive masses, then the implications for a direct attempt to teach for transferable principles can not be neglected.

Summary

The educationally important question of how much guidance is desirable if one is interested in transfer was tested experimentally by a new use of coding. Each of 76 college students as his own control translated into 20 different codes a common four-word sentence, with the rule given for half of the problems and required to be derived solely from example for the other half. As in previous studies on initial learning, the Ss did significantly better on those problems with the rule given. However, a week later on a multiple-choice transfer test consisting of 20 different sentences, one for each of the 20 coding principles of the first test, the selection of the adequate code from three specious ones made by randomizing letters gave very different results. The scores were significantly increased for those problems which had formerly been derived as contrasted with a significant decrease for those problems where the rule had formerly been given. A control group of 24 college students given only the second test proved by significantly poorer performance than the experimental group the value of transfer from the first test. The results give strong support to the postulate of Hendrix that independently derived principles are more transferable than those given. The apparent contradiction with Kittell's study of children was explained by the smaller apperceptive mass in the child, and the prediction was hazarded that as naivete is lost, the probability of transfer from learning which is minimally directed is increased.

REFERENCES

1. CRAIG, R. C. *The Transfer Value of Guided Learning*. New York: Teachers College, Columbia University Bureau of Publications, 1953.

2. CRAIG, R. C. 1956. Directed versus independent discovery of established relations. *J. Ed. Psychol.* 47:223–34.

3. HASLERUD, G. M. 1950. Properties of bi-directional gradients of sub-goals. *J. Genet. Psychol.* 29:67–76.

4. HASLERUD, G. M. 1953. Anticipative transfer of mechanically guided turns. *J. Exp. Psychol.* 45:431–6.

5. HENDRIX, G. 1947. A new clue to transfer of training. *Elem. Sch. J.* 48:197–208.

6. KATONA, G. *Organizing and Memorizing*. New York: Columbia University Press, 1940.

7. KITTELL, J. E. 1957. An experimental study of the effect of external direction during learning on transfer and retention of principles. *J. Ed. Psychol.* 48:391–405.

CHAPTER : 9

Developmental Aspects of Learning

30. The Development of Scientific Concepts in a Young Child*

> The intensive study of the individual over a period of time is a power-
> ful means of investigating certain developmental aspects of learning.
> In Navarra's research the focus is placed upon one particular area of
> conceptual development, and the data gathered are unusually com-
> plete for a two-year period in the life of a young child. His method of
> analysis and interpretation of the detailed records leads to a de-
> velopmental interpretation of process in conceptual learning.

Overview of the Present Study

This study was concerned primarily with continuous, long-term observation of the conceptual development of an individual . . . Essentially the
collection of data was based upon direct observations of a young child . . .
The means employed to cope with the problem are discussed in relation
to various contributing factors . . .

THE STUDY OF AN INDIVIDUAL

. . . In this study, . . . a young child was observed for a period of somewhat more than two years—beginning when he was three years and two
months old and continuing into his sixth year.

The child was a little boy who was born on May 11, 1948. In all records
of the study he has been designated as L. B.

---

* JOHN G. NAVARRA. Reprinted and abridged with permission of the publisher from
The Development of Scientific Concepts in a Young Child, pp. 25–74. Bureau of Publications: Teachers College, Columbia University, 1955.

On December 22, 1952, after the study had been in progress for one and a half years, L. B. was tested by a practicing consulting psychologist. At this time he was approximately four years and seven months of age.

Test results seemed to indicate that he could conservatively be placed in a group that is usually classified as "high average." On the basis of his performance, his verbal ability seemed to be very well developed. A test of vocabulary was passed at the six-year level. He lacked one word for the test at the eight-year level. However, interest and attention seemed better with respect to concrete items. The comment was made that his potential seemed somewhat higher than his performance at this time.

On the whole, L. B.'s adjustment to the testing situation was very good. He was friendly and cooperative. At first he seemed to be shy; then, as the testing progressed, he seemed to feel more at home and he became more spontaneous in what he communicated.

THE MOTHER AS CO-INVESTIGATOR

. . . The decision to involve the mother as investigator was actually necessitated by the requirement of continuous observation. This was, indeed, a twenty-four-hour-a-day task. Any measures for observation which did not employ the mother would lack the necessary comprehensiveness . . .

The training of the mother as an investigator consisted essentially of involving her at each point in the evolution of the study. During the early phases, the co-investigators observed the child together. This practice was also continued periodically throughout the study. Each kept a record of the child's actions, verbalizations, and interactions with those present. Then a comparison and evaluation of the separate records was made in terms of the purpose of the study. It was from such training and evaluation that the skill of both investigators was developed.

THE TECHNIQUES OF INVESTIGATION

Observation of Play

. . . It seemed necessary in the present study that the emphasis be placed on the observation of the behavior of the young child in his typical daily activities. And a little observation of this day-to-day activity was sufficient to indicate the pre-eminence of play in the life of the child. One might say that play seemed to be the child's natural medium. Thus, the observation of the child's play activity provided us with a ready-made technique for studying him.

During play the child seemed to become self-involved in meaningful activity. That is, at times, he devoted long periods to an activity in which he was engaged. He also became completely engrossed in what he was doing. The child concentrated! It might be suggested that this concentration was probably due to the quality of meaning this activity had from the point of view of the child. Basically, this was the assumption upon which the decision to study the child through such activity was based. The study of play activity became the most important device by which insight was gained concerning the conceptual development of the child . . .

Building Confidence

Basic to the whole approach was the necessity for establishing a feeling of permissiveness. The success of the undertaking depended in no small measure on the relationship between the investigators and the child. Every attempt was made to have the child feel secure . . .

On the whole, the role of the investigator was to be present, interested, and helpful, but definitely not "nosy" or domineering. The cues came from the child. L. B. was continually assured by what the investigators did and said that he should follow his inclinations; and, in a sense, lead the way. He was encouraged to assume responsibility and decide what he would like to do . . .

It should be made clear that the matter of asking questions was also considered a part of the process of building rapport. There was a specific attempt to avoid structuring questions which would be directional and provoke particular kinds of responses. Rather, the stress was on asking and answering questions in such a way as to elicit further clarification of the child's ideas . . .

Mechanics of Recording

The stenographic record of the child's overt activities and verbalizations was entered in small bound notebooks as the observations were made. All pertinent information was entered immediately as the activity was taking place. In addition, each observation was identified as to date, time of day, and, in some cases, duration of activity.

No conscious interpretation of the activity was made at the time of recording. Interpretations on the part of the investigator did not become a part of the notebook record. The emphasis in all notebook records was placed on what the child said and did. Other than this, the record included only descriptions of the scene.

Much of the child's activity was not accompanied by verbalization. Photographs became an important part of the study, as they provided a means of recording such nonverbal activity. They were also invaluable in capturing the quality of the fleeting activity and the setting in which the activity was taking place . . .

Reconstruction of the Child's Experience

A descriptive method of analysis has been selected for the following presentation. Since a mere recording of the day-to-day progress, although valuable, would tend to be confusing, the analytic approach was needed to make the numerous, complex records intelligible . . .

The method of analysis was essentially one of making inferences based on aspects of performance or behavior. These inferences may be termed tentative hypotheses. With these inferences as a basis, the analysis was directed toward the formulation of theoretical constructs which were in agreement with and based on the most obvious observations. However, by continual refinement and successive approximations, the theoretical constructs were modified to conform with larger and larger segments of the data . . .

DIFFERENTIATION WITHIN EXPERIENCE

. . . Differentiation may be defined here as movement in L. B.'s thought process from familiar items to those that are less familiar. An item would obviously be less familiar if it was being met for the first time. However, items well within his experience became those which were less familiar when they were seen in a new context.

In the following set of records the aspect of process which deals with differentiation may be traced. Only pertinent aspects of the records will be presented. These records depict facets of the child's long-term growth in the differentiation of smoke and steam . . .

RECORDS	ANALYSIS
August 11, 1951	From the record it is evident that
L. B.'s attention was attracted by	L. B. has some sort of concept of
his aunt as she was using a spray gun	smoke. He has inquired whether the
to dust a rosebush. Puffs of white	puffs from the spray are smoke. The
powder could be seen. L. B. watched	conditions as he sees them must be

and then inquired, "Is that smoke? That looks like a gun. What are you doing with that gun?" . . .

October 20, 1951

The kitchen had become quite smoky as some food was being prepared. L. B., who had been playing in the kitchen, scampered to the door and opened it.

Mother: What are you doing?

L. B.: I have to let out the smoke. Do you want the house to burn down?

October 26, 1951

L. B. was watching his mother iron clothes which had been dampened.

L. B.: What's that—smoke? Where is that coming from? Is there something under that iron that makes it smoke?

Mother: It looks like smoke, but it really is steam.

L. B.: Why do you have to get the iron hot for? Why does it have to be hot? Is it hot now?

October 22, 1951

L. B. and his father were taking a walk when they happened upon a scene which must have been an awesome sight for the child. A mechanic was using steam to clean the motor of a car. The whole car seemed to be surrounded by steam. L. B. very excitedly said, "What's he doing to the car? Is the car burning on fire?" The father replied, "No, he's using steam to clean the car."

somewhat similar to his concept for smoke. However, the fact that he has posed a question as to its identity may mean that he has reservations as to the applicability of his smoke concept to the present situation . . .

Now, one can begin to see what had probably bothered L. B. . . . His concept of smoke must entail that there be a source of heat and fire. In neither of the preceding incidents was there any source of heat for him to see. Thus, although some features were identical, there was disagreement on other basic elements in the concept.

L. B. has used the term "smoke" to apply to the phenomenon known as steam, but he is puzzled as to the source of the "smoke," which he cannot seem to see. It would seem that he makes some sort of connection between smoke and heat, but steam does not seem to be associated with heat. When he was told that the phenomenon was steam, he wanted to know why the iron had to be hot. This might be interpreted as a questioning of the mother's information that it was not smoke.

Here, again, can be seen the child's association of a "smoke-like" phenomenon with heat, fire, and burning. He is now told by his father that such a phenomenon is called steam.

RECORDS

ANALYSIS

February 18, 1952

Celeste was pouring boiling water for tea. Vapor was rising from the boiling water.

L. B.: Hey! Look at all that steam. Are you going to drink that? Where is all that smoke going to? . . .

L. B. has used the word "steam." But as can be noted, he also used the word "smoke" to apply to the same phenomenon. This seems to be a transitional stage in the differentiation. The clue to this may be in the information supplied by his father . . .

April 27, 1952

L. B. had become ill with the croup. A part of the remedy is to inhale moist, warm air. He was taken into the bathroom, which was filled with steam by opening the hot water faucets. L. B. ran his fingers over the mirror on the medicine chest and said, "This is wet." Then he brushed his hand over the wall and repeated, "This is wet, too." In a few moments he turned to his mother and inquired, "Hey, Mommy, where does this steam come from—from the water?" His mother replied that it did, and then L. B. returned to running a finger over the tile wall. Then he very deliberately shook his head and said, "This *is* steamy." Mother inquired, "What do you mean—steamy?" L. B. replied with a very emphatic, "It's all wet." . . .

The child's experience has led him to realize that water is associated with steam. He raised the question himself: "Where does the steam come from . . . ?" A partial answer was also given by L. B. to his own question. The phrase "from the water" can be viewed as both an answer and an hypothesis on the part of the child. However, it seems clear that he has identified the origin of steam as water . . .

May 17, 1952

L. B.'s mother was pressing some clothes. She was using a regular iron and a damp cloth. L. B. seemed to be fascinated. His mother asked, "Do you see something interesting?" L. B. responded, "I see some steam going up—every time you move it." Then he requested, "Pick it up." Mother agreed, "O.K.—it's up." She continued to hold the iron away from the cloth. Then L. B. asked his mother

In this record, L. B. has used the term "steam" to apply to what he has seen. He has also associated the steam with the movement of the iron. In his last statement, L. B. has definitely tied the iron into the scheme of steam-making. However, he has not expressly stated that heat has anything to do with the making of the steam . . .

to place the iron on the cloth again. When asked why he wanted the iron placed on the cloth again, he replied, "Cause when you pick it up and put it down again it makes steam.". . .

July 2, 1952

L. B. was walking along Riverside Drive with his mother. L. B. noticed smoke rising from the Hudson River. He asked, "Where is all that smoke coming from?" He could not see the ship on the river, since he was not close enough to the embankment. Mother said, "Let's go and see." They walked to the railing at the top of the embankment. L. B. pointed and said, "I know where from—out of the pipe.". . .

The differentiation is becoming clear. He is using the terms "smoke" and "steam" more or less for the proper phenomena. Here he has named the phenomenon "smoke" without seeing the source . . .

August 28, 1952

L. B. was watching the steam coming out of the vaporizer.

L. B.: Where is the steam coming from, Mommy?

Mother: From inside.

His mother disconnected the vaporizer and showed him where the water was.

Mother: See the water in there.

Nothing else was said at the time. The vaporizer continued to give off steam and L. B. became interested in other things.

There had not been too much water in the vaporizer and in about half an hour it needed to be filled again. Mother disconnected the vaporizer and got water.

Mother: We'll have to put more water in it.

L. B.: Where did the water go? Into the steam?

Slightly more than one year has elapsed since . . . L. B. inquired about the origin of the steam. He was shown the water but was not told anything explicitly about the water . . . His inquiry concerning where the water had gone was followed by the suggestion that it had gone "into the steam". . . L. B. had hypothesized that steam came from water, but here he seems to be extending it to include the actual change of water to steam.

RECORDS

ANALYSIS

February 21, 1953

As part of his lunch, L. B. had a cup of hot bouillon placed before him on the table.

L. B.: Cool it off!

Mother: Wait until it cools off.

L. B.: O.K.

He continued with the rest of his lunch and, after some time had elapsed:

L. B.: Is it cool now?

Mother: I don't know.

He looked at the cup of bouillon.

L. B.: Yes, it's cool now 'cause there's no steam.

Mother: Does that mean it's cool?

L. B.: Yes.

Mother: Doesn't steam come from cool things?

L. B.: No, only when it's hot . . .

In this record he has given explicit verbalization to still another phase in the differentiation. Steam has now been associated with heat. The concept now has the elements water-into-steam and heat, whereas the smoke concept as identified in these records has the elements heat, burning, and smoke . . .

This sequence of records has been offered to highlight phases in the child's gradual differentiation between smoke and other "smoke-like" phenomena. Steam was the phenomenon the differentiation of which was traced in detail.

On the basis of the records it may be suggested that many phenomena were seen as "smoke-like" by the child. However, the applicability of his smoke concept to these other phenomena gradually began to be questioned by the child. This questioning seemed to arise when his experiences with these other phenomena did not completely agree with his smoke concept. Verbal information from the adults may have helped, but it seems clear from the records that the verbal information alone did not suffice to make the differentiation clear. There seemed to be a web of experiences, with some probably more important than others, which moved the child in the direction of clarifying the differentiation . . .

THE DEVELOPMENT OF EXPECTANCIES

The concept-forming process engaged in by the child seemed, in many instances, to be directed toward gathering and validating information pertinent to concerns which arose during the course of his activity. The concern was, in a sense, a focus around which experiences were integrated. Through his activities the child gradually accumulated a body of information pertinent to the item of concern. This cumulative body of integrated information could be called an expectancy pattern . . .

RECORDS	ANALYSIS
December 13, 1951	This might be said to be an initial
L. B. was playing in the snow which covered the ground. While playing he said that he was thirsty and asked for a drink of water. The mother went into the house and then returned with a cup of water for L. B. to drink. L. B. drank approximately half the water. He still had the cup in his hand when he said, "I think I'll put snow in the cup." His mother cautioned, "Did you have enough water to drink?" L. B. returned a prompt "Yes." He then proceeded to put some snow into the cup. As soon as the snow was placed in the water, it seemed to melt. L. B. laughingly exclaimed, "No more snow.". . .	type of expectancy developed through his experiences with snow, i.e., that when snow is placed in water the snow disappears. On previous occasions . . . L. B. had used water to melt ice. This information may have carried over to the present situation and induced him to place the snow in the water. His actions in this present record may have been, in fact, a test of a previous expectancy which he had developed in relation to ice, i.e., that when ice is placed in water, it melts . . .
December 15, 1951	The child seems to be reaching out
L. B. was looking out the window at the snow. He turned to his father and asked, "Why does it snow now and not in the summer?" The father answered, "Yes, that's right. It doesn't snow during the summer time but it snows at times during the winter." L. B. chuckled to himself and didn't say anything more . . .	and drawing upon great segments of experience. As he lived through the summer he never stated that it was not snowing. He had no cause to make such a statement. But in this record it would seem that he has searched back into his past and made a differentiation between summer and winter in connection with the snow. Thus, it might be said that his summer experiences provided *useful, future information* with respect to this concern although the relationship was not apparent at the time . . .
December 19, 1951	The mother posed the question concerning what had happened to the
There had been a lot of snow the	

RECORDS	ANALYSIS
day before. Mother raised the question, "I wonder where all the snow went?" *John:* It went 'way up in the sky so you couldn't play with it. *L. B.:* No, it didn't. It melted. Snow melts . . .	snow. The question was not directed at anyone specifically, nor would she have insisted upon an answer if none had been volunteered. However, John, L. B.'s playmate, offered a suggestion which L. B. quite emphatically rejected. L. B.'s answer also indicates that some of the information has been integrated into an expectancy that snow melts . . .

The child's expectancies can be traced throughout the development of his concept of melting. The records indicate that expectancies were formulated and used in relation to very specific items within his experiences, but an expectancy should not be considered as an isolated hypothesis about an item. Indications are that expectancy development was a positive and necessary phase in the continued progression of a concept.

The phase of concept formation indicated in this treatment as the development of expectancies is postulated to have operated in the following manner: As information accumulated, it provided the child with an expectation in relation to an event or concern. Then, in future encounters with the items of the concern, the expectation served the child as an hypothesis. Contrasts were made by the child between information derived from his experiences and the expectations which had been formulated on the basis of past information. The testing of his expectation or hypothesis—on the basis of further information derived through more extensive contacts with the items of concern during his activities—was the prime instigator in conceptual growth and revision . . .

THE EXPECTANCY IN PROBLEM FORMULATION

Many of L. B.'s concerns or problems developed in situations in which expectations were not confirmed, i.e., when information derived during his activity did not substantiate what L. B. expected from the event. The information which accrued from such a situation might be thought of as a negative instance which was . . . "expectancy-infirming": such information brought about recognition of an inconsistency or difficulty in the conceptual framework. This inconsistency became a genuine concern or problem the resolution of which impelled the child to seek and relate additional information. Further experiences contributed information which led to expectancy breakdown or revision.

The following record has been chosen as a succinct description of the expectancy function under discussion. It is representative of what happened continuously throughout other activities in which the child engaged.

RECORDS

March 21, 1952

L. B. and his mother and father had just left the shopping district on Broadway in Bayonne. They were walking along Twenty-First Street toward the place where the automobile had been parked. The mother and father were carrying on a conversation. L. B. was holding his mother's hand and was not involved in the conversation. As they walked along, L. B. left his mother and father and walked back to a building which had just been passed.

L. B.: Daddy! Look at that garage! How do they get down there? It looks like some kind of garage. How do they get a car down there? *It's got steps!*

Dad: I don't think the people use it for a garage any more.

The original driveway which led to the garage (located under a house) probably had a dip of approximately two feet downward from the street to the floor of the garage. This driveway had been filled in and made level with the street. As a result, about two feet of the bottoms of the original doors were below sidewalk level. There were a few steps leading down to the doors.

L. B. and his parents continued along Twenty-First Street. Approximately half a block from the previous garage doors, L. B. came to a brief halt and inspected another garage.

L. B.: This garage is O.K. because it *don't* have steps . . .

August 25, 1952

L. B. and his mother were walking along Twenty-Ninth Street in Bayonne when L. B. was attracted by what appeared to be garage doors. The original doors had been covered by imitation brick and a cellar window had been placed in each door so that the door area now appeared to be a part of the regular foundation.

L. B. called his mother's attention to the "doors": "Look at that!" As he walked toward the "doors" he exclaimed, "It's a garage!" and then in a rather quiet questioning way he said, "It's not a fake garage." But as he paused and examined the doors he squinted and sighed, "It has to be a fake garage—'cause I don't see a keyhole.". . .

Thus, it would seem that information which accrues from negative instances during the child's activities may initially be designated as expectancy-infirming. Such incongruous information may lead to the formulation of a problem on the part of the child. However, the expectancy which gives rise to the problem is not immediately discarded. The expectancy may initially be suspect in the eyes of the child, but the child seems to display a good deal of reservation and caution. An analysis of the child's further activities seems to indicate that he responds to a weighted average—that the weight of the information derived from his activities may lead the child to view the expectancy as untenable and impel him to revise his conceptual framework.

CONCERNS POINT A DIRECTION

. . . The conceptual growth which was traced in the records was not merely in terms of the resolution of a given concern. Rather, the concern and resolution of the concern were also the instigatory points of a progression of related events in a larger pattern of growth.

The following set of records is presented to reveal the nature of a concerns-instigatory role. The description includes the development of the initial concern and the concomitant progression of related events.

RECORDS

July 9, 1951

L. B. was playing with water which had been placed in a large circular basin. He used a small pail to scoop water out of the basin. Using various items such as a cup, dipper, and little truck with which to scoop water, he continued to fill the pail.

L. B. turned his attention to a water pistol. The pistol was empty. It had to be filled by pouring water through a little hole at the top of the handle. L. B. used a small red dipper to pour the water into the pistol. After he filled the pistol, he squirted the water at various objects. Over a period of eleven minutes he filled and emptied the water pistol three times. Each time he used the red dipper. He was about to fill the pistol again, but this time he picked up a small reed basket. It was about the

L. B. placed a small plastic truck near the pail of water. The rear of the truck body was built like a rectangular box. L. B. filled the reed basket with water from the pail and then held the basket over the rear section of the truck body. The water streaming from the basket fell into the rectangular carrying section of the truck.

L. B. continued to fill the truck by allowing water to drip from the basket. However, the truck was quite a distance from the pail and a good deal of the water would drip out before he was able to get the backet over the truck. L. B. seemed to become impatient and he was clearly annoyed as he looked up and said, "It comes out."

As he continued, he seemed to increase the speed with which he moved same size as the red dipper, i.e., approximately two inches in diameter. L. B. attempted to use the reed basket for the purpose of filling the water pistol. He dipped the basket into the pail of water. Then he lifted the basket to pour the water into the pistol. Before he could accomplish this, the water dripped out of the reed basket in a rather steady stream.

L. B. seemed to be fascinated by the water streaming from the basket. He immediately filled the basket with water again and held the basket aloft, watching the stream of water strike the terrace. This "filling" and "watching" continued for approximately three minutes.

the basket from pail to truck. But he was still losing water. Eventually L. B. moved the truck closer to the pail. Then he settled down for a time just filling the truck. Each time the truck was filled, he poured the water back into the pail.

L. B. placed a tin box a few feet from the pail. He continued to use the reed basket to transfer water from the pail to the truck as he had done before. However, now when the truck was filled he "drove" the truckload of water over to the tin box. Then he transferred the water from truck to tin box . . .

July 25, 1951

L. B. was in the process of being given a bath. He had taken some toys into the bathtub and he was playing with a metal funnel and a plastic spoon. L. B. scooped a spoonful of water and then dumped the water into the funnel. This was repeated a number of times. L. B. seemed quite interested in the water dropping out of the hole in the funnel stem. As he placed the water in the funnel he watched for it to drop out. After a minute of this type of observation, he held his hand over the hole and proceeded to fill the funnel with water. After the funnel was quite full he removed his hand from the hole and watched the water as it fell from the funnel. He kept repeating this procedure and mother asked, "What are you doing?" L. B. responded, "Watching the water go into the tub."

The water falling through the funnel stem attracted his attention to the hole. In this situation the hole was easily isolated by the child, whereas the reed basket in the previous record was of a perforated construction and the hole could not be as easily isolated and identified with the flow of water. It seems evident from the record that L. B. identified the place at which the water flowed from the funnel. The child exercised a measure of control over the flow of the water in the present record. This control was established by covering and uncovering the hole.

July 30, 1951

L. B. was playing with the reed basket. He was filling the basket with water but as fast as L. B. placed the water in the basket it would flow out of the holes in the weave structure. L. B. placed his hands around the basket in what appeared as an attempt to prevent the flow of water from the basket. However, this action was of no avail and L. B. inquired, "Why can't it stay up in my hand?" Mother said, "What seems to happen?" L. B. replied, "It slips through my hands.". . .

Here we have L. B. encountering the reed basket again. His attempts to control the flow of water in this record are definitely basket-centered: he wrapped his hands around the basket. On the basis of this behavior it may be suggested that he recognizes that water is flowing through the holes. This is in direct contrast to the attempts at control during his initial encounter with the reed basket . . . His actions in the present record seem to be related to the covering and uncovering of the funnel hole . . . and there would seem to be some carryover from the information derived during that experience . . .

September 26, 1951

L. B. was pouring water through the funnel. A number of times he used his hand to cover the hole in the stem and thus hold water in the funnel. L. B. used the funnel in this way to transport water. He moistened some soil and made a muddy mixture. L. B. placed some of this mud in the funnel. He examined the hole in the stem and then shook the funnel. Mother asked, "What's the matter?" L. B. replied, "It doesn't come out.". . .

L. B. has become aware of holes in various contexts. In this record he has used his concept of hole to control the flow of water from the funnel. He has had many encounters with water pouring forth from a hole. However, this record indicates that a new element has come within his experience. L. B. placed mud in the funnel. From his actions it would seem that he expected the mud to come out of the hole in the stem of the funnel; but the information derived from this encounter and other similar experiences gradually led him to realize that many things do not fit through a hole . . .

November 1, 1951

L. B. was playing with a short length of hose. It was approximately three feet long. He placed a nail in the hole at one end of the hose and it came out the other end. L. B. continued doing this. Then he placed

The child is becoming aware of further information that would seem to be pertinent to his developing concept of a space in relation to the item going through that space . . .

two nails in the hole. He shook the hose until both nails moved through the length of the hose and fell to the ground. He commented, "See, they come out—you put two nails in and two nails come out.". . .

A clear indication of the records thus far would seem to be that the initial concern started with an attempt to control the flow of water from the reed basket. This concern had as its concomitant the information that not every container will hold water. In further activities this information led to the isolation and identification of a hole as the means by which water flows from a container. Thus, it might be said that the initial concern has directed the child's inquisitiveness and has led to his recognition that a hole facilitates the passage of water. It should be noted that his generalization has not been specifically stated by the child, but rather is inferred from his behavior. The experiences and information contributing toward this generalization have progressed far beyond the initial item of concern. It is in this sense that the concern can be thought of as initiating further investigations and influencing the direction of the child's activities . . .

PROCESS PERVADES THE CHILD'S ACTIVITIES

The most significant inference that emerged from the records was the persistence of growth and refinement in the child's experience. This growth in L. B.'s understanding of his environment seemed to be directional and systematic. That is, a systematic procedure seemed to be evident as the child learned about his environment . . .

The process evidenced in the child's activities seemed to be one which relied upon interpretation of the events in his environment. This interpretation was based upon the child's own observations and depended heavily upon logically thought out relationships within the child's experience. The process was one which seemed to facilitate growth, since the logical relationships were continually revised as further observation expanded the matrix of experiences. However, growth was not evidenced merely as an additive process in which new experiences were accumulated; the growth was also a matter of integration in which new relationships were drawn among both old and new experiences . . .

The analysis of L. B.'s conceptual growth seems to indicate that with each addition and integration of information, the possibilities for new concerns, progressions, and directions in the child's activities are significantly increased. Many times what appeared to be an insignificant item of concern within L. B.'s experience initiated growth in his conceptual framework which far surpassed the immediate resolution of the concern. The immediate concern or problem became dwarfed in relation to the progression of events which it instigated . . .

A notable feature of L. B.'s conceptual growth seems to be the gradualness with which it occurred. The evolution is characterized by long periods of integration during which the child pulls together diverse but interlocking experiences. Sources of motivation which instigate integration among experiences are the persistent and pervasive concerns which engage the child. With such foci, the continued accumulation and integration of information bring about a gradual growth and refinement in the conceptual framework.

REFERENCES

1. DENNIS, W. 1942. Piaget's questions applied to a child of known environment. *J. Genet. Psychol.* 60:307–20.
2. GUILLET, C. 1917. The growth of a child's concepts. *Ped. Sem.* 24:81–96.
3. HAZLITT, V. 1929. Children's thinking. *Brit. J. Psychol.* 20:354–61.
4. HUANG, I. 1943. Children's conceptions of physical causality: A critical summary. *Ped. Sem.* 63:71–121.
5. MOTT, S. M. 1936. The development of concepts. *Ch. Dev.* 7:144–48.
6. TIEDMANN, D. 1927. Observations on the development of mental faculties of children (1787). Trans. by C. Murchison and S. Langer in *J. Genet. Psychol.* 34:205–30.

31. How Children Form Mathematical Concepts*

Piaget is well-known for his provocative observations on how children of different ages and abilities go about the task of learning. In this article, he synthesizes the results of a number of his experiments on the development and use of mathematical concepts. This and other studies by Piaget lend strong support to a developmental concept of readiness in learning.

* JEAN PIAGET. Reprinted and abridged with permission of the publisher from the *Scientific American,* 1953, Vol. 189, No. 5, pp. 74–9.

It is a great mistake to suppose that a child acquires the notion of number and other mathematical concepts just from teaching. On the contrary, to a remarkable degree he develops them himself, independently and spontaneously. When adults try to impose mathematical concepts on a child prematurely, his learning is merely verbal; true understanding of them comes only with his mental growth.

This can easily be shown by a simple experiment. A child of five or six may readily be taught by his parents to name the numbers from 1 to 10. If 10 stones are laid in a row, he can count them correctly. But if the stones are rearranged in a more complex pattern or piled up, he no longer can count them with consistent accuracy. Although the child knows the names of the numbers, he has not yet grasped the essential idea of number: namely, that the number of objects in a group remains the same, is "conserved," no matter how they are shuffled or arranged.

On the other hand, a child of six and a half or seven often shows that he has spontaneously formed the concept of number even though he may not yet have been taught to count. Given eight red chips and eight blue chips, he will discover by one-to-one matching that the number of red is the same as the number of blue, and he will realize that the two groups remain equal in number regardless of the shape they take.

The experiment with one-to-one correspondence is very useful for investigating children's development of the number concept. Let us lay down a row of eight red chips, equally spaced about an inch apart, and ask our small subjects to take from a box of blue chips as many chips as there are on the table. Their reactions will depend on age, and we can distinguish three stages of development. A child of five or younger, on the average, will lay out blue chips to make a row exactly as long as the red row, but he will put the blue chips close together instead of spacing them. He believes the number is the same if the length of the row is the same. At the age of six, on the average, children arrive at the second stage; these children will lay a blue chip opposite each red chip and obtain the correct number. But they have not necessarily acquired the concept of number itself. If we spread the red chips, spacing out the row more loosely, the six-year-olds will think that the longer row now has more chips, though we have not changed the number. At the age of six and a half to seven, on the average, children achieve the third stage: they know that, though we close up or space out one row of chips, the number is still the same as in the other.

In a similar experiment a child is given two receptacles of identical shape and size and is asked to put beads, one at a time, into both receptacles with both hands simultaneously—a blue bead into one box with his right hand and a red bead into the other with his left hand. When he has more or less filled the two receptacles, he is asked how they compare. He is sure that both have the same number of beads. Then he is requested to pour the blue beads into a receptacle of a different size and shape. Here again we see differences in understanding according to age. The smallest children think that the number has changed: if, for instance, the beads fill the new receptacle to a higher level, they think there are more beads in it than in the original one; if to a lower level, they think there are fewer. But children near the age of seven know that the transfer has not changed the number of beads.

In short, children must grasp the principle of conservation of quantity before they can develop the concept of number. Now conservation of quantity of course is not in itself a numerical notion; rather, it is a logical concept. Thus these experiments in child psychology throw some light on the epistemology of the number concept . . .

Study of the child's discovery of spatial relationships—what may be called the child's spontaneous geometry—is no less rewarding than the investigation of his number concepts. A child's order of development in geometry seems to reverse the order of historical discovery. Scientific geometry began with the Euclidean system (concerned with figures, angles and so on), developed in the 17th century the so-called projective geometry (dealing with problems of perspective) and finally came in the 19th century to topology (describing spatial relationships in a general qualitative way—for instance, the distinction between open and closed structures, interiority and exteriority, proximity and separation). A child begins with the last: his first geometrical discoveries are topological. At the age of three he readily distinguishes between open and closed figures: if you ask him to copy a square or a triangle, he draws a closed circle; he draws a cross with two separate lines. If you show him a drawing of a large circle with a small circle inside, he is quite capable of reproducing this relationship, and he can also draw a small circle outside or attached to the edge of the large one. All this he can do before he can draw a rectangle or express the Euclidean characteristics (number of sides, angles, etc.) of a figure. Not until a considerable time after he has mastered topological relationships does he begin to develop his notions of Euclidean and projective geometry. Then he builds those simultaneously.

Curiously enough, this psychological order is much closer to modern geometry's order of deductive or axiomatic construction than the historical order of discovery was. It offers another example of the kinship between psychological construction and the logical construction of science itself.

Let us test our young subjects on projective constructions. First we set up two "fence posts" (little sticks stuck in bases of modeling clay) some 15 inches apart and ask the child to place other posts in a straight line between them. The youngest children (under the age of four) proceed to plant one post next to another, forming a more or less wavy line. Their approach is topological: the elements are joined by the simple relationship of proximity rather than by projection of a line as such. At the next stage, beyond the age of four, the child may form a straight fence if the two end posts parallel the edge of the table, or if there is some other straight line to guide him. If the end posts are diagonally across the table, he may start building the line parallel to the table's edge and then change direction and form a curve to reach the second post. Occasionally a youngster may make a straight line, but he does so only by trial-and-error and not by system.

At the age of seven years, on the average, a child can build a straight fence consistently in any direction across the table, and he will check the straightness of the line by shutting one eye and sighting along it, as a gardener lines up bean poles. Here we have the essence of the projective concept; the line is still a topological line, but the child has grasped that the projective relationship depends on the angle of vision, or point of view.

One can proceed to study this with other experiments. For instance, you stand a doll on a table and place before it an object oriented in a certain direction: a pencil lying crosswise, diagonally or lengthwise with respect to the doll's line of vision, or a watch lying flat on the table or standing up. Then you ask the child to draw the doll's view of the object, or, better still, ask him to choose from two or three drawings the one that represents the doll's point of view. Not until the age of about seven or eight can a child deduce correctly the doll's angle of vision.

A similar experiment testing the same point yields the same conclusions. Objects of different-shapes are placed in various positions between a light and a screen, and the child is asked to predict the shape of the shadow the object will cast on the screen.

Ability to coordinate different perspectives does not come until the age of 9 or 10 . . . The experimenter sits at a table opposite the child, and between the child and herself she places a cardboard range of mountains. The two see the range from opposite perspectives. The child is then asked to select from several drawings the ones that picture both his own and the opposite person's views of the mountain range. Naturally the youngest children can pick out only the picture that corresponds to their own view;

they imagine that all the points of view are like their own. What is more interesting, if the child changes places with the experimenter and sees the mountains from the other side, he now thinks that his new view is the only correct one; he cannot reconstruct the point of view that was his own just a little while before. This is a clear example of the egocentricity so characteristic of children—the primitive reasoning which prevents them from understanding that there may be more than one point of view.

It takes a considerable evolution for children to come, at around the age of 9 or 10, to the ability to distinguish between and coordinate the different possible perspectives. At this stage they can grasp projective space in its concrete or practical form, but naturally not in its theoretical aspects.

At the same time the child forms the concept of projective space, he also constructs Euclidean space; the two kinds of construction are based upon one another. For example, in lining up a straight row of fence posts he may not only use the sighting method but may line up his hands parallel to each other to give him the direction. That is, he is applying the concept of conservation of direction, which is a Euclidean principle. Here is another illustration of the fact that children form mathematical notions on a qualitative or logical basis.

The conservation principle arises in various forms. There is first the conservation of length. If you place a block on another of the same length and then push one block so that its end projects beyond the other, a child under six will suppose that the two blocks are no longer of equal length. Not until near the age of seven, on the average, does the child understand that what is gained at one end of the block is lost at the other. He arrives at this concept of the conservation of length, be it noted, by a process of logic.

Experiments on a child's discovery of the conservation of distance are especially illuminating. Between two small toy trees standing apart from each other on a table you place a wall formed of a block or a thick piece of cardboard, and you ask the child (in his own language, of course) whether the trees are still the same distance apart. The smallest children think the distance has changed; they are simply unable to add up two parts of a distance to a total distance. Children of five or six believe the distance has been reduced, claiming that the width of the wall does not count as distance; in other words, a filled-up space does not have the same value as an empty space. Only near the age of seven do children come to the realization that intervening objects do not change the distance.

However you test them, you find the same thing true: children do not appreciate the principle of conservation of length or surface until, somewhere around the age of seven, they discover the reversibility that shows the original quantity has remained the same (*e.g.,* the realignment of equal-length blocks, the removal of the wall, and so on). Thus the discovery of logical relationships is a prerequisite to the construction of geometrical concepts, as it is in the formation of the concept of number.

This applies to measurement itself, which is only a derived concept. It is interesting to study how children spontaneously learn to measure. One of my collaborators . . . and I have made the following experiment: We show the child a tower of blocks on a table and ask him to build a second tower of the same height on another table (lower or higher than the first) with blocks of a different size. Naturally we provide the child with all the necessary measuring tools. Children's attempts to deal with this problem go through a fascinating evolution. The youngest children build up the second tower to the same visual level as the first, without worrying about the difference in height of the tables. They compare the towers by stepping back and sighting them. At a slightly more advanced stage a child lays a long rod across the tops of the two towers to make sure that they are level. Somewhat later he notices that the base of his tower is not at the same level as the model's. He then wants to place his tower next to the model on the same table to compare them. Reminded that the rules of the game forbid him to move his tower, he begins to look around for a measuring standard. Interestingly enough, the first that comes to his mind is his own body. He puts one hand on top of his tower and the other at its base, and then, trying to keep his hands the same distance apart, he moves over to the other tower to compare it. Children of about the age of six often carry out this work in a most assured manner, as if their hands could not change position on the way! Soon they discover that the method is not reliable, and then they resort to reference points on the body. The child will line up his shoulder with the top of his tower, mark the spot opposite the base on his thigh with his hand and walk over to the model to see whether the distance is the same.

Eventually the idea of an independent measuring tool occurs to the child. His first attempt in this direction is likely to be the building of a third tower next to and the same height as the one he has already erected. Having built it, he moves it over to the first table and matches it against the model; this is allowed by the rules. The child's arrival at this stage presupposes a process of logical reasoning. If we call the model tower A, the second tower C and the movable tower B, the child has reasoned that B = C and B = A, therefore A = C.

Later the child replaces the third tower with a rod, but at first the rod must be just the same length as the height of the tower to be measured. He then conceives the idea of using a longer rod and marking the tower height on it with his finger. Finally, and this is the beginning of true measurement, he realizes that he can use a shorter rod and measure the height of the tower by applying the rod a certain number of times up the side.

The last discovery involves two new operations of logic. The first is the process of division which permits the child to conceive that the whole is composed of a number of parts added together. The second is the displacement, or substitution, which enables him to apply one part upon others and thus to build a system of units. One may therefore say that measurement is a synthesis of division into parts and of substitution, just as number is a synthesis of the inclusion of categories and of serial order. But measurement develops later than the number concept, because it is more difficult to divide a continuous whole into interchangeable units than to enumerate elements which are already separate.

To study measurement in two dimensions, we give the child a large sheet of paper with a pencil dot on it and ask him to put a dot in the same position on another sheet of the same size. He may use rods, strips of paper, strings, rulers or any other measuring tools he needs. The youngest subjects are satisfied to make a visual approximation, using no tools. Later a child applies a measuring tool, but he measures only the distance of the point from the side or bottom edge of the paper and is surprised that this single measurement does not give him the correct position. Then he measures the distance of the point from a corner of the paper, trying to keep the same slant (angle) when he applies the ruler to his own sheet. Finally, at about the age of eight or nine, he discovers that he must break up the measurement into two operations: the horizontal distance from a side edge and the perpendicular distance from the bottom or top edge. Similar experiments with a bead in a box show that a child discovers how to make three-dimensional measurements at about the same age.

Measurement in two or three dimensions brings us to the central idea of Euclidean space, namely the axes of coordinates—a system founded on the horizontality or verticality of physical objects. It may seem that even a baby should grasp these concepts, for after all it can distinguish between the upright and lying-down positions. But actually the representation of vertical and horizontal lines brings up quite another problem from this subjective awareness of postural space. [We] have studied it with the following experiments: Using a jar half-filled with colored water, we ask our young subjects to predict what level the water will take when the jar is tipped one way or another. Not until the age of nine, on the average, does a child grasp the idea of horizontality and predict correctly. Similar experiments with a plumb line or a toy sailboat with a tall mast demonstrate that comprehension of verticality comes at about the same time. The child's tardiness in acquiring these concepts is not really surprising, for they require not only a grasp of the internal relationships of an object but also reference to external elements (*e.g.,* a table or the floor or walls of the room).

When a child has discovered how to construct these coordinate axes by reference to natural objects, which he does at about the same time that he conceives the coordination of perspectives, he has completed his conception of how to represent space. By that time he has developed his fundamental mathematical concepts, which spring spontaneously from his own logical operations.

The experiments I have described, simple as they are, have been surprisingly fruitful and have brought to light many unexpected facts. These facts are illuminating from the psychological and pedagogical points of view; more than that, they teach us a number of lessons about human knowledge in general.

REFERENCES

1. PIAGET, J. *The Child's Conception of Physical Causality.* New York: Harcourt, Brace, 1930.
2. PIAGET, J. *The Child's Conception of the World.* New York: Harcourt, Brace, 1929.
3. PIAGET, J., CARTALIV, M. E., ESCHER, S. and others. *Judgement and Reasoning in the Child.* New York: Harcourt, Brace, 1928.

32. Physical Maturation and Fine Motor Coordination*

While it is assumed that fine motor coordination plays a basic role in complex manipulative tasks, the relationship of such an ability to specific aspects of physical maturity has not been fully explored for

* JOHN A. FUZAK. Reprinted and abridged with permission of the author and publisher from The role of physical maturation in determining the ability of junior high school boys to perform complex finger coordinative activities in industrial arts, pp. 1–81. *Research Report of the American Technical Society.* Chicago, Ill.: American Technical Society, 1958.

many school tasks. In this article, Fuzak describes an attempt to validate in a longitudinal study a measure of fine motor coordination to predict success in the manipulative tasks involved in a junior high school industrial arts program. He draws several specific conclusions from his study and suggests their implications for teaching in areas requiring fine manipulative skills.

INTRODUCTION

. . . After several years of teaching experience in industrial arts, it was observed that many junior high school pupils did not achieve reasonable success in a number of the manipulative processes which they were expected to perform. It seemed not to matter how hard they tried, how much the teacher varied his teaching techniques, nor how intelligent they were; these pupils still did not achieve satisfactory results. At the same time, it was observed that older beginning pupils achieved satisfactorily on these same manipulative processes, with much less expended effort by teacher and pupils. It was noted that the troublesome processes usually involved finger, wrist, elbow, and shoulder coordinations. The question, therefore, was raised as to the relationship of physical maturity to the readiness of pupils to learn to perform complex coordinative processes in industrial arts classes.

This led to inquiry into the research and writing concerned with motor ability and motor educability, and next led to several informal experiments in junior high school industrial arts classes. These resulted in a strengthening of the idea that physical maturity might be significantly related to the ability to perform activities requiring complex finger coordinations. This study was undertaken to investigate that possibility . . .

MAJOR PURPOSES

1. To determine the role that physical maturity plays in ability of junior high school boys to perform manipulative processes which require complex finger coordinations.

   Hypothesis:

   The level of physical maturity attained by a junior high school boy, determines the level of his ability to perform complex finger coordinative activities.

2. To find an indicator of the level of physical maturity attained by junior high school boys, which is practical for use by the classroom teacher.

Hypothesis:

> Strength of grip, as measured by a simple hand dynamometer, is an effective indicator of the level of physical maturity of junior high school boys, and therefore of the level of their ability to perform complex finger coordinative activities.

Assumptions

As determined by previous research, strength of grip, measured by a hand dynamometer, is a fairly valid and reliable indicator of physical maturity.

While factors such as intelligence, interest, quality of vision, previous experience, general health, and cooperativeness affect any physical performance, their effects can be held to a minimum in the administration of a few simple and carefully selected performance tests.

Industrial arts teachers can identify those of their pupils who are outstandingly weak and those who are outstandingly strong in coordinative ability, when independent judgments by two or more industrial arts teachers are in agreement as to an individual's ability.

A performance test constructed to involve complex finger coordinations, which will discriminate between those judged outstandingly strong or weak in coordinative ability by two or more industrial arts teachers, is a valid test of complex finger coordinative ability . . .

Development and Selection of Performance Tests

The [major] step in the building of the tests was the identification of a number of manipulative processes commonly carried on in industrial arts classes, such as marking, scribing, rotating, tracing, paring, etc. A number of these processes were analyzed as to the involvement of finger, wrist, elbow, and shoulder controls, as well as to the involvement of muscle fibers determining this control. Materials developed in the field of occupational therapy were found especially helpful in this analysis. Those processes involving appropriate coordinations were then put together into . . . test situations, each to be individually administered . . .

Test Number 1

This test represented a very familiar manipulative process to the industrial arts teacher—marking parallel to an edge with a marking gauge . . .

Each pupil was given a brief demonstration in the use of the marking gauge, and then was asked to gauge a line parallel to the edge of a piece of even-grained white pine ten inches long . . . The test was scored by comparison with a product scale which was later developed.

Test Number 2

This test involved starting three nuts on machine screws projecting within the interior of a rectangular box twelve inches long . . . The pupil was not allowed to look while he attempted to start a nut on each of the screws projecting from above, and another nut on one of the screws projecting from the end. He attempted to start the nut on the screw in the lower left-hand corner if right-handed, and on the one in the lower right-hand corner if left-handed. The test was scored in seconds consumed in starting the three nuts.

Test Number 3

This test involved attempting to trace around an irregularly shaped pattern on coordinate paper without raising the pencil, without moving the pattern, or without departing from the pattern . . . This test was scored by comparison with a product scale which was later constructed.

Test Number 4

This test involved attempting to scribe a line perpendicular to the edge of a piece of 20-gauge galvanized iron which had been coated with layout dye. The pupil attempted to align a combination square with a fixed starting point (a fine v notch cut in the metal) and scribe lines with a scratch awl from that point. This test was scored by comparison with a product scale which was later developed . . .

Administration of Tests and Gathering of Data

GENERAL PROCEDURE FOR TESTING

Schools selected for testing were three junior high schools in Lansing, Michigan; Okemos, Michigan, High School; and Laingsburg, Michigan, High School . . .

Seventh, eighth, and ninth grade pupils of these schools, who were enrolled in industrial arts classes during the spring of 1954, were the pupils selected for testing . . .

Each of the industrial arts teachers, whose classes were being tested, was asked to identify his pupils who were outstandingly weak or outstandingly strong in finger coordinative ability. They were asked to make this estimate on the basis of performance alone, and were urged not to attempt to match the number in the two groups. They were also asked not to identify any member of a class as being at the extreme, if they thought that no one in the class could be classified as outstandingly weak or strong.

Data were collected for 392 seventh, eighth, and ninth grade pupils of the schools previously mentioned between May 16, and June 5, 1954. The girls who were enrolled in industrial arts were tested along with the boys. The scores of girls had to be eliminated because of their small number in the total group. There were cases where complete data were not available and this forced elimination of these as well. The final group retained in the study numbered 322 boys . . .

ADMINISTRATION OF DYNAMOMETER TEST . . .

The dynamometer test was administered by the investigator to individual pupils, and performance observed carefully. Motivation was not a problem. All pupils strove to outdo themselves in proving their great strength. Experimentation developed a procedure which seemed to solve the warm-up and fatigue problems satisfactorily. The working of the dynamometer was explained to the pupil, and he was shown how to hold the dynamometer. He was then told to get the feel of the instrument by exerting light pressure—no more than half the pressure he thought he could exert—for three preliminary trials. When he was ready he was asked to exert his greatest strength, which was recorded. He then had two more trials . . .

The preferred hand grip scores were retained for each individual as the scores utilized in the study.

The decision was made to use the mean of the three trials as the individual's score, since this promised greater reliability than the use of the individual's highest score . . .

ADMINISTRATION OF PERFORMANCE TESTS

Each of the four tests was administered by a member of the team of testers who was trained and responsible for that test throughout the gathering of data in the spring of 1954. Each of the group had had a part in the development and selection of the tests, so that each member was thoroughly familiar with the tests and their purpose.

Directions for administration of each of the tests were developed, and each of the testers reviewed the directions regularly to remain consistent in the administration of his test . . .

DEVELOPMENT OF PRODUCT SCALES AND RATINGS OF PERFORMANCE

The dynamometer test, measured numerically in kilograms of pressure exerted, and the screw box test, measured numerically in seconds of time consumed, posed no problem for evaluations of pupils' performances. However, the evaluation of pupils' performances on the marking gauge, tracing, and screw box tests proved quite troublesome. The procedure of over-all judgment based upon previously established criteria, used in determining the discriminative ability of the performance tests, was found not to be effective for this purpose. Although effective in judging extremes of performance, it proved of relatively little value in judging performances scattered throughout the range of possible performance. The development of product scales for evaluating individual performances seemed necessary . . .

[DEVELOPING] A PRODUCT SCALE FOR SCRIBING . . .

. . . A careful selection was first made of 130 samples of scribing, which represented all types of performance. These were rated very carefully by the investigator on . . . a 13-point scale. An assistant recorded placement by the code numbers. The 130 samples were scrambled and put aside for several days, after which the samples were again rated carefully on a thirteen point scale . . . The process was repeated several times with increasing time intervals between next judgments.

It was found that at least one sample had been placed at every one of the thirteen points of the scale in all of the separate judgments . . . The sample representing approximately the midpoint of the several performances consistently placed at the extremes was selected for the product scale. Others selected for the product scale were those consistently placed in the same positions from two to twelve . . .

All of the remaining 309 scribing tests were rated by comparison to the product scale . . .

SELECTION OF SAMPLE FOR RATING BY INDEPENDENT JUDGES . . .

A sample of roughly one-third of all of the performances on the scribing test was drawn by combining stratified and random selection. The frequency of ratings for each of the thirteen points of the scale, in the rating completed by the investigator, was tabulated. One-third of each of these figures was taken to designate the proportion of that level of performance to be included in the sample . . .

After the determination of the number of pieces rated 1, 2, 3, etc. to be included, the identity of the actual pieces was determined by a random process . . . This procedure was an attempt to make the selected sample representative of the total group in terms of levels of performance, and at the same time scatter the selection among the work of pupils from all of the schools involved in the study.

RESULTS OF RATINGS BY INDEPENDENT JUDGES

Two graduate students in industrial education agreed to serve as judges. After a brief explanation, and a few trials in rating performances not to be included in the sample, each judge in turn took the product scale and the selected samples of performance to his home. The judges had no knowledge of the ratings of the performances which had been made by the investigator, nor of the proportions of each level of performance which had been included . . .

Product-moment coefficients of correlation were computed for relationship of ratings between each of the judges and the investigator and between the ratings of the two judges . . .

The product-moment coefficients for this rating were:

Judge 1 and Investigator: $r = +.94$
Judge 2 and Investigator: $r = +.96$
Judge 1 and Judge 2: $r = +.93$

This was deemed to be highly satisfactory; in fact greater agreement than had been expected . . .

Since the procedure had proved satisfactory, a closely similar procedure was followed in developing product scales for the remaining two performance tests . . .

Relationships of Dynamometer Test to [Certain of the] 1954 Data . . .

RELATIONSHIP OF DYNAMOMETER TEST TO PERFORMANCE TESTS

Product-moment coefficients were computed to determine the degree of relationship which existed between the dynamometer test scores and each of the four performance tests. These coefficients were:

Dynamometer test and Scribing test:	$r = +.897$
Dynamometer test and Marking Gauge test:	$r = +.882$
Dynamometer test and Tracing test:	$r = +.742$
Dynamometer test and Screw box:	$r = +.877$

The scores on the four performance tests were then combined and the product-moment coefficient of correlation computed for the four tests in combination and the dynamometer test. The coefficient was:

Dynamometer test and Four Tests combined: $r = +.91$

The conclusion was reached that a high degree of relationship existed between the dynamometer score and the scores on the performance tests. Assuming the validity of the performance tests on the basis of their earlier established discriminative ability, the dynamometer test is an excellent indicator of complex finger coordinative ability in junior high school boys.

RELATIONSHIP OF DYNAMOMETER TEST TO TEACHER'S ESTIMATES

As data were gathered the teachers had been asked to identify pupils they considered outstandingly strong and outstandingly weak in coordinative ability. Of the total group of 322 pupils, 25 were identified as being outstandingly weak in coordinative ability. Twenty pupils were identified as being outstandingly strong in coordinative ability. The coefficient of correlation was computed to determine the degree of relationship between dynamometer test and these estimates. The result was:

Dynamometer test and Teacher's Estimates: $r = +.746$ . . .

COMPARISON OF MEANS OF PERFORMANCE FOR SEVENTH, EIGHTH, AND NINTH GRADERS

While the rate of physical maturation varies widely from one individual to another, the combination of pupils into large groups should serve to average out individual variations in maturation rate. The performance of an eighth group on the dynamometer test and on tests of complex finger coordinative ability, should exceed the performance of a seventh grade group; the performance of the ninth grade group should exceed the performance of the eighth grade. As a further test of the influence of physical maturity upon the level of performance of complex finger coordinative ability, the means of performance for the three grade level groups were compared. The following table indicates these means of performance.

MEANS OF PERFORMANCE ON FIVE TESTS

Group	Number of Pupils	Dynamometer	Tracing	Marking Gauge	Scribing	Screw Box
7th	163	23.908	6.227	4.675	4.055	4.877
8th	136	28.324	8.081	6.985	6.265	5.613
9th	23	36.130	9.174	10.261	9.304	9.565
Total	322	26.646	6.798	6.060	5.363	5.994

In order to determine the significance of the differences between the means of these groups . . . the *t* values were computed for the differences in the means between the 9th and 8th grade groups and between the 8th and 7th grade groups for the dynamometer test and the four performance tests. A table showing the determined "*t* value" for these tests follows:

t VALUES FOR DIFFERENCES IN MEANS

	Dynamometer	Tracing	Marking Gauge	Scribing	Screw Box
9th and 8th grade	5.088	2.333	4.307	4.569	6.447
8th and 7th grade	6.363	5.88	6.363	7.245	2.547

If . . . the critical value is 2.58, it may be seen that all of the values, except two, exceed this. The conclusion was, that the means of performance on the five tests were significantly different for each of the grade level groups being tested.

Interpretation. The data gathered on the 322 junior high school pupils in the spring of 1954 show that a close positive relationship exists between dynamometer test scores and the level of complex finger coordinative ability as measured by the tests, and as indicated by the teacher estimates of pupils outstandingly strong or weak in finger coordinative ability. (Dynamometer test score is preferred by the investigator to strength of grip as a name, because of the element of coordination which enters into the performance.)

The data strongly indicate that the level of physical maturity of junior high school boys determines the level of their ability to perform complex finger coordinative activities.

The Follow-up in 1957

PURPOSES OF THE FOLLOW-UP

The major purposes of the follow-up study were to examine further the hypothesis that level of physical maturity determines the level of ability to perform complex finger coordinative activities, and to test further the effectiveness of the dynamometer test as an indicator of the level of ability to perform complex finger coordinations . . .

If the level of physical maturity determines the level of ability to perform complex finger coordinative activities then one would have certain logical expectations with regard to the data and their relationships. One would logically expect:

1. A decrease in the degree of relationship between the dynamometer test and age, height, and weight as a number of the pupils approached or attained physical maturity.

2. Generally improved performances on the five tests, since all pupils would have attained some further maturation, except those pupils who were already physically mature in 1954.

3. A change in the relative position (or rank) of a number of individuals within the group as to level of complex finger coordinative ability. Some of the pupils may have attained, or been close to attainment, of physical maturity in 1954, while others were much further from its attainment.

4. A narrowing of the range of performances on the five tests, as many of the pupils approached physical maturity.

5. A high positive relationship between the change from a pupil's first performance on the dynamometer to his later performance on the

dynamometer, and the change from a pupil's first performances on the four tests to his later performances on the four tests . . .

PROCEDURE OF THE FOLLOW-UP . . .

After some preliminary investigation, it became obvious that it would not be possible to follow-up all of the 322 pupils without spending six or seven months in gathering the data . . . As a result, the decision was made to select a stratified sample of pupils for re-testing purposes . . .

Of the 156 pupils identified as available, 151 were re-tested . . . Since all except one of these pupils had dynamometer scores near the center of the distribution of scores, where greater numbers of pupils were included in the sample, the sample was judged satisfactory . . .

RELATIONSHIPS OF CERTAIN OF THE 1954 AND 1957 DATA . . .

GENERAL LEVEL OF PERFORMANCE ON THE FIVE TESTS

The mean performance of the group of 151 pupils on the dynamometer test in 1954, was computed and compared to the mean performance of the same group on the dynamometer test in 1957. The mean performance of the group of 151 pupils was also computed for a combination of the four tests in 1954, and compared to the mean performance of the same group for a combination of the same four tests in 1957. These means were:

	1954	1957
Dynamometer Mean	26.34	43.35
Combination of 4 tests (Mean)	23.35	43.62

The increase in the size of the means for the same group shows increase in general level of performance expected if the hypothesis was sound.

RELATIVE POSITION OF INDIVIDUALS WITHIN THE GROUP

The technique selected for determining the relative position of individuals within the group was the computation of product-moment coefficients of correlation between 1957 and 1954 performances on the dynamometer test and between 1957 and 1954 performances on the four tests in combination. If the coefficient was high and positive it would indicate relatively static position of pupils in relation to the group; that is, pupils who were high in performance in relation to the group in 1954 would remain high in performance in relation to the group in 1957, etc.

The coefficients were:

Dynamometer Test, 1954 and 1957:	r = +.28
Tests in Combination, 1954 and 1957:	r = +.225

The size of these coefficients indicate considerable change in the relative position of individual pupils within the group in both the dynamometer test score and in the four performance tests. This was an expected result if the hypothesis was sound.

RANGE OF PERFORMANCE TEST SCORES ON THE FIVE TESTS

An examination of the data for the 1957 tests shows a shift upward in performance of the entire group. A great many of the 1957 group were close to the top performance as previously indicated by the mean performance of the entire group for the four tests in combination. Thirteen points on each of the four tests would result in a score of 52. The mean score for the entire group was 43.62. Better ways of showing decrease in variability exist than range; however, the situation is so evident through direct inspection of test scores that range of scores suffices to present the situation.

	Dyna-mometer	Tracing	Marking Gauge	Scribing	Screw box
1954	14–47	1–13	1–13	1–13	1–13
1957	26–59	6–13	4–13	5–13	5–13

RELATIONSHIP BETWEEN CHANGE IN DYNAMOMETER
SCORE AND CHANGE IN PERFORMANCE

This relationship can be shown through the correlation between the difference in performance on the dynamometer test and re-test and the difference in performance on test and re-test of the four tests of finger coordinative ability. A high positive correlation would indicate that change in the dynamometer test score is accompanied by change, in the same direction, of the finger coordination test scores. Scores for the four finger coordinative tests were combined for 1957 and also for 1954. The combined scores on the four finger coordinative tests for 1954, were subtracted from the combined scores for 1957, for each of the 151 pupils. Then the dynamometer scores for 1954 were subtracted from the 1957 dynamometer scores for each pupil, and the product-moment coefficient of correlation computed to determine the degree of relationship of these differences. The coefficient was:

Dynamometer, 1957–1954, and 4 tests combined, 1957–1954: r = +.87

This indicates the effectiveness of the dynamometer test score as an indicator of the level of finger coordinative ability for junior high school boys. It also promises the tentative value of the dynamometer test score for indicating level of finger coordinative ability for high school boys . . .

Interpretation. The 1957 data fulfilled the expectations in terms of relationships for supporting the hypothesis that level of physical maturity determines level of fine finger coordinative ability in junior high school boys.

A dynamometer test continued to show a high degree of effectiveness as an indicator of level of physical maturity, or, of level of ability to perform complex finger coordinative activities.

CONCLUSIONS AND IMPLICATIONS

MAJOR PURPOSE 1

One of the major purposes of this study was to explore the role played by maturation in determining the ability of junior high school boys to perform complex finger coordinative activities. The following hypothesis was established as a means for directing this exploration:

Hypothesis

The level of physical maturity attained by a junior high school boy determines the level of his ability to perform complex finger coordinative activities.

All of the data of this study support the acceptance of this hypothesis, and on the basis of this study, the investigator concludes that the hypothesis is true.

MAJOR PURPOSE 2

The second major purpose of the study was to find an indicator of the level of ability of junior high school boys to perform complex finger coordinative activities which was practical for use by the classroom teacher. Upon acceptance of the hypothesis related to the first major purpose of the study, level of physical maturity and ability of junior high school boys to perform complex finger coordinative activities are equated. Strength of grip has been identified by a number of investigators as an effective indicator of level of physical maturity. Its effectiveness was checked throughout the conduct of the study.

All of the data support the acceptance of the hypothesis: Strength of the grip as measured by a simple hand dynamometer is an effective indicator of the level of physical maturity of high school boys, or, of their ability to perform complex finger coordinative activities.

The dynamometer test offers promise as an indicator of level of complex finger coordinative ability in senior high school boys, but needs further study.

Data available in the study indicated the relative stability of the dynamometer test score as an indicator of level of physical maturity. It did not seem to be affected by exercise or unusual manipulative experience . . .

The investigator concludes that the hand dynamometer test score is an instrument of great importance to effective teaching of junior high school industrial arts . . .

The investigator has come to several tentative conclusions, based upon the examination of hundreds of performances. Junior high school boys falling below 24 kilograms as a mean dynamometer score should not be expected to perform activities in industrial arts requiring complex finger coordinations. Complex finger coordinative activities should be carefully selected and limited for boys falling below 28 kilograms mean dynamometer score . . .

IMPLICATIONS

The junior high school industrial arts teacher should no longer ignore the readiness of his pupils to learn manipulative processes requiring complex finger coordinations. He should plan his teaching, and the learning experiences he develops, to accommodate a wide range of physical maturation and readiness on the part of his pupils.

The junior high school industrial arts teacher should screen possible learning activities, so that those planned at earlier grade levels concentrate on large muscle coordinations, rather than upon complex finger coordinations.

Implications of a similar sort affect many portions of the junior high school program, where complex finger coordinative activities are carried on. Attention should be given by these teachers to the physical readiness of their pupils to satisfactorily engage in the learning experiences provided. Many pupils are driven away from learning activities involving complex finger coordinations because of their lack of physical readiness to perform them satisfactorily. Much of the time and effort they expend is wasted. This is probably true in particular of the more intelligent pupils. Many of them are somewhat accelerated in school, while duller pupils are somewhat retarded. This must be a deep concern of all teachers who teach activities requiring complex finger coordinations.

CHAPTER : 10

Evaluative Aspects of Learning

33. Measuring the Results of College Instruction*

> Tyler's name has become almost synonymous with evaluation in edu-
> cation. In this article he points out some of the critical needs in de-
> veloping adequate instruments to measure the results of instruction.
> His argument that appraisal instruments must measure the psycho-
> logical processes and outcomes involved in attaining educational ob-
> jectives is fundamental to his concept of validity in educational
> measurement.

It has become almost a tradition to consider as the only necessary equipment for one engaged in educational measurement some ingenuity in
translating subject-matter content into short-answer forms of questions
and familiarity with the statistical methods of computing central tendencies, percentiles, the standard deviation, and the coefficient of correlation. Probably this conception has developed because of the types of
problems which historically have received the focus of attention in the
construction of tests for elementary and secondary schools.

Three avenues of influence have largely dominated educational measurements. The effectiveness, of a comparison of results obtained by using the
same test in several grades, in various schools, and in different cities,
was shown by the spelling investigation of Rice and by the pioneer survey

* RALPH W. TYLER. Reprinted with permission of the author from Measuring the results of college instruction. *Educational Research Bulletin,* Ohio State University, 1932,
11:253–60.

at Cleveland. The result of this influence has been to emphasize standardization of test items and testing conditions. Since spelling and arithmetic were the first subjects to be used in such tests, the problem of validity was concealed by the very nature of the subject-matter. The assumption that a pupil's ability to spell a given list of words was a valid test of his spelling ability was accepted without extended consideration of the psychological nature of the outcomes to be expected, while his response to the request that he perform indicated arithmetic operations upon a given list of numerical exercises was thought to be a valid test of his ability in the fundamental operations of arithmetic. Much study has been given to such problems as the words to be used in the spelling list and to the numerical exercises to be included in the arithmetic test, but the types of mental reaction which should be expected of pupils in a valid test of these subjects has rarely been considered.

A second major influence in educational measurement has been the intelligence-testing movement. Since many persons who had constructed intelligence tests were asked to build educational tests, and because most of the other educational testers were profoundly impressed by the intelligence-test program, certain techniques used by the intelligence testers naturally dominated the procedures in making educational tests. Intelligence tests for school children were commonly validated by getting a fairly high correlation between the test results and the teachers' judgment of the children's brightness, or between the test results and their school marks. Surprisingly enough, educational testers, who are continually criticizing the lack of validity and reliability of teachers' marks, frequently use these same marks as the criteria of good tests for measuring the results of instruction. Another method of intelligence testers has been to validate individual items by their relationship to the total test score. This has been done by calculating bi-serial r or by determining the difference between the percentage of correct responses among the pupils who made high total scores on the test and those who made low total scores. This method, too, has been taken over by those making educational tests. Probably because of this influence of the intelligence-testing movement, when the question of the validity of an educational measurement has been raised, a fairly high correlation between the test results and teachers' marks has been accepted as an assurance for the validity of the test, while a high relation between the response on an individual item and the total test score has been accepted as a guaranty of the validity of the item. Obviously, however, this procedure cannot guarantee a total test which is more valid than the teachers' judgments and can only assure homogeneity of items rather than validity.

The evident lack of objectivity and of reliability in traditional examinations has perhaps been the most potent influence. It was easy to show that the same examination paper when marked by a large number of teachers was given a variety of marks, ranging in some cases from 25 to 95. It was also simple to collect evidence that the same person when marking a set of examinations a second time assigned different marks to many of the papers. The accumulation of such evidence made it clear to those interested in examinations that the mark a student received on a paper was not only a matter of the quality of his answers, but it also depended upon the judgment of the marker, which varied among individuals and varied at different times with the same individual. This criticism of the subjectivity of traditional examinations caused test-builders to give prime consideration to examinations that could be scored objectively. They ignored, however, the fact that the selection of the form of the test and of the test items is a highly subjective process which greatly influenced the test results.

The other deluge of examination criticism was concerned with the adequacy of the sampling of test questions, often called "reliability." The typical examination with five, ten, or twenty questions did not give an adequate sample of the student's responses to serve as a basis for a dependable estimate of his attainments. When the student was given a second set of questions covering the same material, his mark was often widely at variance with that obtained from the first examination. Because this fact was brought home so forcibly, educational testers gave careful study to reliability. Reliability was measured by the correlation between the two sets of scores obtained from two similar tests covering the same field. Measured in this way, reliability was quite distinct from validity.

The accepted techniques used by educational testers have been the translation of subject-matter into forms of questions which may be scored objectively, the standardization of the test items in terms of the percentage of pupils who answer items correctly, the computation of the coefficient of correlation between the test results and the teachers' marks, the determination of the relation between the response on an individual item and the total test score, and the computation of the coefficient of correlation between the results obtained from two similar forms of the test. Obviously, then, in the past the desirable training for one engaged in constructing educational measurements was conceived in terms of these techniques.

The extension of the problem of measuring the results of instruction to the college level is changing the conception of the type of training appropriate for educational testers. An analysis of the mental processes characteristic of a given subject assumes an importance heretofore unrecognized. Many college instructors are suspicious of the so-called "objective examinations," and not without reason. Not only are many objective tests quite different from the examinations to which they are accustomed, but it is also difficult for them to determine whether the tests provide a measure of the objectives of the subject they are teaching. It is, therefore, natural that they should be cautious in relying upon such examinations. Hence, a fundamental task in constructing achievement tests which will be used by college instructors is to make certain that the important objectives of the subject and course are adequately measured.

This is so obvious a requirement for a valid examination that there is nothing new in the suggestion that it is the essential criterion for validity. The difficulty in the past has been the common failure to distinguish between the content of a subject and the mental processes which a student of this subject is expected to exhibit. Often, without recognizing it, testmakers have assumed that all the content treated in a course is to be remembered and that a test of the amount of this material which is remembered by the student is an adequate test of the subject. When the instructors of any college subject formulate their objectives, it is quickly evident that there are other mental processes which students are expected to develop.

Some makers of tests have recognized that there are other objectives of instruction in addition to the recall of information. Many have assumed, however, that there is a high relationship between measurements of information and the measurements of other objectives in the subject. This has not been found true in the elementary biology courses at Ohio State University. The correlation of the scores on information tests with those of tests of applying principles is found to be only .40; with tests of interpretation of experiments, only .41; and of tests of the formulation of experiments to test hypotheses, only .46. It therefore seems apparent that although some college instructors are properly demanding tests which measure the attainment of each objective of their courses, the commonly accepted method of test construction based upon an analysis of informational content alone will not meet this demand.

To measure the attainment of each of the objectives of a course we can no longer conceive of examinations as limited to paper-and-pencil tests.

An educational measure is only a means for obtaining valid evidence of the degree to which students have attained the desired objectives of instruction. We must then begin the task of constructing educational tests by defining those objectives which we expect students to attain as a result of instruction in a given subject. These objectives must be defined in terms of students' behavior; that is to say, the objective must be expressed in terms of an analysis of the psychological processes developed by this subject. For example, in zoölogy, one type of mental process expected of students is the recall of important facts, principles, and technical terms. Another is an ability to formulate reasonable generalizations from the specific data of an experiment. A third type is an ability to plan an experiment which might be used to test a given hypothesis in zoölogy; a fourth, the ability to apply general principles to new situations; and a fifth, skill in the use of the microscope. The nature of these objectives when analyzed determines the variety of achievement tests to be constructed. It is obvious that the measurements of the information which a student recalls may be done with a paper-and-pencil examination, while a test of skill in the use of the microscope would require a different set-up.

When we recognize the fact that the real objectives of instruction are to bring about desired changes in the behavior of students, we are then in a position to consider a valid examination as one which provides situations in which the student may express this. From his behavior in a representative sampling of such situations we judge the degree to which the objectives have been attained. Such a conception of valid measurement will lead to the recognition of the need for a broader equipment for those who are constructing educational tests. It is evident that a primary qualification of one who is to build examinations to be used to measure the results of college instruction is training in analysis of the psychological processes characteristic of college subjects.

Perhaps the type of training which may be expected of a test technician may better be suggested by describing briefly the procedures followed in constructing examinations at Ohio State University. This is a co-operative enterprise of the Bureau of Educational Research with the departments concerned. After the objectives of a given subject have been stated and have been analyzed so as to reveal the nature of the behavior expected of students, samples of specific situations in which a student can be expected to express each of these types of behavior are collected.

The sources for these situations depend upon the nature of the objective. In the case of one of the objectives proposed for zoölogy, the ability to draw inferences from experimental data, the most productive source of situations was the current research in zoölogy. The results of new experiments can be obtained from this source which may be presented to students to test their ability to interpret experiments. Since they are new experiments, the students cannot interpret them from memory of textbook interpretations. Similarly, a productive source for the objective, the ability to propose ways of testing hypotheses, was found in the problems proposed for investigation by various research workers in the field. Since these problems have never been investigated, the student cannot depend upon his memory of the method of attack used by others. The ingenuity of the test-maker and of the instructors was required in order to find productive sources of test situations for each objective.

After selecting the situations, the technician developed a method of administration by which it was possible to present these situations to the students and to get a record of their reactions. Accuracy of observation was tested by experiments which were observed by each student, and his observations were recorded by him on a blank specially prepared for the purpose. A check list of students' reactions was devised to test skill in the use of the microscope, and the observer used it to make a record of each student's actions when using the microscope. Situations which were verbal in character, such as the memory of important principles, were easily presented to students in written examinations.

After a record of the student's behavior had been made, we were then ready to evaluate the student's reactions in the light of each objective. Obviously, many of these evaluations were not wholly objective, but when any significant variation in the evaluation from one instructor to another was found, it was usually possible to develop a method for judging or scoring reactions which largely eliminated the individual biases in judgment . . .

After a satisfactory degree of objectivity has been obtained the next step is to determine the reliability; that is, the adequacy of the sample of test situations used to measure that particular objective. This can be done by the usual method of submitting a second random sample of test situations to the same students and correlating the scores from the two samples. When the correlation coefficient has been calculated, it is possible to determine the number of test situations required to obtain any satisfactory degree of reliability. In case the reliability of the preliminary test is too low, it is necessary to improve the reliability of the preliminary examination by providing a more adequate sampling of test situations.

When these steps have been carried through to completion, an objective, reliable test for each of the course objectives has been obtained. Because this preliminary test is based upon a sampling of the students' behavior of the type expected as an objective of the course, it is much more likely to be valid than the usual set of teachers' marks. Not only are teachers' marks somewhat unreliable, but they are often not diagnostic; that is, they do not distinguish between the student's attainment of different objectives separately. Our work to date has shown quite clearly that the correlation between the student's attainment of one objective and his attainment of another may be quite low. Thus we found a correlation between skill in the use of the microscope and memory of information to be only .02, between an understanding of technical terms and an ability to draw inferences from facts, only .35, between information and ability to apply principles to concrete situations, only .40. These correlations are so low that we are justified in preparing separate tests for each of the objectives so that the instructor may diagnose the difficulties of students in achievement with reference to each objective separately.

This brief description of the methods of test construction employed at Ohio State University is illustrative of the changes in the problems and procedures of educational measurement which have taken place rapidly since the inauguration of attempts to measure the results of college instruction. The problem of validity now assumes major importance in the construction of examinations. With the recognition of the significance of this problem we are no longer satisfied with a validity based upon an analysis of textbook content nor upon a high correlation with teachers' marks, but, instead, increasing emphasis is being placed upon an analysis of the psychological processes which we expect to be developed by instruction in a given field. The task of setting up test situations is no longer considered to be limited to particular forms of paper-and-pencil tests, but we believe them to be as varied as are the typical conditions under which the student has opportunity to express the desired behavior. Furthermore, test construction is a co-operative project involving the whole-hearted participation of the instructors in the subject-matter departments and the test technicians. Because of these considerations it is my belief that we must revise our common conception of the professional training essential for those engaged in educational measurements. Ingenuity in translating subject-matter content into short-answer forms of questions and familiarity with certain statistical methods alone will not suffice. Demands are increasing, and interesting problems exist for those broadly trained in the science of education.

34. Rate, Accuracy, and Process in Learning*

Investigations of the learning and teaching of arithmetic have placed increasing emphasis upon understanding the meaning of arithmetical processes as a major criterion of progress. A pioneer investigator in this area, Brownell, demonstrates that interpretation of the adequacy of a student's performance on his multiplication combinations varies according to what aspect of performance is appraised. He makes a forceful plea for the need for appraising the arithmetical processes of the student.

Group Test Data

Group tests consisting of the eighty-one simple multiplication combinations (the 0-combinations were excluded) were administered to about one hundred fifteen children per half-grade, from Grade IIIA through Grade VA, in two North Carolina school systems. The methods of administration and of scoring yielded the usual measures of rate and accuracy of work. Table 1 summarizes very briefly the data obtained.

TABLE 1

Summary of Data from Group Tests

Measure	Scores, by Half-Grades				
	IIIA*	IVB	IVA	VB	VA
Accuracy (number correct; 81 possible)					
Actual Median	64	80	81	81	81
Actual Q_1	55	75	80	80	80
Rate (time to finish, in minutes and seconds)					
Actual Median	6:20	4:40	2:45	3:25	2:50
Actual Q_1	8:25	5:30	3:50	3:50	3:25
Actual Q_3	5:20	3:30	2:30	2:45	2:30

* At the time of the testing the Grade IIIA pupils were supposed to have mastered only sixty-five of the eighty-one combinations, the remaining sixteen being taught in Grade IVB.

Fig. 1 presents the data in a somewhat different manner. In the construction of all four curves the records made by the Grade VA pupils

* WILLIAM A. BROWNELL. Reprinted and abridged with permission of the author from the *Journal of Educational Psychology*, 1944, 35:321–37.

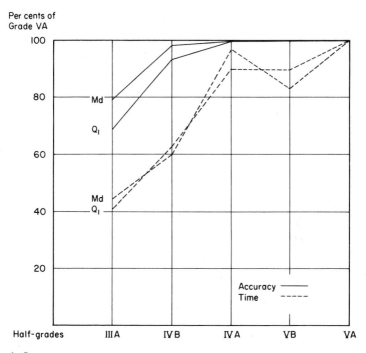

FIG. 1. INCREASE IN ACCURACY AND RATE BY HALF-GRADES EXPRESSED IN TERMS
OF THE GRADE VA MEDIANS AND Q_1'S.

were taken as bases for comparison. The median accuracy score for Grade
VA was 81; that of Grade IIIA was 64, or seventy-nine per cent of the
Grade VA median. The median accuracy score for Grade IVA was 80, or
ninety-nine per cent of the Grade VA standard, and so on. The Q_1-curve
for accuracy and the median-and-Q_1-curves for rate were constructed in
a similar manner, always with the Grade VA measure as the standard.

Inspection of the accuracy curves discloses that progress was most rapid
in Grade IVB, when the average child "knew" the combinations about
as well as did the average child in Grade VA, and when three-fourths of
the children could write correct answers for ninety-three per cent or more
of the eighty-one combinations.

As judged by rate scores, the greatest gains come in Grade IVA, a
half-grade later than in the case of accuracy. In Grade IVB the average
rate score was only sixty per cent of what it was in Grade VA; but in
Grade IVA, ninety per cent. The Q_1-curve also shows the greatest amount

of gain in Grade IVA. As was untrue in the case of accuracy, the children of Grade VB still had some distance to go before they could equal the rate records a half-grade later in Grade VA.

Table 1 and Fig. 1 are typical of reports of research on learning, and the data which they summarized are likewise typical of such reports. They are typical in the sense that they describe two aspects of performance, and only two. Measures of rate and accuracy do, of course, supply information of considerable value with respect to the changes which occur in learning. In the present instance, for example, they tell us: (1) the degree to which the experimental children found correct answers for combinations, and (2) the speed with which they wrote their answers. But they tell us no more than this, and more is needed if learning is to be appraised in anything like a comprehensive manner.

As a matter of fact, measures of rate and of accuracy really describe the efficiency of performance. In this study they tell us how well (how quickly and accurately) these particular children wrote answers, but they do not tell us how the children got their answers. They depict the efficiency with which processes were used, but have nothing to say about what these processes were. Stated differently, measures of rate and of accuracy do not tell us how good a performance is,—whether it is expert or amateurish, mature or immature, close to the limit of possible improvement or near the first stages of improvement. To restrict research data on learning to measures of rate and accuracy is to portray learning incompletely. To neglect the processes employed in learning, while it is characteristic of research to do so, is to tell only part of the story,—and possibly the less important part at that.

INTERVIEW DATA

The Procedure.—The group tests on the combinations were supplemented by individual interviews, designed to procure evidence on a third aspect of learning; namely, processes used. The children, immediately after the group tests, were taken one at a time, one child per interviewer. Preliminary research had demonstrated that practically all children's procedures would fall into one or another of ten categories, but provision was made for recording unusual processes. In all grades, except Grade IIIA where the children had not yet studied some of the "higher" tables, fifteen of the more difficult combinations were employed in the interviews, so selected that all tables would be represented and that no closely related pairs of combinations would appear in succession.

After informal discussion the interviewer placed before the pupil a combination not included in the interview record, with the request, "Can you tell me the answer?" The next questions were of the following types: "How did you get your answer?" . . . "What did you think to find the answer?" . . . "What were you thinking after I showed you the combination and before you told me the answer?" Two more practice combinations were then used, to make sure that the child knew what was expected of him and to make sure also that no undesired emotional states were operative. When rapport and understanding had been established, the fifteen interview combinations (nine in the case of Grade IIIA) were presented, and records were kept.

The eleven categories according to which pupils' responses were classified are presented in the chart on page 392.

After a short period of training, the interviewers (all of whom were graduate students in the writer's course, Investigations in Arithmetic) were able to classify children's processes at once and to record their judgments by means of code letters on a mimeographed Interview Blank . . .

In general, the eleven categories previously mentioned were found to be serviceable and reliable. To begin with those at the bottom of the list, in only one half-grade (IVB) were as many as 1.2 per cent of the responses classified as X (miscellaneous); in Grade IIIA the per cent was 0.7, and in the other three half-grades, 0.1 or less. In only one half-grade (VB) were processes finally classified as I. Of course at the time of the interviews more procedures than these were tentatively identified as indeterminate; but because of the complete records made then, it was possible later to dispose of most of them in one or another of the first nine categories. The fact that in only one half-grade (IVB) I and X together contributed more than one per cent of the classifications may be taken as evidence both of the degree to which the nine other categories were adequately comprehensive and of the degree to which identification in these nine categories was possible.

To continue to read the list of categories upward, it may be said that no difficulty arose in recognizing when children visualized (V), or recited tables (T), or reversed combinations (R), or counted (C), or solved unknown combinations from better known combinations (S). It was, however, not so simple to distinguish among guessing (G), the use of meaningless associations (M), and the use of meaningfully habituated associations (H). However, as will be explained in a later section, means were found to meet this problem, and it is believed that the data for

CHART OF THE ELEVEN CATEGORIES

Code Letter	Description of Class
H	*Habituation, meaningful.*—The correct answer is confidently given at once, with every indication of understanding.
M	*Memory, rote.*—The answer is given at once and with apparent confidence, but there is no evidence of understanding.
G	*Guessing.*—The answer, usually wrong, is given rather promptly, but it is evident that the child is guessing.
S	*Solution.*—The child starts with a familiar combination and adds to, or subtracts from, the product to get the answer. There are many kinds of solution, for example: $3 \times 4 = 2 \times 4 = 8, + 4 = 12.$ $3 \times 4 = 4 \times 4 = 16, - 4 = 12.$
C	*Counting.*—The child adds or counts the same unit several times. $3 \times 4 = 3, 6, 9, 12;$ or, $4, 8, 12.$
R	*Reversal.*—The child interchanges multiplier and multiplicand to get a more familiar order. $6 \times 3 = ?; 3 \times 6 = 18,$ so $6 \times 3 = 18.$
T	*Tables.*—The child starts with a lower combination in the table involved and recites the table to the required point. $4 \times 6 = ?; 4 \times 1 = 4; 4 \times 2 = 8; \ldots 4 \times 6 = 24$ or, $4 \times 4 = 16; 4 \times 5 = 20; 4 \times 6 = 24.$
V	*Visualization.*—The child reproduces groups of objects or figures in clear imagery and works with these. $4 \times 5 = ?; 4 \times 5¢$ (nickel) $= 20¢,$ or $20.$
N	*No attempt.*—The child makes no attempt to state the answer.
I	*Indeterminate.*—The child gives an answer for the combination, but you cannot ascertain how he got it (that is, his process).
X	*Miscellaneous.*—The child reports a process not included in the preceding list—or you are uncertain as to its proper classification. Report what the child said, using the back of the Interview Blank if this is necessary.

these three categories as they are here reported are about as reliable and as valid as are the data for the other categories.

The data obtained.—Table 2 for Grade IVB is typical of the tables which summarize the interview data for the five half-grades (except that in Grade IIIA the interview combinations included only the nine which had

TABLE 2

GRADE IVB: PROCESSES USED WITH SELECTED COMBINATIONS AS REVEALED IN INTERVIEWS (N = 136)

Process	7/5	6/9	3/8	6/5	8/7	6/4	3/7	9/8	7/6	9/2	4/7	5/3	8/6	7/9	3/6	Total
H	79	56	47	78	52	79	60	67	68	93	55	91	63	46	57	991
M	20	18	15	16	17	15	16	24	13	18	16	18	17	27	19	269
G	7	10	6	4	21	4	2	12	14	2	7	1	13	14	2	119
S	11	10	17	22	14	18	15	11	20	6	19	14	15	19	18	229
C	6	4	4	3	5	7	4	6	4	10	4	6	11	4	6	84
R	5	24	41	5	9	5	37	3	4	4	26	2	3	12	30	210
T	5	4	5	2	8	6	2	1	4	3	6	2	2	..	3	53
V	1	1	..	1	..	1	..	1	..	..	..	1	2	1	1	10
N	1	6	..	2	8	..	..	8	5	..	..	..	7	10	..	47
I	..	1	..	..	..	..	..	1	1	..	..	..	..	..	..	3
X	1	2	1	3	2	1	..	2	3	..	3	1	3	3	..	25

been taught). In Grade IVB fewer than half of the combinations (2040 in all,—one hundred thirty-six subjects, fifteen combinations each) were dealt with by processes which could be classified as H. Three other types of procedure, M, S, and R, together contributed about a third of the total, each of the three to about the same extent. Guessing occurred with about six per cent of the combinations, and counting with about four per cent. Answers were not attempted in forty-seven instances (two per cent) and were obtained by some form of counting in fifty-three instances (three per cent).

Theoretically, at least, the teachers of these children had been striving for a year or more to develop the kind of thought process here designated as meaningful habituation (H). True, unwittingly they had encouraged M-responses, for their methods of teaching from the outset stressed repetitive practice on the formulas of the combinations. Still, it is surprising to discover how far these children were in Grade IVB from the expected kind of procedure. In spite of considerable drill (and, correspondingly, in spite of the frequent repetition of the number facts), these children had not yet abandoned immature and, in certain cases, undesirable procedures (M and G, notably). Indeed, in view of the method of instruction one may well ask how these children happened at all to be using other procedures than M, N, and G (and possibly H), for the conditions of learning were not calculated to suggest other procedures.

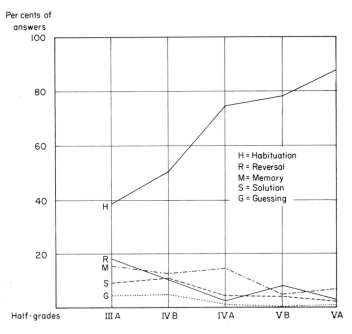

FIG. 2. CHANGES IN PROCESSES USED FROM GRADE TO GRADE,
AS REVEALED IN INTERVIEWS.

Fig. 2 is based upon the five tables of interview data of which Table 2 is a sample. It pictures learning in a different way than does Fig. 1, where the criteria of learning are rate and accuracy. In Fig. 2 the criterion is nature of the processes employed to find answers. The curves for the five major processes represented in the figure need to be studied with due regard for their relationships. As compared with Grade IIIA, there is some gain in the use of H in Grade IVB, with slight compensating losses in use of R and M. The marked gain in use of H in Grade IVA is made possible by the practical abandonment of G and by the tendency to discard R and S. The most striking change in Grade VB is a reduction in the use of M, there being little increase in use of H. The situation in Grade VA is that about twelve per cent of the combinations were still obtained by methods short of H,—which is to say that even after two and a half years of instruction these children had not developed the most desirable and the most mature procedure for all combinations.

Relation of Interview Data to Group Test Data.—The facts revealed by Fig. 2 should now be placed alongside the facts pictured in Fig. 1, for they serve to explain the findings with respect to gains in rate and accuracy. The Grade IIIA children were slow and inaccurate on the group tests because they had meaningful habituations for fewer than half of the (interview) combinations and because they had to employ with combinations which they had not yet habituated meaningfully, processes far short of H in maturity and efficiency. These processes, especially guessing, were susceptible to error, and they were employed clumsily and none too successfully, with the consequence of increased time and mistakes.

The rate curves (Fig. 1) show moderate increases, and the accuracy curves considerable increases in Grade IVB. Improvement in these aspects of learning is explained, less by the abandonment of immature and inefficient processes than by greater control over the same processes which characterized the children in Grade IIIA. That is to say, the children in Grade IVB used the processes of Grade IIIA, but used them more effectively. Use of H increased only from thirty-nine to forty-nine per cent.

In Grade IVA the slight gains in accuracy brought the experimental subjects practically to the point of proficiency evidenced in Grade VA. The gains in rate are very marked. Again, the interview data provide the reasons. Three-fourths of the combinations now were obtained by the use of H, one-fourth more than in Grade IVB. Only one answer in ten was secured by immature (but desirable) processes, and only one in six (compared with one in five in Grade IVB) by undesirable processes.

The group test data for Grade VB (Fig. 1) reveal no changes in accuracy as compared with Grade IVA results. The maintenance of the Grade IVA level of accuracy is consistent with the lack of change in processes (Fig. 2). The temporary loss in rate is explained by the fact that for some time prior to the group testing these children had had little practice on the multiplication combinations.

The Grade VA children had practically ridden themselves of immature processes and of undesirable processes on the interview combinations (and supposedly on the other combinations of the group test as well). Use of H had increased to eighty-eight per cent. These facts together account for the excellent showing in rate and accuracy, but they also disclose that, so far as process is concerned, these children were still short of final maturity of method (H).

SIGNIFICANCE OF PROCESS IN LEARNING

Implicit in the foregoing discussion is the notion that maturity of process is a better index of learning than are the customary indices of rate and accuracy.[1] Certain processes have been described as "mature" and "immature," as "desirable" and "undesirable," as "effective" and "ineffective." For example, G is undesirable, immature, and inefficient (unless by some chance the correct answer is guessed). R is fairly effective but immature (since it is short of H), but not undesirable as an early way of thinking of combinations. M is undesirable (since the formulas may be learned without understanding) and effective only when the correct answer has been memorized and when the given combination is used in situations which to the learner are very similar to the learning situation. S, like R, is immature but relatively effective; and it is desirable in the early and intermediate stages in learning, for R involves the apprehension of relationships and so contributes to understanding. C is immature, none too effective (especially when a good deal of counting is needed to secure the answer), and is desirable only at the outset of learning. T occupies about the same place as C in the scale of maturity, effectiveness, and desirability, except that it is more likely to be associated with memorization. At the bottom of the scale of maturity is G; at the top, H.

Now, there is no necessary relationship between level of process used and scores in rate and accuracy. A process low in maturity (e.g., C) may be so completely mastered as to make both for speedy and for correct responses. On the other hand, a process higher in maturity (e.g., S) may be so imperfectly mastered that errors and excessive time results.[2] It is for these reasons that at an earlier place in this paper the popular measures of

---

[1] Caution requires that this statement be restricted to the kind of learning investigated in this study; namely, the acquisition of meaningful relationships. It is conceivable that level of process is not so good a criterion in the case of other kinds of learning, in which meaning is not an important aspect. But the multiplication combinations are properly learned only when they are meaningfully learned: they must be retained and used in countless differing situations . . .

[2] One consequence of this lack of relationship between level of process and efficiency of performance is that test scores, usually expressed in terms of rate or of accuracy, are frequently misleading. High scores in rate or in accuracy, or in both, are commonly accepted as evidence of sound learning. Such may not be the case at all.

rate and accuracy were termed measures of efficiency: they reveal only how well (promptly and correctly) a given child uses whatever method he does use. It is for these reasons also that the maturity of processes used has been suggested as a sound index of learning. And it is for these reasons, again, that Fig. 2 is offered as a complement to the traditional so-called learning curves which are constructed from measures of rate or of accuracy alone.

Learning as re-organization.—The impression one gets from typical learning curves is that improvement consists simply in the refinement and the mastery of the response with which one starts initially: one practices this response over and over again, and the result is a smoother, quicker, and more accurate performance. The conception of learning which is revealed by Fig. 2 is something quite different: learning consists in the progressive re-organization of processes or procedures. At the outset the learner satisfies the requirements of the task by using relatively cumbersome and ineffective procedures. He practices at this level for a long or short period, thereby getting greater command over (efficiency with) this type of performance. Continued practice will not raise him to the next higher level of process. Instead he must, for one reason or another, reorganize his response in order to move on the next higher level. Here again he may pause to secure more or less mastery of that process,—only again under appropriate motivation, to abandon this level for the next above. Eventually, after a series of re-organizations, he may arrive at an expert, adult-like level of performance.

This conception of learning is to be seen in Fig. 2 for the group of experimental subjects as a whole. It is to be seen too in Table 3, in the case of seventeen pupils who were interviewed in the fall when they were in Grade IVB and again in the spring, six months later, when they were in Grade IVA.

In Table 3 ten categories of process are listed in the first column in the order of their approximate maturity, with H at the top and C, N, V, and X at the bottom. They are listed again (seven, this time) along the tops of the next columns, with the least mature processes at the left. Of the eighteen combinations dealt with by H in the fall sixteen were answered in the same way in the spring, one process being then classified as M, and another as R. S, a comparatively mature way of thinking of the combinations, provided a sound basis later for H: thirty-four of the forty-nine combinations solved in the fall had been meaningfully habituated by spring. Four of the ten combinations answered by R in the fall were dealt with by higher processes (S and H) in the spring. The movement toward more mature procedures is shown also in the case of the use of T and C. On the other hand, the slight contributions of M and G to meaningful habituation are equally as evident in the figures of Table 3. G and M could hardly evolve into H because they themselves are devoid of meaning.

TABLE 3

COMPARISON OF PROCESSES USED, FALL AND SPRING, WITH THE SAME
SEVENTEEN SUBJECTS, OBTAINED BY INTERVIEWS

Fall Processes, with Frequency	Spring Processes, Same Combinations: Frequency						
	G	M	C	T	R	S	H
H (18)	..	1	..	..	1	..	16
S (49)	..	3	..	5	..	7	34
R (10)	..	3	..	..	3	..	3
T (21)	1	4	..	1	4	1	10
C (43)	1	1	1	3	..	4	33
M (58)	..	35	..	..	1	..	22
G (25)	..	11	..	..	2	4	8
N (18)	..	1	2	..	1	7	7
V (3)	..	..	..	..	..	..	3
X (10)	2	4	..	..	1	2	1

While the interview data warrant the conception of learning as a series of progressive re-organizations, one must not go too far in assuming greater uniformity than actually exists. One should not infer, for example, that all children in a given grade are at the same stage of maturity of process with respect to all combinations. The figures of Table 2 discredit any such notion. Nor, again, should one infer that any given child is at the same stage with respect to all combinations . . . And still, again, one should not infer that all children traverse the same series of stages preliminary to final meaningful habituation. On the contrary, beyond any question some children omit one or two types of process (they may, for example, not use R or T with some combinations), and some move toward H much more rapidly than do others. Still, with all these limitations, the general picture of progressive re-organization as revealed in Fig. 2 seems to be sound. The learning of meaningful relationships is no simple straight-line affair. Instead, such learning is characterized by a continuous series of changes from lower or less mature and effective organizations of behavior to steadily higher or more mature and effective types of response.

DISCUSSION

The study of the learning of the multiplication combinations is reviewed here less because of its practical than because of its theoretical implications. Research on learning rarely reports (and probably rarely secures) measures of the kind collected in the present instance by means of the interview. As a consequence, the accounts of learning which emerge from such research must necessarily be incomplete, and they may well be misleading. The nature of the incompleteness and of misinterpretation has been illustrated in the foregoing pages.

It seems curious that learning in the case of meaningful tasks should be so commonly investigated with no regard for what happens with regard to the meanings themselves. Perhaps one reason for neglect of data at this point is that the meaning-aspects of behavior are difficult to quantify. In turn, they are difficult to quantify because meanings are peculiarly subjective. Hence, it is seldom possible through objective tests to secure trustworthy measures. This obstacle will, however, disappear as soon as we are willing to substitute other techniques for that of objective testing,—as soon as we are willing, for example, to employ such evaluation procedures as those of the interview and of direct observation.

There is sound justification for the suspicion which attaches to these procedures. Unless they are carefully planned and managed, observation and the interview are subject to all sorts of error. This fact,—and it is a fact,—merely signifies that proper safeguards must be found and applied. And they can be found and applied.

Attention has already been called in the section, Interview Data, to the difficulty of discriminating among H, M, and G when children quickly gave their answers, correct or incorrect, to number combinations. On this account it became necessary to modify the interviewing technique. Changes were made in the following manner: When children gave answers, correct or incorrect, which they could not justify, instead immediately offering other answers when questioned about their first attempts, it was assumed that they had guessed, and G was recorded as the process. In the case of H and M, (1) a tentative entry of M or H was recorded at once when one of these processes seemed to have been used. At this time questioning was carried only far enough to give a reasonable basis for the preliminary classification. Then, after the subject had responded to all fifteen combinations, he was taken back over the M and H facts. (2) On the second trial the child was asked, "How did you know that . . . was the correct answer?" and "What did you think to get the answer?" If these questions did not elicit an unambiguous report an absurd suggestion was offered. For example, for 8×3 it might be asked, "Did you get your answer by thinking '8 and 3 are 11, and 7 are 18 and 6 are 24'?" The child, in rejecting this absurd procedure, usually explained what he had done. If so, the appropriate entry was made, and the next doubtful combination was presented. If not, the original entry of M or H was allowed to stand until the remaining doubtful facts had been considered. The child was then taken back over the uncertain M and H facts. (3) On the third trial the interviewer said, "But suppose I say that 24 (for 8×3) is not correct. Suppose I say the answer is 25 How could you prove me wrong?" If the child was able by any rational and logical method to prove the correctness of his answer and the incorrectness of the suggested answer, it was assumed that he understood what he was doing, and he was given credit for H. If, on the other hand, he had no way of testing the correctness of answers, his process was recorded as M.

This whole procedure sounds much more complicated in the description than it was in actual use. The children were not aware of the three levels of questioning. Their responses were not distorted by the inquiry, but on the contrary remained true to reality. Indeed, only rarely did children realize that they were asked to deal as many as three times with the same combinations.

The modified technique employed in interviewing is described here in detail in order to demonstrate the feasibility of surrounding this research procedure with safeguards which will insure trustworthiness of data. The peculiar advantages of the interview are not infrequently lost through failure to recognize the dangers which it entails. In research such as that here reported the interview cannot be completely standardized. Instead the questioning, which of course must follow a general pattern, must be left flexible enough to elicit responses even from uncooperative children. Furthermore, it must be flexible enough to allow for individual differences in understanding the situation to which they are to react. But this flexibility must be kept within limits. Otherwise, the interviewer who has no clear insight into his problem can readily ruin his data by suggesting to his subjects processes which, while they are not their own, they will nevertheless claim as their own.

So much for the interview as a research technique in learning research it is exceedingly valuable if it is sagaciously employed. It is valuable because it enables the investigator to secure a kind of data which are usually not collected on the ground that they are likely to be unreliable. But the data which the interview can supply are essential to a complete account of the learning process. They must therefore be secured. Otherwise, we shall continue to over-simplify and to misunderstand the true course of meaningful learning and hence to base instruction upon an imperfect foundation.

REFERENCES

1. The data reviewed here have been published in much more complete form in the following reference: BROWNELL, W. A., CARPER, D. V. *Learning the Multiplication Combinations.* Duke U. Res. St. in Ed., No. 7. Durham, N.C.: Duke U. Press, 1943.

35. Tensions and School Achievement Examinations*

That a certain amount of tension exists in learning is assumed. It might be further assumed that the experience of taking a course examination would tend to maximize tension in the student. Hastings, in a study in which unusual care was taken to validate the measuring instruments used, reports his findings on this little-explored yet realistic aspect of learning. His demonstration that a simple, practicable classroom questionnaire may be constructed for the prediction of tensions in school course examinations is of particular interest.

INTRODUCTION

Experientially there is reason to believe that there are significant differences in tensions felt before and during an examination. Experimentally there has been little objective identification of those individuals who have high or low tensions directed toward, or associated with, the classroom examination. It is true that there have been studies which show that examination tensions do exist, but few of these investigations have attempted to ascertain the degree of tension, or to designate individuals studied as belonging to a "high tension" group or a "low tension" group.

* J. THOMAS HASTINGS. Reprinted and abridged with permission of the author and publisher from the *Journal of Experimental Education,* 1944, 12:143–64.

The use of the word "tension" seems more appropriate to describe the affective state of the individual in certain situations (for example, taking or about to take an examination, applying for a new position, about to step upon the lecture platform) than does the word "emotion," which is commonly reserved for those situations bearing a stronger affect . . .

OBJECTIVES OF THE INVESTIGATION

The primary statement of the problem has two parts: (1) to develop a technique by which the pupils taking an examination can be differentiated in terms of intensity of tension directed toward the examination, (2) to search for relationships which such tension scores may bear to the examination results.

Since the focal point of the study is the regular classroom achievement examination, the technique mentioned under item (1) must be applicable to such situations. Obviously, continuous records of physiological indices throughout the examination would be impossible for a regular examination. For purposes of classroom use, any laboratory method of measuring tension is, at best, awkward and laborious. This is certainly no reason, of itself, to abandon the laboratory methods, but it seems sound to use less awkward or burdensome methods, if they can be shown to correspond to the results of the more complicated procedures. A questionnaire method would solve this problem of practicability, if a sufficient degree of reliability and validity could be demonstrated.

The first three objectives of this investigation concern the development of such a technique; i.e., it was sought (1) to develop a questionnaire which had as its purpose the differentiation of pupils in terms of tensions toward an examination, (2) to demonstrate a reasonable reliability for this instrument, (3) to demonstrate the validity of this instrument. In regard to validity, it is proposed to show:

a. That certain fundamental characteristics of validity are present in the questionnaire results.

b. That differences in tension, as measured by the questionnaire, between examination situations correspond to differences in objective characteristics of these situations.

c. That the results of the questionnaire correspond to the results of a technique which utilizes disturbances in speech and motor reactions as an index of tension.

d. That the results of the questionnaire correspond to the results of an accepted physiological index of affective states.

In connection with the second part of the statement of the problem, three more objectives may be set forth: (4) to demonstrate the existence or lack of existence of concomitant variation between tension scores and examination results . . . ; (5) to compare the reliability of scores on achievement examinations for "low tension groups" with the reliability of scores of "high tension groups" on the same examinations; (6) to examine the predictability of test scores for "high tension groups" and for "low tension groups."

The Sample

All of the ninth grade pupils who were taking mathematics (four were not) in the University of Chicago High School were used as subjects. These pupils were in three mathematics classes: two classes having twenty-nine pupils and the other having twenty-two. Since the study continued for a complete semester, absences caused the total number available for different purposes to vary from seventy-five to eighty . . .

The Examinations

Each class was given four examinations: (1) a Semester examination which was the same for all three classes, given just before the end of the first semester in January, 1942; (2) an examination over a unit of work (three to four weeks of class work)—this examination was different for each of the three classes; (3) a comparable form of this Unit examination on the day following the first Unit examination; (4) a Final examination over the entire year's work—this Final examination was the same for all three classes. These examinations will be referred to as T_s, T_1, T_2, and T_f, respectively; and classes will be designated as Class 1, Class 2, and Class 3 . . .

The experimental examination situations were selected with regard for differences in importance, length, and difficulty. These three characteristics are objective enough to allow for agreement concerning differences, and they can be expected to produce differences, in general, in magnitude of tensions . . .

In order of decreasing amount, all three characteristics were present in the four examination situations as follows: Final, Semester, Unit 1, and Unit 2. This gives a basis for expecting a definite pattern in average tensions in the four situations.

The Questionnaire

A questionnaire was developed as the main technique for differentiating pupils in terms of examination tensions. It was of such a length that it could be taken in approximately eight minutes. This shortness of time was desirable, since the questionnaire could be given at the end of an examination period without seriously limiting the time devoted to the examination. This questionnaire was administered to the pupils in each class at the close of each of the four examination periods. The following excerpt gives the instructions at the top of the questionnaire page and a few example items . . .

Here are some statements concerning your feelings about today's test. In each statement you are to choose one of the three phrases marked a, b, or c. In *each statement* choose the *one* phrase (a, b, or c) which will make the sentence *most nearly describe your feeling.* Indicate your choice by making a *circle around the letter of that phrase.*

2. While taking the test I felt . . .   a. very nervous   b. somewhat nervous   c. not at all nervous

5. For the amount of time we had to work on it, the test seemed to me to be . . .   a. about the right length   b. much too long   c. too short

7. As soon as I began to work on the test I felt . . .   a. very calm   b. not at all calm   c. fairly calm

In order to have valid items in the sense of using the words of the pupils to state conditions which they might have felt, the construction of the questionnaire was started by requesting a group of twenty-five pupils to write out statements of how they felt about taking mathematics examinations in general. They were told that some pupils had stated a preference between doing "home-work" problems and doing "examination" problems, and that we should like to know what factors entered into this preference. The resulting essays were analyzed for common statements of tension, and these statements were incorporated in the first draft of the questionnaire. The wording which the pupils used was allowed to stand as nearly like they had written it as the formality of the questionnaire would allow.

This first draft of the questionnaire was then administered to two of the experimental classes following unit tests which they had taken. The pupils were asked to comment on the items in this draft and to add any statements which they felt were pertinent. The results of these administrations were used to delete one item, change the form of a second item, and add two items. This revised form is the one used in the main experiment. All construction was completed prior to the main experiment.

In order to follow the lead suggested by Brown, this questionnaire is so worded throughout that it applies specifically to the examination which the pupil has just taken, not to examinations in general.

In order to answer each item on the questionnaire, the pupil is required to make a choice among three possible answers. The three answers under each item were each given a value of 1, 2, or 3 points: 1 point for the answer which is indicative of the least tension, 3 points for the answer which is indicative of the greatest tension. The total score is the sum of item scores.

For most items this discrimination of answer values is an easy matter— one answer clearly states high tension and another answer is the opposite. For all items the discrimination between "highest" and "lowest" answers was made on the basis of the original essay statements. The answers were so arranged that no one value had the same position in every item. In the completed questionnaires there was no case of a pupil obtaining the same value on every item, nor was there a case of any pupil marking the same position for every item. This is evidence which substantiates the claim that the pupils responded to the questionnaire items; they did not simply "fill in spaces."

As a check on the correctness of the weights which were assigned to the answers, a measure of internal consistency was computed for each item. After the first administration an item analysis was made of all the papers. The total score on the questionnaire was used to select three groups: (1) the twenty-two pupils who made the highest scores, (2) the twenty pupils who made the lowest scores, (3) the seventeen pupils who made scores around the average. A mean was found for each group on each item. These means are presented in Table I.

TABLE I

MEAN ON EACH ITEM OF THE QUESTIONNAIRE FOR HIGH, LOW, AND AVERAGE GROUPS SELECTED ACCORDING TO TOTAL SCORE

Group	N	Item Number															
		1	2	3	4	5	6	7	8	9	10	11	12	13	14	15	16
High	22	2.8	2.5	2.4	2.4	2.6	2.2	2.4	2.7	2.6	2.2	2.7	2.4	2.6	1.9	2.9	2.7
Average ..	17	2.2	1.9	1.6	2.2	2.0	1.8	1.8	1.7	1.9	1.9	1.9	1.8	2.2	1.8	2.6	2.1
Low	20	1.6	1.2	1.2	1.6	1.2	1.2	1.4	1.2	1.7	1.2	1.7	1.5	1.6	1.4	2.0	1.6

If an item were weighted incorrectly, the item means for the three groups (selected according to total score) would not bear the relation to each other of high, low, and medium for the corresponding groups. This correspondence is evident for each item in the table . . .

LURIA TECHNIQUE

One of the objectives of this investigation was stated: to show how the results of the questionnaire correspond to the results of a technique which utilizes disturbances in speech and motor reactions as a measure of examination tensions. The technique used for this is the one which has been described so thoroughly by Luria that it is designated with his name in the literature . . .

In the present study, pens attached to an air system by means of a Marey tambour recorded the hand pressures on six-inch paper, which was driven by a constant speed motor. Stimulus time and verbal response time were recorded on the same paper by means of a pen which was attached to an electromagnet and operated by the experimenter with a spring key. The experimenter would depress the key as he stated the stimulus word and again, as the subject spoke the response. Each such depression of the key would cause a break in the stimulus-response record line. Time intervals—fifths of a second—were recorded on the paper by a fourth pen, which was in series with a circuit breaker operating on a synchronous, constant speed motor . . .

Each record for each pupil consisted of four lines: (1) a line which showed time in fifth-second intervals; (2) a line which showed, by means of breaks, the interval between stimulus and verbal response; (3) a line which indicated relative pressures for the preferred hand (voluntary)—hereafter called the right-hand pressure line; (4) a line which indicated relative variations in pressure for the non-preferred hand (involuntary)—hereafter called the left-hand pressure line. The pupils' verbal responses were recorded at the time of the experiment as a matter of formality and in order to motivate the individuals to respond properly. These were not used in the subsequent analysis . . .

The Luria technique was used for each pupil twice. The first administration took place two weeks before the Semester examination. At this time no mention had been made of the examination date nor of preparation for the examination. The Luria was given a second time just preceding the examination; namely, on the same day or on the preceding day. These two administrations will be denoted as L_1 and L_2, respectively.

The stimulus words used for L_1 were as follows:

neutral words—also, captain, cedar, clean, deep, design, enjoy, exchange, follow, grocery, house, nourish, nuisance, occasion, path, prefer, prospect, ride, salute, satisfy, table, tiger, true, unseen, watched;
critical words—arithmetic, equation, graph, number, test;
*post-critical words**—costume, cover, mountain, purpose, umbrella.

The stimulus words used for L_2 were as follows:

neutral words—city, cover, design, door, false, grocery, nourish, nuisance, occasion, path, prospect, ride, satisfy, umbrella, watched;
critical words—algebra, arithmetic, equation, graph, number, problem, rectangle, sign, solve, test;
post-critical words—also, clean, costume, exchange, follow, long, prefer, purpose, salute, tree.

The words were selected with careful consideration of two criteria: (1) that the meaning of neutral words should not be connected with mathematics nor examinations, but the critical words should be connected with these areas; (2) that the words should not present equivocal meanings.

As may be seen, the meanings of the critical words in each list are associated with "mathematics" or with "examination." The meanings of neutral words are not so associated . . .

On his first visit to the laboratory, the pupil was shown the apparatus and told that we wished to get a measure of his reaction time to words. He was seated before the hand tambours and made to feel as much at ease as the conditions of the experiment would permit. Next he was instructed in the procedure of responding to the stimulus words verbally and with hand pressure. He was cautioned not to rest his hands elsewhere (after the chair was adjusted so that his fingers could comfortably reach the tambours), and to keep his "left-hand" (non-preferred hand) steady on the tambour. He was requested to face forward and make sure that he was comfortable before the experiment began.

The experimenter sat to the right of the subject and slightly behind him, in order that he could control the signalizing key for stimulus and response without detracting the subject's attention. A practice run of five or six words (not from the regular list) was used to see if directions were being followed. The number of practice words was increased if there was doubt as to instructions. This procedure, which was allowed to remain

---

* Words which follow the critical words but which, otherwise, would be neutral.

informal, was standardized in terms of specific steps. With the exception of the introduction to the apparatus, the procedure was repeated for the second Luria . . .

For the purpose of the present investigation—only three measures were used: (1) verbal reaction-time (VT); (2) height of right-hand response (HR); (3) height of left-hand response (HL). The first of these was estimated in tenths of a second by use of the time interval line; height measurements were made in millimeters.

These three measurements were made for each of the thirty-five words on every record. Two sets of primary scores were tabulated for each individual—one for L_1, the other for L_2. Each set consisted of three scores for each word—VT, HR, and HL scores. The scores which were used as indices of tensions were derived from these primary measurements.

The thirty-five VT scores, the thirty-five HR scores, and the thirty-five HL scores were summarized for each pupil on each Luria by obtaining four statistics: (1) the standard deviation for the thirty-five words (σ_t); (2) the mean of the neutral words (M_n); (3) the mean of the critical words (M_c); (4) the mean of the post-critical words (M_p). Thus, each pupil's responses on each Luria were represented by four numbers on VT, by four on HR, and by four on HL. These means may be considered as "best estimates" of a pupil's responses to the neutral words, to the critical words, and to the post-critical words, respectively.

The Luria technique utilizes differences in response between neutral words and post-critical words as well as between neutral words and critical words. The two types of differences are used on the basis that excess excitation caused by the critical word may carry over to the post-critical word, or, in some cases, actually not appear until the post-critical word is presented. In the present investigation the larger of the two differences . . . was used in all cases. These differences were divided by the standard deviation of the responses for the total word list, in order to make them abstract numbers (independent of the unit of measurement). These derived "tension scores" are represented by D . . .

By this final computation each pupil was represented by three scores for each Luria. Since these D-scores are abstract numbers, the three for one pupil—VT, HR, and HL—may be combined. The advantage of this combined D-score is evident when one realizes that any tension which exists may be evidenced in any one, but not necessarily all, of the three responses. These D-scores were used in showing relationship between the results of the questionnaire and the results of the Luria technique.

Respiration Index

In order to demonstrate correspondence between the results of the questionnaire and results of a respiration measure at examination time, two groups of pupils—a high tension group and a low tension group—were selected from the entire sample for use in the respiration experiment. There were seven boys and seven girls selected for each group . . .

Those in the "high" group had scored above the mean for the total group in each of three questionnaires: Q_s, the one which accompanied the Semester examination; and Q_1 and Q_2, which accompanied the Unit examinations. Those in the "low" group had scored below the means for the entire group in each of these questionnaires.

Arrangements were made for these twenty-eight pupils to come to the laboratory individually just before the final examination. The length of time preceding the examination varied from one-half hour to twenty-four hours. The schedule was arranged so that the individuals of the "high" and "low" groups were treated the same in regard to the lapse of time.

The technique for obtaining the respiration record was very conventional. A respiration bellows attached to the chest of the subject by means of a belt picked up the breathing movements. These changes in pressure were transmitted to a pen by means of an air system. The respiration record was an ink line which showed inhalations and exhalations by corresponding waves.

Besides the respiration line itself, the record consisted of a line which measured time intervals and a line on which breaks signalized the beginning or the ending of the various types of stimulus periods used in the procedure. Rate of respiration could be measured by counting the number of wave crests (or troughs) appearing in conjunction with a given length of the time line.

As each pupil entered the laboratory, the apparatus was shown to him, and its general function was described. After he was seated in a desk-arm chair facing the experimenter, the respiration belt was fastened about his chest. Care was taken to see that the subject was comfortable and that the belt was properly adjusted. A short record was run to assure the proper functioning of all apparatus. The pupil was requested to sit up straight and to remain quiet. This admonition was repeated when necessary during the experiment. The experimental period was comparatively short, and the pupils cooperated well.

The experimental period was divided into six main parts: (1) an initial rest period which lasted almost two minutes (so that the first part could be discarded and three half-minute periods would remain); (2) and (3) a questioning period, which was later divided into two parts (each slightly over two minutes in length); (4) and (5) two one-minute periods during which the pupil worked problems on an addition test; (6) and a final rest period identical with the initial rest period in time and directions given.

For the first period the pupil was directed to "relax and think about as near nothing as you can." Time was allowed for the breathing movements to become more or less regular before the record was started. For parts (2) and (3) the pupil was asked the following questions: Do you know whether this coming examination will count more in terms of grades or about the same in terms of grades as do most of the mathematics tests that you have taken through the year? Do you feel more or less worried about this mathematics examination (the Final examination) than you do about other subject-matter tests in general? Can you think of any type of material on this coming examination which might worry you more than other types? If so, what material? What statement could you make about how well prepared you feel that you are for this math examination? Knowing what grades you have made in general on unit tests in mathematics, what grade (A, B, C, D, F) would you believe or guess that you may make on this coming examination?

These questions were intended as excitation stimuli for those who would express examination tensions. Following the questions, two periods, (4) and (5), were devoted to working an addition test, copies of which were attached to the desk-arm of the chair so that the pupil would only have to use his writing arm. This test had two psychological connections with the coming mathematics examination: it had been used at the time of two previous examinations; and it was arithmetic material. At the end of the fifth period the pupil was instructed to relax "once more—as you did so well at the first part of the experiment." The record of this relaxation period constituted the sixth period. Each of these six periods was marked on the record by means of a signalizing pen, which was operated by the experimenter with a spring key.

Respirations were counted in half-minute intervals for each of the six experimental periods. These counts were averaged for each pupil for each period. The averages, converted into respirations per minute (a more conventional unit for reporting than is the half-minute unit), were used as scores. In this way, the final records show one score for each pupil on each of the experimental periods.

Questionnaire Reliability and Validity

An "odd item—even item" division was used for the split-half method of estimating reliability. Reliability coefficients were obtained for each of five subgroups and for the total number of pupils (seventy-seven pupils completed the questionnaire in each of the four administrations). The five subgroups were: (1) class 1, twenty-eight pupils; (2) class 2, twenty-two pupils; (3) class 3, twenty-seven pupils; (4) all of the boys, forty pupils; (5) all of the girls, thirty-seven pupils. Obviously, the membership of the last two groups overlaps that of the other three. These subgroups were used in order to determine whether any one class or sex presented a notably different pattern of reliability coefficients than did the total group of pupils.

As stated previously, the questionnaire was administered to each group four different times. A further check on the reliability of an instrument is the consistency of the magnitude of reliability coefficients under differing circumstances. Twenty-four reliability coefficients were computed for the questionnaire; one for each administration for each of the six groups. These coefficients were substituted in the Spearman-Brown formula for estimating the reliability of a whole test from the reliability of half of the test. These corrected coefficients are presented in Table II, together with the corresponding standard deviation for each group.

TABLE II

Reliability Coeficient (r),[a] Standard Deviation (σ), and Number of Cases (N)
for Each of Five Subgroups and the Total Group on Each of Four
Administrations of the Questionnaire

Examination Situation	Class 1 N = 28		Class 2 N = 22		Class 3 N = 27		Boys N = 40		Girls N = 37		Total N = 77	
	r	σ	r	σ	r	σ	r	σ	r	σ	r	σ
Semester	.80	6.46	.74	5.59	.78	7.13	.74	6.19	.86	6.69	.80	6.81
Unit 1	.81	7.01	.72	5.34	.76	6.19	.76	5.94	.67	6.07	.74	6.24
Unit 2	.82	5.68	.76	4.68	.56	3.10	.77	4.14	.77	5.20	.76	4.68
Final	.78	5.55	.84	5.27	.61	5.64	.68	4.84	.72	5.55	.75	5.65

[a] By the "split-half" method; corrected for length.

With the exception of four of them, all of the coefficients exceed .70; six of them are .80 or above; and the median value for the twenty-four coefficients is .76. For the Total Group, the coefficient has a range of only .74 to .80. No one group has the highest or lowest correlation in all situations, and for no one situation are the coefficients the highest nor the lowest for all groups. In other words, there is no trend in terms of situations or groups. There is consistency in the magnitude of the coefficient for the twenty-four estimates. The median value of the reliability coefficients is .76 . . .

The foregoing data substantiate the statement that the questionnaire is sufficiently reliable that its scores may be used to differentiate groups of pupils. Furthermore, the reliability coefficients for six groups in four different situations show a consistency of magnitude which supports use of the questionnaire under varying conditions.

VALIDITY

Certain fundamental characteristics of validity are present in the questionnaire: (1) the items in the questionnaire pertain to the characteristics with which the investigation is concerned; (2) the examinees understood the phraseology of items in the questionnaire; (3) the questionnaire results do meet the common-sense expectation of significant relationships—correlations different from zero—between tension rankings of pupils in different examination situations. The six intercorrelations for the four administrations of the questionnaire are presented in Table III together with the reliabilities for the total group of seventy-seven pupils. The intercorrelations are all positive and each exceeds the minimum value necessary for significance at the 1 per cent level of confidence.

TABLE III

INTERCORRELATIONS AND RELIABILITY COEFFICIENTS[a] FROM FOUR ADMINISTRATIONS OF THE QUESTIONNAIRE TO SEVENTY-SEVEN PUPILS

Examination Situation	Semester	Unit 1	Unit 2	Final
Semester	.80			
Unit 1	.49	.74		
Unit 2	.39	.39	.76	
Final	.61	.41	.45	.75

[a] From Table 2, inserted here for comparison with intercorrelations.

Questionnaire-score differences between examination situations corresponded to differences in objective characteristics of these situations. More particularly, when the degree of difficulty, the length, and the importance to the pupil increased or decreased from one examination to another, the questionnaire scores for those examinations increased or decreased, respectively.

Table IV shows the questionnaire means for seventy-seven pupils for each of the four examination situations. The standard deviation and standard error of the mean are presented for each situation in the same table. It may be seen by inspection that the four means for the total group do indicate that average tension (as measured by the questionnaire) does vary from situation to situation. In order of decreasing magnitude of tension, the situations are ranked as follows: Final, Semester, Unit 1, Unit 2. This order is the same as that suggested by ranking the examination situations on the basis of the characteristics of length, difficulty, and importance. The differences in means are statistically significant.

TABLE IV

QUESTIONNAIRE MEAN, STANDARD DEVIATION, AND STANDARD ERROR OF MEAN
FROM FOUR EXAMINATION SITUATIONS FOR SEVENTY-SEVEN PUPILS

Examination Situation	Mean	Standard Deviation	Standard Error of Mean
Semester	31.7	6.81	0.78
Unit 1	29.1	6.24	0.71
Unit 2	23.1	4.68	0.53
Final	34.3	5.65	0.64

For further validation of the questionnaire it was proposed to show the correspondence between the results of the questionnaire and the results of a technique which utilizes disturbances in speech and motor reactions as an index of tension. The Luria technique, which was chosen for this demonstration, has been described.

There were seventy-three pupils who completed both Lurias and the questionnaire at the time of the Semester examination. In order to make a comparison between questionnaire results and Luria results, these pupils were divided into two groups, a high tension group and a low tension group, according to the scores which they made on the questionnaire at the time of the Semester examination. The mean questionnaire score for the total group was 31.7. Of the seventy-three who completed the Lurias and the questionnaire there were thirty-seven who scored 32 or above on the questionnaire. These compose the high tension group. The other thirty-six pupils, who scored 31 or below on the questionnaire, form the low tension group.

If the questionnaire results correspond to the results of the Luria, the scores on the second Luria must show that these two groups differ significantly. Table V presents the mean D-score (combined measure) for each group on that Luria which was taken immediately before the examination. This combined D-score is the most appropriate measure to compare with questionnaire results, since tension as measured by the Luria may be expressed in any one, but not necessarily all three, of the indices (VT, HR, and HL). It can be seen that the high tension group, according to the questionnaire, scored higher on the Luria than the low tension group and that this difference is significant at the 9 per cent level of confidence . . .

TABLE V

MEANS AND DIFFERENCES BETWEEN MEANS FOR HIGH AND FOR LOW TENSION GROUPS (BY QUESTIONNAIRE) ON THE COMBINED D-SCORE OF THE SECOND LURIA

| | Tension Group | |
	High	Low
Number of Cases	37	36
Mean	0.20	0.08
Standard Deviation	0.31	0.28
Standard Error	0.05	0.05
Difference of Means	0.12	
Standard Error of Difference	0.07	
t-value	1.71	
Level of Confidence	9%	

The results of the questionnaire corresponded to the results of a technique which utilized disturbances in speech and motor reactions as an index of tension. The groups selected as high and low in tension according to the questionnaire showed the same order in terms of their mean score on the Luria method.

It was proposed to show correspondence between the results of the questionnaire and a respiration index used as a measure of tensions. The apparatus, the experimental setup, and the scoring of the respiration records were described in a foregoing section.

If this respiration measure is an index of tension, the number of respirations per minute during the middle four "disturbance" periods (questions and addition) should be greater than the number during the two rest periods. To determine whether this was so or not, the respiration scores for the two rest periods were averaged for each pupil, and the scores for the other four periods (disturbance periods) were averaged for each pupil. These averages are given in Table VI. The average number of respirations per minute is larger for each of the twenty-seven pupils in the disturbance periods of questioning and addition than it is in the rest periods.

TABLE VI

AVERAGE NUMBER OF RESPIRATIONS PER MINUTE FOR THE TWO PERIODS
OF REST AND FOR THE FOUR PERIODS OF DISTURBANCE
(QUESTIONS AND ADDITION) FOR EACH PUPIL

| | High Tension Group[a] | | | Low Tension Group[a] | |
Case Number	*Rest Periods*	*Disturbance Periods*	*Case Number*	*Rest Periods*	*Disturbance Periods*
04	15.0	30.0	14	18.0	27.5
07	19.5	25.8	17	11.5	18.5
29	15.0	18.0	19	18.0	24.5
30	28.5	31.5	22	15.0	17.0
38	11.0	18.2	26	17.0	20.0
39	10.0	26.8	35	14.0	19.8
43	15.5	20.5	46	14.5	22.0
45	16.0	27.0	52	16.0	23.2
53	20.0	27.0	55	20.5	24.0
54	12.5	25.0	56	12.5	18.0
61	23.0	25.2	57	15.0	15.8
62	18.5	26.2	59	22.5	27.0
73	10.0	25.2	79	19.0	23.8
77	22.5	24.5			

[a] Selected by questionnaire scores.

The average respirations per minute during the rest periods for the high tension group (questionnaire) and the same statistic for the low tension group are shown in Table VII together with the difference between the means and the t-value of this difference. Since this t-value (for twenty-five degrees of freedom) indicates a level of confidence between 70 per cent and 80 per cent, it can be stated that the two groups, high and low, did not differ in average number of respirations per minute during the rest periods. The two groups were alike on this respiration measure at the time of the rest periods.

TABLE VII

MEAN, STANDARD DEVIATION, AND NUMBER OF CASES FOR HIGH AND FOR LOW
TENSION GROUPS[a] ON RESPIRATIONS PER MINUTE DURING REST PERIOD:
DIFFERENCE BETWEEN MEANS, t-VALUE, AND LEVEL OF
CONFIDENCE FOR THE TWO GROUPS

| | Tension Groups | |
	High	Low
Number of Cases	14	13
Mean	16.9	16.4
Standard Deviation	5.42	3.15
Difference of Means	0.5	
t-value	0.29	
Level of Confidence	70% to 80%	

[a] Selected by questionnaire scores.

Table VIII presents the same statistics for the two groups as those in the preceding table, except that the disturbance periods of questioning and addition were used for the means in Table VIII. The two groups, as selected by the questionnaire results, differed in terms of respirations per minute during the disturbance periods of the experiment. This is especially significant, since the two groups were shown to be alike in the rest periods.

TABLE VIII

MEAN, STANDARD DEVIATION, AND NUMBER OF CASES FOR HIGH AND FOR LOW
TENSION GROUPS[a] ON RESPIRATIONS PER MINUTE DURING DISTURBANCE
PERIODS[b]; DIFFERENCE BETWEEN MEANS, t-VALUE, AND LEVEL
OF CONFIDENCE FOR THE TWO GROUPS

| | Tension Groups | |
	High	Low
Number of Cases	14	13
Mean	25.1	21.6
Standard Deviation	3.89	3.75
Difference of Means	3.5	
t-value	2.38	
Level of Confidence	2% to 5%	

[a] Selected by questionnaire scores.
[b] Two periods of questioning and two periods of addition.

The results of the questionnaire corresponded to the results of a respiration measure of tension in that groups selected as high and low in tension according to the questionnaire showed the same order in terms of their mean scores on the respiration measure. Although the groups did not differ significantly when the measure was applied during a rest period, they did differ significantly in the direction which demonstrated correspondence between questionnaire and respiration measures, when the respiration measure was applied during periods which should incite examination tensions.

TENSION INTENSITY AND EXAMINATION RESULTS

The second objective of this investigation was "to search for relationships which tension scores may bear to the examination results." The validity of the questionnaire which was developed has been demonstrated, and it was shown to have a reliability which is sufficiently high to justify group selection. Consequently, high tension and low tension groups were selected by means of questionnaire scores for this study of relationships between tension intensity and examination results . . .

TABLE IX

CORRELATION COEFFICIENTS BETWEEN EXAMINATION SCORES AND QUESTIONNAIRE SCORES FOR VARIOUS GROUPS IN EACH OF THE FOUR EXAMINATION SITUATIONS

Examination Situation	GROUP					
	Class 1 $N = 28$	Class 2 $N = 22$	Class 3 $N = 27$	Boys $N = 40$	Girls $N = 37$	Total $N = 77$
Semester	—.40	—.38	—.26	—.47	—.42	—.46
Unit 1[a]	.11	—.25	—.12	. . . .
Unit 2[a]	.05	—.52	—.21	. . . .
Final	—.06	—.51	—.09	—.38	—.03	—.20

[a] Since the Unit examinations were different for each class, correlations could not be computed for the last three groups.

The correlation coefficients between tension scores and examination scores are presented in Table IX. It appears that concomitant variation between tensions and examination scores tends to be inverse, although high tensions are certainly not confined to those making low marks on the examination. Only seven of the eighteen coefficients are larger than the magnitude required for significance at the 5 per cent level; the meaning of these is rather lost in the inconsistency with which they appear for any one group or for any one examination situation.

Of course, the correlation coefficients give no sure basis for an interpretation of causal relationship; they merely indicate the degree of association between the two variables. However, for those who investigate the causation of tensions, the main implication of the foregoing findings is that other factors than lack of ability on the examination must enter into such causation. Studies directed toward the areas of "ego involvement" and "level of aspiration" might help answer the question as to why these tension-examination correlations tend to vary so much. On the other hand, for those who infer causation in the other direction—higher tensions resulting in lower scores—the findings indicate that this might be true only in certain situations, not in all situations . . .

TENSIONS AND PREDICTIONS OF EXAMINATION SCORES

Because the Semester examination and the Final examination are of similar difficulty and importance and differ mostly in amount of material sampled, one should expect fairly high predictive value from the former to the latter. The interest of the present investigation, however, is not in the absolute value of the prediction. It is in the difference of predictability between those with high tensions and those with low tensions.

As in the previous parts of this investigation, high and low tension groups were selected on the basis of scores on the questionnaire. In this instance an average score for two administrations of the questionnaire was used. The two administrations were those in the Semester situation and in the Final situation, since it seems reasonable to suppose that prediction might be affected by tensions at either time. Three sets of high and low tension groups were used: (1) all of those who scored above the mean of the entire group, thirty-nine cases, and all of those who scored below this mean, thirty-eight cases; (2) those who scored 36 or above, twenty-nine cases, and those who scored 30 or below, thirty cases; (3) those who scored 37 or above, twenty-one cases, and those who scored 28 or below, twenty-two cases. Sets (2) and (3) were used in order to see if widening the gap between high and low groups on the tension scale would affect the differences in prediction.

For each of these groups—three high and three low in tension scores—three statistics are presented in Table X: (1) the correlation between

Semester examination scores and Final examination scores; (2) the standard deviation for the group on the Final examination; (3) the standard error of estimate in predicting Final from Semester. The first of these shows the degree of association between the two variables. The second, together with the first, is used in obtaining the third, which is a measure of the value of the prediction: the higher the standard error of estimate of a prediction, the poorer is the prediction. Groups to be compared have the same group identification number in the table; namely, high tension group 1 should be compared with low tension group 1, etc. The data in the table have been so arranged that the size of the groups decreases as one reads up or down from the center of the table, just as the size of the extreme group decreases as one moves up or down from the center of the tension scale.

TABLE X

STANDARD ERROR OF ESTIMATE AND CORRELATION COEFFICIENT IN PREDICTING
FINAL FROM SEMESTER SCORES, AND STANDARD DEVIATION ON FINAL
EXAMINATION FOR HIGH AND LOW TENSION GROUPS
AND FOR TOTAL SAMPLE

Tension Group	Number of Cases	Tension Score Limits	Correlation Coefficient	Standard Deviation on Final	Standard Estimate Error of
High					
3	21	37 or above	0.52	14.9	12.7
2	29	36 or above	.61	15.0	11.8
1	39	34 or above	.63	13.9	10.7
Low					
1	38	33 or below	.71	14.4	10.2
2	30	30 or below	.77	15.9	10.2
3	22	28 or below	.76	14.4	10.5
Total Group	77	———	0.71	14.9	10.6

The correlation coefficients for the high tension groups (Table X) decrease in magnitude as the group selection moves toward the upper end of the tension scale; that is, as more of the middle group are excluded from the high group. The coefficients for the low tension groups increase as the selection is made farther down the tension scale (going from group 1 to group 2 or group 3). Comparisons between correlations for paired high and low tension groups show that the high tension group produces a smaller coefficient in each case than does the low tension group. In other words the high tension group presented a lower association between Semester and Final scores than did the low tension group, and this difference was increased when the selection was such that the groups represented greater divergence in tension.

The differences between coefficients for paired high and low groups are not statistically significant . . . Lack of significance is of less importance than it might be under other circumstances because of consistent trends in the data . . . It seems reasonable to conclude that significance would be clearer, if a greater number of cases at the extremes could be utilized . . .

Scores were available for seventy-four of the pupils in the ninth grade on the American Council Psychological Examination, the Reavis-Breslich Arithmetic Tests, and both Semester and Final examinations. The first two tests were administered to these pupils early in the first semester of the same year as the present investigation. It was decided to use these two scores plus the Semester examination scores to predict the Final examination scores, and then to examine the differences between predicted and obtained scores in relation to intensity of tension . . .

An F score (predicted score on Final Examination) was computed for each pupil in the group of seventy-seven for whom there were tension scores from the questionnaire in the Final situation. For each pupil there was also, of course, an obtained score, $\bar{F}$, on the Final examination. The absolute value of the difference between predicted score and obtained score was computed for each pupil. This value, $|(F - \bar{F})|$, represents the deviation from prediction of the pupil's obtained score. It was these scores which were examined in relation to intensity of tension on the hypothesis that pupils having higher tensions at the time of an examination produce examination results which tend to be less predictable than the examination results of pupils who exhibit lower tensions.

The pupils were divided into a high tension group and a low tension group on the basis of their scores on the questionnaire which was administered at the time of the Final Examination. These groups consisted of thirty-nine and thirty-eight cases, respectively. Those in the high group had scores on the tension scale of 35 or above; those in the low group had scores on the tension scale of 34 or below. The mean value of $|(F - \bar{F})|$ and the standard error of the mean were found for each group. These were used to compute the difference between the means for the groups, the standard error of the difference, and the t-value of the difference. These statistics are presented in Table XI.

TABLE XI

MEAN $|(F - \bar{F})|$ VALUE AND STANDARD ERROR OF THE MEAN FOR HIGH
AND FOR LOW TENSION GROUPS, AND DIFFERENCE BETWEEN MEANS,
STANDARD ERROR, AND THE t-VALUE OF THE DIFFERENCE

Tension Group	N	Mean $|(F - \bar{F})|$	Standard Error of Mean	Difference Between Means	Standard Error of Difference	t-value of Difference	Level of Confidence
High	39	8.6	1.04				
				2.2	1.2	1.8	7%
Low	38	6.4	0.77				

It is evident that the high tension group had a higher average deviation of obtained score from predicted score, $|(F - \bar{F})|$, than that of the low tension group. The difference is significant at the 7 per cent level of confidence. In other words, when the scores on the Final mathematics examination were predicted from scores on a psychological examination, a diagnostic arithmetic examination and the Semester mathematics examination, those pupils who showed high tensions deviated more from this predicted score than did those pupils who showed low tensions . . .

In summary, all of the results in the study of the relationship between intensity of tension and predictability of examination results point to the fact that those showing higher tensions at the time of an examination produced examination results which tended to deviate further from prediction than did the examination results of those who gave evidence of lower tensions, when tensions were measured by means of a questionnaire and the examinations were in ninth grade algebra. These results support the general hypothesis that pupils who undergo higher tensions than other pupils at the time of an examination tend, on the whole, to turn out a "less standard" examination product.

Conclusions

The following conclusions are based on the findings of the study:

1. The questionnaire which was developed for this study does afford a technique for differentiating pupils in terms of examination tensions.

a. This technique is a practical one for classroom examination situations in that it is easy to administer, it is easy to score, it consumes little time in the examination period, and it may be applied at the time and in the setting of the examination.

b. The questionnaire results do pertain to the particular examination situation for which the questionnaire is used, not to examinations in general.

c. The questionnaire which was developed is sufficiently reliable to justify its use in the selection of high tension and low tension groups.

d. Certain fundamental characteristics of validity are present in the questionnaire.

e. The questionnaire is valid in the sense that results of the questionnaire correspond to the results of a speech-motor disturbance technique and to the results of a respiration (rate) index of affect, when the latter two are used for the same purpose as the questionnaire.

2. Concomitant variation between tension scores and examination scores tends to be inverse, but the magnitude of this relationship, as shown by correlation, is so small that little importance can be attached to the degree of relationship. High tensions do not necessarily accompany low examination scores, nor contrariwise.

3. There is a definite tendency for a "high tension" group, as selected by the questionnaire, to yield a lower reliability coefficient on an examination than a "low tension" group shows on the same examination. Although the magnitude of the difference in reliability coefficients is too small to be statistically significant for the size of the groups used, the direction of the difference shows a high consistency.

4. Pupils showing higher tensions, as measured by the questionnaire, at the time of an examination produce examination results which tend to deviate further from prediction than do the examination results of those who give evidence of lower tensions.

a. This appears to be true at each score level within the examination.

DISCUSSION

It will be remembered that the questionnaire used in this study was developed as a practical technique, in terms of the classroom examination situation, for differentiating pupils in regard to tensions directed toward an examination situation . . . The present investigation has shown that this particular example of the technique meets certain criteria of practicability, reliability, and validity. It should not be considered, however, as *the* method of obtaining the desired ends.

If the questionnaire were to be used in further experimentation, certain cautions should be observed. The questionnaire used in the present work was constructed specifically for the group being tested; that is, essay statements by this group (a representative sample) were used as a basis of construction. If the technique were to be used for other groups, essay statements by those groups should be used in the construction of the schedule as a precaution against failure to take into account different forms of expression and modes of thinking. Undoubtedly, many of the items would remain the same for different groups, but this precaution should be observed.

Also, it would be well to attempt to expand the questionnaire: (1) in order to account for a greater number of specific indices of tension, so that the entire picture for each pupil would be more complete; (2) so that the length being greater, the reliability of the instrument might be increased sufficiently to justify greater discrimination.

One other point in connection with the use of the questionnaire technique bears emphasis: it is especially necessary in using this type of technique to gain rapport with the examinees. In the present investigation every effort was made to obtain real cooperation on the part of the pupils. The successfulness of this effort was due largely to respect which the three teachers had engendered in their pupils previously, and to their straight-forward manner of enlisting the pupils' willing participation.

Except in one area, the data from the investigation of relationships between tension and examination results are suggestive rather than conclusive. The one area is that of predictability of examination scores. The lack of finality in some of the data is unfortunate, of course, in terms of completely solving problems, but it is not surprising in consideration of scarcity of previous work in this field.

The importance of locating and describing these relationships is great. Examinations are being utilized more and more as bases for certification of accomplishment, for directing and counseling the individual in his plans for further work, for alteration and construction of curriculums, and for comparing the effectiveness of procedures. It is important that all aspects of the examination situation be understood, and that aberrations in results be interpreted properly.

This investigation offers evidence which should allow for an improved control of the use and interpretations of examination results. Sufficient clues have been given to justify more extensive investigation in this area. It would be well to expand the study to include examination material in other subject matter fields and at other school levels. Research should be undertaken to show whether or not there is change in relative amount of tension at different grade levels, and, if so, whether or not the magnitude of the relationships (e.g., predictability variation as associated with intensity of tension) is affected. It may well be that with greater tensions the "reliability" relationship might be of more apparent significance. In any event, the results of this study indicate that the value of interpretation of examination results may be enhanced by acquiring knowledge of the incidence and magnitude of tensions . . .

REFERENCES

1. BROWN, C. H., GELDER, D. V. 1938. Emotional reactions before examinations: I. Physiological changes. *J. Psychol.* 5:1–9.
2. BROWN, C. H. 1938. Emotional reactions before examinations: II. Results of a questionnaire. *J. Psychol.* 5:11–26.
3. BROWN, C. H. 1938. Emotional reactions before examinations: III. Intercorrelations, *J. Psychol.* 5:27–31.
4. GARDNER, J. 1937. An experimental study of the Luria technique for detecting mental conflict. *J. Exp. Psychol.* 20:495–506.
5. OLSEN, D., JONES, V. 1931. An objective measure of emotionally toned words. *J. Genet. Psychol.* 39:174–96.
6. SHARP, D. L. 1937. Group and individual profiles in the association-motor test. *U. Iowa St. Ch. Welf.* 15:97–196.

Text Correlation

The correlation of articles with selected current texts in educational psychology is given below to facilitate the use of the articles. The chapters cited appear to be those most relevant to each article. Instructors and students may also discover additional chapters in certain texts to which specific articles may be usefully related.

Cronbach: *Educational Psychology*
(Harcourt) 1954

CHAPTER
1.
2.
3. 1,2,3,4
4–7. 30,31,32
8.
9. 5,6,7,8,9,23,29

10. 13,14,15,30,31
11. 19,20,21
12. 16,17,18,28
13. 28
14. 25,26,27
15. 22,23,24
16. 32,33,34,35
17.
18.
19.

Frandsen: *How Children Learn* (McGraw-Hill) 1957

1.
2. 1,2,3,4
3. 30,31,32
4. 5,6,7,8,23,34
5. 16,17,18
6. 27
7. 29
8. 25,26
9.
10. 9,10,11,12
11. 28
12.
13.
14. 23,24,32,33,34,35

Garrison and Gray: *Educational Psychology* (Appleton) 1955

1.
2.
3. 32
4.
5.
6. 30,31
7. 24
8. 19,20,21
9.
10.
11. 1,2,3,4,28
12. 22,23,25,26,27
13. 16,17,18
14. 13,14,15,28
15. 5,6,7,8,9,10,11,12,23
16. 29
17. 32,33,34,35
18.
19.
20.

Gates, Jersild, McConnell, Challman: *Educational Psychology* 3rd ed. (Macmillan) 1948

1.
2. 30,31
3. 32
4.
5.
6. 31
7.
8.
9–10. 1,2,3,4
11. 16,17,18
12. 13,28
13. 13,14,15
14. 5,6,7,8,9,10,11,12,23
15. 29
16. 32,33,34,35
17. 19,20,21
18. 25,26,27
19.
20.
21.
22.

Kingsley and Garry: *The Nature and Conditions of Learning* 2nd ed. (Prentice-Hall) 1957

1. 1,2,3,4
2. See, for example, 5,13,20,27, 29,30
3. 32,33,34,35
4. 1,2,3,4
5. 30,31,32
6–7. 25,26,27,28,29
8.
9.
10. 16,17,18

11. 27
12. 28
13. 13,14,15
14. 5,6,7,8,23
15.
16. 19,20,21,22,23,24
17. 29

Klausmeier: *Learning and Human Abilities* (Harper) 1961

  1. 1,2,3,4
  2.
  3. 4
  4.
  5. 22,23,24
  6. 13,14,15,30,31
  7. 5,6,7,8,9,10,11,12
  8. 16,17,18,32
  9. 19,20
10. 21
11. 25,26,27
12. 28,29
13. 9,11
14.
15. 33,34
16. 32,35

Lindgren: *Educational Psychology in the Classroom* (Wiley) 1956

  1.
  2. 27
  3. 30,31,32
  4.
  5.
  6.
  7. 28,29
  8. 1,2,3,4,5,6,7,8,23
  9. 13,14,15,16,17,18,19,20,21,26

10.
11. 22,25
12.
13. 22,23,24
14. 32,33,34,35
15.
16.
17.
18.

McDonald: *Educational Psychology* (Wadsworth) 1959

  1.
  2.
  3. 1,2,3,4
  4. 25,26,27
  5. 13,14,15
  6. 28
7–8. 19,20,21
  9. 16,17,18
10. 5,6,7,8,23,29
11. 30,31,32
12.
13. 22,23,24
14. 33
15. 32,34,35
16.
17.
18.

Morse and Wingo: *Psychology and Teaching* (Scott, Foresman) 1955

	SECTION
1.	1.
2.	2.
3.	3. 28
4.	4. 25,26

5.   5. 35
6. 30,31   6.
7. 32   7.
8. 1,2,3,4,25,26   8. 4,9
9. 22,23,24   9. 1,2,3,4
10. 28,31
11. 27,29
12. 13,14,15,16,17,18,19,20,21,23
13.
14. 32,33,34,35
15.

Mouly: *Psychology for Effective Teaching* (Holt-Dryden) 1960

1.
2. 27
3.
4. 32
5.
6. 22, 23, 24
7. 30,31
8. 1,2,3,4
9.
10. 25,26
11. 28,29
12. 5,6,7,8,9,10,11,12,13,14,15,16, 17,18,23
13. 19,20,21
14. 32,33,34,35
15.
16.
17.
18.

Pressey, Robinson, Horrocks: *Psychology in Education* (Harper) 1959

1.
2. 32
3.
4.
5.
6.
7. 25,26,27,30,31
8. 1,2,3,4,5,6,7,8,23,27
9. 28,29
10. 22,23,24
11.
12.
13. 32,33,34,35
14.
15.
16.
17.
18.
19.

Stephens: *Educational Psychology* rev. ed. (Holt) 1956

1.
2.
3.
4. 16,32
5. 30,31
6. 32,33,34,35
7.
8–9. 1,2,3,4,27
10. 25,26
11.
12. 5,6,7,8,23
13. 13,14,15,30,31
14. 28,29
15.
16.
17. 19,20,21
18. 22,23,24

19.
20.
21.
22.

Thompson, Gardner, DiVesta: *Educational Psychology* (Appleton) 1959

1. 32
2.
3.
4. 32,33,35
5. 34
6.
7.
8.
9. 24
10.
11. 1,2,3,4
12. 25,26,27
13. 28,29
14. 5,6,7,8,23
15. 13,14,15,30,31
16. 19,20,21
17. 16,17,18
18.
19.
20.
21.
22. 22,23,24
23.
24.

Trow: *Psychology in Teaching and Learning* (Houghton Mifflin) 1960

1.
2. 19,20,21
3.

4.
5. 26,32
6. 33,34,35
7. 30,31
8. 21,23,27
9. 25,26,27,35
10. 16,17,18
11. 13,14,15,28,29
12. 5,6,7,8,29
13.
14. 22,23,24

Woodruff: *The Psychology of Teaching* 3rd ed. (Longmans) 1951

1.
2.
3.
4. 4,24
5. 5,22
6.
7–10. 25,26,27
11. 21
12.
13.
14.
15. 1,2,3,4
16. 5,6,7,8,9,10,11,12,13,14,15,16, 17,18,19,20,21,23,30,31,32
17. 25,26,27,28,29
18.
19.
20.
21.
22.
23.
24.
25. 32,33,34,35
26.
27.

DATE DUE

AP 30 '70		
NO 10 '70	NO 3 '74	
JA 18 '71		
AP 2? '71		
AG 13 '71		
N. 2 '70		
MR 13 '74		
		PRINTED IN U.S.A.
GAYLORD		